International Criminal Justice Series

Volume 34

The *International Criminal Justice Series* aims to create a platform for publications covering the entire field of international criminal justice. It, therefore, deals with issues relating, among others, to:

- the work of international criminal courts and tribunals;
- transitional justice approaches in different countries;
- international anti-corruption and anti-money laundering initiatives;
- the history of international criminal law.

It is peer-reviewed and seeks to publish high-quality works emanating from excellent scholars.

Editorial Office

Prof. Dr. Moritz Vormbaum
University of Münster
Faculty of Law
Bispinghof 24-25
48143 Münster, Germany
vormbaum@uni-muenster.de

International Criminal Justice Series

Volume 34

Series Editors

Gerhard Werle, Berlin, Germany

Moritz Vormbaum, Münster, Germany

The *International Criminal Justice Series* aims to create a platform for publications covering the entire field of international criminal justice. It, therefore, deals with issues relating, among others, to:

- the work of international criminal courts and tribunals;
- transitional justice approaches in different countries;
- international anti-corruption and anti-money laundering initiatives;
- the history of international criminal law.

It is peer-reviewed and seeks to publish high-quality works emanating from excellent scholars.

Editorial Office

Prof. Dr. Moritz Vormbaum
University of Münster
Faculty of Law
Bispinghof 24-25
48143 Münster, Germany
vormbaum@uni-muenster.de

Victoria Ojo-Adewuyi

Criminal Justice Responses to the Boko Haram Crisis in Nigeria

ASSER PRESS

Springer

Victoria Ojo-Adewuyi
Berlin, Germany

ISSN 2352-6718 ISSN 2352-6726 (electronic)
International Criminal Justice Series
ISBN 978-94-6265-614-7 ISBN 978-94-6265-615-4 (eBook)
https://doi.org/10.1007/978-94-6265-615-4

Published by T.M.C. ASSER PRESS, The Hague, The Netherlands www.asserpress.nl
Produced and distributed for T.M.C. ASSER PRESS by Springer-Verlag Berlin Heidelberg

This T.M.C. ASSER PRESS imprint is published by the registered company Springer-Verlag GmbH, DE, part of Springer Nature.
The registered company address is: Heidelberger Platz 3, 14197 Berlin, Germany

Paper in this product is recyclable.

Contents

Abbreviations

AC	Appeals Chamber
ANC	African National Congress
Art(s)	Articles
ASP	Assemblies of States Parties
AU	African Union
BBC	British Broadcasting Corporation
CNN	Cable News Network
CTJF	Civilian Joint Task Force
DRR	De-radicalisation, Rehabilitation and Reintegration
DTM	Displacement Tracking Matrix
ECOWAS	Economic Community of West African States
Ed(s).	Editor(s)
edn.	Edition
et al.	And others (et alia)
et seq.	And the following (et sequens; et sequentes)
FATF	Financial Action Task Force
HRVIC	Human Rights Violation Investigation Commission
i.e.	That is (id est)
Ibid./ibid.	In the same place (Ibidem)
ICC	International Criminal Court
ICRC	International Committee of the Red Cross
ICTR	International Criminal Tribunal for Rwanda
ICTY	International Criminal Tribunal for (the former) Yugoslavia
IMF	International Monetary Fund
IMT	International Military Tribunal (at Nuremberg)
IOM	International Organisation for Migration
ISIL	Islamic State of Iraq and the Levant
ISIS	Islamic State of Iraq and Syria
ISWAP	Islamic States' West Africa Province
JIBWIS	Jama'at Izalat al-bid'a wa Iqmat al-Sunna
JTI	Jama'atul Tajdidi Islam

LCBC	Lake Chad Basin Commission
MEND	Movement for the Emancipation of the Niger Delta
MNJTF	Multinational Joint Task Force
NEDC	North East Development Commission
NGO	Non-Governmental Organisation
OHCHR	Office of the United Nations High Commissioner for Human Rights
OTP	Office of the Prosecutor
PCNI	Presidential Committee on the North East Initiative
PINE	Presidential Initiative on the North East
SACP	South African Communist Party
SCSL	Special Court for Sierra Leone
STL	Special Tribunal for Lebanon
SWAPO	South West Africa People's Organisation
UN	United Nations
UNICEF	United Nations International Children's Emergency Fund
UNOCHA	United Nations Office for the Coordination of Humanitarian Affairs
UNODC	United Nations Office on Drugs and Crime
UNSC	United Nations Security Council
VSF	Victims Support Fund

Chapter 1
Introduction and Overview

Contents

Abstract This chapter sets the context and provides a general overview for the crisis perpetrated by the *Jama'atul Alhul Sunnah Lidda'wati Wal Jihad* (Boko Haram) group in Nigeria and in areas around the Lake Chad Basin region. It provides a critical background to the crisis while exploring the methodology, answering the research questions and situating the crisis firmly within the context of international criminal law. The chapter also addresses the objectives and provides a general outline of the book.

Keywords African Union · Boko Haram · Civilian Joint Task Force (CJTF) · Criminal Code · Kidnapping · Penal Code · Terrorism Prevention Act · International Criminal Court

1.1 Context

On 19 January 2015, the president of the United Nations Security Council (UNSC) condemned the escalation of the Boko Haram attacks and acknowledged that the violence constituted threats to international peace and security.[1] By 2015, Boko Haram had developed from what was regarded as a local irritation into an international phenomenon with a recognisable name. Its violence had become recurrent in

[1] United Nations Security Council 2015.

V. Ojo-Adewuyi, *Criminal Justice Responses to the Boko Haram Crisis in Nigeria*, International Criminal Justice Series 34, https://doi.org/10.1007/978-94-6265-615-4_1

the Nigerian security sphere since it started in 2009.[2] Regarded as a domestic terrorist group, the Boko Haram crisis defied predictions including the report of a technical defeat by the Nigerian government.[3] From the government's initial lukewarm reaction towards the group's violence, to recognising the impacts of its activities, the anti-terror efforts mainly consisted of an armed offensive against the group. While Boko Haram gained its early members due to its provisions of social and other critically required services,[4] it grew to become increasingly confrontational and utilised terror to achieve its aims of holding territory from its operational base in Northeastern Nigeria and the Lake Chad Basin region. Boko Haram combatants carried out large-scale violent attacks on civilians, government agents and public and private infrastructure alike. Its violence was the focus of a number of United Nations resolutions and statements, reports of international governmental and non-governmental organisations, countless anti-terror efforts and strategic high-level security conferences.[5] However, civilians in Northeast Nigeria bore the brunt of the Boko Haram campaign of terror and violence. Domestically and internationally, Nigeria's response to the Boko Haram violence led to far-reaching challenges. Access to arms for this purpose was at the centre of a diplomatic incident between Nigeria and the United States for a number of years.[6] The lack of progress in addressing the violence was arguably one of the factors responsible for the loss of the second term bid by the then incumbent President Goodluck Jonathan in 2015.[7] Commentators have provided varying perspectives for the rise of the group and suggested a number of approaches to combat Boko Haram's violence.[8] However, not much appreciable progress was made, and the group continued to reinvent its strategies to fit new tactics utilised by the Nigerian government.

In its anti-terror efforts, the Nigerian military operated jointly with the police and other law enforcement agencies. A Civilian Joint Task Force (CJTF) was also set up. The CJTF included members of the affected communities tasked with assisting in

[2] From a relatively unknown religious group into one based on expressing local grievances, Boko Haram grew to commit large scale violence responsible for destabilising Northeast Nigeria since 2009. The group's history and early activities are well documented in articles, news reports and reports of international non-governmental organisations operating in Northeast Nigeria. See generally Cook 2011, p. 3, Onuoha 2010, p. 55, and Walker 2012.

[3] See BBC 2015, and Punch Newspaper 2018.

[4] Apart from preaching the Q'uran, Boko Haram gained its early following especially among the youth due to the lure of the social services it provided. The group provided free Islamic education, business loans and arranged marriages among its members without the lengthy and expensive traditional processes. See generally, Washington Post 2016, TRT World 2017, Mercy Corps Report 2016, and Matfes 2017a.

[5] United Nations Human Rights Council Resolution on the atrocities committed by the terrorist group Boko Haram and its effects on Human Rights in the affected states. Adopted by the Human Rights Council at its twenty-third special session, 1 April 2015 A/HRC/RES/S-23/1. United Nations Security Council Resolution 2349 2017, and United Nations Human Rights Office of the High Commissioner 2017.

[6] See generally, BBC 2014, The New York Times 2015, and The New York Times 2016a, b.

[7] See VOA 2015, and The Guardian 2015.

[8] See Forest 2012, Solomon 2012, and Agbiboa 2013.

the identification of suspected members and/or sympathisers of Boko Haram.[9] Thousands of detainees with alleged Boko Haram links were remanded in custody, in jails and military facilities. A few cases were also instituted. However, a minute percentage of these cases were completed in a timely manner. In response to these challenges, the Nigerian government in 2017 set up special courts with civilian judges sitting in military facilities exclusively for trials of Boko Haram related suspects and detainees. On the whole, although the violence has been described as 'localised'[10] and its activities an 'African insurgency rather than a prototypical terrorist organization',[11] at the beginning, the sustained nature of the violence and the sheer resilience of Boko Haram attacks since 2009 suggests that the characterisation has since changed.

In the domestic sphere, majority of the egregious acts of violence committed by Boko Haram fits the characterisation as crimes of terrorism and may be addressed partly by domestic legislation.[12] However, depending on categorisation, whether or not terrorism, which lacks a definition for the purpose of international criminal justice, should be considered as a crime within the contemplation of international criminal law has been a subject of spirited academic debate. It is settled that there is no *sui generis* crime of terrorism in the sense of a *delicta juris gentium*. The traditional view is that terrorism committed in peacetime is a crime within the domestic jurisdiction. Additionally, terrorist crimes have been described as amounting to acts of national criminal law which may or may not be of international concern.[13] The necessity of international prosecution of terrorism has been called into question as terrorism is viewed as a crime against the 'security, stability, sovereignty and integrity, institutions and structures or economy and development' of the state.[14] The idea of terrorism as a form of political violence was legitimised by the 1994 Declarations on Measures to Eliminate International Terrorism where a distinction of acts of terrorism from other acts of violence through its 'political aims' was made by the General Assembly in the annexed declaration.[15] The definition of terrorism in the United Nations Convention for the Suppression of the Financing of Terrorism is widely recognised partly due to its abstract nature[16] and it also received judicial acknowledgement by the Appeal

[9] Agbiboa 2018, Bamidele 2016, and Omenma and Hendricks 2018.

[10] See Thomson 2012, p. 57.

[11] Matfes 2017b, p. 1.

[12] Terrorism is specifically addressed in Section 15 of the Economic and Financial Crimes Commission (Establishment) Act 2004 and wholly in the Terrorism Prevention Act 2011 and the Terrorism (Prevention) (Amendment) Act 2013.

[13] UNODC Handbook on Criminal Justice Responses to Terrorism 2009.

[14] Margariti 2017, p. 7.

[15] 'Criminal acts intended or calculated to provoke a state of terror in the general public, a group of persons or particular persons for political purposes are in any circumstance unjustifiable, whatever the considerations of a political, philosophical, ideological, racial, ethnic, religious or any other nature that may be invoked to justify them;' UN General Assembly Resolution 49/60 1990.

[16] 'Any person commits an offence within the meaning of this Convention if that person by any means, directly or indirectly, unlawfully and willfully, provides or collects funds with the intention that they should be used or in the knowledge that they are to be used, in full or in part, in order to carry out: (a) An act which constitutes an offence within the scope of and as defined in one of the treaties

Chamber of the Special Tribunal for Lebanon.[17] The Tribunals' basis for the finding that terrorism is a crime under customary international law especially during peace time includes: commission of a criminal act or the threat of such an act, the intent to spread fear, coerce an authority to take action or refrain from taking an action and a transnational element.[18] According to the Chamber, purely domestic attacks do not qualify to be regarded as crimes under international law.[19] Some commentators rejected the approach of the Special Tribunal for Lebanon on the existence of a customary international crime of terrorism.[20]

Boister[21] proposes a transnational criminal legal framework for accountability for the crime of terrorism by utilising the structure inherent in the international anti-terrorism conventions which oblige states to criminalise prohibited terrorist acts. In his view, transnational criminal law consists of horizontal treaty obligations between states and vertical application of criminal law by states to individuals to meet its

listed in the annex; or(b) Any other act intended to cause death or serious bodily injury to a civilian, or to any other person not taking an active part in the hostilities in a situation of armed conflict, when the purpose of such act, by its nature or context, is to intimidate a population, or to compel a government or an international organization to do or to abstain from doing any act.' Article 2(1) United Nations Convention for the Financing of Terrorism 1999 UN General Assembly Resolution 54/109 of 9 December 1999. The annex specifies the following conventions: Convention for the Suppression of Unlawful Seizure of Aircraft, done at The Hague on 16 December 1970. 2. Convention for the Suppression of Unlawful Acts against the Safety of Civil Aviation, done at Montreal on 23 September 1971. Convention on the Prevention and Punishment of Crimes against Internationally Protected Persons, including Diplomatic Agents, adopted by the General Assembly of the United Nations on 14 December 1973. International Convention against the Taking of Hostages, adopted by the General Assembly of the United Nations on 17 December 1979. Convention on the Physical Protection of Nuclear Material, adopted at Vienna on 3 March 1980. Protocol for the Suppression of Unlawful Acts of Violence at Airports Serving International Civil Aviation, supplementary to the Convention for the Suppression of Unlawful Acts against the Safety of Civil Aviation, done at Montreal on 24 February 1988. Convention for the Suppression of Unlawful Acts against the Safety of Maritime Navigation, done at Rome on 10 March 1988. Protocol for the Suppression of Unlawful Acts against the Safety of Fixed Platforms located on the Continental Shelf, done at Rome on 10 March 1988. International Convention for the Suppression of Terrorist Bombings, adopted by the General Assembly of the United Nations on 15 December 1997.

[17] Special Tribunal for Lebanon Interlocutory Decision on the Applicable Law: Terrorism, Conspiracy, Homicide, Perpetration, Cumulative Charging 2011.

[18] Werle and Jessberger 2014.

[19] Special Tribunal for Lebanon Interlocutory Decision on the Applicable Law: Terrorism, Conspiracy, Homicide, Perpetration, Cumulative Charging 2011.

[20] See compelling arguments in Ambos 2011, and Saul 2011.

[21] Boister 2012, See similar arguments in Boister 2003, p. 14, Bossard 1990, and Luban et al. 2014.

treaty obligations and this may be applied regarding responsibility for terrorism.[22] However, the need for an international mechanism for terrorism has been highlighted to prevent the possibility of terrorist offenders escaping accountability. This might occur should third states make decisions regarding the obligation of '*aut dedere aut judicare*'[23] for political reasons rather than a due consideration of the intent of criminal justice. While consensus seem to have been achieved regarding acts of terror committed in peacetime within the borders of one state, the same cannot be said for the applicability of terrorism in time of armed conflict[24] or with regards to acts of terror that results in a situation of armed conflict within the borders of a state.

Depending on the context, acts of terror may amount to a specific war crime, when committed during an armed conflict or crimes against humanity, when committed in peacetime, as part of a widespread or systematic attack against a civilian population with the required mental element.[25] Generally, for definitional purposes, a number of international instruments, while avoiding a general definition of terrorism, describe the phenomenon either in terms of prohibited acts committed or threat of violence

[22] Boister 2012, p. 13.

[23] Deriving from several multi-lateral conventions, '*aut dedere aut judicare*' refers to the legal obligation of States under international law either to surrender a suspect accused of serious international crimes to another State with the jurisdiction and willingness to prosecute or to adjudicate the cases before its national courts. It is often commonly expressed as the obligation to 'extradite or prosecute' and has been described as a *jus cogens* principle. See generally Bassiouni and Wise 1995. See also International Law Commission 2014.

[24] For example, see Cassese 2006. See also Scharf 2004.

[25] Article 7 The Rome Statute of the International Criminal Court 2002 hereinafter referred to as the Rome Statute.

utilised.[26] This approach was also used in a number of national legislations addressing terrorism.[27]

Whether the crimes committed by Boko Haram may be addressed by Nigeria's domestic criminal legal regime notwithstanding, the transnational dynamics to the conflict is also especially noteworthy. Similar to its violent campaign within Nigeria, Boko Haram committed egregious crimes in states outside the territorial borders of Nigeria most especially Cameroon, Niger and Chad. In this vein, it may be inadequate to only envision the response of Nigeria's domestic legal framework to the Boko Haram violence; rather, a more broad-based perspective may be more appropriate.

---

[26] See for example Article 1(2) of the Arab Convention for the Suppression of Terrorism 2002 which states that Terrorism is 'Any act or threat of violence, whatever its motives or purposes, that occurs in the advancement of an individual or collective criminal agenda and seeking to sow panic among people, causing fear by harming them, or placing their lives, liberty or security in danger, or seeking to cause damage to the environment, or to public or private installations or property, or to occupying or seizing them, or seeking to jeopardize a national resources.' Article 1(3) of the OAU Convention on the Prevention and Combating of Terrorism 1999 describes Terrorist acts as 'any act which is a violation of the criminal laws of a State Party and which may endanger the life, physical integrity or freedom of, or cause serious injury or death to, any person, any number or group of persons or causes or may cause damage to public or private property, natural resources, environmental or cultural heritage and is calculated or intended to: (i) intimidate, put in fear, force, coerce or induce any government, body, institution, the general public or any segment thereof, to do or abstain from doing any act, or to adopt or abandon a particular standpoint, or to act according to certain principles; or (ii) disrupt any public service, the delivery of any essential service to the public or to create a public emergency; or (iii) create general insurrection in a State; (b) any promotion, sponsoring, contribution to, command, aid, incitement, encouragement, attempt, threat, conspiracy, organizing, or procurement of any person, with the intent to commit any act referred to in para (a) (i) to (iii)'. Article 1(2) of the Convention of the Organisation of Islamic Conference on Combating International Terrorism 1999 states, '"Terrorism" means any act of violence or threat thereof notwithstanding its motives or intentions perpetrated to carry out an individual or collective criminal plan with the aim of terrorizing people or threatening to harm them or imperiling their lives, honour, freedoms, security or rights or exposing the environment or any facility or public or private property to hazards or occupying or seizing them, or endangering a national resource, or international facilities, or threatening the stability, territorial integrity, political unity or sovereignty of independent States'. See also Article 2(1) (a) and (b) of the United Nation's International Convention for the Suppression of the Financing of Terrorism. It states that '1. Any person who commits an offence within the meaning of this Convention, if that person by any means, directly or indirectly, unlawfully and willfully, provides or collects funds with the intention that they should be used or in the knowledge that they are to be used, in full or in part, in order to carry out: (a) An act which constitutes an offence within the scope of and as defined in one of the treaties listed in the annex; or (b) Any other act intended to cause death or serious bodily injury to a civilian, or to any other person not taking an active part in the hostilities in a situation of armed conflict, when the purpose of such act, by its nature or context, is to intimidate a population, or to compel a government or an international organization to do or to abstain from doing any act'.

[27] A number of national anti-terrorism legislation in both civil and common law countries also defines terrorism along this line. See for example Section 1(2) Nigeria's Terrorism (Prevention) Act 2011, Section 2(1) Kenya's Prevention of Terrorism Act, No. 30 of 2012 (Rev 2015). Article 137 of Belgium's Terrorism Offences Act of 29 December 2003 defines a terrorist offence as acts which 'by its nature or context may cause serious harm to a country or an international organization.'

In the international sphere, some of the crimes committed by Boko Haram may also fulfil the requirements as crimes within the contemplation of the Rome Statute.[28] This necessitates an exploration of the potential jurisdiction of the International Criminal Court ('the ICC'). The possibility of the exercise of jurisdiction of the ICC is worthy of investigation, particularly due to the focus of the Rome Statute of the ICC on the individual perpetrator specifically and generally on individual criminal responsibility as international crimes are not committed by abstract entities.[29] Conversely, mechanisms available under public international law are typically more focused on the general obligations on states to create measures to address terrorism. Should the state not carry out its treaty obligations effectively, it may be logical to explore the response of international criminal justice to hold those who commit grave crimes accountable.

Generally, the International Criminal Court does not have the mandate to address all crimes, rather, investigating and prosecuting the 'most serious crimes of international concern'.[30] Accountability for international crimes is the driving force of its activities and the jurisdiction of the International Criminal Court is 'complementary to national criminal jurisdiction'.[31] Cases may be admissible before the ICC if the state with primary jurisdiction is 'unwilling or unable to genuinely carry-out the investigation or prosecution' according to the principle of complementarity.[32] The crimes within the jurisdiction of the Court include the crime of genocide, crimes against humanity, war crimes and the crime of aggression.[33] The jurisdiction of the ICC may be triggered by a state party referral in accordance with Article 12 of the Rome Statute,[34] by the Security Council under Chapter VII of the United Nation Charter,[35] or by the prosecutor acting *suo motu* in accordance with Article 15.[36] Its jurisdiction extends not only to the individuals accused of the crimes, but others who may be liable through aiding and abetting or otherwise assisting in the commission of the crimes as provided for in Article 25. The jurisdiction of the ICC may be exercised when the accused is a national of a state party or a state otherwise accepting the jurisdiction of the court, and when the conduct in question occurred in the territory of a state party or a state otherwise accepting the jurisdiction of the court.[37] The jurisdiction is non-retroactive and its temporal jurisdiction may be applied only in

---

[28] Rome Statute of the International Criminal Court 2002.

[29] Article 1, 25, Rome Statute of the International Criminal Court 2002. Determined to put an end to impunity for the perpetrators of international crimes, the Rome Statute has a mechanism for establishing degrees of responsibility elaborately provided for in Article 25. See generally Van Sliedregt 2012, and Werle and Burghardt 2014.

[30] Preamble, Rome Statute of the International Criminal Court 2002.

[31] Preamble, Rome Statute of the International Criminal Court 2002.

[32] Article 17 (1)(a), Rome Statute of the International Criminal Court 2002.

[33] Article 5, Rome Statute of the International Criminal Court 2002.

[34] Article 13(a), Rome Statute of the International Criminal Court 2002.

[35] Article 13(b), Rome Statute of the International Criminal Court 2002.

[36] Article 13(c), Rome Statute of the International Criminal Court 2002.

[37] Article 12, Rome Statute of the International Criminal Court 2002.

respect to crimes committed after July 1, 2002.[38] Although, terrorism does not exist as a stand-alone crime within the Rome Statute, commentators have proposed that terrorist acts and conducts may be prosecuted if they amount to prohibited acts within the definition of crimes in the Rome Statute regardless of legal characterisation.[39]

Although, the Boko Haram crisis is ongoing as at the time of writing, Nigerian authorities are also exploring certain measures that may amount to classic transitional justice mechanisms[40] as a response to the crisis. The contribution of these mechanisms to restorative justice will be further explored later in this book.

1.2 Background

Officially named *Jama'atul Alhul Sunnah Lidda'wati Wal Jihad*,[41] the moniker, Boko Haram, is generally expressed to mean 'western education is forbidden'.[42] Since the group became a phenomenon in Nigeria, it has imprinted itself into national and international consciousness through grave acts of violence and terror. From systematic murders, inflicting grievous bodily harm, to suicide bombings optimised for large-scale casualties, abductions of women and girls, malicious destruction of properties, the group has acquired a reputation as a law unto itself. Since 2009 when Boko Haram began to wage violent conflict against Nigeria and its nearest

---

[38] Article 11(1) Rome Statute of the International Criminal Court 2002.

[39] See generally Arnold 2004, Cohen 2012, and Kenny 2017.

[40] Transitional justice mechanisms are typically utilised in post-conflict societies or post-authoritarian societies. Classic transitional justice mechanisms include judicial proceedings, utilising truth commissions, reparations for victims, vetting and lustrations, including amnesties. Regarding the Boko Haram crisis, the Nigerian government made a declaration promising amnesty for repentant Boko Haram members. The process commenced through the De-radicalisation, Rehabilitation and Reintegration Program (DRR) and Operation Safe Corridor (OSC) inaugurated by the Defense Headquarters in 2015. The programme has been widely criticised by commentators. See generally Hassan 2018, and Punch Newspaper 2017.

[41] "People committed to spreading the heritage of the prophet and Jihad or people committed to preaching of the Sunnah and Jihad".

[42] There is no generally acceptable meaning of the word Boko Haram. The term "boko" is usually rendered as a translation of the Hausa word for "book", while "haram" is generally accepted to connote the Arabic word for "forbidden" or "sinful". Although this interpretation has been disputed, the idea that western education is forbidden has come to be generally accepted as embodying the ideology of the group. Paul Newman in his dissent examined the etymology of the word "boko" and opines that it does not connote the Hausa word for "book" but rather means "sham", "fraud" or "inauthentic" which, according to him, the group uses to represent western education and learning. See Newman 2013, 1–13. In a 2009 statement, a so-called spokesperson for the Boko Haram group also affirmed that the name did not imply 'Western education is forbidden' but rather implies that 'western civilization' is forbidden. He also asserted that the focus of the group is to stress the supremacy of Islamic culture over all others. See Vanguard 2009. The name has also been described as a dismissive name for members of the group by its early neighbours as a critique of its activities. The argument is that Boko Haram could not connote the sinful nature of western civilisation as the group still utilised modern tools such as phones, cameras, social media platforms and the internet including vehicles and modern weapons. See Walker 2012, p. 7.

neighbours, the group became 'sophisticated, coordinated and menacingly daring in its operations'.[43] As of early 2017, about two million Nigerians were reportedly displaced[44] as a result of the violent conflict. The healthcare and educational system was also completely shut down in a number of states during the period due to Boko Haram's campaign of terror.[45] Additionally, humanitarian workers in 2017 warned of a hunger and famine crisis as major challenges in the region.[46]

The Nigerian government's response to the crisis was lukewarm in the beginning. It took mass international attention for significant anti-terror action to begin. The government declared a state of emergency first for six months in 2011; another for twelve months in 2013, but rather than the situation improving, it worsened considerably and the civilian casualty figures tripled during the period.[47] A number of cases were instituted against suspects on terror-related charges in Nigeria during the period. A large percentage of accused persons also remained in custody for years without the cases being charged to court or the matters dispensed with. Additionally, there were allegations of mistreatment of suspects and detainees including reports of summary executions of Boko Haram suspects in custody in Cameroon and Chad.[48]

Attempts have been made by the Nigerian government to negotiate with the group,[49] the efforts seemed successful as it facilitated the exchange of eighty-two of the infamously abducted Chibok girls with some alleged senior Boko Haram detainees in custody in May 2017.[50] While this achieved a temporary pause in the violence, the group returned to the commission of violent acts thereafter. The terms of the agreement and whether the negotiations were related to putting an end to the violence or were merely utilised to facilitate the return of some of the hostages remained unclear.

The crisis has had wide-ranging political and diplomatic implications for Nigeria. Additionally, since the group's evolution into transnational terrorism, Boko Haram has metamorphosed from a wholly Nigerian problem into a regional concern. The African Union boosted Nigeria's anti-terror efforts by contributing to renaming and improving the erstwhile Multinational Joint Security Force created by the Lake Chad Basin Commission ("the LCBC") in 1994.[51] The mandate of the new Multinational Joint Task Force ("the MNJTF") was expanded to include the fight against Boko

---

43 Aghedo and Osumah 2012, p. 859.

44 See International Organization for Migration 2017.

45 See generally Human Rights Watch Report 2016, UNICEF 'Nigeria Co-Situation Report' 2016, UNHCR 2016, Médecins Sans Frontières 2015, and The Guardian 2014.

46 Food and Agriculture Organisation of the United Nations 2017.

47 New York Times 2012, BBC 2013, and Deutsche Welle 2014.

48 Amnesty International Report 2016, and Vanguard Nigeria 2015.

49 New York Times 2016a, b.

50 Vanguard Nigeria 2017.

51 The Lake Chad Basin Commission (LCBC) is a regional inter-governmental organisation comprising of countries jointly bordering the Lake Chad. It was established in 1964 and its members include Nigeria, Niger, Chad, Cameroon, Libya and Central African Republic. The Boko Haram violence is rife in the region around the Lake Chad in Nigeria, Northern Cameroon and Niger due to a number of factors including porous borders and high mobility. See Galeazzi et al. 2017.

Haram in 2012. Troops were contributed by the LCBC countries to assist Nigeria and its nearest neighbours in the fight against Boko Haram. The Multinational Joint Task Force was effectively operationalised in 2015[52] with its operative headquarters in N'Djamena, the Republic of Chad.[53]

The conduct of the Boko Haram group was first addressed by the International Criminal Court in its 2012 report of preliminary examination activities. It is clear that the jurisdiction of the International Criminal Court may be triggered if the State which possess jurisdiction over the crimes committed is unwilling or unable to genuinely carry out investigation or prosecution.[54] The Office of the Prosecutor received communications under Article 15 of the Rome Statute and opened preliminary examinations in Nigeria inclusive of the Boko Haram violence. The preliminary examination was completed in December 2020, a decade after they started, with the prosecutor's acknowledgement that there was a reasonable basis to believe that conduct amounting to war crimes and crimes against humanity were committed within the context. Throughout the preliminary examination, the Office of the Prosecutor placed its focus on assisting Nigeria to strengthen its investigative and prosecutorial abilities through its complementarity activities. The decision of the Pre-Trial Chamber with regards to the request of the prosecutor for the authorisation of full investigation is at the time of rounding up this book, being awaited.

1.3 Methodology and Research Questions

In conducting this normative study, the assessment of the Boko Haram crisis was approached in a number of ways. While the main purpose of the book is to conduct an evaluation, and legal analysis of the Boko Haram problem, the utilisation of a multidisciplinary approach in the early chapters became crucial. The historical, theological and socio-legal perspectives were analysed to assist in addressing the context and overview of the Boko Haram crisis. This aided in the understanding of the Boko Haram situation, including providing answers to the pertinent research questions.

Regarding the analysis chapters, while relying on both primary and secondary sources, this study described and prescribed the challenges of the domestic, regional and international criminal legal regime as a response to the crisis. This study interpreted the lesser-known domestic regime in accordance with established jurisprudence of international criminal law. Empirical data was also utilised particularly in the assessment of the efforts of the domestic legal system in relation to the crisis. With regards to potential crimes under the jurisdiction of the ICC, contextual elements of the crimes against humanity and war crimes were specifically and systematically addressed.

---

52 African Union 2015b.

53 For more on the MNJTF, see generally African Union 2015a, and Institute for Security Studies West Africa Report 2016.

54 Article 5, Rome Statute of the International Criminal Court 2002.

This book seeks to answer three key questions. The first is focused on the adequacy of Nigerian legal responses. Assessing whether Nigeria's domestic legal framework is adequate to ensure genuine investigation and prosecution of the grave crimes committed by Boko Haram. The Rome Statute implementation bill is undomesticated and stalled at the National Assembly. The pertinent question then is whether the Criminal and Penal Code and the Terrorism Prevention Act (2013) are adequate and whether Nigeria can discharge its duty to prosecute those bearing the greatest responsibility for the crimes in question based on its available domestic legal regime?

The second question is based on the potential intervention of the International Criminal Court. Do the violent crimes of Boko Haram meet the requirements as core crimes within the contemplation of the Rome Statute on the basis of the available facts? Do they have the sufficient gravity, and will they meet the jurisdictional and interests of justice bar?

The third question is focused on an assessment of other potential alternatives and adjuncts to domestic or international criminal prosecution. The potential usage of transitional justice mechanisms other than criminal prosecution is explored. Additionally, the usefulness of utilising other transitional justice mechanisms in a situation where there has been no transition yet is analysed.

1.4 Literature Survey

Commencing effectively in 2009, the Boko Haram problem is a relatively recent phenomenon. Serious discourse relating to the Boko Haram group and its activities generally did not seem to emerge until the crisis reached alarming and ferocious dimensions around 2013–2014. Since then, a high volume of academic writings addressing the crisis from varying perspectives have emerged.[55] Fiction[56] and non-fiction[57] writers also seemed to find the Boko Haram crisis an irresistible subject. However, academic literature specifically addressing the legal perspectives of the crisis and the role of the ICC were few and far between. Even fewer, were those addressing the crisis from the perspective of international criminal law. For clarity's sake, a rough categorisation of literature addressing the Boko Haram problem in relation to this study will be addressed in a two-pronged manner. The first will explore the central thesis dominating selected literature addressing the domestic legal perspectives, while the second will explore relevant literature on the role of international law generally and the ICC more particularly.

Generally, the literature seems to suggest a lack of public understanding and consensus relating to Boko Haram, its motivations, internal structure including the

[55] See generally, for example, Loimeier 2012, p. 47, Barna 2014, Montclos and Magrin 2018, Dunn 2018, p. 12, and Mantzikos 2013.

[56] See for example Davieson 2014.

[57] See generally Matfes 2017c, and Walker 2016.

preferred response of domestic law. Iocchi[58] opined that the religious label which Boko Haram carries and the conceptualisation of the conflict as religious inspired terror is incorrect. The author suggested an understanding of Boko Haram as a terror franchise, with economic interests in the 'bush-economy' of the Lake Chad Basin region. Ebeku[59] addressed the Boko Haram crisis as an agitation for Islamic legal regime in Nigeria and proposed a sovereign national conference to resolve the constitutionalism and Islamism question. Ike[60] explores the role of Nigeria's domestic law and the criminal justice system. Noting the inadequate nature of Nigeria's major anti-terrorism legislation and the challenges plaguing the law enforcement and judicial authorities' insufficient response to the conflict, the author concluded on the need for further collaborative work among relevant agencies and the need for further study on the role of the law in countering terrorism in Nigeria. Adesoji[61] noted that the regular recurrence of religious fundamentalism in Nigeria is symptomatic of the inadequate handling of the government and the lack of decisiveness in dealing with perpetrators of such violence in the past while Niworu went as far as stating that the crisis is a manifestation of the failure of the Nigerian state.[62] The author of this book previously explored the capacity of national laws to address the Boko Haram violence and noted that while the domestic option may be desirable and available in a limited manner, not much progress has been made in that regard.[63] Sampson[64] also noted the non-domestication of key international treaties as a major contributor to the perceived inadequate legal framework and recommended the development of a more robust counter-terrorism strategy and accountability mechanisms. A common theme in the literature is the highlighted inadequacy of the response of the domestic legal regime and the need for a more robust assessment and decisive action.

On the role of the international legal regime, Ajigboye[65] noted the justifiable need for intervention on the Boko Haram crisis. The author opined that the principle of responsibility to protect may be interpreted under international law to allow third states' intervention to protect Nigerian citizens from the violence of Boko Haram and the failure of the Nigerian government to address same. However, the author suggested a regulation mechanism for such powers in order that it does not lend itself to abuse. Ezeani[66] similarly argued that although Boko Haram is a home-grown problem in Nigeria, the group has plugged into the international terror franchise. The author also recognised Nigeria's inability to deal decisively with the group using its own internal mechanism extolled the merits of a potential intervention by the African Union and the ICC in the crisis. In a review of the crimes committed by

58 Iocchi 2015, p. 15.

59 Ebeku 2011, p. 23.

60 Ike 2018, p. 6.

61 Adesoji 2010, p. 45.

62 Niworu 2013, p. 6.

63 Ojo 2015.

64 Sampson 2015, p. 59.

65 Ajigboye 2014.

66 Ezeani 2017.

Boko Haram and international humanitarian law, Abiodun and Abila[67] examined the armed conflict based on the regime of the Geneva Conventions and the UN Charter. They assessed Boko Haram's terrorism as a non-international armed conflict; and suggested the prioritisation of the provisions of the relevant treaties and their roles in the protection of the rights of civilians and combatants.[68] In a similar approach, Taiwo[69] advocated an integration of both international human rights and international humanitarian legal remedies to effectively respond to the crisis. Oke[70] noted specifically the crucial role of the ICC. In his view, the ICC is a neutral international forum, with uncontested jurisdiction over crimes against humanity committed by Boko Haram in Nigeria. Although the author addressed the crimes committed only as crimes against humanity, without recourse to conduct constituting war crimes under the statute, he advocated for an ICC prosecution of perpetrators. In a similar vein, Badar, Amin and Higgins[71] noted that while the ICC is working hard to change the perceived imperialistic image of the Court, its handling of the Boko Haram crisis must be done with an acknowledgement that the conducts in question are also prohibited under Islamic law. Sverdlov[72] specifically addressed sexual violence against women noting that the Boko Haram crisis presents an opportunity for the ICC to be decisive about the crimes and to prosecute Abubakar Shekau, the leader of Boko Haram, for sexual violence as war crimes and crimes against humanity under the statute. Bakare[73] also singled out the conduct of Boko Haram violating the rights of children to education since the conflict started. The author focused on the nature of Boko Haram as a non-state armed group and recommended varying approaches for accountability including the domestication of the Rome Statute. In a crucial contribution to the discourse around Boko Haram and international law, a 2018 edited volume was published.[74] The chapters addressed the crisis from a variety of viewpoints including violence and statehood, a classification of armed conflicts in international law, an examination of Boko Haram's ideology and an analysis of the weaponization of women and children in the conflict. While the contribution of the volume to the Boko Haram discourse is particularly noteworthy, since it is the first to address the subject matter in such a broad-based manner, other important perspectives such as an international criminal legal perspective, an analysis of potential crimes before an international forum and the potential utilisation of other transitional justice mechanisms were not addressed.[75]

In the general literature and discourse of the Boko Haram crisis since inception, an analysis of the crimes committed by Boko Haram both from the perspective of the

---

[67] Abiodun and Abila 2018, p. 73. See also Archibong and Ibanga 2018, p. 137.

[68] See Taylor 2014, p. 21, Owie 2018, p. 85, and Okebukola 2018, p. 155.

[69] Taiwo 2018, p. 33.

[70] Oke 2012–2013, p. 12.

[71] Badar et al. 2014, p. 3.

[72] Sverdlov 2017, p. 50.

[73] Bakare 2018, p. 18.

[74] Iyi and Strydom 2018.

[75] See also Iyi 2018, p. 415.

domestic and international sphere seems missing. From the domestic perspective, most literature simply addressed the crimes as terrorism without an assessment of the Boko Haram crimes committed before Nigeria's anti-Terrorism legislation was passed into law in 2011 hence ignoring Boko Haram crimes committed between 2009 and 2011. Regarding discourse around international humanitarian law and international criminal law, there also seem to be an inherent gap in the assessment of the crimes committed both as war crimes and crimes against humanity. Additionally, so far, the existence of literature assessing other transitional justice mechanisms which take into account the local context and the reality of Northeast Nigeria also seems insufficient.[76] This book is conceptualised to fill these identified gaps.

1.5 Significance and Contribution to Scholarship

The goal of this book is to interpret the existing domestic criminal legal regime as it relates to the crimes under review. Additionally, it is envisaged that a contribution to the field of transnational terrorism in international criminal law will be made. The landscape of international criminal law especially as it relates to transnational terrorism is a very unique one. The inter-relation of international criminal law with violent crimes committed by domestic and transnational terrorist groups would benefit from further illumination. While assessing the Boko Haram situation, the violent crimes committed by Boko Haram are placed first within the context of domestic criminal law. This is composed of a critical assessment of how the domestic legal regime and the international treaties that have been domesticated in Nigeria view the acts committed by Boko Haram. Although, there have been some academic literature on the Boko Haram crisis from varying perspectives, very few address the violent conflict from an international criminal legal viewpoint. This book contributes to bridging this lacuna in a comprehensive manner.

The response of the international criminal law to the violent conflict may be viewed in two-fold manner. First, international criminal law as it relates to the Boko Haram violence is addressed as a source of law for the domestic legal regime, and secondly as a distinct area of law. Prosecutions on the basis of international criminal law as a useful response to the crisis for the most serious offenders is also explored. Additionally, uniquely, this book assesses specific crimes committed by Boko Haram against crimes in Articles 6, 7 and 8 of the Rome Statute of the International Criminal Court. Placing the violent crimes committed within the appropriate context of domestic and international criminal law is an original contribution to scholarship.

[76] See Hassan and Tyvoll 2018.

1.6 Organisation of the Chapters

To achieve the aims and objectives, this book is organised into six chapters. The first chapter has provided an essential introduction, set the context to the violent crisis of Boko Haram and gave a critical background to the book. Chapter 2 provides a context and general overview of the crisis under review. It further addresses the historical background to the Boko Haram crisis, while giving an essential chronological, historical, social and religious context of the issues that have culminated into the Boko Haram. It presents an insight into the specific acts of Boko Haram and its impacts on Nigeria and in the Lake Chad Basin region.

Chapter 3 is devoted to an assessment of the options of ensuring criminal accountability for the crimes of Boko Haram at the domestic level. This includes an assessment of Nigeria's legal regime and how the domestic legal regime as at the time these crimes were committed; view them within its jurisdiction. Whether Nigeria's investigative and prosecutorial institutions are willing and able to investigate and prosecute the perpetrators of the heinous crimes committed are additionally accessed. Chapter 4 is devoted to the response of international criminal law. The Boko Haram situation before the ICC is analysed and the significant legal issues of both procedural and substantive nature addressed. These include but are not limited to issues of trigger mechanism, gravity, complementarity, jurisdiction and interests of justice. Additionally, this chapter attempts a contribution to the discourse on whether situations of transnational terrorism as evidenced by the Boko Haram violence can be regarded as international crimes in the strict sense. Furthermore, this chapter assesses whether the acts of Boko Haram fulfil the requirement as core crimes within the contemplation of the Rome Statute. Chapter 5 is devoted to alternatives and adjuncts to domestic or ICC prosecutions. It assesses the interplay between the two levels of justice and provides an outlook for future research by exploring other transitional justice responses to the violent crisis. It highlights the appropriateness of utilising other transitional justice mechanisms when there has not yet been any transition. The book closes with Chap. 6 concluding the discourse on the Boko Haram violence by calling for a focus on the victim within the responses to the Boko Haram crisis.

References

Abiodun A, Abila S (2018) A Review of the Boko Haram Insurgency and Armed Conflicts in Nigeria under International Humanitarian Law. (2018) 73 Journal of Law, Policy and Globalization.

Adesoji A (2010) The Boko Haram Uprising and Islamic Revivalism in Nigeria'. 45 African Spectrum.

African Union (2015a) The AU and the LCBC sign an Agreement for the Operationalization of the MNJTF, 21 October 2015, available at http://www.peaceau.org/en/article/the-au-and-the-lcbc-sign-an-agreement-for-the-operationalization-of-the-mnjtf.

African Union (2015b) Inauguration of the Headquarters of the Multinational Joint Task Force against the Boko Haram Terrorist Group, 26 May 2015, available at http://www.peaceau.org/en/article/inauguration-of-the-headquarters-of-the-multinational-joint-task-force-against-the-boko-haram-terrorist-group.

Agbiboa D (2013) The Ongoing Campaign of Terror in Nigeria: Boko Haram Versus the State' (2013) 2(3). Stability International Journal of Security and Development.

Agbiboa D (2018) Eyes on the Streets: Civilian Joint Task Force and the Surveillance of Boko Haram in Northeastern Nigeria. Intelligence and National Security.

Aghedo I, Osumah O (2012) The Boko Haram Uprising: How Should Nigeria Respond? (2012) 33, Third World Quarterly 859.

Ajigboye O (2014) International Law and the Responsibility to Protect: Legal and Theoretical Basis for International Intervention in Nigeria. Afe Babalola University, Journal of Sustainable Development Law and Policy.

Ambos K (2011) Judicial Creativity at the Special Tribunal for Lebanon: Is There a Crime of Terrorism under International Law? (2011) Leiden Journal of International Law, 24(3).

Amnesty International (2016) Amnesty International Report 'Cameroon: More than 1000 People Accused of Supporting Boko Haram held in Horrific Conditions, Some tortured to Death', July 2016, available at https://www.amnesty.org/en/latest/news/2016/07/cameroun-conditions-de-detention-effroyables-voire-tortures-a-mort-pour-plus-de-1-000-personnes-accusees-de-soutenir-boko-haram/.

Archibong J, Ibanga M (2018) The Boko Haram Insurgency: Characterization and Implications under Municipal and International Laws. In: Iyi J, Strydom H (eds) Boko Haram and International Law. Springer.

Arnold R (2004) The ICC as a New Instrument for Repressing Terrorism. Transnational Publishers Inc.

Badar M, Amin E, Higgins N (2014) The International Criminal Court and Nigeria's Crisis. 3, International Human Rights Law Review.

Bamidele O (2016) Civilian Joint Task Force (CJTF) - A Community Security Option: A Comprehensive and Proactive Approach of Reducing Terrorism. Journal for Deradicalization.

Bakare S (2018) Boko Haram and the Child's Right to Education in Africa: Examining the Accountability of Non-State Armed Groups. 18, African Human Rights Law Journal.

Barna J (2014) Insecurity in Context: The Rise of Boko Haram in Nigeria. European Parliament Directorate-General for External Policies DG EXPO/B/PolDep/Note/2014_113.

Bassiouni MC, Wise EM (1995) *Aut Dedere Aut Judicare*: The Duty to Extradite or Prosecute in International Law. Brill – Nijhoff.

BBC (2013) 'Nigeria Goodluck Jonathan Declares Emergency in States' 15 May 2013, available at http://www.bbc.com/news/world-africa-22533974.

BBC (2014) Boko Haram Crisis: Nigeria Fury over US Arms Refusal', 11 November 2014, available at https://www.bbc.com/news/world-africa-30006066.

BBC (2015) 'Nigeria's Boko Haram: Militants Technically Defeated-Buhari', 24 December 2015, available at https://www.bbc.com/news/world-africa-35173618.

Boister N (2003) Transnational Criminal Law? EJIL 14.

Boister N (2012) An Introduction to Transnational Criminal Law. Oxford University Press.

Bossard A (1990) Transnational Crimes and Criminal Law. Office of International Criminal Justice, University of Illinois at Chicago.

Cassese A (2006) The Multifaceted Criminal Notion of Terrorism in International Law. 4, Journal of International Criminal Justice.

Cohen A (2012) Prosecuting Terrorists at the International Criminal Court: Reevaluating an Unused Legal Tool to Combat Terrorism. (2012), Michigan State International Law Review.

Cook D (2011) The Rise of Boko Haram in Nigeria. (2011) Vol 4(9) CTC Sentinel.

Davieson A (2014) Boko Haram and its Suicide Squad: The Confession of a Jihadist. Createspace Independent Publishing Platform.

Deutsche Welle (2014) 'Nigeria's State of Emergency a Failure', 21 November 2014, available at http://www.nytimes.com/2012/01/01/world/africa/boko-haram-attacks-force-emergency-in-4-nigeria-states.html.

Dunn G (2018) The Impact of the Boko Haram Insurgency in Northeast Nigeria on Childhood Wasting: A Double Difference Study. (2018) 12 Conflict and Health.

Ebeku K (2011) Beyond Terrorism: Boko Haram Attacks and National Constitutional Questions in Nigeria. (2011) 23, Sri Lanka Journal of International Law.

Ezeani E (2017) Responding to Homegrown Terrorism: The Case of Boko Haram. (2017) 22 Annual Survey of International and Comparative Law.

Food and Agriculture Organisation of the United Nations (2017) 'Nigeria Hunger Crisis Deepens, Spills into Lake Chad Basin', 24 February 2017, available at http://www.fao.org/news/story/en/item/472006/icode/.

Forest J (2012) Confronting the Terrorism of Boko Haram in Nigeria. JSOU Press.

Galeazzi G, Medinilla A, Ebiede TM, Desmidt S (2017) Understanding the Lake Chad Basin Commission (LCBC): Water and Security at Inter-Regional Crossroads. (2017) European Centre for Development Policy Management background paper.

Guardian (2014) 'Nigerian State Closes Schools amidst Fears of Boko Haram Attacks' 18 March 2014, available at https://www.theguardian.com/world/2014/mar/18/nigeria-state-closes-schools-fears-boko-haram.

Guardian (2015) 'How Goodluck Jonathan Lost the Nigerian Election', 1 April 2015, available at https://www.theguardian.com/world/2015/apr/01/nigeria-election-goodluck-jonathan-lost.

Hassan I (2018) What is Justice? Exploring the Need for Accountability in the Boko Haram Insurgency. Harvard Human Rights Law Journal 31 (2018), available at http://harvardhrj.com/what-is-justice-exploring-the-need-for-accountability-in-the-boko-haram-insurgency/.

Hassan I, Tyvoll J (2018) After Boko Haram: Prospects for Transitional Justice in North-East Nigeria. Centre for Democracy and Development.

Human Rights Watch Report (2016) Human Rights Watch Report 'They Set the Classrooms on Fire: Attacks on Education in North-East Nigeria', April 2016, available at https://www.hrw.org/sites/default/files/report_pdf/nigeria0416web.pdf.

Institute for Security Studies West Africa Report (2016) Institute for Security Studies West Africa Report 'Assessing the Multinational Joint Task Force against Boko Haram', September 2016, available at https://issafrica.s3.amazonaws.com/site/uploads/war19.pdf.

International Law Commission (2014) The Obligation to Extradite or Prosecute (*aut dedere aut judicare*). (2014), Yearbook of the International Law Commission, Vol. 2 (Part Two).

International Organization for Migration (IOM) (2017) Displacement Tracking Matrix (DTM) Nigeria Round XIV Report January 2017, available at https://nigeria.iom.int/sites/default/files/dtm_reports/01%20DTM%20Nigeria%20Round%20XIV%20Report%20January%202017.pdf.

Ike TJ (2018) Reconceptualizing the Role of Law in Countering Terrorism: A Case Study of Boko Haram in Nigeria. (2018) 6, Journal of Law and Justice.

Iocchi A (2015) The Boko Haram Franchise and the War on Terror in Nigeria. (2015) 15 Diritto & Questioni Pubbliche.

Iyi J, Strydom H (eds) (2018) Boko Haram and International Law. Springer.

Kenny C (2017) Prosecuting Crimes of International Concern: Islamic State at the ICC? (2017), Utrecht Journal of International and European Law.

Loimeier R (2012) The Development of a Militant Religious Movement in Nigeria. (2012) 47, African Spectrum.

Luban D, O'Sullivan J, Stewart D (2014) International and Transnational Criminal Law. Wolters Kluwer Law & Business.

Mantzikos I (ed) (2013) Boko Haram: Anatomy of A Crisis. E-International Relations.

Margariti S (2017) Defining International Terrorism: Between State Sovereignty and Cosmopolitanism. T.M.C. Asser Press.

Matfes H (2017a) Boko Haram: History and Context. Oxford Research Encyclopaedia of African History.

Matfes H (2017b) Women and the War on Boko Haram: Wives, Weapons and Witnesses. Bloomsbury.

Matfes H (2017c) African Arguments 'Rescued and Deradicalized Women are Returning to Boko Haram. Why?', 1 November 2017, available at https://africanarguments.org/2017/11/01/rescued-and-deradicalised-women-are-returning-to-boko-haram-why/.

Médecins Sans Frontières (2015) 'Nigeria: There are only two doctors in the whole of North Borno State', 13 January 2015, available at http://www.msf.org/en/article/nigeria-%E2%80%9Cthere-are-only-two-doctors-whole-north-borno-state%E2%80%9D.

Mercy Corps (2016) Mercy Corps Report 'Motivations and Empty Promises: Voices of Former Boko Haram Combatants and the Nigerian Youths', April 2016, available at https://www.mercycorps.org/sites/default/files/Motivations%20and%20Empty%20Promises_Mercy%20Corps_Full%20Report.pdf.

Montclos M, Magrin G (eds) (2018) Crisis and Development: The Lake Chad Region and Boko Haram. Agence Francaise de Developpement.

Newman P (2013) The Etymology of Hausa Boko. Mega-Chad Research Network.

New York Times (2012) 'Emergency Declared in Four Nigerian States', 31 December 2011, available at http://www.nytimes.com/2012/01/01/world/africa/boko-haram-attacks-force-emergency-in-4-nigeria-states.html

New York Times (2015) 'Boko Haram Helped by US Policies', 23 July 2015, available at https://www.nytimes.com/2015/07/24/world/africa/muhammadu-buhari-says-us-should-arm-nigeria-against-boko-haram.html.

New York Times (2016a) 'After Years of Distrust, the US Military Reconciles with Nigeria to Fight Boko Haram', 15 May 2016, available at https://www.nytimes.com/2016/05/16/world/africa/boko-haram-nigeria-us-arms-sales-warplanes.html.

New York Times (2016b) 'Nigeria Describes 3 Failed Negotiations with Boko Haram on Kidnapped Girls', 16 September 2016, available at https://www.nytimes.com/2016/09/17/world/africa/nigeria-boko-haram-chibok.html.

Niworu S (2013) Boko Haram Sect: Terrorists or a Manifestation of the Failed Nigerian State? (2013) 6, Journal of Politics and Law.

Ojo V (2015) The Boko Haram Violence from the Perspective of International Criminal Law. University of the Western Cape.

Oke Y (2012-2013) International Criminal Court, Crimes against Humanity and the Nigerian Boko Haram Islamist Group: Can Two Wrongs Make a Right? 12 ISIL Yearbook of International Humanitarian and Refugee Law.

Okebukola E (2018) Calibrating the Legal Obligations in the Ongoing Non-International Armed Conflicts in Nigeria. In: Iyi J, Strydom H (eds) Boko Haram and International Law. Springer.

Omenma J, Hendricks C (2018) Counterterrorism in Africa: An Analysis of the Civilian Joint Taskforce and Military Partnership in Nigeria. (2018) 31(3) Security Journal.

Onuoha FC (2010) The Islamist Challenge: Nigeria's Boko Haram Crisis Explained. (2010) 19 (2), African Security Review, 55.

Owie U (2018) International Law Response Terrorism: Boko Haram in Perspective. In: Iyi J, Strydom H (eds) Boko Haram and International Law. Springer.

Punch Newspaper (2017) Boko Haram: De-radicalization, A Misplaced Strategy. 2 August 2017. Available at https://punchng.com/boko-haram-deradicalisation-a-misplaced-strategy/.

Punch Newspaper (2018) 'Boko Haram and the Concept of "Technical Defeat"' September 18, 2018, available at https://punchng.com/boko-haram-and-the-concept-of-technical-defeat/.

Sampson I (2015) Between Boko Haram and the Joint Task Force: Assessing the Dilemma of counter-Terrorism and Human Rights in Northern Nigeria. (2015) 59, Journal of African Law.

Saul B (2011) Legislating from a Radical Hague: The United Nations Special Tribunal for Lebanon Invents an International Crime of Transnational Terrorism. (2011), Leiden Journal of International Law, 24(3).

Scharf MP (2004) Defining Terrorism as the Peacetime Equivalent of War Crimes: Problems and Prospects. (2004) 36 Case W. Res. J. Int'l L.

Solomon H (2012) Counter-Terrorism in Nigeria: Responding to Boko Haram. (2012), the RUSI Journal.

Sverdlov S (2017) Rape in War: Prosecuting the Islamic State of Iraq and the Levant and Boko Haram for Sexual Violence against Women. (2017)50, Cornell International Law Journal.

Taiwo O (2018) Two is Better than One: Systemic Integration of International Humanitarian Law and International Human Rights Law to Boko Haram Conflict. (2018) 33, American University International Law Review.

Taylor L (2014) Boko Haram Terrorism: Reaching Across International Boundaries to aid Nigeria in the Humanitarian Crisis. (2014) 21 ILSA, Journal of International and Comparative Law.

Thomson V (2012) Boko Haram and Islamic Fundamentalism in Nigeria. (2012) 3 Global Security Studies.

TRT World (2017) 'Boko Haram Timeline: From Social Welfare to International Terrorism', 12 April 2017, available at https://www.trtworld.com/mea/boko-haram-timeline-from-social-welfare-to-international-terrorism-6304.

UNHCR (2016) 'Nigeria: Regional Refugee Response Plan', December 2016, available at http://www.unhcr.org/56a2351b9.pdf (accessed 31 August 2017).

UNICEF (2016) 'Nigeria Co-Situation Report', January 2016, available at https://www.unicef.org/appeals/files/UNICEF_Nigeria_Humanitarian_Situation_Report_Jan_2016.pdf.

United Nations Security Council (2015) Statement by the President of the Council S/PRST/2015/4 January 19, 2015, available at http://undocs.org/S/PRST/2015/4.

United Nations Human Rights Office of the High Commissioner (2017) 'UN Experts call on Nigeria to ensure release of all those still under Boko Haram Captivity', 9 May 2017, available at https://www.ohchr.org/en/NewsEvents/Pages/DisplayNews.aspx?NewsID=21598&LangID=E

Van Sliedregt E (2012) Individual Criminal Responsibility in International Law. Oxford University Press.

Vanguard (2009) 'Boko Haram Resurrects: Declares Total Jihad', 14 August 2009, available at https://www.vanguardngr.com/2009/08/boko-haram-ressurects-declares-total-jihad/.

Vanguard (2015) 'Chad Executes 10 Boko Haram suspects by Firing Squad', 29 August 2015, available at https://www.vanguardngr.com/2015/08/chad-executes-10-boko-haram-suspects-by-firing-squad/.

Vanguard (2017) '82 Chibok Girls; Why we Helped Nigeria Negotiate with Boko Haram-Swiss Government', 10 May 2017, available at https://www.vanguardngr.com/2017/05/82-chibok-girls-helped-nigeria-negotiate-boko-haram-swiss-govt/.

VOA (2015) 'Insurgency, Corruption Challenge Jonathan in Nigerian Reelection Bid', 18 March 2015, available at https://www.voanews.com/a/nigeria-jonathan-profile/2685769.html.

Walker A (2012) What is Boko Haram? United States Institute of Peace.

Walker A (2016) Eat the Heart of the Infidel: The Harrowing of Nigeria and the Rise of Boko Haram. C Hurst & Co Publishers Ltd.

Werle G, Burghardt B (2014) Establishing Degrees of Responsibility: Modes of Participation in Article 25 of the ICC Statute. In: Van Sliedregt E, Vasiliev S (eds) Pluralism in International Criminal Law. Oxford University Press.

Werle G, Jessberger F (2014) Principles of International Criminal Law, 3rd edn. Oxford University Press.

Other Documents

Arab Convention for the Suppression of Terrorism (2002).

Convention of the Organization of Islamic Conference on Combating International Terrorism 1999.

Convention on the Physical Protection of Nuclear Material, adopted at Vienna on 3 March 1980.

Convention on the Prevention and Punishment of Crimes against Internationally Protected Persons, including Diplomatic Agents, adopted by the General Assembly of the United Nations on 14 December 1973.

Convention for the Suppression of Unlawful Acts against the Safety of Civil Aviation, done at Montreal on 23 September 1971.

Convention for the Suppression of Unlawful Acts against the Safety of Maritime Navigation, done at Rome on 10 March 1988.

Convention for the Suppression of Unlawful Seizure of Aircraft, done at The Hague on 16 December 1970. 2.

Economic and Financial Crimes Commission (Establishment) Act 2004.

High Level Conference on the Lake Chad Region in Berlin Results in 2.1 Billion US Dollars in Pledges of Assistance' 3 September 2018, available at https://www.auswaertiges-amt.de/en/aussenpolitik/themen/humanitaerehilfe/lake-chad-conference/2132000.

International Convention against the Taking of Hostages, adopted by the General Assembly of the United Nations on 17 December 1979.

International Convention for the Suppression of Terrorist Bombings, adopted by the General Assembly of the United Nations on 15 December 1997.

OAU Convention on the Prevention and Combating of Terrorism (1999).

Prevention of Terrorism Act, No. 30 of 2012 (Rev 2015) Kenya.

Protocol for the Suppression of Unlawful Acts against the Safety of Fixed Platforms located on the Continental Shelf, done at Rome on 10 March 1988.

Protocol for the Suppression of Unlawful Acts of Violence at Airports Serving International Civil Aviation, supplementary to the Convention for the Suppression of Unlawful Acts against the Safety of Civil Aviation, done at Montreal on 24 February 1988.

Rome Statute of the International Criminal Court (2002).

Special Tribunal for Lebanon Interlocutory Decision on the Applicable Law: Terrorism, Conspiracy, Homicide, Perpetration, Cumulative Charging STL-11-01/1/AC/R17bis 16 February 2011. Available at file://w7server/dfs/homedir/Downloads/20130530_F0936_PUBLIC_PRES_Interlocutory_Decision_Corrected_WEB_EN.pdf.

Terrorism Offences Act of 29 December 2003 Belgium.

Terrorism Prevention Act 2011

Terrorism (Prevention) (Amendment) Act 2013.

UN General Assembly Resolution 49/60 (1990), A/RES/49/60 9 December 1994 annexed Declaration, par 1.3.

UN General Assembly Resolution 54/109 of 9 December 1999. Available at http://www.un.org/law/cod/finterr.htm.

United Nations Convention for the Financing of Terrorism 1999.

United Nations Human Rights Council Resolution on the atrocities committed by the terrorist group Boko Haram and its effects on Human Rights in the affected states. Adopted by the Human Rights Council at its twenty-third special session 1 April 2015 A/HRC/RES/S-23/1.

United Nation's International Convention for the Suppression of the Financing of Terrorism.

United Nations Security Council Resolution 2349 (2017) March 31, 2017 S-23/1 (2015). United Nations Security Council 'Statement by the President of the Security Council' May 13, 2016, available at https://documents-dds-ny.un.org/doc/UNDOC/GEN/N16/137/47/PDF/N1613747.pdf?OpenElement.

UNODC Handbook on Criminal Justice Responses to Terrorism 2009.

Chapter 2
The Boko Haram Crisis: An Overview

Contents

Abstract This chapter provides an introduction and factual background to the crimes committed by the Boko Haram group. It historicises the crisis while addressing the conduct by typology in a manner easily prosecutable. It also provides a view of the general impacts of the crisis.

V. Ojo-Adewuyi, *Criminal Justice Responses to the Boko Haram Crisis in Nigeria*, International Criminal Justice Series 34, https://doi.org/10.1007/978-94-6265-615-4_2

Keywords Almajiri · Al Qaeda · Civilian Joint Task Force (CJTF) · Islamic State in the West Africa Province (ISWAP) · Maitatsine · Political Islam · Salafi Jihadism · Salafism · Shari'a

2.1 Introductory Remarks

On the night of 14 April 2014, armed men overran Government Girls Secondary School Chibok, North-Eastern Nigeria. They approached in a blaze of gunfire, invaded the dormitories and abducted 276 girls who were scheduled for their examinations.[1] While this was not the first time Nigerians or the rest of the world heard about Boko Haram, it represented a new scale in its campaign of violence.[2] As of 2014, Boko Haram had carried out a sustained campaign of violence in the North-East and the North-Central regions of Nigeria for about five years. Although, these attacks were usually primed to maximise casualties, they were mostly carried out by lone suicide bombers, car bombs and sporadic shootings carried out by few gunmen. By abducting the girls, Boko Haram effectively communicated to Nigeria and the world that it was no longer a small fry but had now metamorphosed into a group capable of bringing the nation to its knees. This chapter sets the context for the development of the group by focusing particularly on the historical perspectives to the violent crisis of Boko Haram. It provides the factual background and explores the violent acts of the group.

Structurally, the first section focuses on the historical and political context of the Northern Nigerian region. This is set to contribute to an understanding of the complexities of the social, political and religious issues that together created a viable environment for the emergence of Boko Haram. In the section, due to the fact that Boko Haram first introduced itself to the nation as an Islamic group and its ideologies are patterned after the Salafi Jihadism, the history of the introduction of Islam in Northern Nigeria, political Islam in the region, the development of Islamic fundamentalism as a major challenge is explored. Additionally, the perceived contribution of the Islamic educational system to the crisis and the rise of the use of violence for religious ends are also examined.

The next section of the chapter traces the framework to the development of the Boko Haram group itself and provides a factual background to the violent crisis. It contextualises the conflict to provide a case study analysis. The section concentrates on tracing the trajectory of the development of Boko Haram as a phenomenon which developed in North-Eastern Nigeria against the backdrop of the complexities of the

---

[1] The Chibok abductions were widely reported by mainstream media. See for example, BBC 2014a, The Guardian 2014a, b, and BBC 2017. During transportation, 57 girls managed to escape in a daring move, the Boko Haram group took 219 girls into captivity. In May 2017, the Nigerian government was able to negotiate for the release of 82 girls. Since then, more than 100 girls are still in Boko Haram custody. See Washington Post 2017.

[2] BBC 2014b, and Aljazeera 2014.

issues mentioned above. It also delves into the structure of the group of which admittedly, not much information is within the purview of the public yet. Additionally, the ideology of Boko Haram and its purported alignment with global jihadist movements are explored. Finally, the section concludes on the evolution of the group into a transnational concern and its attempts to export its ideology by carrying out attacks and abductions into territories of Nigeria's nearest neighbours.

While the group has carried out varying acts of violence, the third section attempts to identify a common theme between the acts and structure them in a way in which they can potentially be easily prosecuted. These include killing of civilians, sexual and gender-based violence, proliferation of abductions and hostage taking, violent acts against children including the conscripting and enlisting of children and attacks against civilian properties and protected objects. The section is limited to a mere description of the acts. The domestic and international criminal legal analyses of the identified acts are addressed in later chapters. The chapter concludes with a cursory look at the general consequences of the Boko Haram violent conflict and its impacts on the affected areas, the country and the West African sub-region.

2.2 Historicising the Development of Boko Haram

2.2.1 Islam in Northern Nigeria

North-Eastern Nigeria encompasses an area that extends from Lake Chad in the North, the Mambilla Plateau in the South and the Nigeria-Cameroon borders in the East.[3] The region consists of numerous ethnic groups and religious communities, dominantly the Hausa, Fulani and Kanuri and other smaller groups.[4] While the three largest ethnic groups are predominantly Muslim, the smaller groups include Christians and animists. The earliest known records show that Islam made its first inroads into the region in the eleventh century during the reign of Hume. The influence came from different directions, through the pilgrim traffic and the trans-Saharan trade routes including the political influence of Songhay and Bornu.[5] The Hausa, who were said to have migrated into the region, became an identifiable group around the twelfth century. The rulers of the Kanem-Borno Empire were recorded to have commenced an extensive process of Islamisation of their subjects and developed strong diplomatic contacts with the Islamic world at that time.[6] By the thirteenth century, the Hausa states gained control over most of the region and managed to

[3] Alkali et al. 2012, p. 4.

[4] The tribal and ethnic formulation of Northern Nigeria has been discussed in varying texts including famously the two-volume publication of Meek, a British government anthropologist in Northern Nigeria. See generally Meek 1931. Meeks identified more than 50 non-Muslim tribes in the region in his research.

[5] Trimingham 1962, p. 132.

[6] See generally Alkali, KawuMonguno and Mustafa 2012.

assimilate some of the smaller groups. The empire further became a force to be reckoned with in the seventeenth century because it significantly traded in salt, gold and slaves.[7] According to Trimingham, however, Islam had existed within the ruling and the upper class earlier and the first Muslim ruler appeared in Kano in 1370. Kebbi and Katsina also had rulers who referred to themselves as Muslims in 1510 and Zamfara in 1640.[8] Despite this early influence, the form of Islam that existed before the sixteenth century was described as a relaxed and permissive form.[9] Thomas Hodgkin gave an account of the sixteenth-century kingdom of Kanem Bornu where he stated that there was 'a rebirth of Islam greatly emphasising sharia, the transfer of judicial powers from the tribal chiefs to the Qadis (Muslim judges), the introduction of Purdah (practice of female seclusion and veiling) in Kano and the public celebration of Muslim festivals.'[10] The dynasty of the Kanem Bornu empire was compared in longevity to the greater empires of western Sudan.[11]

The popular account of this history is usually traced to the notable period of the resurgence of Islam in the early nineteenth century when the greater part of the modern-day Northern Nigeria and Northern Cameroon was conquered in a jihad by Uthman dan Fodio (ibn fudi). This led to the creation of the Sokoto Caliphate and the introduction of an austere form of Islam to the region.[12] The Caliphate marked the beginning of cohesion in the region under the Islamic movement even though it consisted of autonomous emirates with their own Emirs and administration.[13] Uthman dan Fodio was an esteemed fulanin gidda (town Fulani)[14] of a group that settled in the Hausa kingdom of Gobir, a member of the qadriyyah sect.[15] Between the early days of Islamic contact with the region and the nineteenth century, the religion had acquired a mix of animism and paganism and it was this weakened form of Islam that Uthman dan Fodio reportedly objected to.[16] As a result of the Jihad,

---

7 International Crisis Group 2010, p. 2.

8 Trimingham 1962, p. 107.

9 Even though many scholars have disagreed with the earlier historical account for lack of solid records, it is apparent that it existed in the Islamic monuments and literature in the State of Bornu which was not conquered by Uthman dan Fodio and the traditions of the descendants of Muhammed al-Amin al-Kanemi. For more on this, see generally Schacht 1957.

10 See Hodgkin 1960, p. 27.

11 Trimingham 1962, p. 107.

12 Schacht 1957, p. 123.

13 International Crisis Group 2010, p. 3.

14 The Fulanis are a nomadic tribe present in the Sahel and West Africa predominantly in Nigeria, Guinea, Guinea-Bissau and Mali and other West African countries. They were the first set of West Africans to contact Islam and they facilitated the spread of Islam in the region. On the Fulani tribe see generally, Ibrahim 1966.

15 Means 1965, p. 14.

16 Means 1965, p. 17. It has been argued that the so-called Fulani Jihad was not only for religious reasons, but rather that it was a pretext for a Fulani rebellion against economic liberty and the way of life in a predominantly Hausa kingdom. For more on these thoughts, see generally Olaosebikan 2011, and Audu and Osuala 2014.

Uthman Dan Fodio was proclaimed Amir al-Mu'minin in Hausa Sarkin Musulmi.[17] The Sheikh of Bornu, a Muslim scholar with ties to the Arab world was the only leader to successfully resist Uthman dan Fodio's famous Jihad.[18] After the Jihad, the Hausa rulers were replaced by members of the Fulani Muslim elite. Uthman dan Fodio was quoted as describing the situation thus:

> The government of a country is the government of its king without question. If the king is a Muslim, the land is Muslim; if he is an unbeliever, his land is a land of unbelievers. In this circumstance, it is lawful for anyone to leave it for other country. There is no dispute that the Hausa kings worshipped many pieces of idols, and trees, and rocks, and sacrificed to them. This constitutes unbelief according to the general opinion... The above description was applicable to the condition of the Hausa peoples as we found them before the jihad. Since then, we have fought them, and put them to flight, and killed some, and driven others from the land by the power of God...We have appointed Muslim governors over the land and it has become a land of Islam without doubt.'[19]

The Caliphate promoted a culture of Islamic knowledge and intellectualism and Islamic education became the benchmark for opportunities including political leadership.[20] The Caliphate was resisted in part because of intense taxation and revolts over Islamic doctrinal issues. Additionally, the success of its economy was mostly based on plantation labour and the use of captured slaves from so-called heathen territories.[21] A major legacy of the Caliphate is the structured system of traditional governance based on Islam which was founded on the Emirs and their descendants. Although, the Caliphate was defeated in 1903, the British utilised its structure albeit with some restructuring, to administer the region through its policy of indirect rule.[22]

The political idea of 'One North' or 'Jama'ar Arewa' was pioneered by Ahmadu Bello, the former Premier of the new Northern Nigeria region which emerged after the Nigerian independence from British colonisation in 1960. This led to what some regarded as a forceful marriage between the diverse groups in the region and what seemingly became an imposition of the Hausa-Fulani hegemony including the imposition of Islam on the rest of the region.[23] This idea pursued a 'northernisation' strategy which favoured Northerners over Southern migrants who were being increasingly perceived to be a threat in the region.[24] Although the strategy had benefits, it undermined the agitations of the religious and ethnic minorities within the region in favour of a collective agitation against the so-called outsiders. Additionally, the leadership system in the North was firmly in the hands of the Muslim Fulani

---

[17] This title also rendered as 'Amir-ul Momineen' means the 'defender of the faithful' and it remains one of the ceremonial titles of the Sultan of Sokoto in Northern Nigeria till date. See Oliver and Atmore 2005, Trimingham 1962, p. 199.

[18] Means 1965, p. 18.

[19] Quote from Means 1965, p. 19.

[20] International Crisis Group 2010, p. 3.

[21] International Crisis Group 2010, p. 4. See also Lovejoy 1983, p. 195.

[22] The idea of indirect rule in the then Northern Nigeria protectorate was pioneered by Sir Fredrick Lugard. The ideology is explained in Lugard 1922, p. 121, See also Reynolds 2001, p. 604.

[23] For more on these issues, see Kwanashie 2002, p. 204.

[24] See generally Loimeier 2012a, b, Harnischfeger 2008.

nobility and the Hausa majority, thus excluding almost completely a representation of the other minority tribes and religious leanings. The Northern Peoples' Congress (NPC) of Ahmadu Bello also embarked on a policy to promote Islam as a means to preserve the cultural identity of the region. It established the Jama'atu Nasril Islam (Unity for Islam) in 1962 to unite the various Muslim sects under an umbrella body. This body also provided an ideological base for the political party and remains the largest Islamic umbrella body in Nigeria till date. Additionally, intense conversion campaigns intended for the 'pagan' minority groups was embarked upon. These were recorded as being widely successful as they were supported by state resources. Collective pilgrimages to Mecca were encouraged and sometimes funded. Ahmadu Bello himself campaigned and won as Vice President of the World Muslim League in 1963.[25] Predictably, fears of an Islamic hegemony both in Northern Nigeria and in the rest of the country rose as a result and have continued to surface periodically since then. Ideologically, the Sufi brotherhoods of Quadiriya and Tijaniyyah dominate Muslim identity in Northern Nigeria.[26] The Izala movement was the first non-Sufi sect to emerge in the region.[27] The Shiites also emerged in the early 1980s reportedly through the influence of the writings of Egyptian scholars.[28]

2.2.2 *Political Islam in Northern Nigeria*

Political Islam also described as internal jihadi[29] or religious nationalism[30] is a form of Islamic activism that attempts to capture the apparatus of the nation-state and all its institutions as a response to its perceived corruption and secularism. This system operates under the belief that political sovereignty is of God and as such, Islamic law should be comprehensively implemented within the state system. The state can be captured through activities such as education, propaganda, political mobilisation

[25] International Crisis Group 2010, p. 7.

[26] Sufism represents traditional Islam in Northern Nigeria, commonly practiced by the Quadiriya and the Tijaniyyah sects. Sufis refer to other groups like the Salafis as radicals. Sufism has deep roots in Nigeria as it was the state form of Islam practised in the Caliphate of Uthman dan Fodio. The brotherhoods choose a saint to revere and emulate. The Qadiriyya is named after Abdul-Qadir Jilani, a scholar who rose to prominence in Baghdad in the late 11th and early 12th centuries, the Tijaniyya after Ahmad al-Tijani from the Western Maghreb between 1737 and 1815. Both are global movements. See Hill 2010, Mohammed in Perouse de Montclos 2014, p. 11.

[27] The *Izala* movement is otherwise known as Jama'at 'Izalat al-Bid'a wa-Iqamat al-Sunna (Association for the removal of innovation and the establishment of the Sunna). The group was established in 1978 in response to the introduction of innovations such as the worship of saints by the Sufi sects. See generally Amara 2012.

[28] Shiites are united under a foundation organisation called The Islamic Movement of Nigeria led by Ibrahim El Zaky Zaky. See Alao 2013.

[29] International Crisis Group 2005.

[30] See Juergensmeyer 1994, p. 50. See also Fawaz 2005.

including through political violence.[31] Islam is then maintained through the apparatus of the nation-state. This can be clearly distinguished from Islamic fundamentalist movements such as Salafism which rejects and seeks to abolish the modern state and its apparatus while attempting to entrench the Muslim collective (ummah) as the administrative entity. The nineteenth century Jihad of Dan Fodio is an example of the utilisation of what became the ideology of political Islam. He was instrumental to the establishment of a single political authority, the Caliphate, over the region which was made up of a large number of nominally subordinate separate Islamic states. The Emirs who led the emirate system governed their territory with a large measure of autonomy with occasional interference particularly relative to the issue of succession. They also paid a bi-annual tribute to the Caliph.[32] As a result, traditionalism and conservative Islam in a feudal and aristocratic institution with an elaborate administrative system developed and became entrenched in the region.[33] Under Muhammad Bello and his successors, so-called 'religious imperialism' became institutionalised. This state-centred form of Islam continued to develop until the advent of British colonisation and the system was also utilised for governance purpose by Sir Frederick Lugard.[34] This was in direct contrast to the system utilised in the rest of present-day Nigeria, the so-called southern protectorate. With regards to law, Lugard stated that the practice of indirect rule will not interfere with matters of religion and Shari'a (the legal expression of Islam), except for punishments regarded as inhumane, particularly criminal penalties such as slavery and amputation as a punishment.[35] True to its form and the evolution of its history in Northern Nigeria,[36] Islam in the region is geared towards every sphere of life including the political order. Thus, in Northern Nigeria, Islam and politics are historically rooted and intrinsically linked.[37] Nigerians classify themselves principally by ethnic, religious and gender rather than national identity,

---

[31] Armborst 2009, p. 54.

[32] Huntwick 1992, p. 146.

[33] Means 1965, p. 22.

[34] Sir Frederick Lugard was the High Commissioner of the Protectorate of Northern Nigeria from 1899 to 1906. He also became the Governor with the mandate to amalgamate the Northern and Southern protectorates in 1912. He was successful by promoting the ideal of Islamic system of self-government and using the forms of administration already in place in Northern Nigeria instead of replacing the system with British institutions and officers. The available British officers played a rather sparing supervisory role behind the scene in the administration of the region. His ideas on the development and suitability of indirect rule in occupied colonies are articulated in 1922 book.

[35] Sir Frederick Lugard 1922, p. 121 See also Reynolds 2001, p. 604. See also Anderson 1959, p. 443.

[36] The history of the development of the sharia legal regime and the subsequent conflict with English law has been exhaustively addressed by scholars. See generally Anderson 1959, Christelow 2002, and Ubah 1982.

[37] Examples abound in the world where the continued presence of Islamic political parties lends credence to this argument. For example, Hamas in Palestine is arguably a political entity, the Muslim Brotherhood in Egypt, the *Jama'at-i-Islami* in Pakistan and Bangladesh etc. all commenced as political institutions using Islam as an ideological basis. The concept of political Islam has been discussed in an earlier section of this work.

this is also very apparent in Northern Nigeria.[38] In Northern Nigeria, religious identity has the tendency to 'override citizenship, and access to opportunity, entitlements and participation may be principally based on the religion of the seeker.'[39] Northern Nigeria as with other parts of the country epitomises a society where the citizens are greatly polarised across religious and ethnic lines. The over-exertion of religion on other spheres of life also creates a situation where religion and religious sentiments are not immune from manipulations by politicians for their own gain.[40] Principally, in Northern Nigeria, Islam is politicised, politics is Islamised and Islam has been used as a tool to legitimise power.

2.2.3 Development of Islamic Fundamentalism in Northern Nigeria

In Nigeria, it is difficult to make sweeping generalisations about the root cause and the development of fundamentalism. However, commentators on the Northern Nigerian region have identified a fusion of both internal and external factors which in their view have contributed strongly to the development of Islamic fundamentalism. Additionally, a combination of these factors with the social, economic, political and religious upheavals in Nigeria provided a breeding ground for the phenomenon.

The root of Islamic fundamentalism is typically traced to the inception of colonial rule when Islamic resistance (taqqiya) played a major role in the opposition to the British incursion which led to the eventual defeat of the Sokoto Caliphate.[41] The resistant groups were however not homogeneous. Before the Nigerian independence in 1960, doctrinal differences between Islamic sects especially the Quadriyya and Tijaniyya created a lot of violence which persisted until the independence.[42] From 1967 to 1970, the civil war broke out and it devastated major parts of the country. The next decade was spent rebuilding vast parts of the country after the ravages of war. These among other factors were identified as contributing to an environment in which fundamentalism and radicalisation could freely thrive. In 1978, the rise of the Wahabbi-inspired Izala movement was a pivotal point in the development of Islamic fundamentalism in Nigeria. Under the leadership of Sheik Abubakar Gumi,

---

38 Blanco-Mancilla 2002.

39 Agbiboa 2013a, b, p. 7.

40 An example of this is the introduction of Shari'a legal regime first in Zamfara state in Northern Nigeria. Commentators have noted that this was not due to the religious devotion of the then governor, Ahmed Sani Yerima, but rather as a political decision taken on the recognition of his reducing popularity and support in a bid to sustain his re-election campaign. It is a common view additionally that politicians are also usually responsible for some of the violent uprising in Northern Nigeria either by using gangs of young thugs to stir up religious related violence and also to seek a pay-out from the federal government once the violence is spent. See for example these and related arguments in Kendhammer 2013, and Ntamu et al. 2014.

41 Mohammed 2014, p. 21.

42 Alao 2013, p. 130.

the group became critical of the traditional Islamic system, perceived corruption in government, and so-called declining moral values in the society.[43] The 1979 revolution against the Shah of Iran and the subsequent establishment of an Islamic republic also became a model of how Islam could be used as a vehicle for social reform. During this period, Nigeria experienced an increase in Islamic revolutionary literature. The writings of Sayyid Qutb and Hassan al-Banna of Egypt inspired many revolutionary Islamic movements including Ibrahim El-Zakyzaky and the so-called Nigerian Muslim Brotherhood, a *Sunni* group that rejected the Nigerian constitution, flag and legal institutions and accepted the shari'a legal regime as the only recognised legal authority.[44] Politically, the period between 1980 and 2000 was also fraught with instability. There were two civilian administrations, five military coups (two executed, one attempted and two alleged), an annulled general election, an interim administration and a dictatorship.[45]

The emergence of the Maitatsine group signalled the beginning of the utilisation of organised violence against the Nigerian State.[46] Using Salafism as its basis, the group preached a complete rejection of affluence, so-called western education, materialism and any form of technology. The leader, Mohammed Marwa, originally from Cameroon, presented himself as a liberator and a voice for the lower class. The members carried out violent attacks against Muslims who did not share their beliefs, considered as pagans, non-Muslims and the police, who were seen as a tool of the so-called secular state. Although the leader was killed in one of the early attacks in December 1980, violent acts continued in his name and on his behalf for several years after his death. Other internal factors include the introduction of the Structural Adjustment Program of the World Bank and the International Monetary Fund (IMF) adopted in 1986. Many Nigerians blamed the SAP for the adverse impacts it had on the economy at that time. These programmes led to mandatory devaluation of Nigeria's currency, the Naira, high inflation rate, lower purchasing power and created an economic crisis which impoverished a large percentage of the populace.[47]

A new wave of fundamentalism was awakened between 1999 and 2000 with the introduction of Shari'a law with a full criminal jurisdiction in Zamfara state and its rapid adoption by eleven other states.[48] Although, the British colonial system preserved many elements of Shari'a after the fall of the Sokoto Caliphate, its scope was greatly reduced by a Common Law Code that was introduced for the whole country. After independence, the Islamic Court of Appeal was abolished in 1967

[43] Mohammed 2014, p. 22.

[44] Kenny 1996, p. 344.

[45] See generally Alao 2013, p. 130, Ogbeidi 2012, and Dawood 2015.

[46] The leader of the group was a dissident preacher who hailed from Marwa in Cameroon. The name of the group developed from the saying of the leader, '*wanda bata yarda ba Allah ta Tchine*' in Hausa which means 'May Allah curse anyone who disagrees with this version', later rendered as 'Maitatsine'. See Isichie 1987, p. 195.

[47] Alao 2013, p. 130.

[48] Bauchi, Borno, Gombe, Jigawa, Kaduna, Kano, Katsina, Kebbi, Niger, Sokoto, Yobe, and Zamfara States in Northern Nigeria have all adopted full implementation of Shari'a as at 2002. See further Mohammed 2014, p. 22.

and the new Constitution in 1978 recognised no religion. The Federal Constitution defined Shari'a law in terms of civil and personal matters only, with no criminal jurisdiction. In 1999, some states exploited a legal loophole in Section 277 of the Constitution and conferred full criminal jurisdictions on their Shari'a courts. First, by Zamfara state government in Northern Nigeria and swiftly followed by other states, some also established Shari'a law enforcement agencies.[49] The adoption of Shari'a with full criminal jurisdiction, including a Shari'a Penal Code was marketed as a tool for the improvement of the quality of the lives of the populace of the majority Islamic states. The Code restored the offences and the punishments as prescribed in Islamic traditions including prescriptions on homicide and bodily harm.[50] However, in practice, the system suffered from lost hopes and an uneasy coexistence with the so-called secular institutions and the Nigerian Constitution. There was also scant evidence that the Code was successful in achieving the expectations of enhancing socio-economic welfare, reducing grassroots crime, ensuring efficient dispensation of justice and stemming the tide of corruption in government.[51] This resulted in a fervent call by radical groups for the full adoption of Shari'a law as against the Zamfara model. Proponents of full adoption opine that Shari'a will not be truly realised except it is implemented, not by politicians, but by religious leaders leading to an Islamic State.[52] This call has remained a major pillar of the ideology of radical groups such as Boko Haram.

Intra-Islamic rivalry also played a major role in the leanings towards fundamentalism. Violence leading to massive loss of lives and properties in Northern Nigeria were sparked in many instances by doctrinal differences between Islamic sects. Majority of these crises were between the Sunnis and the Shiites with devastating consequences in 1996, 2005 and 2007.[53] Differences between each group's appreciation and understanding of religious norms and practices including alignment with sympathetic international Islamic organisations resulted in faithfuls' taking up arms to defend their version of Islam.

The influences of certain external elements are also noteworthy. A number of Middle East and North African countries like Iran, Egypt, Saudi Arabia and Libya in the 1980s massively sponsored Islamic missions in West Africa. This was in the form of sponsorship of radical texts and offer of scholarships to youths to study in

[49] The Hisbah is an Islamic law enforcement group similar to the religious police common in Islamic countries. The group was tasked with the enforcement of the Shari'a code while operating with the consent and support of the state governments. Hisbah officers were accused of assaulting women perceived to have been inappropriately dressed, destroying alcohol merchant's shops and goods and carrying out summary punishment for anyone accused of insulting Islam. All these created a lot of chaos and widespread allegations of human rights abuses during the high point of the Shari'a crisis. It was also unclear where the functions of the Hisbah stopped and those of the police started. The Hisbah crisis eventually settled down and its officers work more in terms of social mediation. See International Crisis Group 2010, and Adamu 2008.

[50] Weimann 2007, p. 240.

[51] International Crisis Group 2010.

[52] International Crisis Group 2010, p. 23.

[53] Alao 2013, p. 135.

the North Africa and the Middle East, building of Islamic schools and the sponsoring of Islamic Literature.

Similarly influential was the so-called American factor. The United States of America's foreign policy in the Middle East, its support for Israel coupled with the perception of Israel's actions in Palestine enraged fundamentalists in Nigeria. The American invasion and occupation of Afghanistan after the September 11, 2001 attack attributed to Al-Qaeda and the subsequent 'global war on terror' was interpreted as a war against Muslims and Islam everywhere. This contributed to the fundamentalism pool and evoked considerable anti-western feelings. American support for the state of Israel was a unifying and rallying cause among radical Muslims in Nigeria regardless of section. Due to strong ties to the Arab world and the high concentration of Muslims in the region, the worldview in Northern Nigeria has been described as 'pan-Islamic.' Most Muslims in the region are viewed as having a strong sense of solidarity with religious causes across the world and gives thought to his place in the global Islamic community. Wide scale anti-American rhetoric was used in propaganda by radical Islamic groups in Nigeria towards recruiting new members. After the September 11, 2001 attacks on the United States, there were celebrations in some parts of Northern Nigeria with many hailing Osama bin Laden as a new hero that will demystify the United States of America.[54] In December 2008, a large number of Shiite protesters marched through Kano, calling on the Nigerian government to cut ties with the Israel during the Israeli blockade of Gaza.[55]

Abiodun Alao while categorising the manifestation of Islamic radicalisation in Nigeria noted three categories of radicals. The first group he describes as the genuine radicals committed to reacting to what they consider a desecration of their religion. This group abandons families to take up the cause of Islam by joining radical groups such as Boko Haram fully. The second category he described as ad-hoc radicals. According to the author, these individuals live normal lives and only choose to go on a rampage when there is an instruction from a spiritual leader to that effect and afterwards revert to their normal lives. This category also includes sympathisers who are eager to provide support, funding and sometimes participate in violence in defence of their beliefs. The third category describes opportunistic radicals, who sometimes utilise the chance of an ongoing violence to loot and vandalise properties. This characterisation is instructive because regardless of the membership strength of a radical Islamic group per time, the percentage of so-called ad-hoc radicals and sympathisers in Northern Nigeria is typically very high. This usually puzzles investigators who find it difficult to reconcile the massive violence carried out with the seemingly small numerical strength of the responsible radical group.

[54] See also Harnischfeger 2012.

[55] All Africa, 2008. See also The Guardian 2017a, b.

2.2.4 *Islamic Education and the Influence of the Almajiri System in Northern Nigeria*

Since the rise of fundamentalism in Nigeria, there has been vigorous debate about the role of the traditional Quranic educational system as a feeder for fundamentalism. Writers and researchers have argued that Islamic fundamentalists find easy recruits in the traditional Quranic educational schools where students are at the bottom rung of the societal ladder, loosely supervised and due to their relatively young age and harsh living conditions, they are potentially easily radicalised.[56] Additionally, it has being contended that a good number of members of the so-called terrorist groups in the past like the Maitatsine group including known members of Boko Haram were former students of the almajiri system.[57] Other writers have argued, however, that there is no systematic evidence to support these assertions and that the almajiri have merely become convenient scapegoats in the discourse around Islamic fundamentalism and terrorism in Nigeria.[58] It is important to understand the traditional Qur'anic educational system in order to understand why these group of Nigerian citizens are usually quickly blamed for facilitating the spread of radicalisation and consequently for acts of terrorism.

The word 'almajiri' is borrowed from the Arabic word 'Al Muhajir' denoting a seeker of Islamic knowledge or a travelling student. Referencing the Hijra of Prophet Muhammad from Mecca to Medina, his fellow migrants were regarded to as 'Al Muhajirrun'—'the emigrants'.[59] The practice was described as a religiously legitimate exercise and one of the Hadith of Prophet Muhammed states; 'seeking knowledge is an obligation upon every Muslim'.[60] The traditional Islamic system of education had been in existence before the Jihad of Dan Fodio and it continued to wax stronger and became more standardised in the Caliphate. Dan Fodio is credited with strengthening the heritage of the Quranic educational system and transforming it into a well-organised Islamic primary educational system before his death in 1817. The almajiri heritage is not exclusively Nigerian and it exists in different names and forms in most of Islamic West Africa previously under the political control of the Sokoto Caliphate.[61] The system has also been described as similar in structure to the madrassahs in Pakistan and central Asia, and the talibe system in Senegal, Gambia, Guinea, Mauritania, Mali and Guinea-Bissau.[62]

This system of Islamic education continued and remained in operation after the incursion of the British. Teaching is provided by religious scholars known as mallams. The system is very fluid but the major focus is on learning the Quran by heart with

---

[56] See Akubor 2016.

[57] See generally Asogwa et al. 2015, Gomment et al. 2017, and Aghedo and Eke 2013.

[58] For more on the arguments and counter arguments, see Hoechner 2014. See also Awofeso et al. 2003, p. 311.

[59] Taiwo 2013, p. 67.

[60] Sunan Ibn Majah 224. English Reference Vol 1 Book 1 Hadith 224. Arabic Book 1 Hadith 229.

[61] Awofeso et al. 2003, p. 314.

[62] See generally, Mbow 2009.

much attention paid to recitation and memorisation. In principle, the instruction is private, free and informal. The teacher depends on charity (sadaka) extended by parents and the student's assistance in the exercise of his trade. The system typically comprises a large number of boys and very few girls who leave the system earlier than the boys.[63] There is no stated age of enrolment but students are usually aged four to early teens and the academic ability of a student determines the duration of the study. The educational system is usually composed of three major stages; learning the Quran by heart (tilawa), memorising (hafizi) and perfecting the ability to write the whole Quran with no error either on a slate or more recently on paper (darasi).[64] An important distinguishing feature from any other educational system is that children relocate away from their families and friends, usually in the villages to live under the custody of the mallams in the city.

After the incursion of the British, the more established traditional Islamic educational system began an uneasy coexistence with the new secular educational system that was introduced. The practice of indirect rule by Lord Lugard which attempted not to interfere with the cultural, religious and educational structures of Northern Nigeria inadvertently pioneered a secular educational system based on class. The initial introduction to western secular education was done by founding six-month training in Roman script and elementary science open only to the children of the upper class. This system quickly metamorphosed into the so-called emir schools which became elite schools. The children of peasants and the descendants of former slaves continued to acquire their education through the almajiri system. Graduates from the emir schools found employment in the budding colonial system which needed translators and workers. Most of who became powerful players in the Northern Nigeria society while graduates of the almajiri system could not be employed in the rapidly growing colonial system. Thus, the deep gulf between the elites and the so-called peasants continued to widen. The almajiri heritage began to be seen as an important element in the opposition to the colonial system and its hegemony. Consequently, there was widespread resistance to subsequent attempts of its incorporation into the secular educational system. After Nigeria's independence in 1960, the almajiri system was not standardised and thus not formally recognised as part of the educational system nor was funding provided for their operations. The almajiri system has become quite different from the organised system of the past and as Taiwo described:

> Almajiri pupils learn the Quran under a teacher three times a day without good shelter, food or good health care and away from their parents, some of whom are hundreds of kilometers away. His consolation lies in the belief that his suffering in the world is for the reward that awaits him in heaven.[65]

Some mallams (teachers) have as many as a hundred students who they are expected to feed and accommodate. Due to the fact that this became practically impossible in the post-independence Nigerian economy, the mallams began to allow

[63] Schacht 1957, p. 131.

[64] Taiwo 2013, p. 68.

[65] Taiwo 2013, p. 68.

the students carry out menial jobs around the town where they study during the day time when there are no classes. These students also typically engage in begging for food and loose change.[66]

The Federal Government constituted tribunal of inquiry into the 1980s Maitatsine uprising noted in its reports that a large number of the perpetrators of the violent attacks in the early 1980s were almajiri who were learning the Quran, including adult followers who were former students.[67] Most of the children from very poor backgrounds that have exclusively gone through the almajiri system typically involve themselves in anti-social activities such as drug abuse, due to lack of meaningful job opportunities and many end up as beggars (Almajiranchi), hawkers or wanderers.[68] In major Northern cities like Kano and Kaduna, many of the alms-begging Almajiri have graduated into Yandaba, adolescent groups that in the past socialised teenagers into adulthood but have metamorphosed into gangs.[69] The National Council for the Welfare of the Destitute in 2005 estimated that there were at least seven million Almajiri children in Northern Nigeria. Even though the almajiri system continues to undergo reform in the democratic dispensation in Nigeria,[70] it has produced generations of citizens who are ill-equipped to cope with the practical realities of the times. It is, therefore, not far-fetched that terrorist groups like the Boko Haram may find easy recruits for its purposes among the group.

2.2.5 Terror for Religion's Sake

As previously shown, religious-related violence is not a novel occurrence in Northern Nigeria. The cocktail of factors, notably religious pluralism mixed with fierce ethnic and tribal identity in a complex society, produce the volatile situation evident in the region. Since the 1980s, violent conflict has flared up periodically in Northern Nigeria. Agbiboa argued that Islam in the region is emblematic of the religious-political nexus.[71] Other factors identified include, but are not limited to political manipulation of religion and ethnicity, corruption, failure of the State to ensure public order, economic decline and absence of viable employment opportunities and

[66] Yusha 'u et al. 2013, p. 126.

[67] Report of the Ministerial Committee on Madrassah Education 2010, para 287.

[68] Yusha'u et al. 2013, p. 129.

[69] International Crisis Group 2010. See also Last 1991, p. 19.

[70] The governments of a number of Northern states have embarked on reform programmes intended to improve the Almajiri system including for example, infusing it into the Universal Basic Education Program (UBE), introducing a dual curriculum of Islamic and Western studies, payment of salaries to the teachers (Mallams) etc. During the Presidency of Goodluck Jonathan, he continued the reform of the Almajiri system and embarked on ambitious project of building Almajiri model schools. Whether this will have a lasting impact remains to be seen as they were not widely accepted in the North. See generally, Taiwo 2013, and Daily Post 2016a, b, c.

[71] Agbiboa 2013a, b, p. 3.

inequality.[72] Bassam opine that Islam as a majority religion has a leading role in the incessant religious conflict in the region because, in his view, Islam never ceased to have an impact on political life.'[73] Religious pluralism in Northern Nigeria and the presence of citizens of differing tribal and religious affiliations are among major factors at the root of age-long tensions and among other causes have led to major violent conflict in the past. Since independence, Nigeria has dealt with a continuum of religious conflicts and civil unrests which usually commences from the Northern region. Christians in the North argue that among other risks, they are compelled to live in segregated areas and forced to place their children in separate schools. This forceful segregation makes them a sitting target whenever violence commences. Usually, violence erupts for many reasons including perceived slight on Islam in many forms as well as the unwillingness of non-Muslims to be subject to any form of Islamic control or the Shari'a legal regime.[74] These acts of violence are usually of a collective nature and non-Muslims and ethnic minorities are frequently sought out for killing, relocation and destruction of properties.[75] The areas susceptible to incessant violence are typically the large urban centres(especially Kaduna, Kano and Bauchi) with a large migrant population and a plurality of religious beliefs and practices.

The first major inter-ethnic crisis occurred in 1953 in the period leading up to independence. Hausa and Igbo migrants clashed in Kano over the attempts by the 'southerners' anti-colonial and pro-independence rallies. The crisis led to the death of at least thirty-six people and left about two hundred people injured.[76] The crisis was a result of the initial opposition of the Northern elites to independence due to the perceived fear that an end to British rule could terminate its hegemony over the arguably more developed and better educated South. The lack of consensus over the readiness of Nigeria for independence was also responsible for its late independence

[72] International Crisis Group 2010.

[73] Bassam 2007, p. 17.

[74] The dynamics of the interrelations between Christians and Muslims were historically fraught with tension and suspicions. Controversial challenges include the native and settler dichotomies and the use of indigeneity which has disenfranchised and delegitimised certain non-Muslim communities in Northern Nigeria. According to complaints, Land for Christian religious activities were granted outside the desirable areas of town, in many instances, individual Christians acquiring lands and properties were required to sign clauses in contracts such as 'not to be used for church or hotel'. Christian's resident in the North strongly resisted the implementation of the Shari'a legal regime in the North. They complained that mission schools and hospitals were stripped of their Christian identity and symbols and were replaced by 'more befitting Hausa-Muslim ones'. Public expression of Christian faith raised suspicion and Christians several times alleged that they were unable to get slots on public radio and television stations for evangelising purposes regardless of how much they were willing to pay, while public funds were being used to sponsor Islamic programmes on the same stations. Muslim leaders argued, however, that non-Muslims had nothing to do with Shari'a and were not to be affected by it. Both sides view each other with deep suspicion. On these and related issues, see, for example, Ludwig 2008, Yusuf 2007, and Harris 2013.

[75] Agbiboa 2013a, b, p. 8.

[76] See generally Lynn 2006.

compared to its smaller neighbour Ghana which began to agitate for self-government as early as 1948.[77]

In January 1966, a military coup led by Christian Igbo leaders from the Eastern region led to the killing of several Northern political and military leaders. This served to further fracture the already strained relations between the North and the rest of the country. Incidentally, it halted the control of the Northern People's Congress on minorities in the North. In July of the same year, there was a counter coup which led to the installation of a Christian from the middle belt, Lieutenant Colonel Yakubu Gowon, in what was interpreted as an act of concession by the Muslim leaders in an attempt to retain the solidarity of the non-Muslim minorities. Between July and October 1966, mobs of Northerners descended heavily on Southerners in the region, mostly Igbos, killing thousands and forcing survivors to flee from the region. Part of the reactions to the killings was the call to secession by the Igbo dominated Eastern region, declaring itself the Republic of Biafra. This led to the infamous three year long civil war from 1967 to 1970.[78]

In October 1982, two prominent churches were burnt and six more destroyed after the Archbishop of Canterbury, Robert Runcie visited Kano to lay the foundation stone of an Anglican Church. Violent protest by the Muslim Student's Society led to the death of at least forty-four people.[79] Similarly, in 1991, protests over the invitation of the late controversial American-based German revivalist, Reinhard Bonnke, to a Christian crusade in Kano left more than two hundred Southern Christians dead and about twenty churches destroyed.[80] Violence is typically deployed in Northern Nigerian to purportedly defend Islam for varying reasons and with little provocation. For instance, In September 2001, the appointment of a Christian local council chairman led to massive violence that resulted in the death of about one hundred and sixty people.[81] In November 2002, massive violent riots arose on the eve of the Miss World beauty pageant which was to be hosted by Nigeria. Infuriated Northerners took to the street in the Northern city of Kaduna and unleashed violence on symbols of modernity including churches, clubs and on their Christian neighbours. Over one hundred people were killed in the attacks and more than five hundred were reportedly injured.[82] Similarly, in April 2011, the aftermath of the presidential elections led to the death of over eight hundred people and the displacement of about sixty-five

---

[77] The 1948 Accra riots marked the formal beginning of the agitation of Ghana for independence from British rule. It gained independence and self-government in March 1957. Although a Southerner, Anthony Enahoro, moved the motion in the Nigerian Parliament in 1953 for independence by 1956, this was vehemently opposed by the Northern members and the Sardauna of Sokoto moved a counter motion for independence 'as soon as practicable'. See generally, Chazan 1989, and Feit 1968.

[78] See Heerten and Moses 2014.

[79] See Sandah 2013, and The New York Times 1982.

[80] The Washington Post 1991. See generally Deegan 2011.

[81] See generally, Human Rights Watch 2005, and Ludwig 2008.

[82] The violence was motivated by an article in a Lagos-based newspaper. The author, while exploring what Prophet Muhammed could think of the pageant, suggested that he could have chosen a wife from among the contestants. See The Guardian 2002.

thousand people. The violence reportedly started by followers of Northern Muslim candidate, Muhammadu Buhari, in protest of the election of Goodluck Jonathan, a Christian from the South.[83]

2.3 Factual Background to the Boko Haram Crisis

2.3.1 Trajectory of the Development of Boko Haram

The roots of Boko Haram have been traced to an extremist youth group that gathered to pray in the Alhaji Muhammadu Ndimi mosque in Maiduguri, North-East Nigeria. A part of the group in 2002 announced that the Islamic establishment and the town had become corrupt. Declaring a hijra,[84] the group moved to Kanama, a village in Yobe state. They established a community administered according to their version of strict Islamic principles. The site which seemed to have been chosen for its remoteness and defensibility and 'an eye for military details' was in a forest area, surrounded by two bodies of water at the Nigeria-Niger border area.[85] The group in turn extended an invitation to other Muslims to join them and live according to what they termed true Islamic belief in other to create a perfect society, away from the alleged corrupt political and religious institutions.[86] Initially, the group was focused on da'wa (preaching of Islam) and the creation of a micro-society exemplifying their idea of pure Islam.[87] In 2003, however, as a result of a dispute over fishing rights, the group overpowered a local police unit, seized their weapons and engaged in massive violence. They attacked other police stations and government buildings and wreaked havoc in about five local government areas of Yobe State. This resulted in a clash with the Nigerian military and led to the death of about seventy members of the group including the leader at that time, Muhammad Ali. The incident brought them to national attention and the group quickly earned the moniker, 'the Nigerian Taliban'. The survivors joined the members who remained in Maiduguri under the leadership of Muhammed Yusuf and built a mosque of their own. The mosque attracted a lot of young people and became a centre of education for a new crop of jihadists. Soon, membership spread to other states such as Bauchi and Yobe in the Northeast region. The group became known as 'Boko Haram' because of its stance and ideology regarding western education and lifestyle. However, they formally called themselves Jama'atul Alhul

[83] Human Rights Watch 2011.

[84] The concept of *hijrah* can be loosely translated to the English word emigration. This implies leaving a land of sin to a land of Islam. This is inspired by the emigration of the Prophet Muhammad and his followers to the city of Medina in 622 A.D. after the opposition they received from the polytheist Mecca traders. The arrival in Medina symbolises the official beginning of the Islamic era and the starting point of the Islamic calendar (year 1AH that is *Anno Hegirae*), Moosa 2004.

[85] Mohammed 2014, p. 12.

[86] Doukhan 2012, p. 6.

[87] Pate 2014.

Sunnah Lidda'wati wal Jihad.[88] They were able to establish an organisation that functioned just as a modern state would, with their own quasi-governmental institutions, Islamic educational bodies, system of welfare, agricultural economy, including an internal religious law enforcement unit. The group attracted new members by giving out welfare, food, free Islamic education, and shelter. Arguably resulting from their actions, thousands of Christians were said to have fled from the area where the group held sway. Eventually, the group succeeded in purging parts of Yobe and Borno of the Christian population who had resided there for decades. They also eliminated symbols of the central government from some areas.

According to Kyari Mohammed, the evolution of Boko Haram can be understood in three distinct, but sometimes overlapping phases: the *Kanama* phase, the da'wah phase and the phase of armed struggle.[89] He described the period between 2002 and 2005 as the *Kanama* phase. During this period, Muhammad Ali, a Nigerian, believed to have been radicalised in Saudi Arabia and was said to have fought alongside the mujahideen in Afghanistan, led the group. It was during this phase that the group declared the hijra and moved to Kanama hence the name. Starting after the collapse of the Kanama uprising and the death of Ali, the da'wah (preaching and proselytising) phase ended with the suppression of Boko Haram proper in July 2009. The phase according, to Kyari Mohammed, was characterised by intense preaching, recruitment, indoctrination and radicalisation of its members.[90] During this period, the teachings of the group focused on critiquing the existing secular, religious and political system, intense debates with opposing clerics on the propriety or otherwise of western education, westernisation, democracy and secularism. In his view, the third phase took off with the 2009 suppression of the group's violence and the killing of its leadership. As a result, the group went underground, re-structured and resurfaced in 2010 becoming more militant and commenced the bombing of high-profile targets, indiscriminate killings and large-scale kidnappings. Kyari Mohammed describe the period as characterised by systematic violence against the Nigerian state. The diversification of the typologies of the violence of the group seems to signal a fourth phase characterised by the trans-nationalisation and regionalisation of the violence. Clear indicators are that the violent attacks are carried out in a more coordinated and sophisticated manner including attacks in neighbouring countries in the Lake Chad Basin region (Niger, Chad and Cameroon). This led to the shift of Boko Haram into a transnational and regional concern.

[88] Literal meaning 'People committed to spreading the heritage of the prophet and Jihad'.

[89] Mohammed 2014, p. 9. Although other writers have discussed the evolution of Boko Haram using different terms and benchmarks, the ideas are similar. See generally Voll 2015, Matfes 2017, Loimeier 2012a, b, and Magrin and Pérouse de Montclos 2018.

[90] Mohammed 2014, p. 10.

2.3.2 *Structure of Boko Haram*

There are a variety of speculation relating to the hierarchy of Boko Haram and its leadership structure. Due to the paucity of verifiable information about the internal workings of the group, it is very difficult to ascertain the reliability of statements and reports which claim to give a definitive idea of the structure of the group. In July 2012, Johnnie Carson, the US Department of State's assistant secretary for African affairs, noted that while information on Boko Haram was limited, he believed the group was composed of at least two branches: a "larger organization" that aims to discredit the Nigerian government and a smaller more dangerous group that is increasingly sophisticated and lethal.[91] Doukhan[92] also described the leadership structure of Boko Haram as a network of cells controlled by a shura (consultation), a council of 30 members who do not share one location. The members of the council, he described as capable of travelling easily in Nigeria and the neighbouring countries tend to use mobile phones rather than hold face-to-face meetings. Each member of the council, in his opinion, is in charge of a cell, and each cell attends to a specific task in a geographic region. In his view, the compartmentalisation of the cells is so strict that a member of the lowest rank in a cell might not know another member of the same rank. Doukhan believes that the organisation's activities are generally discussed in the forum of the council, but sometimes Abubakar Shekau, the new leader that succeeded Muhammad Ali, makes operative decisions without consulting the members of the shura. In Doukhan's view, an Amir (leader) is positioned in every state where the organisation is active.[93]

Regardless of the veracity of this differing information, in 2011, a splinter group emerged from Boko Haram. Said to comprise of a faction of Al-Qaeda trained members of Boko Haram, the splinter group, Jama'atu Ansaril Muslimina Fi Biladis Sudan or Ansar al-Muslimin fi Bilad al-Sudan (Supporters of the Muslims in the Land of Black Africans) is known as Ansaru. Although, Ansaru utilised the same strategy as Boko Haram, it seemed geared towards foreigners, foreign interests and the Nigerian government. Unlike Boko Haram, it seemed to only attack Nigerian Muslims and Christians in the instance of self-defence.[94] The group equally utilised violence against the State, focusing especially on targeted kidnappings usually in response to military action by western nations in solidarity with Islamic countries. This group is said to be led by Abu Usmatul Al-Ansari and has carried out deadly attacks since its emergence. The splinter group is believed to be responsible for the killing of seven hostages it captured in March 2013.[95]

The rebranding of Boko Haram in 2015 is also noteworthy. As a result of its pledge and alliance with the Islamic State, it took on the name Islamic State in the West African Province (ISWAP). As a result of certain doctrinal differences,

[91] US Congressional House Hearing Report 2012.

[92] Doukhan 2012, p. 10.

[93] Doukhan 2012, p. 10.

[94] Zenn 2014, p. 100.

[95] The Guardian 2013.

Abubakar Shekau the leader of Boko Haram was claimed to have been forced out of the leadership of the rebranded ISWAP.[96] Abu Musab al-Barnawi became the Islamic State recognised leader of ISWAP. Boko Haram, Ansaru and ISWAP have taken responsibility for violent crimes committed and they have engaged the Nigerian military in combat at different times.[97]

2.3.3 *Ideology of Boko Haram*

The founder of Boko Haram, Mohammed Yusuf, published a book in Arabic as the manifesto of its ideology. The book articulated the doctrine of the group along the lines of Salafi Jihadism, aligning itself with global Salafi movements like Al-Qaeda while remaining principally focused on local complaints.[98] The word Salafism refers to the first generation of Muslims addressed as al-Salaf al Saleh denoting the pious predecessors including the companions of the prophet, his followers and the followers of the followers of the prophet.[99] The idea of Sunni Muslims which gave rise to Salafism is that temporal proximity to the prophet is associated to the truest form of Islam including the urge to return to the original form of Islam. Salafism is an extreme form of Islamic denomination which aims to purge Islam of outside influence and strives for a return to the Islam practiced by the holy ancestors. It is characterised by three main features; a strict disapproval to concessions of modernism and so-called secularism, a perception that societal pluralism is a threat to Islam and a scriptural interpretation of the holy text to the exclusion of supposed blasphemous influences.[100] Salafists apply foundational Islamic texts literally in their day-to-day life and do not adhere to recognised Islamic legal schools. They also reject other approaches to Islam.[101] Salafism has evolved in the course of the history of Islam. It adheres to a rigorous interpretation of the Quran; the hadith and it aims to change the personal behaviour of Muslims. Women and girls under Salafism are regarded as lesser beings requiring male guardianship and female sexuality is regarded as a threat to male spirituality and family honour.[102]

---

[96] See generally Zenn 2018.

[97] See Zenn 2017.

[98] The book is titled '*Hadhihi aquidatuna wa manhaju da'awatin*' 2009. The title is loosely translated to mean 'This is our creed and method of preaching'. There is no clear information as to when exactly it was published but it is commonly agreed that it was published by Yusuf. The ideas in the book are not novel and its ideas are said to have been taken from the writings of Saudi clerics active when Yusuf was there in 2003–2004. The book was published in Arabic, and it was translated by Prof Sani Umar of Ahmadu Bello University, Zaria.

[99] Barkindo 2013, p. 16.

[100] Armborst 2009, p. 58.

[101] Thurston 2016, p. 9.

[102] Barkindo 2013, p. 17.

Salafism in all its forms shares a core conception of Tawhid, the concept of the unity of God. This concept is a foundational principle and a gateway into the religion of Islam. Tawhid is customarily expressed in the pronouncement that: 'There is no god but Allah and Muhammad is the Messenger of Allah'. Although, the Tawhid is universally accepted by all Muslims, its meanings and implications are understood and applied differently. For the Salafists, the interpretation of the Tawhid has been divided broadly into three categories, affirming that Allah is the only (a) Lord of the universe; (b) proper recipient of worship; (c) absolutely incomparable in name and essence. According to Salafists, this translates that the belief in Allah as the only Lord of the universe carries a practical implication of rejecting any authority other than that of Allah, whether political, legal or otherwise. It also implies that humans should obey only the law of Shari'a as the law of God and reject all others.[103] There are many brands of Salafism, but only Salafi Jihadism advocates the utilisation of violence to achieve its aims of returning to the original form of Islam.[104]

One of the early proponents of Salafism in Nigeria is Sheik Abubakar Gummi who studied Islamic law in a British colonial school for aspiring judges conducted in Arabic language. After serving as a senior Muslim judge in Northern Nigeria, he became an anti-Sufi thinker after 1966. Subsequently, his followers founded the Jama'at Izalat al-bid'a wa-Iqmat al-Sunna,[105] commonly referred to as the Izala group (the Yan-Izala, or JIBWIS): this organisation worked tirelessly towards the dissemination of anti-Sufism in Northern Nigeria.[106] While accusing Sufi Muslims of innovation and apostasy, the Izala movement fought against novelties such as the Sufi kneeling in greeting elders, practice of keeping concubines by traditional rulers, celebration of the Prophet's birthday, visiting graves and tombs of dead scholars, and the promotion of women's rights and education.[107] Due to intense competition and debates between Salafis and Sufis and the subsequent death of Sheik Gummi, the Izala group became fragmented.

Mohammed Yusuf, the founder of Boko Haram, was a protégé of Ja'far Mahmud Adam, a member of the Izala group who studied at the Saudi Islamic University of Medina and returned to Nigeria to build a following.[108] However, a rivalry ensued between Yusuf and his mentor and a divergence of opinion over Salafist doctrine particularly with regards to the so-called western education began to surface. Soon, both became estranged.[109]

Other accounts claim that Yusuf was a member of the Shiites under the leadership of Ibrahim El-Zakzaky initially and that when Jama'atul Tajdidi Islam (JTI) of Abubakar Mujahid which was based in Kano broke away from the Shiites in the 1990s, he became a member of the new group and eventually became an Amir

[103] Umar 2015, p. 2.
[104] Onuoha 2014, p. 160.
[105] The Society for the removal of heretic innovation and the establishment of the prophet's model.
[106] Thurston 2016, p. 10.
[107] Barkindo 2013, p. 15.
[108] Thurston 2016, p. 10.
[109] Zenn 2014, p. 103.

(Emir or leader) for Borno State. What is undisputed, however, is that Yusuf revered and drew inspiration from Al-Qaeda, Osama bin laden and the Taliban and he was recorded as stating directly that all Islamic scholars who undermine ibn Taymiyya, Sayid Qutb, Hassan al-banna and Osama bin Laden are not authentic Muslim Scholars.

The major themes of Yusuf's book as interpreted from Arabic and explained by Prof. M. Sani Umar[110] are five and they embody the pillars of the ideology of Boko Haram as it is known today. They include: (1) subscription to the doctrine of Tawhid; (2) opposing democracy as a pagan system of unbelief; (3) impermissibility to acquire modern secular education as well as employment in the service of the modern secular state particularly in the military and the law enforcement sectors; (4) views that shi'ism and sufism are un-Islamic and are paganism; and (5) the belief that the Shari'a legal regime embodies the perfect Islamic system that should be followed.

Mohammed Yusuf also contends that the colonial origins of modern secular education made it religiously prohibited for Muslims to acquire. Claiming that it amounts to unbelief, he urged all Muslims to denounce modern education and refrain from sending their children to the so-called secular schools. The ideas of the group are not only limited to western education, but additionally the perceived fruits of western education and its incompatibility with traditional Salafist ideology.[111] Yusuf objected to the contents of most systems of western-style education while singling out ideas like Darwinism as contradicting the Quran and blamed secular schools for allowing Muslim students to adopt the mannerisms of 'Jews and Christians'. Additionally, the system of gender mixing and interactions at western-style schools was blamed for encouraging 'fornication, lesbianism, homosexuality, and other corruptions.' The almajiri Islamic system of education was preferred over the western-styled schools.

In a 2011 leadership statement issued by Boko Haram, the group outlined its specific objectives:

> We want to reiterate that we are warriors who are carrying out Jihad (religious war) in Nigeria and our struggle is based on the traditions of the holy prophet. We will never accept any system of government apart from the one stipulated by Islam because that is the only way that Muslims can be liberated. We do not believe in any system of government, be it traditional or orthodox, except the Islamic system which is why we will keep on fighting against democracy, capitalism, socialism and whatever. We will not allow the Nigerian Constitution to replace the laws that have been enshrined in the Holy Quran: we will not allow adulterated conventional education (Boko) to replace Islamic teachings. We will not respect the Nigerian government because it is illegal. We will continue to fight its military and the police because they are not protecting Islam. We do not believe in the Nigerian judicial system and we will fight anyone who assist the government in perpetrating illegalities.[112]

On democracy, Yusuf stated directly:

> We do not believe in democracy and we do not work with or employ democracy because it is the way of the infidels. Following democracy, working with it or utilizing its systems are

[110] Umar 2015, p. 6.

[111] Thurston 2016, p. 15.

[112] Agbiboa 2013a, b, p. 4.

> all acts of infidelity. Therefore, it is not permissible for a Muslim to nominate himself as a candidate or vote for another candidate in a democratic system.'

According to him, popular sovereignty directly usurps the divine sovereignty of Allah. Politics, in his perspective, should conform to the idea of Islam and the Shari'a as a perfect blueprint for the society as opposed to democracy. A true Muslim should not only condemn democracy, but it is essential to go further to oppose it. He also believed that the Nigerian government needed to be replaced by a government according to Salafism:

> We follow the Ideology of the Salafist and any fatwa issued by a Salafist scholar. No matter how important a Muslim scholar is, we need to know if he is guided by Salafist principles before we accept such a scholar. As a group, we will not accept personal interpretations, opinions and judgements. Every teaching of a scholar must be supported by the writings and teachings of a Salafist scholar.[113]

On employment in the services of a modern secular state, Yusuf opines in his book that it is not permissible under Islam for any Muslim to be employed in any system of government that does not obey Allah's will as expressed in Shari'a. He singled out employment in the military, security and the law enforcement sectors as being particularly intolerable because these sectors are the instruments used to impose the so-called infidel rule on Muslims. He contended additionally that acceptance of such employment negates the Islamic faith and it amounts to unbelief. Successive Boko Haram leader after Abubakar Shekau continued to uphold the ideology and expressed famously that he strives for the day that the government in Nigeria will be replaced by 'government of Allah, by Allah and for Allah'.[114]

2.3.4 The Practice of Jihad by Boko Haram

There is no easy definition for the concept of Jihad and the available descriptions are usually as varied as the authority defining it. This section, while not bidding to undertake a general definition on the doctrine of jihad, will, however, attempt to convey an understanding of the practice of jihad by Boko Haram. Jihad has been described in many forms to include struggle or to strive in the religious sense. It has been described as jihad-fisabillah meaning struggle in the way of God.[115] The term is usually used in terms of fighting in the path of God in the Quran. It is describing warfare against the enemies of the early Muslim community (ummah*)*.[116] The hadith is also generally understood to address jihad as armed action and this obligation has been interpreted in the military sense. Islamic scholars describe the obligation of Jihad

113 Zenn 2014, p. 104.

114 Pointblank News 2013.

115 Also spelt *Jehad* or *Jiohad*, the doctrine has been widely defined, debated and contested. See Palival 2007 for an exploration of various definitions from differing perspectives.

116 Knapp 2013, p. 82.

not as an individual obligation, but rather an obligation of the Muslim community -fard kifaya. However, in emergency situations when the Muslim community comes under attack, the individual is obliged to participate and bear arms in defence of the community. In this sense, Jihad is interpreted as a tool to be used defensively not offensively.[117]

There have been various philosophical perspectives describing Jihad from different viewpoints. Notorious among these is the fatwa of Ibn Taymiyyah whose works and arguments laid the foundation for the modern radical Islamist and has been cited repeatedly by jihadists including Osama bin Laden to justify their attacks.[118] Bassiouni[119] opines that the activities of contemporary religious fundamentalists linking their struggles with non-Muslim states with a religious obligation are largely responsible for the current perspective that jihad is synonymous with Islamic violence. These new advocates of Jihad utilise, allow or excuse indiscriminate or targeted violence against civilians and impermissible objects, which, according to him, are religiously prohibited.

Initially, the focus of Boko Haram was not on Jihad in the military sense against the Nigerian government; rather, Yusuf, in the early days, stated that: an Islamic system of government should be established in Nigeria and if possible, all over the world, but through preaching of the faith (dawa'a).[120] This became obvious because regardless of their extreme views, the group sparingly attacked the Nigerian government and there was no apparent coordinated plan of broader insurgency initially. However, towards 2009, shortly before Yusuf's death, he seemed to be leaning more towards the notion of violent Jihad. He was quoted as saying:

> The only thing that can stop the killing of Muslims and the insults against their prophet is Jihad. However, the group must exercise patience until there is the strength to carry out the Jihad. We are for Jihad, and our Jihad is to put an end to democracy, to western education and to western civilization. The Jihad is intended to make Muslims return to our basics and the original state of Islam.'

The extra-judicial killing of Yusuf while in government custody in July 2009 and the transition to the leadership of the more militant Abubakar Shekau ushered Boko Haram into a period of tactical transformation and intense and violent Jihad in the military sense. In July 2010, Abubakar Shekau declared famously that Jihad has begun. Shekau is also notoriously anti-western and specifically anti-America and he called for continuation of violent Jihad saying; 'Do not think Jihad is over, rather, Jihad has just begun. Oh America, die with your fury.'[121] He is also credited with operationalising Yusuf's thinking into a jihadist insurgency.

[117] Bassiouni 2007.

[118] Sivan 1990, p. 101. See also Bassiouni 2014.

[119] Bassiouni 2014, p. 199.

[120] Zenn 2014, p. 103.

[121] Zenn 2014, p. 108.

2.3.5 *Spreading the Germ: Boko Haram Evolution into Transnational Terrorism*

Although, Boko Haram initially focused primarily on the Northern Nigeria region, the unique features of the Lake Chad Basin region made it relatively easy for the group to carry out acts that transcend the national borders of Nigeria.[122] In 2007, two members of Boko Haram were arrested and tried on charges relating to terrorism. The first, Muhammad Yusuf, was indicted for being a member of the so-called 'Nigerian Taliban' and was charged for receiving $300,000 US dollars reportedly from Al-Qaeda to fund the training and recruitment of terrorists in Nigeria. Mohammed Damagun was additionally indicted for acts including receiving money from operatives belonging to Al-Qaeda.[123] In June 2010, Abdelmalek Droukdel, the *emir* of Al-Qaeda in the Islamic Maghreb announced that talks were ongoing with Boko Haram with regards to possible assistance for the group. There were also reports of a Boko Haram relationship with al-Shabaab in Somalia, particularly in terms of training. The use of suicide bombers, a major strategy utilised by global Salafist jihadi groups, previously unheard of in Nigeria, was adopted and popularised by Boko Haram in 2011.[124] By 2012, Boko Haram allegedly had a modest following in Niger Republic.[125] The group also reportedly sent its members to support Al-Qaeda in the Islamic Maghreb and the Movement for Unity and Jihad and West Africa in their attacks in Mali in 2012.[126] Likewise, regular attacks, raids and a high spate of kidnapping attributed to Boko Haram became the order of the day in Niger and Cameroon by 2013. The report of the United Nations High Commissioner on Human Rights (OHCHR) stated that between April 2013 and July 2014, its office conducted interviews which indicated that over 770 civilians were massacred by Boko Haram in the three most affected divisions in Northern Cameroon.[127] The notorious kidnapping of a French family in Northern Cameroon was a pivotal point in the extension of its activities outside Nigeria.[128] In March 2015, the leader of Boko Haram Abubakar Shekau made an official pledge (bayat) to the so-called Islamic State (ISIS), and officially recognised the leader of the Islamic State al-Baghdadi, as the Caliph of Muslims.[129] In this vein, the group took on the name Islamic State's West Africa

[122] Some of the peculiarities of the Lake Chad basin region includes ease of movement due to the ECOWAS agreement and porous borders, similarities in language, weak states and massive poverty, corruption among many other challenges. These intricacies are further discussed in Thurston 2016, p. 22–23.

[123] Minteh and Perry 2013, p. 10.

[124] Siegle in Mantzikos 2013, p. 87.

[125] Some suspected sect members were arrested by Nigerien authorities in Diffa, close to the southeastern capital near Maiduguri. Thurston 2016, p. 22.

[126] Zenn 2013. See also The Daily Beast 2015.

[127] Report of the UN High Commissioner for Human Rights on the Violations and Abuses Committed by Boko Haram and the Impact of Human Rights in the Affected Countries 2015.

[128] Reuters 2013.

[129] BBC 2015b, and BBC 2015c.

Province (ISWAP). Although, it is unclear how much of an advantage such a pledge was to its day-to-day operations, however, aligning its activities with the Islamic State has made Boko Haram very attractive for synergy and linkage with Al-Qaeda collaborators in the Islamic Maghreb and the West African region.[130]

Boko Haram consequently began to tailor its propaganda towards global jihad, professionalising its media products and emphasising Arabic over Hausa language.[131] Additionally, this led to a period of intensified attacks outside the national borders of Nigeria, principally in Cameroon, Chad and Niger, changing the group from a purely Nigerian problem into a massive regional concern. Al-Qaeda in the Islamic Maghreb reportedly provided training and some financing for Boko Haram.[132] According to the 2015 Global Terrorism Index, Nigeria experienced a 300% increase (the biggest year-on-year increase) in terrorism deaths between 2014 and 2015. It also showed countries like Chad and Cameroon which had little to no recorded terrorism related fatality before 2013 experiencing a sudden spike in 2014 and 2015 principally through the activities of Boko Haram.

2.4 Boko Haram Crisis by Typology

2.4.1 Killings of Civilians

Boko Haram became known for killing Christians and other so-called infidels, government authority figures, law enforcement agents, Muslims who disagree with its ideology, members of the traditional leadership structure and civilians generally. Initially using rudimentary weapons like cutlasses and stones and knives and motorcycles to attack civilians, Boko Haram became increasingly sophisticated and began to employ high calibre weapons, improvised explosive devices, land mines, guns mounted on trucks and subsequently graduated to military grade helicopters, armoured vehicles for the purpose of killing and maiming. As a result, civilians have been shot, beheaded, amputated, stoned, drowned, burnt, and bombed among other heinous acts. In certain instances, the killings came as a result of the refusal of the civilians in the area to heed the call of the group to join them 'in the work of Allah'.[133] Boko Haram typically focuses on soft targets such as markets and shopping centres, churches, bars, government offices, relaxation centres and schools. They utilise suicide bombers, including children, to create the highest possible casualties.[134]

[130] Centre for Democracy and Development 2016.

[131] Thurston 2016, p. 24.

[132] Counter Extremism Project Report 2015. See also Reuters 2014.

[133] Report of the UN High Commissioner 2015, p. 6.

[134] The Washington Post 2016a, b, c.

The five-day standoff between the so-called Nigerian Taliban and the law enforcement authorities in 2009 marked the dramatic national introduction of the group. The attack left in its wake about eight hundred civilian casualties in Maiduguri.[135] More civilians were attacked and killed in Bauchi, Yobe and Kano during the period. According to the Human Rights Watch Report, between July and December 2010, at least eighty-five people were killed in thirty-five separate attacks in four states in Northern and Central Nigeria, as well as in Abuja, Nigeria's capital city.[136] The year 2010 ended on a bloody note when the group attacked a church during Christmas Eve prayers.[137] Attacks attributed to Boko Haram in 2011 left about five hundred and fifty people dead in a hundred and fifteen separate incidents. End of the year attacks were also repeated in 2011 leading to the death of at least 40 worshippers in a church.[138] In a daring suicide car bomb attack at the United Nations building in Abuja, Boko Haram killed about twenty people while injuring others in August 2011.[139] Utilising suicide car bombs in coordinated attacks in April 2012, Boko Haram also attacked Thisday, a private newspaper in its offices in Abuja and in Kaduna leaving about seven people dead.[140] In the first nine months of 2012 alone, more than eight hundred and fifteen people died in two hundred and seventy-five separate attacks in twelve northern and central states, and Abuja.[141] Attacks in 2013 led to the death of forty-three students and fifty teachers in a boarding school in Mamudo and in an agricultural college in Gujba, both in Yobe state.[142] A survivor who was reportedly abducted in 2013 when she ran into a roadblock near Bama recounted her experience in a 2014 Human Rights Watch report:

> The blockade was up to 40 vehicles long. When the men separated the Muslims from the Christians, we knew then that they were Boko Haram; all young men including Muslims were told to either join them or be killed. They slit the throat of some of the men saying they'd not waste bullets on them. Christian women wearing pants were shot in the legs and left to die. Older Muslim men and women wearing veils were released to go, while the rest of us were driven to their camp in Sambisa Forest.[143]

The activities of Boko Haram were described as been responsible for nearly half of all the civilian deaths in African war zones in 2014.[144] A particularly fierce attack in February 2014 saw the killing of about sixty male students of the Federal Government College, Buni Yadi in Yobe state.[145] Another 2014 estimate gave a figure of 20,000

[135] Reuters 2009.

[136] Human Rights Watch 2012, p. 32.

[137] Aljazeera 2010.

[138] BBC 2011a.

[139] BBC 2011b.

[140] BBC 2012.

[141] Human Rights Watch 2012.

[142] Human Rights Watch Report 2014, p. 22.

[143] Human Rights Watch Report 2014, p. 25.

[144] The Guardian 2015a, b.

[145] Reuters 2014.

civilian fatalities between 2009 and 2014.[146] In a 2017 report,[147] the United Nations documented accounts of three thousand nine hundred and nine killed and seven thousand three hundred and thirty-three children maimed during the period under review.[148]

In a yearly review, the Washington post reported one hundred and fourteen civilians' dead in thirty-two attacks in 2011, nine hundred and ten civilian casualties in one hundred and forty-eight attacks in 2012, one thousand and eight in one hundred and eight attacks in 2013, three thousand four hundred and twenty-five in two hundred and twenty attacks in 2014 and six thousand and six in two hundred and seventy attacks in 2015.[149] Between January 2014 and April 2015, Amnesty international in its report documented at least three hundred raids and attacks carried out by Boko Haram against civilians.[150] These raids were usually accompanied by widespread burning and looting of properties. The United Nations High Commissioner report provides similar statistics of civilian casualties of Boko Haram in Niger, Chad and Cameroon.[151]

The Office of the Prosecutor of the International Criminal Court in its 2016 report identified three hundred and fifty-six separate incidents of killings attributed to Boko Haram in North-Eastern Nigeria as well as in Cameroon and in Niger which led to the killings of over eight thousand civilians between 2009 and 2016. Some of the territory liberated from Boko Haram following military operations in February 2015 were found with mass graves sites and decomposing bodies of civilians killed by Boko Haram.[152] In December 2016, the President of Nigeria declared Boko Haram finally crushed, however, the attacks continued unabated. This was later dubbed by the presidency as a 'technical defeat'.[153] Boko Haram continued to carry out violent attacks on civilians in the affected region despite this.

2.4.2 *Sexual and Gender-Based Violence*

Sexual and gender-based crimes have been treated as an accompanying and troubling aspect of armed conflict for centuries.[154] The United Nations Security Council in its resolution 2331 (2016) acknowledged the nexus between terrorism and sexual and gender-based violence and recognised that sexual and gender-based violence is an integral tactic and a recognised part of the ideology of terrorist groups to perpetrate

[146] Report of the UN High Commissioner 2015, p. 6.

[147] Report of Secretary-General on Children and Armed Conflict in Nigeria 2017.

[148] Report of the Secretary General on Children and Armed Conflict in Nigeria 2017, p. 9.

[149] The Washington Post 2016a, b, c.

[150] Amnesty International Report 2015a, b.

[151] Report of the UN High Commissioner 2015, p. 7.

[152] Office of the Prosecutor Report on Preliminary Examination Activities 2015.

[153] Premium Times 2016.

[154] Bensouda 2007.

terrorism.[155] For Boko Haram, its direct focus on women and children first began to emerge in 2013.[156] Although initially, it was unclear whether the group had a strategic policy towards women and children, or whether they simply proved to be convenient objectives. However, the continued targeting of women and children soon became a feature emblematic of the conflict. In North-East Nigeria, a pattern of abductions, forced conversions, rape, sexual violence, sexual exploitation, forced marriages and forced pregnancy was established. The focus on women and their roles in the Boko Haram episode changed as the crisis transformed. Initially, women and girls were targets for abductions; it also became apparent that the role of women in the organisation became increasingly serious as some became recruiters for the group and eventually suicide bombers. Women and young girls were also used as 'wives' for male operatives and sex slaves who also procreate a new generation of children for the insurgents.[157]

The United Nations estimated that at least seven thousand women and children have suffered from sexual violence perpetrated by Boko Haram between 2009 and 2017especially following abductions and during forced marriages.[158] Reports of rape and other sexual abuses of abducted women who are yet to be 'married' to members of Boko Haram were also rife. Needless to say, rape and sexual violence have been used by members of Boko Haram for a myriad of reasons including punitive aims.[159] Varying examples include the rape of a 44 year old woman who was abducted and raped by teenage combatants because she did not give money to the cause of Boko Haram in the early days of the group.[160] The areas with the highest abduction rate of sexual and gender-based violence were the predominantly Christian areas and it appeared that the victims were targeted for their religious affiliations and western lifestyle.[161] Before Boko Haram became a highly organised group that moved away to form its own community, its youth members engaged in physical abuse for so-called provocative dressing including beatings, rapes and throwing acid on unveiled faces. Burning of shops and business premises belonging to non-Muslim women based on the so-called Islamic principle that the woman's role was in the home, including accusations of acts of blasphemy leading to the mobbing of the suspect were widespread.[162] With the metamorphosis of the group, married women were

[155] Report of the Secretary General on conflict-related sexual violence United Nations Security Council 2017.

[156] Zenn and Pearson 2014, p. 47.

[157] See generally, Iyi and Strydom 2018.

[158] Report of the Secretary General on Children and Armed Conflict in Nigeria 2017, p. 11.

[159] These reasons include 'providing an incentive for recruitment, supporting financing through the sale, trade and trafficking of women, girls and boys, destroying, punishing, subjugating, or controlling communities, displacing populations from strategically important zones, extracting information for intelligence purposes from male and female detainees, advancing ideology which includes the suppression of women's rights and the use of religious justification to codify and institutionalise sexual slavery and exert control over women's reproduction.' See UN resolution S/RES/2331 2016.

[160] Human Rights Watch Report 2014, p. 35.

[161] Human Rights Watch Report 2014.

[162] Barkindo 2013, p. 18.

abducted as a punishment for not supporting the ideology of Boko Haram while single women and girls were abducted to provide wives to their fighters, usually after providing a hasty dowry, which the families in question were too fearful to reject. Sometimes, these paltry dowries were offered to the girls in question themselves after abduction.[163] A 19-year-old girl abduction survivor told Human Rights Watch that she was offered some money as dowry to be married to a combatant:

> I refused the dowry and asked them to go pay it to my father if they wanted to marry me. A member of Boko Haram who knows my family accepted it on their behalf. He told me he was afraid I could be killed if I continued to refuse…

In many other instances, the charade of dowry was completely dispensed with and the abducted girls were married to whomever the camp leader saw fit. Survivors who managed to escape or were rescued chronicled experiences of physical and psychological violence, sexual abuse, forced conversions, forced labour and forced participation in military operations. Women and girls were utilised as bait to lure soldiers into ambush, rape and forced marriages were rife and they were forced to take part in raiding and sacking of other towns including the provision of assistance with the loot from these attacks. A survivor in an account of the means by which she was forcefully converted to Islam detailed the experience by describing how members of Boko Haram placed a noose around her neck and threatened her with death until she renounced her Christian faith. Others were constantly beaten or threatened with beatings until they renounced their previous religious beliefs and complied with Boko Haram sanctioned dressing rules. The practice of forcefully marrying off abducted girls to Boko Haram combatants irrespective of age is rife and has resulted in the high rate of rapes and sexual violence after such marriages. According to survivors, without prejudice to the age of the girls involved, they were deemed suitable to be married. A survivor's account is quoted verbatim:

> When one of the victims, a 15-year-old girl, complained to a Boko Haram commander that she and the other abducted girls were too young for marriage, he pointed at his 5-year-old daughter, and said: if she got married last year and is only waiting till puberty for its consummation, how can you at your age be too young to marry?

In May 2014, a video message released by Boko Haram, its leader and spokesman Abubakar Shekau stated that 'young women and girls are slaves who would be sold, western education is sin, it is forbidden and all women must go and marry'. Abducted women have also been forced to participate in military operations; young girls with the advantage of the ability to evade suspicion and detection have been increasingly utilised for suicide bombing attacks.

A number of women and girls who managed to escape or were rescued returned pregnant or with babies including some having contracted varying sexually transmitted infections including HIV/AIDS.[164] These women as well as the children fathered by Boko Haram members live with shame and stigma and discrimination

[163] Human Rights Watch Report 2014, p. 3.

[164] Report of the Secretary General on conflict-related sexual violence United Nations Security Council 2017.

and as outcasts in the internally displaced camps and in their communities.[165] The women and children face ostracism and guilt by association as well as victim status in the violent conflict. Despite the information available, it is a widely held belief that rape and sexual abuse have been grossly under-reported in the Boko Haram crisis in Northern Nigeria. This is due to the culture of silence, stigma and shame that accompanies sexual issues and abuse and the conservative and deeply religious nature of the region. These socio-cultural issues have contributed immensely to the under-reporting of issues relating to sexual and gender-based violence in North-East Nigeria. According to the United Nations, only about two percent of the survivors of sexual and gender-based violence seeking medical care were able to access it and almost half of all survivors decline to report sexual violence.[166] Another troubling dimension of the conflict is the use of women and girls as suicide bombers; also regarded as person-borne improvised explosive devices representing the highest record of any terrorist group in history.[167]

The United Nations Security Council's approach to conflict-related sexual violence refers to rape, sexual slavery, forced prostitution, forced pregnancy, forced abortion, enforced sterilisation, forced marriage, and any other forms of sexual violence of comparable gravity perpetrated against woman, men, girls or boys that is directly or indirectly linked to a conflict.[168] The indices of the link include the targeting of the victim on the basis of gender identity. It is clear that the United Nation does not exclude sexual violence and gender-based violence perpetrated against men and boys. However, in the case of North-East Nigeria, there is scant information available on sexual violence against men and boys due to the socio-cultural issues and the reluctance of survivors to discuss such matters. Although, men and boys have been targeted specifically by Boko Haram as well as girls and women, there is very little available information on whether these targeting also involve sexual violence.[169] The true scale of the events of the past few years particularly as it relates to sexual violence may never be completely known.

---

165 News24 2016.

166 Report of the Secretary General on conflict-related sexual violence United Nations Security Council 2017.

167 Warner and Matfes 2017.

168 Report of the Secretary General on conflict-related sexual violence United Nations Security Council 2017.

169 Since the beginning of the conflict, Boko Harm members have abducted and executed and forcibly conscripted boys and men including the notorious killing of at least 29 male students in Federal Government College, Buni Yadi; attack on Government Secondary School (GSS) Damaturu; Government Secondary School (GSS), Mamudo; the College of Agriculture in Gujba among many other similar instances of targeting boys and men for a myriad of purposes. See generally Premium Times 2014, and Chidi Anslem Odinkalu 2017. UNICEF 2018.

2.4.3 *Abductions/Hostage Taking*

Abduction seemed to be an important part of the strategy of Boko Haram from inception. Initially, this was advanced through kidnapping of women and children for ransom. However, schools and students eventually became an important target. In an October 2014 report, Human Rights Watch reported that Boko Haram has abducted at least five hundred women and girls between 2009 and 2014.[170] Initially, the group gave the impression that the abductions were in retaliation of the arrests and detention of the family members of key Boko Haram members especially in 2011 and early 2012.[171] In a January 2012 video, Shekau was quoted as saying,

> Since you are now holding our women, just wait and see what will happen to your own women…to your wives, according to Shari'a law[172]

Additionally, in May 2013, he was quoted saying,

> No one in the country will enjoy his women and children…if the relatives of Boko Haram were not released by the security officials[173]

Subsequently, an attack on a police barrack in Bama, Borno State led to the capture of twelve Christian women and children for which the group promptly claimed responsibility.[174] The largest single recorded incident of abduction occurred in April 2014 when members of Boko Haram stormed a government secondary school in Chibok, Borno State and abducted two hundred and seventy-six students.[175] Abductions of women and children including medical professionals (doctors, nurses, and pharmacists) have been widely reported in the region.[176] The infamous abducted Chibok girls are believed to be a small fraction of the women, girls, young boys and men abducted by Boko Haram.[177] Between January 2014 and March 2015, the Office of the Prosecutor recorded fifty-five incidents of abductions leading to at least one thousand eight hundred and eighty-five abductees. While the abduction persisted, some of the abductees were murdered, underwent forced conversion, sexual violence, outrages upon personal dignity and general cruel treatments.[178] Cross-border abductions were also widespread and in January 2015 about 60 people were abducted in Northern Cameroon.[179] Between October 2015 and June 2016, the United Nations documented accounts of eight thousand seven hundred and seven children who were rescued, escaped or surrendered to the Nigerian security forces out of the clutches

---

[170] Human Rights Watch 2014.

[171] Human Rights Watch Report October 2014.

[172] Human Rights Watch Report, October 2014.

[173] Human Rights Watch Report October 2014.

[174] Human Rights Watch Report October 2014.

[175] BBC 2014c.

[176] Daily Trust 2014, and Information Nigeria 2014.

[177] Amnesty International 2015.

[178] Office of the Prosecutor Report on Preliminary Examination Activities 2015.

[179] Time 2014, BBC 2015a, and The Telegraph 2015.

of Boko Haram. Abductions were used as a punishment for students for attending western-style schools, as a means to forcibly recruit children and for use of children as human shields during military operations.[180] In its 2017 report, the United Nations verified five hundred and sixty-seven incidents of abductions affecting eight hundred and thirty-six children.[181] The data on women and men are not readily available. Additionally, the report attributes the abduction of at least four thousand girls, boys and women to Boko Haram.

2.4.4 Violence Against Children/Conscripting and Enlisting of Children

Boko Haram has also directed its actions at and has had tremendous impact on children within the affected region since the inception of the violence. Additionally, the group made attacks against and utilisation of children a part of its strategy. According to the estimate of the United Nations Secretary General by December 2014, 54% of the internally displaced persons identified in four states were children. By February 2015, about eight hundred thousand children were displaced in the region.[182] This number increased to more than one million by December 2016. The expansion of the attacks and violence of Boko Haram into Cameroon, Chad and Niger also brought with it a consequence of cross-border recruitment, killing, maiming and abduction of children as well as attacks on schools. The evolution of the tactics of Boko Haram from lone attacks into wider scale attacks and holding territory from late 2014 also saw increased incidences of the recruitment and use of children and abduction of children. It was reported that children were used in direct hostilities, for planting improvised explosive devices, burning of schools and houses and in support roles such as cooks, messengers and lookouts. Some children were also reportedly used as human shields to protect Boko Haram combatants during military operations. According to the United Nations International Children Emergency Fund (UNICEF), boys were forced to attack their own families to demonstrate their loyalty to Boko Haram and the use of children especially girls, as suicide bombers have become a defining feature of the conflict.[183] While Boko Haram was being resisted and pushed back from mid-2015, they reverted to lone attacks and there was a spike in the incidences of using underage girls as suicide bombers, and the use of person-borne improvised explosive devices.[184] The report of the Secretary General estimated that since the start of the crisis in 2009, at least eight thousand children have been recruited and used by Boko Haram. Additionally, with the increase of

---

[180] Report of Secretary-General on Children and Armed Conflict in Nigeria 2017, p. 13.

[181] Report of the Secretary General on Children and Armed Conflict in Nigeria 2017, p. 13.

[182] Report of the Secretary-General on Children in Armed Conflict in Nigeria 2017, p. 3.

[183] UNICEF Report 2016, p. 1.

[184] France 2015, and Huffington Post 2015.

the spread of Boko Haram into the Lake Chad Basin region, cross-border recruitment and use of children was also documented by the report.[185] UNICEF, in an April 2016 publication, stated that since the beginning of the violence, at least 1.3 million children have been uprooted in Nigeria, Niger, Cameroon and Chad.[186] The Office of the Prosecutor of the International Criminal Court in its 2015 Preliminary Examination report acknowledged that Boko Haram has recruited and utilised children as young as twelve years old in its operations. In a propaganda video by Boko Haram, child soldiers were being trained in the use of firearms. An August 2017 report by UNICEF also raised concerns on the use of children as so-called 'human bombs'. According to the report, since January 2017, eighty-three children have been used by Boko Haram for this purpose, fifty-five of whom are girls under the age of fifteen, twenty-seven boys and one a baby strapped to a girl.[187] About eighty children were reportedly rescued from a Boko Haram camp in Cameroon where they were undergoing military training.[188]

2.4.5 *Attacks Against Civilian and Protected Objects*

One of the pillars of the ideology of Boko Haram as evidenced by the literal translation of its name is its condemnation of western education and so-called western civilisation and ideals. From 2011, Boko Haram began to attack facilities and premises which, in their opinion, symbolised western education and civilisation. These include schools, hospitals, churches and government offices. Schools and educational facilities perceived to provide a western curriculum were fatally attacked. According to the Office of the Prosecutor of the International Criminal Court, between January 2012 and October 2013, at least one hundred students and at the minimum seventy teachers were reportedly killed or maimed. At least sixty schools were either completely damaged or burnt down and about sixty more were forced to close.[189]

Throughout 2013, Boko Haram attacks on schools rose exponentially in Borno and Yobe states. The United Nations estimated that about 1500 schools were destroyed by the group since 2014.[190] The group created a pattern of attacking educational facilities, killing and maiming students including committing arson against educational facilities and libraries. By March 2014, due to the continuing attacks and threats of attacks against schools, students and educational personnel, the government announced the closure of all primary and secondary schools in Borno State one of the major hotbed of Boko Haram activities.[191] The following month, Boko Haram,

---

185 Report of the Secretary-General on Children in Armed Conflict in Nigeria 2017, p. 7.
186 UNICEF Report 2016.
187 UNICEF 2017.
188 Office of the Prosecutor Report on Preliminary Examination Activities 2015.
189 Office of the Prosecutor Report on Preliminary Examination Activities 2015.
190 Report of the Secretary-General on Children in Armed Conflict in Nigeria 2017, p. 12.
191 The Guardian 2014a, b.

in an attack against Government Secondary School, Chibok Borno State, where the students were writing their final examinations, infamously abducted 276 girls and completely burnt down the school buildings and facilities.[192] Most of the schools targeted were either government run or Christian mission schools. Boko Haram also seized control of some of the schools it attacked and used them for military objectives, to detain its captives, harbour stolen goods and store and manufacture weapons.[193] In May 2014, the Nigerian Union of Teachers reported one hundred and seventy-three teacher fatalities between 2009 and 2014. In February 2015, an attack on Euga Primary School in Bauchi State disrupted the education of over eight hundred students as Boko Haram took the school as a base for its activities.[194] Attacks on schools also took place in neighbouring countries especially in the Diffa region of Niger where three incidents were reported in 2016. According to UNICEF, over one thousand eight hundred schools were closed, damaged, looted, set on fire or used to shelter displaced persons in North-East Nigeria and Cameroon between 2009 and 2016.[195] Additionally, about one hundred and twenty schools were reportedly forced to close down in the Northern region of Cameroon due to direct Boko Haram threats.[196]

Boko Haram similarly attacked hospitals, killed or abducted personnel including doctors, nurses and pharmacists, and engaged in large-scale looting of medication and vaccines from medical facilities. According to the UN Report, by the end of 2013, the healthcare system in Borno State had ceased to function in 12 of the 27 local government areas.

Acts of religious-related violence directed at places of religion perpetrated including against Christians, churches, Muslim critics and persons deemed to engage in 'un-Islamic' behaviour. Religion was a central factor of the Boko Haram violence and especially in its early days, the crisis was perceived as a religious conflict. In an August 2013 report, the United States of America Commission on International Religious Freedom estimated that between January 2012 and August 2013, fifty churches were bombed, burnt, or attacked, killing three hundred and sixty-six people. There were thirty-one separate attacks on Christians or southerners perceived to be Christians which resulted in the death of at least one hundred and sixty-six persons. There were twenty-three targeted attacks on clerics and senior Islamic figures critical of Boko Haram killing at least sixty persons and twenty-one attacks on so-called un-Islamic institutions or persons engaged in what was perceived to be un-Islamic conduct killing at least seventy-four persons.[197] In a first of its kind bomb attack, on Christmas day in 2011, twenty-six worshippers and seventeen passers-by were killed

---

192 BBC 2014d.

193 Human Rights Watch Report 2016a, b.

194 Report of the Secretary-General on Children in Armed Conflict in Nigeria 2017, p. 12.

195 UNICEF Report 2016, p. 5.

196 Office of the Prosecutor Report on Preliminary Examination Activities 2015.

197 United States Commission on International Religious Freedom Factsheet 'Nigeria: Boko Haram's religiously-motivated attacks' August 2013, p. 1.

in St Theresa Catholic Church, Madalla, Niger State.[198] Consequently, members of Boko Haram created a pattern of shooting into churches during services in an effort to maximise fatality. For three consecutive years after the first Christmas day attack of 2011, churches were attacked during Christmas festivities and also during Easter services in April 2012 leading to the killing and maiming of scores of worshippers in separate incidents.[199] This was repeated a number of times. Additionally, the practice of attacking churches was also carried out across the border in Cameroon.[200]

2.5 Impacts of the Boko Haram Crisis

Nigeria is the most populous country and the largest economy in Africa, with the eleventh largest oil reserves in the world and a myriad of natural resources. It is apparent that Nigeria with her almost two hundred million citizens is of strategic importance to the stability of the West African region and Africa as a whole. While Nigeria is no stranger to violent conflicts, the Boko Haram crisis is unique in a number of ways. The uniqueness is evidenced in the scale of the crisis, the sustained nature of the violence, the ferocity of the crimes committed and the introduction of a terrorist dimension into the criminal sphere of Nigeria. Additionally, the large-scale abductions all highlighted the massive unpreparedness of Nigeria for high-level violence and armed conflict on its own soil. The violent conflict that Boko Haram has waged actively since 2009 has led to a number of consequences. The impact of the ongoing Boko Haram conflict have and is likely to continue to have wide-ranging consequences for the North-Eastern region of Nigeria, Nigeria as a whole and the Lake Chad Basin region in West Africa. Symptomatic evidence of the crisis includes massive forced displacement within Nigeria and in the West African region, increased unemployment, an immense refugee crisis, public health challenges, compromised national security, crisis in the educational sector including a major socio-economic impact with implications for Nigeria and the region.

2.5.1 Forced Displacement and Refugee Crisis

The United Nations Office for the Coordination of Humanitarian Affairs (UNOCHA) in its March 2017 crisis update assessed the Boko Haram crisis and identified the main causes of forced displacement in the region to include mainly the violent attacks by

[198] New York Times "Nigerian Group Escalates Violence with Church Attacks" 25 December 2011, available at http://www.nytimes.com/2011/12/26/world/africa/explosion-rips-through-catholic-church-in-nigeria.html.

[199] Time 2011, CNN 2012a, b, CBS News 2012, and The Guardian 2015a, b.

[200] VOA 2016.

Boko Haram and the military operations in response to these attacks.[201] The persistent insecurity also made humanitarian efforts difficult. More than two million civilians were forcefully displaced internally in North-Eastern Nigeria, directly affecting more than four hundred thousand households in the region. Additionally, about 55% of internally displaced persons are women and children.[202] According to the UNOCHA, as a whole, about 10.7 million people required humanitarian assistance in the region. The internally displaced camps were also considered to be dangerous. There were allegations of large-scale sexual abuse of displaced women and girls by camp officials with displaced women forced to exchange food for sex.[203] Accusations of helpless female refugees being utilised as unpaid domestic workers by camp officials including security challenges in the camps were rife.[204] Additionally, there was an acute lack of food and non-food essential items and poor sanitation facilities in the camps.[205] More than 75% of the displaced persons live in makeshift tents and self-made shelters. Some of the displaced persons have also experienced forceful secondary displacement especially in situations where the first place of refuge was no longer safe for them.[206]

By March 2017, about two hundred thousand Nigerians were externally displaced within West Africa, with over eighty-five thousand Nigerian refugees in the far North region of Cameroon. There were allegations of mass forced return of about one hundred thousand Nigerian refugees by the government of Cameroon.[207] The governments of Nigeria, Cameroon and the United Nations High Commissioner for Refugees earlier signed a tripartite agreement for voluntary repatriation of Nigerian refugees in Cameroon to alleviate this challenge.[208] It is unclear, however, how much of a positive impact the tripartite agreement had. In the Republic of Chad, according to a 2017 estimate, about one hundred and four thousand people have been forcefully displaced. Similarly, in the Diffa region of Niger, about three hundred and forty thousand people were displaced and about ninety-two thousand two hundred and twenty children were separated from their families.

---

[201] UNOCHA 2017a, b, p. 2.

[202] International Organization for Migration (IOM) Displacement Tracking Matrix Report 2017, p. 3.

[203] See Human Rights Watch Report 2016a, b.

[204] Internally displaced camps have been routinely attacked by suicide bombers creating an unsafe environment, killing some occupants and leaving the survivors in fear for their lives. See for example Aljazeera 2017. For example, an airstrike by the Nigerian military mistakenly targeted an Internally Displaced Persons Camp in January 2017 leading to the death of at least 50 people. See The Guardian 2017a, b.

[205] International Organization for Migration (IOM) Displacement Tracking Matrix Report 2017.

[206] See International Organization for Migration (IOM) Displacement Tracking Matrix Report 2017, p. 9.

[207] Human Rights Watch Report 2017.

[208] UNHCR 2017.

2.5.2 *Educational Crisis*

The educational crisis consequent upon the Boko Haram violent conflict can be viewed in a two-pronged manner. The first relates to the direct targeting of educational facilities by Boko Haram while the second emanated from the violent conflict itself including the role of large-scale forced displacement on access to education. In the first view, the violent campaigns of Boko Haram against students and educational facilities resulted directly in a major crisis in the educational sector principally in the North-East of Nigeria. Beginning in 2009 when Boko Haram began to deliberately target schools, the educational situation in the region began to deteriorate and completely collapsed for some time in some states in the region. The group not only killed students and teachers, it also massively destroyed educational facilities. Additionally, when it lost its members to a major government crackdown in 2012, it began to forcibly recruit male students, intimidate and abduct female students.[209] Students were targeted, to prevent them from attending schools and there were a number of suicide bombings at educational institutions. As a result, by March 2016, in Borno State alone, government authorities reported that five hundred and twelve primary schools, thirty-eight secondary schools and two tertiary institutions had been destroyed in the conflict.

In the second view, the Boko Haram conflict also contributed to the fact that about one million displaced students are unable to access education in North-Eastern Nigeria and the Lake Chad Basin region. Schools were forcibly closed down or relocated; students of some of the schools managing to stay open were compulsorily withdrawn by parents as a result of insecurity. This is deeply concerning because Northern Nigeria has historically low school enrolment, attendance and retention including low levels of literacy which predates the Boko Haram crisis.[210] The Nigerian government through the Universal Basic Education programme and the education related Millennium Development Goals was providing a critical response to this specialised problem. However, the activities of Boko Haram in the region might have erased decade-long progress and have presumably made the educational problem in the region direr than before its inception.

2.5.3 *Healthcare Crisis*

The healthcare sphere has also suffered greatly since the violent crisis of Boko Haram began in 2009. Health care centres were unable to provide the critically required services, while centres that were running were generally understaffed and short of acutely needed supply.[211] In Borno State alone, about 50% of the previously available health facilities became inaccessible. Similarly, in Cameroon, five of the eighteen

[209] Human Rights Watch Report 2016a, b, p. 22.

[210] Oladunjoye and Omemu 2013, p. 5.

[211] Business Insider 2016.

health districts in the far North region were closed down.[212] The celebrated massive progress recorded in the polio vaccination campaign in Northern Nigeria began to slowly unravel. Vaccination officers were unable to carry out vaccination drives due to the violent crisis of Boko Haram and on the heels of the celebration of no new cases of polio in Northern Nigeria in two years, new cases of polio emerged in Borno State.[213] Access to critically required health care services for internally displaced persons was also largely inadequate. UNICEF noted a food crisis in the region and the fact that about half a million children under the age of five were at the risk of severe acute malnutrition, with malnutrition related mortality reportedly high.[214] By September 2017, a full cholera outbreak was reported by UNOCHA in North-East Nigeria with about two thousand three hundred confirmed and/or suspected cases and forty-four fatalities.[215] Basic health services in the affected areas of Nigeria, Niger, Chad and Cameroon were reportedly severely lacking or where available, strictly limited.[216]

2.5.4 Socio-economic Impact

The activities of Boko Haram created an uncertain business environment not only in Northern Nigeria, but similarly in the whole of Nigeria and the Lake Chad Basin region. Economic activities reduced, foreign investors were unsure of the viability of their investments and led to a general lull of socio-economic activities especially in the region.[217] Tourism including business visits drastically reduced; parks, restaurants and bars were also shut down in the region. The large-scale kidnappings and assassinations including suicide bombings made international agencies and foreign countries issue warnings regarding travel to and conducting business in Nigeria.[218] This massively reduced the foreign direct investment making its way into the country affecting the economy.[219] Transportation of farm produce became a major challenge due to insecurity leading to a high rate of wastage because the scarce produce could

---

[212] Awosusi 2017, p. 1.

[213] UNICEF 2016, See also World Health Organization 2016.

[214] UNICEF Report 2017.

[215] UNOCHA 2017a, b.

[216] World Health Organization 2017.

[217] Oluwadare 2016, p. 48.

[218] Almost all major countries with consulates and embassies in Nigeria issued essential travel warnings relating to North-East Nigeria and the Lake Chad Basin region. These are constantly updated regarding the severity of the situations. Examples include: United States Department of State 2017. The New Zealand government categorized areas in Nigeria according to criterion of 'extreme risk', 'high risk' and 'some risk'. The Canadian government advised its citizens to 'avoid non-essential travel' to Nigeria and to 'avoid all travel' to the North-East due to the high threat of terrorism. The Australian government also advised its citizens to 'reconsider the need to travel' to Nigeria as a whole.

[219] See generally Joseph et al. 2015, Koko et al. 2017, and Financial Nigeria 2016.

not make it to markets as logistics lines were frequently disrupted.[220] Regarding local economic activities, many banks in the North-Eastern region closed down and those brave enough to stay open worked a few hours at a time. Major markets reportedly shut down due to the high rate of insecurity.[221] The cost of conducting business in the region generally has skyrocketed. This had wide ranging implications for the economic growth of Nigeria and the Lake Chad Basin region and contributed significantly in destroying Nigeria's reputation as a desirable destination for investment. The refugee and internal displacement crisis also created a critical challenge for the region and a major strain on the resources not intended for the influx of people it saw.

2.5.5 *Threat to Regional Stability*

The role of Nigeria in the Lake Chad Basin region and in West Africa cannot be over-emphasised. It had the largest growing economy, the largest population both in the Lake Chad Basin region and in West Africa. Before the violent conflict of Boko Haram, Nigeria was well respected for its military capabilities in Africa and was a major contributor to United Nations peacekeeping operations. The implications of the Boko Haram insurgency were not only been problematic for Nigeria and the Lake Chad Basin region, it also affected the regional stability of West Africa as a whole. Apart from the instability in North-Eastern Nigeria, the Lake Chad Basin region generally became a hotbed of terror. Regional security deteriorated, the territorial integrity of Nigeria, Niger, Chad and Cameroon severely compromised and the Nigerian law enforcement agencies and the military unfortunately demystified.[222] The alleged connection of Boko Haram with other terrorist groups in West Africa also created potential for creating troubling synergy to further destabilise the region.[223]

2.6 Summary and Conclusion

This chapter was developed on four core cornerstones, historicise the phenomenon, provide a factual background, evaluate its typology and assess its impacts. Regarding the history and the development of Islamic fundamentalism in the affected region, the contrasting quality of novelty and familiarity with violence for religion's sake was

220 Dauda 2014, p. 253.

221 Othman et al. 2015, p. 41.

222 Boko Haram has consistently attacked police stations and army bases including most notoriously, the Baga base where the group murdered soldiers, destroyed the facilities and looted weapons. See BBC 2015d.

223 Boko haram reportedly has ties with the Al-Qaeda in the Islamic Maghreb (AQIM), the Movement for Oneness and Jihad in West Africa (MUJAO) and the National Movement for the Liberation of Azawad (MNLA) in Mali and Niger. See generally Aduloju et al. 2014, p. 105.

explored. On the Boko Haram group itself, significant information is known but much more is unknown. Speculations are rife with regards to its numerical strength and a rounded understanding of the structure of the group is largely unavailable. This chapter provided a broad-based view on easily verifiable significant information regarding the group. While attempting to make sense of an otherwise senselessly committed acts, the third part introduced some of the crimes committed by typologies. While the ongoing nature of the crisis made it practically impossible to attempt more than a cursory assessment especially with regards to the impact of the violent conflict, providing a foundation is useful.

References

Adamu F (2008) 'Gender, Hisbah and the Enforcement of Morality in Northern Nigeria'. (2008), Vol. 78, No. 1, Africa: The Journal of the international African Institute.

Aduloju A, Opanike A, Adenipekun L (2014) 'Boko Haram Insurgency in North Eastern Nigeria and Its Implication for Security and Stability in West African Sub-Region'. (2014), 4, International Journal of Development and Conflict.

Agbiboa D (2013) 'The Nigerian Burden: Religious Identity, Conflict and the Current Terrorism of Boko Haram'. Conflict, Security and Development.

Agbiboa D (2013) 'The Ongoing Campaign of Terror in Nigeria: Boko Haram versus the State', 2 Stability: International Journal of Security and Development.

Aghedo I, Eke S (2013) 'From Alms to Arms: The Almajiri Phenomenon and Internal Security in Northern Nigeria' (2013) The Korean Journal of Policy Studies.

Akubor E (2016), 'Poverty and Terrorism in Northern Nigeria: Reflections and Notes on the Manipulation of the Almajirai System and its Implication for National Development' Modern Africa: Politics, History and Society, Vol. 4 Issue 1.

Alao A (2013) 'Islamic Radicalization and Violent Extremism in Nigeria' Conflict Security and Development.

Aljazeera 'Muslim Group Claims Nigeria's Blast', 28 December 2010, available at http://www.aljazeera.com/news/africa/2010/12/20101228123525363633.html.

Aljazeera 'Boko Haram Exploits Nigeria's Leadership Deficit', 14 May 2014, available at http://america.aljazeera.com/opinions/2014/5/boko-haram-nigeriachibokgirlsgoodluckjonathanelection.html.

Aljazeera 'IDP Camps in Nigeria hit by Suicide Bombers', 24 July 2017, available at http://www.aljazeera.com/news/2017/07/idp-camps-nigeria-hit-suicide-bombers-170724090127650.html.

Alkali M, KawuMonguno A, Mustafa B (2012) 'Overview of Islamic Actors in North-Eastern Nigeria', Nigerian Research Network Oxford Department of International Development Working Paper, No. 2 5.

All Africa 'Shiites in Kano Protest Gaza Blockade', 16 December 2008, available at http://allafrica.com/stories/200812160541.html.

'Al Qaeda in the Islamic Maghreb' Counter Extremism Project Report, 9 January 2015, 21. See also Reuters 'How Boko Haram is beating US efforts to choke its financing', 1 July 2014, available at http://www.reuters.com/article/us-usa-nigeria-bokoharam-insight-idUSKBN0F636920140701.

Amara R 'Shaykh Ismaila Idris (2012) '(1937-2000): The Founder of the Izala movement in Nigeria' 11 Annual Review of Islam in Africa.

Amnesty International (2015a) 'Nigeria; Abducted Women and Girls Forced to Join Boko Haram Attacks' 14 April 2015, available at https://www.amnesty.org/en/latest/news/2015/04/nigeria-abducted-women-and-girls-forced-to-join-boko-haram-attacks/.

Amnesty International Report (2015b) 'Our Job is to Shoot, Slaughter and Kill: Boko Haram's Reign of Terror', 14 April 2015 AFR 44/1360/2015.

Anderson J (1959) 'Conflict of Laws in Northern Nigeria: A New Start' The International and Comparative Law Quarterly, Vol. 8, No. 3.

Armborst A (2009) 'A Profile of Religious Fundamentalism and Terrorist Activism', 2(1), Defence against Terrorism Review.

Asogwa I et al. (2015) 'The Almajiri Schools and National Security: A Critical Analysis and Social Development Implication' Global Journal of Management and Business Research, Vol. 15(5).

Audu M, Osuala U (2014) 'Historicizing the Views of Scholars on the Origins the Jihad of Shehu Uthman Dan Fodio' Vol. 3, No. 6 Academic Journal of Interdisciplinary Studies.

Awofeso N et. al (2003) 'The Almajiri Heritage and the Threat of Non-State Terrorism in Northern Nigeria: Lessons from Central Asia and Pakistan' Studies in Conflict & Terrorism.

Awosusi A (2017) 'Aftermath of Boko Haram Violence in the Lake Chad Basin: A Neglected Global Health Threat' BMJ Global Health.

Barkindo A (2013) 'Our Bodies, Their Battleground; Boko Haram and Gender Based Violence Against Christian Women and Children in North-Eastern Nigeria since 1999' (2013) Nigeria's Political Violence Research Network Working Paper No. 1.

Bassam T(2007) 'Political Islam, World Politics and Europe' Routledge.

Bassiouni C (2007) 'Evolving Approaches to Jihad: From Self Defense to Revolutionary and Regime-Change Political Violence', 8, Chicago Journal of International Law.

Bassiouni C (2014) 'The Shari'a and Islamic Criminal Justice in Time of War and Peace' Cambridge University Press.

BBC (2011a) 'Abuja Attack: Car Bomb Hits Nigeria's UN Building', 27 August 2011, available at http://www.bbc.com/news/world-africa-14677957.

BBC (2011b) 'Nigerian Churches Hit by Blast During Christmas Prayers', 25 December 2011, available at http://www.bbc.com/news/world-africa-16328940.

BBC (2012) 'Nigeria's Boko Haram Militants Claim Thisday Attacks', 2 May 2012, available at http://www.bbc.com/news/world-africa-17926097.

BBC (2014a) 'Chibok Abductions in Nigeria: More than 230 seized', 21 April 2014, available at http://www.bbc.com/news/world-africa-27101714.

BBC (2014b) 'Chibok Abductions: Nigeria's Goodluck Jonathan under Pressure', 28 April 2014, available at http://www.bbc.com/news/world-africa-27187255.

BBC (2014c) 'Jonathan: Nigerian girls Abduction a Turning Point', 8 May 2014, available at http://www.bbc.com/news/world-africa-27328003.

BBC (2014d) "Nigerian Villagers Killed in Boko Haram Church Attack", 4 June 2014, available at http://www.bbc.com/news/world-africa-27690687.

BBC (2015a) 'Boko Haram Seizes Army Base in Nigerian town of Baga', 4 January 2015, available at http://www.bbc.com/news/world-africa-30672391.

BBC (2015b) 'Boko Haram in Cameroon Kidnappings', 18 January 2015, available at http://www.bbc.com/news/world-africa-30873243.

BBC (2015c) 'Nigeria's Boko Haram Pledge Allegiance to ISIS', 7 March 2015, available at http://www.bbc.com/news/world-africa-31784538.

BBC (2015d) 'Islamic State 'accepts' Boko Haram's Allegiance Pledge', 13 March 2015, available at http://www.bbc.com/news/world-africa-31862992.

BBC 'Nigeria's Chibok Abductions, What We Know', 8 May 2017, available at http://www.bbc.com/news/world-africa-32299943.

Bensouda F (2007) Gender and Sexual Violence under the Rome Statute. In: Decaux E, Dieng A, Sow M (eds) From Human Rights to International Criminal Law/Des droits de l'homme au droit international penal.

Blanco-Mancilla G (2002) 'Citizenship and Religion in Nigeria: Comparative Perspectives of Islam and Christianity in Kaduna State' Institute of Development Studies, University of Sussex.

'Boko Haram's Pledge to the Islamic State and its Implication for West Africa' Centre for Democracy and Development, 10 September 2016, available at http://www.cddwestafrica.org/2016/09/10/boko-harams-pledge-to-islamic-state-and-implications-for-west-africa/.

Business Insider 'Boko Haram is leaving a major Healthcare Crisis in its Wake', 24 August 2016, available at http://www.businessinsider.com/boko-haram-is-leaving-a-major-healthcare-crisis-in-its-wake-2016-8?IR=T.

CBS News "Easter Bombing near Church in Nigeria Kills 38", 8 April 2012, available at http://www.cbsnews.com/news/easter-bombing-near-church-in-nigeria-kills-38/.

Chazan N (1989) 'Planning Democracy in Africa, a Comparative Perspective on Nigeria and Ghana' 22 Policy Sciences.

Christelow A (2002) 'Islamic Law and Judicial Practice in Nigeria: An Historical Perspective' Journal of Muslim Minority Affairs.

CNN (2012a) '12 Killed in Attacks on Two Churches in Nigeria', 26 December 2012, available at http://edition.cnn.com/2012/12/25/world/africa/nigeria-christmas-attack/index.html.

CNN (2012b) 'As Many as 200 girls Abducted by Boko Haram, Nigerian Officials Say', 16 April 2014, available at http://edition.cnn.com/2014/04/15/world/africa/nigeria-girls-abducted/index.html.

Congressional House Hearing Report, US Policy towards Nigeria: West Africa's Troubled Titan, 10 July 2012. https://www.gpo.gov/fdsys/pkg/CHRG-112hhrg74961/html/CHRG-112hhrg74961.htm.

Daily Beast (2015) 'How ISIS ate Al-Qaeda', 3 December 2015. Available at http://www.thedailybeast.com/articles/2015/03/12/how-isis-ate-al-qaeda.html.

Daily Post (2016) 'Why we are not operating Jonathan's Almajiri Schools-Adamawa Government', 8 September 2016, available at http://dailypost.ng/2016/09/08/not-operating-jonathans-almajiri-schools-adamawa-government/.

Daily Trust (2014) 'Doctors Exiting North-East in Droves', 8 November 2014, available at www.dailytrust.com.ng/weekly/index.php/new-news/18129-doctors-exiting-n-east-in-droves.

Dauda M (2014) 'The Effect of Boko Haram Crisis on Socio-Economic Activities in Yobe State', Vol. 1, (4), Valley International Journals.

Dawood E (2015) 'Leadership ad Ethno-Religious Crises: Implication for National Integration in Nigeria', African Research Review.

Deegan H (2011) 'Religious Conflict in Kano: What are the Fundamental Issues?' 49 Commonwealth and Comparative Politics.

Doukhan D (2012) 'Who Are You, Boko Haram?' International Center for Counter-Terrorism.

Fawaz G (2005) 'The Far Enemy: Why Jihad Went Global' Cambridge University Press.

Feit E (1968) 'Military Coups and Political Developments: Some Lessons from Ghana and Nigeria' World Politics.

Financial Nigeria (2016) 'Why Nigeria no longer attracts Foreign Direct Investment', 7 December 2016, available at http://www.financialnigeria.com/why-nigeria-no-longer-attracts-foreign-direct-investment-blog-194.html.

France 24 (2015) 'Female Suicide Bombers, Boko Haram's Weapon of Choice', 25 February 2015, available at http://www.france24.com/en/20150224-nigeria-boko-haram-female-suicide-bombers.

Gomment T et al. (2017) 'Nigeria: Breeding Future Terrorists: A Study of Almajiri of Northern Nigeria and Islamic Militia', Conflict Studies Quarterly, Issue 18.

Guardian (2002) 'Miss World: Nigerian Odyssey Abandoned after Three days of Fighting Leave 100 dead', 23 November 2002, available at https://www.theguardian.com/world/2002/nov/23/jamesastill.

Guardian (2013) 'Nigerian Islamists Kill Foreign Hostage'. 9 March 2013, available at https://www.theguardian.com/world/2013/mar/09/nigerian-islamists-kill-foreign-hostages.

Guardian (2014a) 'Nigerian State Closes Schools Amidst Fears of Boko Haram Attacks', 18 March 2014, available at https://www.theguardian.com/world/2014/mar/18/nigeria-state-closes-schools-fears-boko-haram.

Guardian (2014b) 'Chibok: The Village that Lost its Daughters to Boko Haram' 15 May 2014, available at https://www.theguardian.com/world/2014/may/15/chibok-nigeria-200-kidnapped-schoolgirls-boko-haram.

Guardian (2015a) 'Nigeria Suffers Highest Number of Civilian Deaths in African War Zones', 23 January 2015, available at https://www.theguardian.com/global-development/2015/jan/23/boko-haram-nigeria-civilian-death-toll-highest-acled-african-war-zones.

Guardian (2015b) 'Boko Haram kill at least 14 in Christmas Day attack', 26 December 2015, available at www.theguardian.com/world/2015/dec/26/boko-haram-kills-at-least-14-in-christmas-day-attack-in-nigeria.

Guardian (2017a) 'Nigerian Airstrike: Dozens Dead as Camp for Internally Displaced Person hit by mistake', 18 January 2017, available at https://www.theguardian.com/world/2017/jan/17/nigeria-military-jet-mistakenly-bombs-displaced-families-camp-boko-haram.

Guardian (2017b) 'Shiites Protest against Israel's Occupation of Palestine, Demand Release of El-Zakyzaky', 23 June 2017, available at https://guardian.ng/news/shiites-protest-against-israels-occupation-of-palestine-demand-release-of-el-zakzaky/.

Harris C (2013) 'Violence in a Religiously Divided City: Kaduna Nigeria-from the Sharia Riots of 2000 to the Post Election Clashes of 2011' (2013) 17 Space and Polity.

Harnischfeger J (2008) 'Democratization and Islamic Law; the Sharia Conflict in Nigeria' Campus Verlag.

Harnischfeger J (2012) '9/11 in Nigeria: Translating Local into Global Conflicts' Afrikanistik online 2012, available at https://www.afrikanistik-aegyptologie-online.de/archiv/2012/3292/Nigeria.

Heerten L, Moses D A (2014) 'The Nigeria-Biafra War: Post-Colonial Conflict and the Question of Genocide'. (2014), 16, Journal of Genocide Research.

Hill J (2010) 'Sufism in Northern Nigeria: Force for Counter Radicalisation?' Strategic Study Institute. Available at https://www.files.ethz.ch/isn/116410/pub989.pdf.

Hodgkin T (1960) Nigerian Perspectives; an Historical Anthology Oxford University Press.

Hoechner H (2014) Experiencing inequality at close range; Almajiri Students and Qur'anic Schools in Kano. In: Mustapha A (ed) Sects and Social Disorder: Muslim Identities and Conflicts in Northern Nigeria. James Currey Publications.

Huffington Post (2015) 'How Boko Haram uses Female Suicide Bombers to Terrorize Nigeria', 28 February 2015, available at http://www.huffingtonpost.com/2015/02/28/boko-haram-female-suicide-bombers_n_6763386.html.

Human Rights Watch (2005) 'Nigeria: Revenge in the Name of Religion: The Cycle of Violence in Plateau and Kano States', 25 May 2005. Available at https://www.refworld.org/docid/42c3bd230.html.

Human Rights Watch (2011) 'Nigeria: Post Election Violence Killed 800', 16 May 2011, available at https://www.hrw.org/news/2011/05/16/nigeria-post-election-violence-killed-800.

Human Rights Watch (2012) 'Spiralling Violence: Boko Haram Attacks and Security Forces Abuses in Nigeria', October 2012.

Human Rights Watch Report (2014) 'Those Terrible Weeks in their Camp; Boko Haram Violence against Women and Girls in North-East Nigeria', October 2014.

Human Rights Watch Report (2016a) 'They set the Classrooms on Fire; Attack on Education in North-East Nigeria' April 2016.

Human Rights Watch Report (2016b) 'Nigeria: Officials Abusing Displaced Women, Girls', 31 October 2016, available at https://www.hrw.org/news/2016/10/31/nigeria-officials-abusing-displaced-women-girls.

Human Rights Watch Report (2017) 'The Forced us unto Trucks like Animals': Cameroon's Mass Forced Return and Abuse of Nigeria's Refugees', 27 September 2017, available at https://www.hrw.org/report/2017/09/27/they-forced-us-trucks-animals/cameroons-mass-forced-return-and-abuse-nigerian.

Huntwick J (1992) An African Case Study of Political Islam. The Annals of American Academy of Political and Social Science.

Ibrahim M (1966) 'The Fulani-A Nomadic Tribe in Northern Nigeria' Vol. 65, No. 259, African Affairs.

Information Nigeria (2014) 'Doctors, Nurses Flee Borno amid Boko Haram Attack', 9 March 2014, available at http://www.informationng.com/2014/03/doctors-nurses-flee-borno-amid-boko-haram-attacks.html.

International Crisis Group (2005) (ed) 'Understanding Islamism' in Middle East/North Africa Report (2005).

International Crisis Group (2010) 'Northern Nigeria: Background to Conflict' (2010) International Crisis Group Africa Report 2.

International Organization for Migration (IOM) Displacement Tracking Matrix Report round XVI, May 2017.

Isichie E (1987) 'The Maitatsine Risings in Nigeria 1980-1985: A Revolt of the Disinherited', 17 Journal of Religion in Africa.

Iyi J, Strydom H (eds) (2018) 'Boko Haram and International Law' Springer.

Joseph E et al (2015) 'The impact of National Security on Foreign Direct Investment (FDI) in Nigeria', IOSR, Journal of Business and Management.

Juergensmeyer M (1994) 'The New Cold War? Religious Nationalism Confronts the Secular State' Comparative Studies in Religion and Society.

Kendhammer B (2013) 'The Shari'ah Controversy in Northern Nigeria and the Politics of Islamic Law in New and Uncertain Democracies' Comparative Politics.

Kenny J (1996) 'Sharia and Christianity in Nigeria: Islam and a 'Secular' State', 26, Journal of Religion in Africa.

Koko M et al (2017) 'Political Risk and Foreign Direct Investment in Nigeria: New Empirical Evidence', Growing Science.

Knapp M (2013) 'The Concept and Practice of Jihad in Islam' Parameters: US Army War College.

Kwanashie G (2002) 'The Making of Northern Nigeria 1900-1965' (2002) Arewa House, Ahmadu Bello University.

Last M (1991) 'Adolescents in a Muslim City: The Cultural Context of Danger and Risk', (1991), Kano Studies (special issue).

Loimeier R (2012) 'Boko Haram: The Development of a Militant Religious Movement in Nigeria', African Spectrum.

Loimeier R (2012) 'Islamic Reform and Political Change in Northern Nigeria' Northwestern University Press.

Ludwig F (2008) 'Christian-Muslim relations in Northern Nigeria since the Introduction of Shariah in 1999', 76, Journal of American Academy of Religion.

Lugard F (1922) 'The Dual Mandate in British Tropical Africa' William Blackwood and Sons, 1st edn.

Lynn M (2006) 'The Nigerian Self Government Crisis of 1953 and the Colonial Office', 34, Journal of Imperial and Commonwealth History.

Magrin G, Pérouse de Montclos M-A (eds) (2018) 'Crisis and Development: The Lake Chad Region and Boko Haram' (2018), available at https://www.afd.fr/sites/afd/files/2018-08-04-37-14/Crisis%20and%20Development.%20The%20Lake%20Chad%20Region%20and%20Boko%20Haram.pdf.

Matfes H (2017) 'Boko Haram: History and Context' Oxford Research Encyclopedia African History 2017. Available at http://oxfordre.com/africanhistory/view/10.1093/acrefore/9780190277734.001.0001/acrefore-9780190277734-e-119?print=pdf.

Mbow P (2009) 'Secularism, Religious Education and Human Rights in Senegal' (2009) Institute for Study of Islamic Thought in Africa (ISITA) Working Paper No. 09-007.

Means J (1965) Study of the influence of Islam in Northern Nigeria Georgetown University.

Meek C (1931) Tribal Studies in Northern Nigeria and A Sudanese Kingdom: An Ethnographical Study of the Jukun Speaking Peoples of Nigeria, Kegan Paul, Trench, Trubner & Co., Ltd., London.

Minteh B, Perry A (2013) 'Terrorism in West Africa-Boko Haram's Evolution Strategy and Affiliations' Mid- West Political Science Conference Proceedings.
Mohammed K (2014) 'The Message and Methods of Boko Haram'. In: Perouse de Montclos M-A (ed) 'Boko Haram: Islamism, Politics, Security and the State in West Africa' Vol 2 West African Politics and Society Series.
Moosa N (2004) 'Unveiling the Mind: A Herstory of the Historical Evolution of the Legal Position of Women in Islam' University of the Western Cape.
News24 (2016) 'Women, Children 'tainted' by Boko Haram become outcasts in Nigeria', 26 August 2016, available at https://www.news24.com/Africa/News/women-children-tainted-by-boko-haram-become-outcasts-in-nigeria-20160826-2.
New York Times (1982) '300 believed killed in religious rioting in Nigeria', 30 October 1982, available at http://www.nytimes.com/1982/10/30/world/300-believed-killed-in-religious-rioting-in-nigeria.html.
New York Times (2011) 'Nigerian Group Escalates Violence with Church Attacks', 25 December 2011, available at http://www.nytimes.com/2011/12/26/world/africa/explosion-rips-through-catholic-church-in-nigeria.html.
Ntamu G, Abia O, Edinyang S et al (2014) Religion in Nigerian Political Space: Implication for Sustainable National Development. (2014) Vol. 4, No. 9, International Journal of Academic Research in Business and Social Sciences.
Ogbeidi M (2012) 'Political Leadership and Corruption in Nigeria since 1960-A Socio-Economic Analysis', Journal of Nigerian Studies.
Oladunjoye P, Omemu F (2013) 'Effect of Boko Haram on School Attendance in Northern Nigeria', British Journal of Education.
Olaosebikan A (2011) 'The Fulani Jihad and its Implications for National Integration and Development in Nigeria', Vol. 5, No. 22, African Research Review.
Oliver R, Atmore A (2005) 'Africa since 1800', 5th edn. Cambridge University Press.
Oluwadare A (2016) 'Boko Haram Terrorism in the Lake Chad Basin Region: Implications for Sub-regional Security', Vol. 8(1), Journal of International and Global Studies.
Onuoha F (2014) 'Boko Haram and the evolving Salafi-Jihadist threat in Nigeria'. In: Perouse de Montclos M-A (ed), Boko Haram: Islamism, Politics, Security and the State in Nigeria IFRA Nigeria.
Othman M et al (2015) 'An analysis of the Impact of Boko Haram Insurgents on Business Entrepreneurship Environment in Nigeria' Vol. 4(3), Academic Journal of Interdisciplinary Studies.
Pate A (2014) 'Boko Haram: An Assessment of Strengths, Vulnerabilities, and Policy Options.' Report to the Strategic Multilayer Assessment Office, Department of Defense, and the Office of University Programs, Department of Homeland Security. College Park MD: START, January 2014.
Paul E Lovejoy (1983) 'Transformations in Slavery: A history of Slavery in Africa' Cambridge University Press.
Perouse de Montclos M-A (ed) (2014) Boko Haram: Islamism, Politics, Security and the State in West Africa. West African Politics and Society, Series Vol. 2. African Study Centre, Leiden.
Pointblank News (2013) 'Boko Haram Leader Shekau Alive; Says No One Can Kill Me Except Allah', 25 September 2013, available at http://pointblanknews.com/pbn/exclusive/boko-haram-leader-shekau-alive-says-nobody-can-kill-me-except-allah/.
Premium Times (2016) 'Buhari declares Boko Haram's 'Final Crushing'; Says Sambisa Last Stronghold Fallen', 24 December 2016, available at http://www.premiumtimesng.com/news/headlines/218799-breaking-buhari-declares-boko-harams-final-crushing-says-last-sambisa-stronghold-fallen.html.
Premium Times (2017) 'In Memory of the Children Massacred in FGC Buni-Yadi on 25 February 2014' Chidi Anslem Odinkalu, 25 February 2017, available at https://opinion.premiumtimesng.com/2017/02/25/177120/.

Reuters (2009) 'More than 700 killed in Nigeria Clashes: Red Cross', 2 August, 2009 http://www.reuters.com/article/us-nigeria-sect-idUSTRE5710AV20090802.

Reuters (2013) 'Nigerian Islamists get $3.15 Million to Free French Hostages: Document', 26 April 2013. Available at http://www.reuters.com/article/us-france-hostages-idUSBRE93P10320130426.

Reuters (2014) 'Nigeria Islamists kill about 59 Pupils in Boarding School Attack', 23 February 2014, available at http://www.reuters.com/article/us-nigeria-violence-idUSBREA1P10M20140226.

Reynolds J (2001) 'Good and Bad Muslims: Islam and Indirect Rule in Northern Nigeria' 34 International Journal of African Historical Studies.

Sandah Z (2013) 'Northern Nigeria: The Conflict Within' African Arguments', 17 January 2013, available at http://africanarguments.org/2013/01/17/northern-nigeria-the-conflict-within-by-zainab-sandah/.

Schacht J (1957) 'Islam in Northern Nigeria' Studia Islamica No 8.

Siegle J (2013) 'Boko Haram and the Isolation of Northern Nigeria: Regional and International Implications' in Mantzikos I. (Ed) 'Boko Haram: Anatomy of a Crisis' E-International Relations.

Sivan E (1990)'Radical Islam: Medieval Theology and Modern Politics' Yale University Press.

Sunan Ibn Majah 224. English Reference Vol 1 Book 1 Hadith 224. Arabic Book 1 Hadith 229.

Taiwo F (2013) 'Transforming the Almajiri Education for the Benefit of the Nigerian Society' Journal of Educational and Social Research Vol 3. No. 9 67.

Telegraph (2015) 'Boko Haram Kidnap at least 60 and Kill three in Cameroon', 18 January 2015, available at http://www.telegraph.co.uk/news/worldnews/africaandindianocean/cameroon/11354185/Boko-Haram-kidnap-at-least-60-and-kill-three-in-Cameroon-raid.html.

Thurston A (2016) 'The Disease is Unbelief: Boko Haram's Religious and Political Worldview' The Brookings Project on US Relations with the Islamic World Analysis Paper.

Time (2011) "Hell on Christmas day: Nigeria's Deadly Bombing", 25 December 2011, available at http://content.time.com/time/world/article/0,8599,2103091,00.html.

Time (2014) 'Boko Haram Kidnap Wife of Cameroon's Deputy Prime Minister', 28 July 2014, available at http://time.com/3045718/boko-haram-cameroon-nigeria/.

Trimingham J (1962) History of Islam in West Africa, Oxford University Press, London.

Ubah C (1982) 'Islamic Legal System and the Westernization Process in the Nigerian Emirate', Journal of Legal Pluralism.

Umar S (2015) 'Salafi Narratives against Violent Extremism in Nigeria' monograph of the Center for Democracy and Development CDDM01/August 2015.

UNICEF (2016) 'New Polio Cases in North-Eastern Nigeria Underline Risk for Children in Conflict', 11 August 2016, available at https://www.unicef.org/media/media_92087.html.

UNICEF (2017) 'Use of Children as Human Bombs Rising in North-East Nigeria', 22 August 2017, available at https://www.unicef.org/nigeria/media_11621.html.

UNICEF (2018) 'More than 1000 children in Northeastern Nigeria abducted by Boko Haram since 2013', 13 April 2018. Available at https://www.unicef.org/nigeria/media_12050.html.

UNHCR (2017) 'UNHCR Concerned about return of Nigerian Refugees from Cameroon', 21 March 2017, available at http://www.unhcr.org/news/briefing/2017/3/58d0ece64/unhcr-concerned-return-nigerian-refugees-cameroon.html.

UNOCHA (2017a)'Lake Chad Basin Crisis Update' No. 13 United Nations Office for the Coordination of Humanitarian Affairs (OCHA) Crisis Update 07 March 2017.

UNOCHA (2017b) 'US $9.9 Million Urgently Needed to Respond to Cholera Outbreak in North-East Nigeria', 18 September 2017, available at https://www.unocha.org/story/us-99-million-urgently-needed-respond-cholera-outbreak-north-east-nigeria.

VOA (2016) 'Christmas Attacks in Cameroon Underscore Continuing Boko Haram Threat', 26 December 2016, available at www.voanews.com/a/christmas-attacks-cameroon-boko-haram/3650882.html.

Voll J (2015) 'Boko Haram: Religion and Violence in the 21st Century' Religions Available at file://w7server/dfs/homedir/Downloads/religions-06-01182.pdf.

Warner J, Matfes H (2017) 'Exploding Stereotypes: The Unexpected Operational and Demographics Characteristics of Boko Haram Suicide Bombers' Combating Terrorism Center August 2017.
Washington Post (1991) 'Planned Christian Revival Sparks Riot in Nigeria', 20 October 1991, available at https://www.washingtonpost.com/archive/politics/1991/10/20/planned-christian-revival-sparks-riots-in-nigeria/c5023a4a-08c9-45d2-bfcf-667bfaec89cb/?utm_term=.ed1a973db824.
Washington Post (2016a) 'The Brutal Toll of Boko Haram Attacks on Civilians', 3 April 2016. Available at https://www.washingtonpost.com/graphics/world/nigeria-boko-haram/.
Washington Post (2016b) 'Boko Haram is forcing more children to carry out suicide bombings', 12 April 2016, available at https://www.washingtonpost.com/world/africa/un-report-huge-surge-in-boko-haram-child-suicide-bombers-in-west-africa/2016/04/12/b0856ee0-4ac7-49d0-9d3f-9b423631eded_story.html?utm_term=.7ec7883d8b9a.
Washington Post (2017) 'Some girls are now free-but hundreds more abducted by Boko Haram are still missing', 7 May 2017, available at https://www.washingtonpost.com/news/worldviews/wp/2017/05/07/some-chibok-schoolgirls-are-now-free-but-hundreds-more-abducted-by-boko-haram-are-still-missing/?utm_term=.559a9e1618a6.
Weimann G (2007) 'Judicial Practice in Islamic Criminal Law in Nigeria-A Tentative Overview', (2007), 14, Islamic Law and Society.
World Health Organization (2016) 'Government of Nigeria Reports two Wild Polio Cases, First since July 2014', 11 August 2016, available at http://www.who.int/mediacentre/news/releases/2016/nigeria-polio/en/.
World Health Organization (2017) 'Lake Chad Basin Humanitarian Response Plan 2017', available at http://www.who.int/emergencies/response-plans/2017/lake-chad-basin/en/.
Yusha'u M et al. (2013) 'Problems and Prospects of the Integrated Almajiri Education in Northern Nigeria' 2(3), Scientific Journal of Pure and Applied Science.
Yusuf H (2007) 'Managing Muslim-Christian Conflict in Northern Nigeria: A case Study of Kaduna State', Islam and Christian-Muslim Relations.
Zenn J (2013) 'Boko Haram's International Connections' Combating Terrorism Centre January 14, 2013.
Zenn J (2014) 'Nigeria al-Qaedaism', 16, Current trends in Islamist Ideology.
Zenn J, Pearson E (2014) 'Women, Gender and the Evolving Tactics of Boko Haram', 5, Journal of Terrorism Research.
Zenn J (2017) 'Demystifying al-Qaida in Nigeria: Cases from Boko Haram's Founding, Launch of Jihad and Suicide Bombing', 11, Terrorism Research Initiative, (2017).
Zenn J (2018) 'Boko Haram, to Ansaru to ISWAP: A Post-Mortem Analysis of Abu Fatima' 9 Militant Leadership Monitor (2018) Available at https://jamestown.org/wp-content/uploads/2018/10/September-2018_MLM-.pdf?x87069.

Other Documents

Global Terrorism Index (2015) Institute for Economics and Peace November 2015. Available at http://economicsandpeace.org/wp-content/uploads/2015/11/Global-Terrorism-Index-2015.pdf.
Report of the Ministerial Committee on Madrassah Education (2010).
Report on Preliminary Examination Activities 2015 12 November 2015 Office of the Prosecutor, available at www.icc-cpi.int/iccdocs/otp/OTP-PE-rep-2015-Eng.pdf.
Report of Secretary-General on Children and Armed Conflict in Nigeria S/2017/304 10 April 2017.
Report of the Secretary General on conflict-related sexual violence United Nations Security Council S/2017/249 15 April 2017.
Report of the UN High Commissioner for Human Rights on the Violations and Abuses Committed by Boko Haram and the Impact of Human Rights in the Affected Countries. 29 September 2015, Human Rights Council Agenda Item 2. 7.

United States Commission on International Religious Freedom Factsheet 'Nigeria: Boko Haram's Religiously-Motivated Attacks' August 2013.

United States Department of State 'Nigeria Travel Warning'. Updated 5 April 2017, available at https://travel.state.gov/content/passports/en/alertswarnings/nigeria-travel-warning.html.

UN resolution S/RES/2331 (2016) 20 December 2016. Available at https://www.un.org/sc/suborg/en/s/res/2331-%282016%29.

Chapter 3
Domestic Criminal Legal Responses to the Boko Haram Crisis

Contents

Abstract This chapter focuses on Nigeria's domestic legal regime as a response to the Boko Haram crisis. It evaluates the domestic criminal system while assessing an interplay between Nigeria's distinct system of laws. It also explores the domestic legal characterisation of the Boko Haram crimes.

Keywords Common Law · Criminal Code · Criminal Procedure (Northern States) Code Act · Domestic Prosecution · Domestication of ICC Statute · Evidence Act · Nigerian Constitution · Northern Nigeria Penal Code Law · Prosecutions · Terrorism Prevention Act

V. Ojo-Adewuyi, *Criminal Justice Responses to the Boko Haram Crisis in Nigeria*, International Criminal Justice Series 34, https://doi.org/10.1007/978-94-6265-615-4_3

3.1 Introductory Remarks

Since the arrival of the British, Nigeria has grappled with the application of three distinct systems of laws namely Islamic/Maliki law, customary law including native law and customs and the received English law. Today, the Nigerian legal system is a unique fusion of the three. Received English Law comprises of the doctrine of common law developed by the old common law courts of England, doctrine of equity developed by the old English court of chancery, statutes of general application in force in England as at 1 January 1900, statutes and subsidiary legislation on specified matters including English statutes made before 1 October 1960 that had not yet been repealed. Customary law of the Ethnic and non-Muslim societies relates to the traditional cultural practices in parts of the country which were largely unwritten and has now been developed by case law. The third category is Shari'a law which is written and became a distinct system in states in Northern Nigeria since 1956. The fragmented nature of the development of the legal system contributed to a system of unequal application of legal regime to the same sets of facts depending on geographical location of the conduct of the crimes. The multifaceted nature of Nigeria's legal system is inherent and the influences of its colonial origins are still present. Before 2015, the system functioned in a varied manner, developing at different phases and applying unequally depending on geographical location within the country.[1] Currently, modes of criminal responsibility generally involve two distinct codes: the Criminal Code[2] which applies in the Southern States and the Penal Code of the Northern States.[3] While both codes have common law backgrounds, the Penal Code also includes religious traditions of the largely Islamic North and it criminalises conducts such as adultery, drunkenness among others which are not crimes under the other system. The law of evidence is provided for by the Evidence Act.[4]Regarding procedure, the regime is also applied unequally within the country. The Criminal Procedure (Northern States) Code Act[5] applies in the courts of the Northern States relative to federal offences in it, while the Criminal Procedure Act[6] applies generally in the rest of the country. The Administration of Criminal Justice Act was signed into law in May 2015 as part of the efforts to end the dual application of the Criminal Procedure Code and the Criminal Procedure Act. It is currently the unifying criminal procedure law for Nigeria. The approach of Nigeria's domestic legal system to

[1] Previously, the major sources of criminal procedure law in Nigeria included the following: The Criminal Procedure Ordinance (applicable in Ogun, Ondo and Oyo State), the Criminal Procedure Act (applicable throughout the country as federal law with regards to federal matters and in force in the old Bendel State as State law), the Criminal procedure law of Eastern Nigeria (applicable in Anambra, Cross River, Imo and Rivers State, the Criminal Procedure of Lagos State and the Criminal Procedure Code applicable in Bauchi, Benue, Borno, old Gongola, Kaduna, Kano, Kwara, Niger, Plateau and Sokoto States. See generally Obilade 2011, p. 245.

[2] Criminal Code Act Cap C38, Laws of the Federation of Nigeria 2004.

[3] Penal Code Law, Northern Nigeria Cap 89 Laws of the Federation of Nigeria 1963.

[4] Evidence Act Cap E14 Laws of the Federation of Nigeria 2004.

[5] Criminal Procedure (Northern States) Act 1960, Cap C42.

[6] Criminal Procedure Act Cap C41 Laws of the Federation of Nigeria 2004.

the Boko Haram violence necessitates an exploration of the history and the development of the legal regime and its applicable forms today. This chapter explores other pieces of legislation that may be applicable to varying acts of the Boko Haram violence since inception including the Economic and Financial Crimes Commission Act, Terrorism Prevention Act, and the Rome Statute Implementation. The chapter also explores the available legal and institutional framework to respond to the Boko Haram conflict from two distinct perspectives. The first standpoint to be explored is substantive criminal law particularly with regards to conduct criminalised according to the available laws. Here, a definition of crime as envisaged by Nigerian law in the Criminal Code, the Penal Code, the Economic and Financial Crimes Commission Act and the latest Terrorism Prevention Act which mirrors the AU Convention on Prevention and Combating of Terrorism will be explored. The second viewpoint is that of legal procedure under which the Criminal Procedure Code, the Criminal Procedure Act, the Administration of Criminal Justice Act including the inherent justice delivery challenges in the Nigerian system.

3.2 Brief Overview of Nigeria's Legal History

The Nigerian legal system is historically a pluralistic one.[7] Before the nineteenth century, the territories that were amalgamated to become Nigeria already had separate though largely unwritten systems of administration of justice. In most parts of the North, the Islamic law typically of the Maliki School held sway while in the South and in a minority part of the North, unwritten customary law enforced by tribal elders was in force.[8] In 1861, King Dosumu signed a treaty of cession which ceded the Lagos Island to Her Majesty's government, consequently making Lagos a British Colony.[9] Although, there had been considerable European and British presence on the shore of Nigeria before 1860, their interests were recorded to have primarily been of business concerns. However, the merchants began dispensing justice as they saw fit. The foray of the British into influencing the judicial system was eventually alleged as intended to protect their business interests and insulate new European and British immigrants from the harshness of the local customary system.[10]

[7] On the intricacies of the Nigerian legal system, see generally Elias 1963, Adewoye 1977, Allott 1962, Asein 1998, and Otu 1999.

[8] Obilade 1979, p. 17.

[9] Although there was British presence in Lagos and an embassy was officially set up in 1851, Lagos became a British domain about ten years later. King Dosumu was purported to have asked for British support to overcome his internal issues, however, he allegedly signed the treaty on the threat of war. The British claimed that their intervention in Lagos was a part of their efforts against slave trade which the region was well known for. There are varying accounts of these events and the dates are frequently recorded differently. The general consensus is that the treaty of cession was signed in 1861. On the succession dispute and a history of Lagos, see generally Smith 1979, Umozurike 1962, Whiteman 2012, and Adekoya 2016.

[10] Asein 1998, p. 159.

Under Ordinance No. 3 of 1863, English Law was introduced and through the Supreme Court Ordinance of 1863, the first Supreme Court with civil and criminal jurisdiction was established.[11] The Court of Civil and Criminal Justice was established in 1866 to replace the Chief Magistrate's Court when Lagos, Gold Coast (Ghana), Sierra Leone and Gambia were placed under a unified administrative system headquartered in Sierra Leone. Even though the British administration did not completely discard local laws and customs including those relating to criminal regime, they were subjected to newly created tests of repugnancy to natural justice,[12] equity,[13] good conscience[14] and incompatibility with local statutes created by the British. Between 1886 and 1899, the Royal Niger Company which comprised of British firms trading along the Banks of River Niger and its basins, operated in the southern parts of what became known as Nigeria. The company was incorporated into the National African Company in 1882. It received a Royal charter for the administration of justice in the territories it functioned in and it established consular courts for civil and criminal matters from which appeals laid to the Supreme Court of the colony of Lagos. With effect from January 1, 1900, the territories previously administered by the Niger Coast Protectorate and the Royal Niger Company were amalgamated to form the protectorate of Southern Nigeria by the Southern Nigeria Order in Council 1889. This acted to fuse the administration of criminal justice regimes under the two territories. In 1906, the colony and the Protectorate of Lagos and the Protectorate of Southern Nigeria were amalgamated to form the Colony and the Protectorate of Southern Nigeria.

Through the Native Courts Proclamation of 1906, a new native Courts system which pioneered the Alkali court and the Judicial Council was introduced. In the North, the Northern Nigeria Order in Council of 1899 established the Protectorate of Northern Nigeria to take effect from January 1, 1900. A Supreme Court, Provincial Courts and cantonment courts were created as a result. On January 1, 1914, the Colony and the Protectorate of Southern Nigeria and the Colony and the Protectorate of Northern Nigeria were amalgamated creating the Colony and the Protectorate of Nigeria. As a result, efforts were made to unify the administration of justice and the court systems of the previously separate colonies. This was done by drawing

[11] Obilade 1979, p. 18.

[12] The concept of natural justice is amorphous, Nigerian courts in their interpretation have utilised the doctrines expressed in the Latin maxims '*audi alteram partem*' (commonly expressed as hear the other side) and '*nemo iudex in causa sua*' (expressed as a person cannot be a judge in his own cause) to express it. See generally Ogoja v. Adamuwa, N. A. 1958, N.R.N. L.R.35. Re Native Court of Onitsha 1928, 9 N.L.R. 65. Modibbo v. Adamawa N.A. 1956 N.R.L.R. 101. Bauchi v. Bauchi N.A. 1957 N.R.N.L.R 156.

[13] The idea of equity has been explained from two different standpoints, the narrow technical sense and the broad sense. From a broad perspective, equity relates to the rules of natural justice, morality and fair play. While the concept of equity is not a part of the law, it is intended to mitigate the harshness of the law. Tobi 1996, p. 38–41.

[14] Good conscience in this regard relates to the consciousness that something is offensive and distasteful to humanity. While this may seem like a relative concept, Nigerian courts developed a legal approach to address the repugnancy question. See Edet v. Essien 1932, 11 N.L.R. 47. Dawodu v. Danmole 1962, 1 W.L.R. 1053.

from varying elements of the previous colonies and fusing them together to form a new distinctive system. A broad-based reform of the court system was completed by legislation in 1933 and a High Court, Supreme Court and increased civil jurisdiction for the native courts was introduced. On 1 October 1954, Nigeria became a federation under the Nigeria (Constitution) Order in Council 1954 and acquired a Federal Constitution. The Constitution established an elaborate system of administration of justice, new courts and an intricate appeal system. The Criminal Procedure Code Law of 1960 established the Magistrate courts to replace pre-existing one to exercise criminal jurisdiction at the lowest level. The Nigerian Criminal Code is applicable in Nigeria alongside the Penal Code which is valid in Northern states. While attempts have been made to harmonise the two codes and thus the criminal system, these efforts have been principally unsuccessful particularly due to the interest of the North in protecting the elements of Islamic law inherent in the Penal Code.

The Northern Nigerian Penal Code[15] is the primary applicable penal legislation in the Northern part of Nigeria. Regarded as a product of 'compromise and amalgamation', it came into force on September 30, 1960.[16] Before 1960, Alkali's Courts in Northern Nigeria applied Islamic Criminal Law from the traditional sources with certain limitations on penalties that could be prescribed.[17] Alongside the Alkali Courts, the Native Courts also applied customary law. In non-Islamic communities, customary law referred to the norms and customs of the society while in the Islamic communities, Islamic law was applied as customary law. In communities with mixed ethnic and religious leanings, a curious mix of Islamic Law and native Law and custom was applied. Appeals from Alkali courts including the native courts typically lay, particularly relating to homicide decisions, to the colonial judicial government mainly the West African Court of Appeal which was governed by English law.[18]

Unlike the Criminal Code applied by the Magistrates and High Courts, Islamic Criminal Law was not codified in one source and the Alkalis discretionarily applied it from its basic sources, resulting in a high level of unpredictability and legal uncertainty.[19] Consequently, resulting from the material differences between received English law and the Islamic Law, jurisdictional issues, choice of applicable law and comparable punishments regarding similar set of facts, there was an apparent need for a codified Penal system based on Islam and addressing the specific concerns of the Northern Nigerian society. For instance, conducts unknown to English criminal law were criminal under Islamic law, acts like adultery, consuming alcoholic beverages, insulting the modesty of women among others. Similarly, under Islamic law, women were not regarded as competent witnesses and could not give testimony

[15] Penal Code Law Cap 89.

[16] Essien 1983, p. 88.

[17] The traditional sources of Islamic criminal law are the *Qur'an*, *Hadith* and the *Sunnah* of the Prophet, (regarded as the divine component of shari'a) *Ijmah*, *Qiyas*, *Marsalah -Mursala*, *Istihsan*, *Istishab*, *Al-Urf*, *Mashabul-Sababi*, *Shar'u-Man-kablana* (regarded as the human component and also the rules of procedure). On the application of State Penal Codes in Nigeria see generally Sada in Ostien 2007, p. 22.

[18] Weimann 2010, p. 88.

[19] Ostien 2007, p. 3.

in court, under the English system in practice, this was not the case. In Islamic criminal procedure in Nigeria, a person accused of highway robbery for example was not allowed to enter a defence. This was eventually overturned in 1959. Additionally, the well-established concept of provocation in homicide cases under the English system was unknown to Islamic law; this issue came into the limelight in the famous 1947 *Tsofo Gubba* case.[20] In many cases, the system applied to a case typically determined life or death for an accused person with the same set of facts in the same geographical location depending on which court it was instituted.[21]

The Penal Code contains elements of the Maliki School of Islamic law and certain characteristics of English criminal law. It was based on the Sudan Penal Code of 1899 which was also centred on the Indian Penal Code of 1834.[22] It incorporated English legal principles alongside principles of Islamic Law and conceded in some instances to Islamic law principles.[23] It introduced religion-based applications of certain provisions which were protected from constitutional ban. However, un-codified Islamic law from the basic sources continued to be applied in civil cases.[24] An elaborate Criminal Procedure Code was also introduced alongside the Penal Code. The Northern Nigerian Penal Code today applies to nineteen Northern states. Islamic law over the years has acquired significant religious and political influence over Muslims in the North and has metamorphosed into a symbol of regional and political identity. Consequently, the re-introduction and full implementation of Shari'a commonly expressed as Islamic Criminal Law after 1999 by some state governors in Northern Nigeria was a clear reflection of the role of Islam in the Nigerian society.

In Nigeria today, a unique fusion of the features and elements of the three distinct systems are apparent in the administration of criminal justice structures, the court systems including the applicable codes in the Nigerian legal system. The classification of the crimes of Boko Haram determines whether they will be treated as ordinary crimes that may fall under the Northern Nigerian Penal Code or the Criminal Code or as specialised offences under newer legislation such as the anti-corruption legislation addressing corruption leading to financing of terrorism, or under the new

[20] Gubba v. Gwandu Native Authority 1947, 12 West African Court of Appeal. In this case, an Alkali Court sentenced the appellant to death for murder. His defence of provocation was not considered by the court as it was unrecognized by Islamic law. Had the case been instituted in a customary court applying the criminal code, the defence could have been recognized and if properly proven may have resulted in a mitigation of sentence from murder to manslaughter. The West African Court of Appeal quashed the decision of the Alkali Court and held that customary law, inclusive of Islamic law, could only be applied in cases not covered by the criminal code.

[21] On the jurisdictional conflicts between English Law and Islamic Law, see generally Anderson 1959, Okonkwo and Naish 1980, Ijaodola 1970, and Milner 1969.

[22] Anderson 1959, p. 453.

[23] Seduction and enticement which were merely torts under the English system were criminalized in S389 of the Penal Code. Adultery and Fornication were also criminalized for persons 'subject to any native law and customs in which extra-marital intercourse is recognised as a criminal offence'. Drunkenness was specifically criminalised for Muslims and there were specific penalties applicable only to Muslims. Ostien 2007, p. 6.

[24] Weimann 2010, p. 89.

anti-terrorism legislation. In most cases, the classification determination and prosecutorial discretion is exercised by officers in the directorate of public prosecution in the Federal Ministry of Justice.

The criminal justice regime in Nigeria functions as a collaboration of numerous agencies at different stages. In a systematised manner, it includes law making agencies, law enforcement agencies, investigation and detection of crimes, prosecution, defence, legal interpretation, judgement delivery and execution.[25] These includes the agencies involved in administering the criminal justice system, the legislature, police, security, intelligence and regulatory agencies, prosecutors and defence attorneys, the judges, and the prison system. Aside from the police, organisations empowered with limited specialised policing powers include, for example, the Economic and Financial Crimes Commission, the States Security Services, the Independent Corrupt Practices and Related Offences Commission, the National Drug Law Enforcement Agency, the Customs Authority, Immigrations Authority, the Civil Defense Corps among others.[26] Ideologically, the Nigerian criminal justice system is geared towards a seeming combination of retribution and deterrence.[27]

3.3 Substantive Criminal Law

3.3.1 The Nigerian Criminal Code

Prior to the enactment of the Terrorism Prevention Act, prevention and combating acts amounting to terrorism in Nigeria rested on the Criminal Code, the Northern Penal Code and other available federal legislations. Although, both the Criminal Code and the Penal Code do not directly address terrorism as a singular phenomenon, neither do they contain provisions directly relating to counter-terrorism, a critical look at their provisions reveals that some acts of violence that may amount to terrorism are already generally criminalised. In this Section, the relevant provisions within the Criminal Code will be highlighted to assist in the understanding of the domestic legal framework relating to anti-terrorism before the Terrorism Prevention Act came into force in 2011. It is noteworthy that the provisions of the Criminal Code take effect subject to the provisions of the Penal Code and cannot be applied in areas of Northern Nigeria under the auspices of the Penal Code.[28] The framework of the Penal Code is addressed in the next section. The provisions explored under this section will be addressed broadly under their headings as contained in the Criminal Code. These include treason and related offences, offences relating to unlawful societies and assemblies, offences relating to religious worship, homicide and unlawful killing,

[25] Alemika 2014.

[26] See generally Alemika 2014, and Inyang 2013.

[27] Alemika 2014, p. 7.

[28] First Schedule Commencement 1A Criminal Code Act Cap C38.

assault on females, abductions, stealing and arson. The offences provided for by the Criminal Code can be instituted in customary courts (which addresses offences relating to violation of local government bye laws and rules), Magistrate courts, State High courts, Federal High courts (which since 2011 has the primary jurisdiction to try specific terrorism offences under the Terrorism Prevention Act). Appellate jurisdiction is also available at the Court of Appeal, Supreme Court and in a limited manner to special criminal courts such as Juvenile courts, Coroners courts, Court Martials and special tribunals and commissions.

3.3.1.1 Treason, Treasonable Felony and Related Offences

Varying categories of offences against public order are addressed in the Criminal Code as treason and treasonable felony. Treason and related offences are provided for in Chapter 6, Section 37 of the Criminal Code.[29] Treasonable felony is also specifically addressed in Section 41.[30] Generally, read together, these provisions can be interpreted to address certain elements of acts of Boko Haram terrorism, particularly as it relates to acts of violence committed in other to intimidate or force the government into taking decisions. These could also address the elements of use of force or threats of violence by Boko Haram to intimidate or outrightly take over the Nigerian government. The activities of Boko Haram after it moved to Kanama, the acts of training and equipping and its members and the subsequent attacks on police and civilians may be charged under the heading of treasonable felony. The rhetoric of Boko Haram on levying war in Nigeria may also be charged under these provisions. Section 42 also addresses the promotion of inter-communal war.[31] It prohibits preparation or carrying out war or any warlike efforts against citizens or the government of Nigeria. The resultant liability is a felony which carries life imprisonment. This implies that the attacks against civilians and the violent engagement of the Boko Haram group against members of the Nigerian military may be prosecuted either as felonies or treasonable felony under the Criminal Code. Unfortunately, as provided for by the Criminal Code, a major challenge to the application of the provisions to the Boko Haram conflict is that a person cannot be tried for treason or treasonable felony unless the prosecution is commenced within two years of the commission of

[29] 'Any person who levies war against the State, in order to intimidate or overawe the President or governor of a state, is guilty of treason and liable to the punishment of death' Section 37 Criminal Code Act Cap C38.

[30] 'Any person who forms an intention to effect any of the following purposes, that is to say (c) to levy war against Nigeria in order by force or constraint to compel the president to change his measures or counsels, or in order to put any force or constraint upon or in order to intimidate or overawe any House of the National Assembly or any other Legislature or Legislative authority; And manifests such intention by an over act, is guilty of a felony and is liable to imprisonment for life' Section 41 (c) Criminal Code Act Cap C38.

[31] 'Any person who, without lawful authority, carries on, or makes provision for carrying on, or aids in or advises the carrying on of, or preparation for, any war or warlike undertaking with, for, by, or against, any traditional chief, or with, for, by, or against any band of citizens, is guilty of a felony, and is liable to imprisonment for life.' Section 42 Criminal Code Act Cap C38.

the offence as stated in Section 43.[32] As long as the charges under these headings relating to some of the early criminal conduct of Boko Haram were not filed within two years of the commission of the offences, the statute of limitation applies and they can no longer be filed under the provision.

3.3.1.2 Offences Relating to Unlawful Societies

Section 62 addresses offences relating to unlawful societies.[33] The aims of Boko Haram as evidenced by its actions, public statements and publications include some of those addressed by the section. By definition, an unlawful society includes one set up for the following aims: to levy war against Nigeria or assist in doing so, to kill or encourage killing, to destroy or encourage destruction of property, subvert government and its officials, commit acts of violence and intimidation and to disturb public peace. According to Section 62, these criteria for an organisation or group to be regarded as an unlawful society are clearly fulfilled by Boko Haram as a group. Section 63 addresses the management of such unlawful society and imposes a liability on conviction of seven years imprisonment.[34] Section 64 also prohibits membership of such unlawful society with a liability of three years imprisonment for convicted members.[35] For prosecution to be instituted under this category of offences, the consent of the Attorney General of the Federation must be sought and received.[36] By virtue of the provisions of Sections 62 to 65 of the Criminal Code, the Boko Haram group may be prosecuted as an unlawful society and its followers for membership of an unlawful society.

[32] 'A person cannot be tried for treason, or for any of the felonies defined in the three last preceding sections, unless the prosecution is commenced within two years after the offence is committed.'

[33] 'A society includes any combination of ten or more person whether the society is known by any name or not. (1) A society is an unlawful society- (i) If formed for any of the following purposes- (a) Levying war or encouraging or assisting any person to levy war on the Government or the inhabitants of any part of Nigeria or (b) Killing or injuring or encouraging the killing and injuring of any person; (c) Destroying or injuring or encouraging the destruction or injuring of any property; or (d) Subverting or promoting the subversion of the government or its officials; or (e) Committing or inciting to acts of violence or intimidation; or (f) Interfering with, or resisting, or encouraging the disturbance of peace and order in any part of Nigeria; or (g) Disturbing or encouraging the disturbance of peace or order in any part of Nigeria; (ii) If declared by an order of the President to be a society dangerous to the good government of Nigeria or of any part thereof.'

[34] 'Any person who manages or assist in the management of an unlawful society is guilty of a felony and is liable to imprisonment for seven years.'

[35] 'Any person who, (a) Is a member of an unlawful society; or (b) Knowingly allows a meeting of an unlawful society, or of members of an unlawful society, to be held in any house, building, or place belonging to, or occupied by him or over which he has control, is guilty of a felony and is liable to imprisonment for three years.' Section 64 Criminal Code Act Cap C38.

[36] Section 65 Criminal Code Act Cap C38.

3.3.1.3 Unlawful Assemblies and Breach of Peace

Chapter 10 defines unlawful assemblies and breach of peace and provides penalties upon conviction. It also addresses threat of violence,[37] intent to intimidate alarm or annoy,[38] and provoking breach of peace by offensive publication.[39] The provisions relating to unlawful assemblies under this heading directly deal with assembling to disturb the peace in the sense of a riot. Although, this may not apply to the Boko Haram violence specifically; the provisions regarding other breaches of the peace in the section are crucial. Section 86 prohibits threatening violence with a penalty of three years imprisonment upon conviction.[40] A major challenge with the provision under this heading relates to its express mention of the unlawful act been carried out in a dwelling house, to the exclusion of all other locations. This implies that gross acts of violence with intent to intimidate and annoy carried out by the Boko Haram group may not be charged under this section. Additionally, a curious difference in the penalty is prescribed depending on whether the offence was committed in the day or in the night. Offences of this nature committed during the day is a misdemeanour, liable to imprisonment for a year, but amounts to a felony when committed during the night with a liability upon conviction of three years. Unlawful processions are also prohibited including bearing of firearms and publicly exhibiting certain emblems and banners.[41]

3.3.1.4 Acts Injurious to the Public

While enumerating acts injurious to the public in general, Chapter 19 in Section 204–206 addresses offences including insult to a religion, offering violence to officiating ministers of a religion and disturbing religious worship.[42] Under these headings,

[37] Section 86 Criminal Code Act Cap C38.

[38] 'Any person who- (1) With intent to intimidate or annoy any person, threaten to break or injure a dwelling-house; or with intent to alarm any person in a dwelling–house, discharges loaded firearms or commits any other breach of the peace; is guilty of a misdemeanour; and is liable to imprisonment for one year, if the offence is committed in the night the offender is guilty of a felony, and is liable to imprisonment for three years.'

[39] Section 88(A) Criminal Code Act Cap C38.

[40] 'Any person who- (1) with intent to intimidate or annoy a person, threaten to break or injure a dwelling-house; or (2) with intent to alarm any person in a dwelling–house, discharges loaded firearms or commits any other breach of the peace; is guilty of a misdemeanour, and is liable to imprisonment for one year, if the offence is committed in the night the offender is guilty of a felony, and is liable to imprisonment for three years.'

[41] Section 88 Criminal Code Act Cap C38.

[42] 'Any person who does an act which any class of persons consider as a public insult on their religion, with the intention that they should consider the act as an insult, and any person who does an unlawful act with the knowledge that any class of persons will consider it such an insult, is guilty of a misdemeanour and is liable to imprisonment for two years 'Any person who- (1) by threats or force prevents or attempts to prevent any minister of religion from lawfully officiating in any place of religious worship, or from performing his duty in the lawful burial of the dead in any

the violent attacks on churches in the early days of Boko Haram particularly the Christmas attacks of 2011 and 2012 which led to the death of hundreds of people may be charged. However, the Criminal Code, by definition treats these offences as misdemeanour and the penalty for assault in a religious service upon conviction is two years imprisonment.

3.3.1.5 Homicide and Related Offences

Homicide, unlawful homicide and related offences are addressed in Chapter 27 of the Code. Murder is defined as unlawful killing or killing in the prosecution of an unlawful purpose.[43] Conviction for murder under the Criminal Code has the liability of a death sentence. Regarding grievous harm, it is defined as a felony with a liability upon conviction of seven years in prison.[44] Individual cases in the context of the various violent attacks of Boko Haram carried out by shooting, by setting bomb and person-borne explosives which led to killings and maiming of civilians may be prosecuted as homicide and related offences under Chapter 27. Injuring or attempting to injure by explosive substances is also criminalised in Section 336 with a liability on conviction of fourteen years imprisonment.[45] In the event that the offender in this Section has not attained the age of seventeen years old as at the time of commission of the offence, and has been found guilty, instead of a death penalty, the underage convict may be detained at the pleasure of the president subject to the provisions of Section 401 of the Criminal Procedure Act.

cemetery or other burial place; or (2) by threats or force obstructs or attempt to obstruct any minister of religion while so officiating or performing his duty; or ....is guilty of a misdemeanour and is liable to imprisonment for two years.' 'Any person who wilfully and without lawful justification or excuse, the proof of which lies on him, disquiets, or disturbs any meeting of persons lawfully assembled for religious worship, or assaults any person lawfully officiating at any such meeting, or any of the persons there assembled, is guilty of a simple offence, and is liable to imprisonment for two months, or to a fine of ten naira.'

[43] 'Except as hereinafter set forth, a person who unlawfully kills another under any of the following circumstances, that is to say- (1) if the offender intends to cause the death of the person killed or that of some other person; (2) if the offender intends to do to the person killed or to some other person some grievous harm; (3) if death is caused by means of an act done in the prosecution of an unlawful purpose, which act is of such a nature as to be likely to endanger human life; is guilty of murder' Section 316 Criminal Code Act Cap C38.

[44] 'Any person who unlawfully does grievous harm to another is guilty of a felony, and is liable to imprisonment for seven years.' Section 335 Criminal Code Act Cap C38.

[45] 'Any person who unlawfully, and with intent to do any harm to another, puts any explosive substance in any place whatever, is guilty of a felony, and is liable to imprisonment for fourteen years.'

3.3.1.6 Assaults and Offences Against Liberty

Broadly assaults on females, the offence of abduction specifically and offences against liberty generally are criminalised by Chapter 30 of the Criminal Code. Section 357 criminalises the offence of rape;[46] with the liability on conviction of life imprisonment with or without caning.[47] Indecent assault on females is criminalised by Section 360 as a misdemeanour with a liability of two years imprisonment.[48] Kidnapping and deprivation of liberty is addressed by Section 364 and 365 with a liability upon conviction of two years imprisonment. Abduction with intent to marry or have carnal knowledge is similarly criminalised in Section 361,[49] while underage abduction of girls under the age of sixteen is specifically criminalised in Section 362.[50] Kidnapping is broadly criminalised by Section 364 with a liability upon conviction of ten years imprisonment.[51] Regarding deprivation of liberty, Section 365 prescribes a liability of two years imprisonment.[52] Slave dealing is also expressly criminalised by the Criminal Code, an offence which Boko Haram members have been accused of, in Section 369 with a penalty on conviction of fourteen years imprisonment.[53] The infamous kidnapping of the Chibok girls, the Dapchi

---

46 'Any person who has unlawful carnal knowledge of a woman or girl, without her consent, or with her consent, if the consent is obtained by force, or by means of threats or intimidation of any kind, or by fear of harm, or by means of false or fraudulent representation as to the nature of the act, or, in case of a married woman, by impersonating her husband, is guilty of an offence which is called rape.' 'Any person who commits the offence of rape is liable to imprisonment for live, with or without caning' See also the decision of the Court of Appeal in Adeoti v. The State (2009) All FWLR Pt 454, 1450. In State v. Ogwudiegwu 1968 NMLR 117 the Court held that corroboration of evidence of evidence implicating a person accused of rape was no longer necessary as long as other material elements are fulfilled.

47 Section 358 Criminal Code Act Cap C38.

48 'Any person who unlawfully and indecently assaults a woman or girl is guilty of a misdemeanour, and is liable for imprisonment for two years.'

49 'Any person who, with intent to marry or to carnally know a female of any age, or to cause her to be married, or carnally known by any other person, takes her away, or detains her, against her will, is guilty of a felony, and is liable to imprisonment for seven years.'

50 'Any person who unlawfully takes an unmarried girl under the age of sixteen years out of the custody or protection of her father or mother or other person having the lawful care or charge of her, and against the will of such father or mother or other person, is guilty of a misdemeanour, and is liable to imprisonment for two years.'

51 'Any person who (1) unlawfully imprisons any person within Nigeria in such a manner as to prevent him from applying to a court for his release or from discovering to any other person the place where he is imprisoned, or in such a manner as to prevent any person entitled to have access to him from discovering the place where he is imprisoned; is guilty of a felony, and is liable to imprisonment for ten years.'

52 'Any person who unlawfully confines or detains another in any place against his will, or otherwise unlawfully deprives another of his personal liberty, is guilty of a misdemeanour, and is liable to imprisonment for two years.' Section 365 Criminal Code Act Cap C38.

53 'Any person who- (1) deals or trades in, purchases, sells, transfers or takes any slave; (2) deals or trades in, purchases, sells, transfers or takes any person in order or so that such person should be held or treated as a slave; … is guilty of slave dealing and is liable to imprisonment for fourteen years.'

girls, among others still believed to be in the custody of Boko Haram may be prosecuted within the provisions of Sections 364 and 365 of the Criminal Code. Rape is the only act of sexual violence specifically provided for within the provision of Sections 357 and 358. Other acts of sexual violence, including enforced pregnancy are not expressly addressed by the Criminal Code. Additionally, although abduction with intent to marry or to have carnal knowledge with a person of majority age is specifically prohibited by the Criminal Code, it is felony with a liability upon conviction of seven years imprisonment. Underage abduction of a girl under the age of sixteen on the other hand is a misdemeanour and liable to imprisonment on conviction of two years. In this vein, abduction of any of the Chibok or the Dapchi girls under the age of sixteen may only be tried under this provision as a simple misdemeanour. Boko Haram reportedly operated a slave market, with the group quoted speaking of its plans to 'sell' some of the abducted women and girls in its custody.[54] Under the provisions of Section 369, members of Boko Haram may be prosecuted for this crime and will be liable upon conviction for fourteen years imprisonment.

3.3.1.7 Stealing and Arson

Although, stealing and arson are not typically categorised together, in the case of Boko Haram, cases of looting have been accompanied by widespread arson in many instances. Regarding stealing generally, Section 382 provides for a legal categorisation of things capable of being stolen, which includes movable inanimate things or properties and immovable inanimate things after it has been made movable among others. Stealing itself is defined in Section 383 (1) as the action of fraudulently taking or fraudulently converting a thing with an intention to permanently deprive the owner of it.[55] Under the Code, stealing is a felony, liable upon conviction to a term of three years.[56] Stealing with violence regarded as robbery is prohibited by Section 401 and 402. Both the act in question and the use or the threat of violence to steal is prohibited.[57] Robbery with firearms or offensive weapons which lead to wounding

[54] BBC 2014a, and The Telegraph 2015.

[55] '(1) A person who fraudulently takes anything capable of being stolen, or fraudulently converts to his own use or to the use of any other person anything capable of being stolen is said to steal that thing.' Section 383 (1)Criminal Code Act Cap C38.

[56] 'Any person who steals anything capable of being stolen is guilty of a felony, and is liable, if no other punishment is provided, to imprisonment for three years.' Section 390 Criminal Code Act Cap C38.

[57] 'Any person who steals anything, and, at or immediately before or immediately after the time of stealing it, uses or threatens to use actual violence to any person or property in order to obtain or retain the thing stolen or to prevent or overcome resistance to its being stolen or retained, is said to be guilty of robbery.' (1) any person who commits the offence of robbery shall upon conviction be sentenced to imprisonment for not less than twenty –one years. (2) if- (a) any offender mentioned in subsection (1) of this section is armed with any firearms or any offensive weapon or any obnoxious or chemical materials or is in company with any person so armed; or (b) at or immediately before or immediately after the time of robbery, the said offender wounds any person, the offender shall upon conviction be sentenced to death.' Section 402 Criminal Code Act Cap C38.

is deemed more grievous and the offender upon conviction is liable to be sentenced to death.

As provided for by Section 443 of the Criminal Code, arson is a felony, which carries a liability on conviction of a life sentence.[58] On malicious injury, Section 451 prohibits wilful and unlawful destruction and damage to property. This is a misdemeanour, with a liability upon conviction of two years imprisonment. If the property in question is a dwelling house or a vessel and has been destroyed by explosives, and the damage endangers life, the liability of the offender upon conviction is life imprisonment.[59] Members of the Boko Haram group have invaded markets to steal produce and money from traders, villages have been attacked for spoil, sacked and then burnt, and explosives have been set to banks in other for them to access the vaults. These acts of violence may be prosecuted either as stealing, robbery, arson or malicious injury.

While it is apparent that some of the conducts of Boko Haram such as individual acts of killings, abductions, some acts of rape and robbery have been expressly criminalised by provisions in the Criminal Code, the challenges with utilising it to respond to the Boko Haram situation are numerous and the question of suitability particularly in addressing the scale of criminality would arise. The provisions in the Code were not crafted specifically to respond to situations of terrorism. Some of the crimes of Boko Haram, such as other acts of sexual and gender-based violence (other than rape), are not criminalised. For some of those criminalised, the severity and the egregious nature of the crimes committed are not addressed by the provisions of the Criminal Code. This can be illustrated for example in Section 206 of the Criminal Code which provides for the offence of disturbing religious worship. This has been done countless times by Boko Haram and it has led to assaults of officiating ministers and members, killing of congregants and arson of religious buildings.[60] However, under the Code, this is classified as a simple offence with a liability of two months' imprisonment or a fine of ten Naira (about 20 Eurocents). Additionally, the Criminal Code did not envisage killings as a result of the disruption, it only provides for assault of persons lawfully officiating in the religious worship or lawfully assembled. Similarly, the dichotomy between the classification and categorisation of offences has created a system where penalties accruing to certain so-called simple offences, misdemeanour felonies may be insufficient when contextualised within a terrorism

---

[58] 'Any person wilfully or unlawfully sets fire to any of the following things- (a) any building or structure whatever, whether completed or not; (b) any vessel whether completed or not; (c) any stack of cultivated vegetable produce, or of mineral or vegetable fuel; (d) a mine or the workings, fittings, or appliances of a mine; is guilty of a felony, and is liable to imprisonment for life.' Section 443 Criminal Code Act Cap C38.

[59] 'Any person who wilfully and unlawfully destroys or damages any property is guilty of an offence, which unless otherwise stated, is a misdemeanour, and he is liable, if no other punishment is provided, to imprisonment for two years.' 'if the property in question is a dwelling house or a vessel and the injury is caused by the explosion of any explosive substance and if- (a) any person is in the dwelling house or vessel; or (i) the destruction or damage actually endangers the life of any person; the offender is guilty of a felony and is liable to imprisonment for life.' Section 451(1) Criminal Code Act Cap C38.

[60] For example, Daily Post Nigeria 2017, and CNN 2012.

situation such as the violent acts of Boko Haram. A prime example relates to the provision of the Criminal Code in Section 428 relating to unlawful possession of firearms. By virtue of the provision and its four subsections, the offence is classified as a simple offence and it is only criminalised to the extent of which such unlawful arms or ammunition belonged to the armed forces or the police. This implies that arms which have been smuggled into Nigeria through other means are not covered by this provision. The reality of this specific context is that only a fraction of the arms and ammunition utilised by Boko Haram members in its attacks have previously belonged to the army or police and were stolen or captured in raids. The majority of weapons in Northern Nigeria thought to be in possession of members of Boko Haram have been allegedly smuggled through a vast and sophisticated network of arms smuggling through the Sahel region and Nigeria's international border with Niger.[61] This dimension is not addressed by the Criminal Code. Additionally, the penalty on conviction for unlawful possession of firearms is a fine of forty Naira (about 80 Eurocents) and payment of a double value of the articles/arms and ammunition. The Code does not address situations where such arms and ammunitions may have been utilised to commit grave crimes like in the case of Boko Haram.

In the same vein, Section 451 criminalises destroying inhabited properties with explosives. However, this is only specifically criminalised to the extent that the properties in question are dwelling houses or vessels. This implies that the provision may not apply for instance to most acts of Boko Haram destruction and bombing of properties such as bombing of churches, office buildings, marketplaces including the notorious bombing of the United Nations' building with a car bomb in Abuja in August 2011. Although the Criminal Code specifically criminalises some of the criminal conduct attributed to Boko Haram, other serious acts of violence have not been criminalised by the Code. Additionally, the provisions of the Criminal Code do not apply to most of the states in Northern Nigeria where majority of the crimes of Boko Haram were committed in Nigeria.

3.3.2 *The Nigerian Penal Code*

As previously stated, the applicability of the Penal Code[62] is limited to the states of the former Northern region of Nigeria. It is applied to the states relating to prohibited criminal acts committed in the areas under its temporal jurisdiction. Under the Penal Code, criminal cases may be tried before Native court, Area courts and the Magistrate courts. The Native court grade A is empowered to try simple criminal cases relating to members of an indigenous community or tribe. In 1967, four grades of Area courts were created by the Area Courts Edict 1967. The Area courts' jurisdiction applies principally to persons who are members of an indigenous community or

[61] Aljazeera Centre for Studies available at De Tessieres 2017.

[62] Penal Code (Northern States) Federal Provisions Act (No. 25 of 1960) 30 September 1960.

tribe. The Area courts are not empowered to try homicide cases, however, other criminal conducts under the Code are within its jurisdiction.

The Magistrate courts in the Northern states also try criminal cases relating to offences contained in the Penal Code. In many cases, however, the same offences are also capable of being tried in the High courts of the states. The major difference affecting the determination of the appropriate court to institute the action is typically based on the fact that the punishment for the offence cannot exceed the punishment which the court in question is capable of prescribing. This is because jurisdiction to try a case has been interpreted as being coterminous with the jurisdiction to punish.[63] In the event where the presiding Magistrate opines that the accused ought to receive a more severe punishment than what the court is capable of prescribing, the facts of the case, recommendation and the proceedings would be forwarded to the High Court or another Court with the appropriate powers of punishment to pass a sentence according to the law.

The Penal Code contains some provisions which are similar by all intents and purposes to provisions in the Criminal Code although with different categorisation. However, it also contains provisions relating to certain conducts that are not criminalised under the jurisdiction of the Criminal Code. Offenders sentenced under the Penal Code can be liable for the punishment of death, forfeiture of property, imprisonment, detention in a reformatory, fine, caning/haddi lashing as prescribed by Islamic law for offenders who are of Muslim faith.[64] Nomenclature in the Penal Code is also radically different from those of offences in the Criminal Code. Additionally, the courts where actions can be instituted under the Penal Code include the Islamic courts while this is not the case under the Criminal Code. A major distinguishing element of the provisions in the Penal Code compared with the Criminal Code is the so-called moral/religious elements. A number of criminal conducts prohibited by the Penal Code are defined along these lines and contain elements that are nebulous and extremely fluid creating definitional and application challenges.[65] The sections of the Penal Code that criminalise conducts that may include some of the Boko Haram crimes will be highlighted broadly under the headings of offences against the public peace, culpable homicide, wrongful restraint and confinement, and rape.

---

[63] See generally Odiai v. Commissioner of Police 1962, NNLR 9. Lamidi Olukun v. Commissioner of Police 1974, NNLR III. Bakare v. Inspector General of Police 1968, NMLR 99.

[64] Haddi lashing may be imposed for Muslim offenders found guilty of specific offences under the code including: adultery (Zina), defamation, injurious falsehood, consumption of alcoholic drinks and drunkenness in public or private places.

[65] For example, Section 354 of the Penal Code prohibits the offence of assault or criminal force to a woman with intent to outrage her modesty. On the face of it, it is unclear what crime this provision addresses and it can be interpreted to suit varying scenarios. It has been generally described as part of the legal framework for sexual and gender-based crimes in Northern Nigeria. See generally Akpoghome 2016, p. 22. Other examples of imprecise offences are the provisions relating to so-called unnatural offences in Section 284 and prohibition of acts of gross indecency in Section 285 which both fail to state specifically the conduct criminalized. Both the prohibitions relating to so-called unnatural offences and acts of gross indecency are typically interpreted as addressing same-sex relations, however, it is unclear from the text. See generally ILGA Report 2007.

3.3.2.1 Offences Against the Public Peace

Chapter 9 of the Penal Code criminalises offences against the public peace generally. Section 100 prohibits an assembly of five or more persons with an objective of a show of criminal force to achieve stated purposes.[66] Under the provisions in this Section, a participant in an unlawful assembly is liable upon conviction to imprisonment for a term which may extend to one year or an unspecified fine or both. The gathering together of members of Boko Haram intended to intimidate members of the public in its early days may be charged under this provision.[67] Another offence of interest to the Boko Haram crisis is described as impersonating a public servant including wearing the clothing or token used by specific public servants. This unauthorised usage is expressly prohibited by Sections 132 and 133 of the Penal Code. Members of Boko Haram have been recorded to cart away police and military uniforms and weapons in its attacks. Members of Boko Haram allegedly showed up for both the Chibok and the Dapchi kidnap operations in police and military uniforms.[68] However, like the Criminal Code, regarding this crime, the Penal Code is silent on situations where the uniforms and weapons have been utilised to commit offences. The Penal Code also criminalises injuring and defiling places of worship, disturbing religious assembly and trespassing in places of worship under the broad categorisation of offences against the public peace, with a penalty of two years imprisonment with or without fine upon conviction.

3.3.2.2 Culpable Homicide

Killing and culpable homicide under the Penal Code is punishable by death generally; with an exception for situations where it may be proven that it was occasioned by grave and sudden provocation. Under this section, individual cases of the varying acts of Boko Haram violence through shootings, bombings among other attacks, which resulted in the death of thousands of civilians in Northern Nigeria, may be prosecuted as culpable homicide. The Penal Code also prohibits for an offence of hurt. This relates directly to causing bodily pain or impairment, and any hurt that causes suffering or endangers the life of the sufferer.[69] Cases of so-called hurt, resulting from

---

[66] 'An assembly of five or more person is designated an unlawful assembly if the common object of the person composing that assembly is- (a) to overawe by criminal force or show of criminal force the government or the government of the federation, or any government of Nigeria or any public servant in the exercise of this lawful powers; or (b) to resist the execution of any law or of any legal process; or (c) to commit any mischief or criminal trespass or other offence (d) by means of criminal force or show of criminal force to enforce any right or supposed right (e) by means of criminal force or show of criminal force to compel any person to do what he is legally entitled to do.' Section 100 Penal Code (Northern Nigeria) Act Cap 89.

[67] See generally US Army Intelligence Report 2015.

[68] The Guardian 2018, and The Telegraph 2013.

[69] 'Whoever causes bodily pain, disease or infirmity to any person is said to have caused hurt. The following kinds of hurt are designated as being grievous- (a) emasculation; (b) permanent

Boko Haram attacks may also be prosecuted within the provisions of Section 241. The liability upon conviction for voluntarily causing grievous hurt without provocation in offence of hurt is an imprisonment for a term which may extend to fourteen years and the possibility of a fine.[70]

3.3.2.3 Wrongful Restraint and Confinement

The offences with characteristics similar to the offence of abduction under the Criminal Code are described as wrongful restraint and confinement in the Penal Code.[71] These offences are regarded as simple offences and their penalties do not exceed three years imprisonment or fine or both. The Penal Code further prohibits criminal force, assault, rape among other crimes. Regarding assault or criminal force to women with intent to outrage modesty, Section 268 prescribes a penalty of three years imprisonment with a fine, or both, upon conviction.[72] Kidnapping, abduction, confining kidnapped persons, slave dealing, trafficking in persons including unlawful compulsory labour is duly criminalised with varying punishment and sentences.[73]

3.3.2.4 Rape

Regarding the offence of rape, the Penal Code prohibits sexual intercourse with a woman against her will, without her consent or obtaining such consent in a climate of fear of death or hurt.[74] The offence of rape carries a penalty of fourteen years imprisonment and the possibility of a fine. A major challenge with this framework of rape as it relates to the Boko Haram crisis is the provision in Section 282 (1)(d)

---

deprivation of the sight of an eye, of the hearing of an ear or the power of speech; (c) deprivation of any member or joint (d) destruction or permanent impairing of any member or joint; (e) permanent disfiguration of the head or face; (f) fracture or dislocation of a bone or tooth; (g) any hurt which endangers the life or which causes the sufferer to be during the space of twenty days in severe bodily pain or unable to follow his ordinary pursuits…'. Section 241 Penal Code (Northern Nigeria) Cap 89.

[70] Section 248 (2) Penal Code (Northern Nigeria) Cap 89.

[71] Section 254–261 Penal Code (Northern Nigeria) Cap 89.

[72] 'Whoever assaults or uses criminal force to any woman intending to outrage or knowing it to be likely that he will thereby outrage her modesty, shall be punished with imprisonment for a term which may extend to three years or with fine or with both' Section 26 Penal Code (Northern Nigeria) Cap 89.

[73] Section 271–281 Penal Code (Northern Nigeria) Cap 89.

[74] '(1) A man is said to commit rape who, save in the case referred to in subsection (2), has sexual intercourse with a woman in any of the following circumstances- (a) against her will; (b) Without her consent; (c) With her consent, when her consent has been obtained by putting her in fear of death or of hurt; (d) With her consent, when the man knows that he is not her husband and that her consent is given because she believes that he is another man to whom she is or believes herself to be lawfully married; (e) With or without her consent, when she is under fourteen years of age or of unsound mind.' Section 282(1) (a-e) Penal Code (Northern Nigeria) Cap 89.

of the Penal Code which can be interpreted to imply that a husband cannot rape a wife.[75] This is a very problematic viewpoint for the context due to the fact that most of the women abducted by members of Boko Haram were either previously or subsequently married by them, the group created a very specific pattern of forced marriages accompanying varying sexual abuse. These forced marriages often involving women young and old including children under the legal age of consent were widespread in the heydays of Boko Haram.[76] Thousands of sham marriages were carried out with women who were in no place to refuse and involving family members who were left with no choice. Sexual abuse, pregnancies and children were a result of these unions. Although, there is a limited possibility that if the so-called marriages are deemed invalid, these situations might be addressed by the provisions of adultery criminalising extra-marital sexual intercourse in Sections 387–388 of the Penal Code. However, the offence of adultery in the Penal Code is a simple offence with a penalty of two years imprisonment or fine or both. Clearly, this cannot be deemed an appropriate response to the gross sexual crimes perpetrated by members of Boko Haram even if the so-called marriages are deemed unlawful. The possibility that this key provision can be interpreted thus creates a huge lacuna for the protection of thousands of women whose rights have been infringed and the course of their lives side-tracked before the coming into force of the Terrorism Prevention Act in 2011. The Penal Code as the primary penal legislation address crimes committed by Boko Haram in Northern Nigeria before the coming into force of the Terrorism Prevention Act in 2011 presents an acutely inadequate response to the problem. Similar to the Criminal Code, while the legal framework of some of the criminal conduct has been provided by its provisions, the degree of criminality, the extent of victimisation and the scale of the Boko Haram violence have not been envisaged by the Penal Code and thus cannot be said to proffer an adequate legal response to the conflict.

3.3.3 The Economic and Financial Crimes Commission (Establishment) Act 2004

The Economic and Financial Crimes Commission Act addresses economic and financial crimes generally; however, its Section 15 provides for offences relating to terrorism financing. It prohibits wilful provision or collection of money with intent or knowledge of its use for any act of terrorism. It prescribes a liability upon conviction of life imprisonment.[77] Although, the presence of this provision in the Act is laudable, its usefulness is limited. Its first and third subsections addresses

[75] '(d) With her consent, when the man knows that he is not her husband and that her consent is given because she believes that he is another man to whom she is or believes herself to be lawfully married.' Section 281(1) (d) Penal Code (Northern Nigeria) Cap 89.

[76] Human Rights Watch Report 2014, The Guardian 2014, The Washington Post 2016, and Mirror 2016.

[77] '(1) A person who willfully provides or collects by any means, directly or indirectly, any money from any other person with intent that the money shall be used or is in knowledge that the money

terrorism linked with economic and financial crimes while the second subsection lacks this nexus. A close look at Section 15(2) suggests a general criminalisation of commission of terrorist acts as its wording lacks a suggestion of connection to an economic or financial crime. The interpretation section of the Act[78] defines economic and financial crimes in terms of 'non-violent criminal and illicit activity committed with the objective of earning wealth illegally…' This is significant due to the fact that the entire Act is intended to address economic and financial crimes which are non-violent in nature. The same interpretation section proceeds to define terrorism in terms of the violation of the criminal or penal code, especially from the criminal and violent perspective.[79] It is difficult to understand the intendment of the drafters of this provision, the rationale for its inclusion in the Act and the practical purposes it is intended to serve. It must be noted, however, that in the legal sphere in Nigeria, the provision of Section 46 of the Act represents the first clear criminalisation of terrorism as a phenomenon. Regrettably, from the poor drafting and the lack of sufficient clarity, the perfunctory introduction of this provision in the Economic and Financial Crimes Commission Act relating to terrorism suffer from a real inability to provide a suitable legal protection.

3.3.4 Terrorism Prevention Act (2011)

The Terrorism Prevention Act 2011 addresses offences relating to acts and purposes connected with terrorism. While it does not define terrorism, it prohibits specific

shall be used for any act of terrorism, commits an offence under this Act and is liable on conviction with imprisonment for life. (2) Any person who commits or attempts to commit a terrorist act or participates in or facilitates the commission of a terrorist act, commits an offence under this Act and is liable on conviction to imprisonment for life (3) Any person who, makes funds, financial assets or economic resources or financial or other related services available for use of any other person to commit or attempt to commit, facilitate or participate in the commission of a terrorist act is liable on conviction to imprisonment for life.' Section 15 Economic and Financial Crimes Commission (Establishment) Act 2004.

78 Section 46 Economic and Financial Crimes Commission (Establishment) Act 2004.

79 According to the Act, 'terrorism means- (a) any act which is a violation of the Criminal Code or the Penal Code and which may endanger the life, physical integrity, and freedom of, or cause serious injury or death to, any person, any number or group of persons or cause or may cause damage to public or property, natural resources, environmental or cultural heritage and is calculated and intended to- (i) intimidate, put fear, force, coerce or induce any government, body institution, the general public or any other segment thereof, to do or abstain from doing any act or to adopt or abandon a particular standpoint or to act according to certain principles, or (ii) disrupt any public service, the delivery of any essential service to the public or to create a public emergency, or (iii) create general insurrection in the state; (b) any promotion, sponsorship of, contribution to, command, aid, incitement, encouragement, attempt, threat, conspiracy,, organization or procurement of any person, with the intent to commit any act referred to in paragraph (a) (i)(ii) and (iii).

acts of terrorism in its first section.[80] It criminalises organisational participation and collaboration in acts of terrorism.[81] The Act vests the power to declare a collective as a proscribed organisation in a judge in chambers on application by the Attorney General, the National Security Adviser or the Inspector General of Police.[82] Accordingly, in May 2013, Boko Haram and its splinter group, Ansaru, were officially proscribed and the order for the proscription duly gazetted pursuant to the provisions of the Act.[83] The Act further criminalises participation in international terrorism, membership or linkage with an international terrorist group, or involvement in participation of any terrorist acts subject of any resolution of the United Nations' Security Council, an instrument of the African Union (AU), and the Economic Community of West African States (ECOWAS).[84] The pledge of the Boko Haram group to the Islamic State in 2015 may be prosecuted under the provisions of Section 9 of the Terrorism Prevention Act. Criminal conducts analogous to terrorism such as terrorism financing[85] and funding[86] (both in the domestic and international sphere) including dealing with terrorism property[87] are also criminalised by Sections 10, 12, 13 and 15 of the Terrorism Prevention Act. Under the Act, financial institutions are required to report suspicious transactions relating to terrorism.[88] The Act also set

[80] '(2) In this Section, "act of terrorism means an act which is deliberately done with malice, aforethought and which: (a) May seriously harm or damage a country or an international organization; (b) Is intended or can reasonably be regarded as having been intended to- (i) Unduly compel a government or international organization to perform or abstain from performing an act; (ii) Seriously intimidate a population; (iii) Seriously destabilize or destroy the fundamental political, constitutional, economic or social structure of a country or an international organization; or (iv) Otherwise influence such government or international organization by intimidation or coercion; and (c) Involves or causes, as the case may be- (i) an attack upon a person's life which may cause serious bodily harm or death; (ii) kidnapping of a person; (iii) destruction to a government or public facility, a transport system, an infrastructure facility, including an information system, a fixed platform located on the continental shelf, a public place or private property, likely to endanger human life or result in major economic loss; (iv) the seizure of an aircraft, ship or other means of public or goods transport and diversion or the use of such means of transportation for any purposes in paragraph (b) (iv) of this subsection; (v) the manufacture, possession, acquisition, transport, supply or use of weapons, explosives or of nuclear, biological or chemical weapons, as well as research into, and development of biological and chemical weapons without lawful authority; (vi) the release of dangerous substance or causing of fire, explosions or floods, the effect of which is to endanger human life; (vii) Interference with or the disruption of the supply of water, power or any other fundamental natural resource, the effect of which is to endanger human life; (viii) an act or omission in or outside Nigeria which constitutes an offence within the scope of the counter terrorism protocols and conventions duly ratified by Nigeria.

[81] Section 3.2 Terrorism (Prevention) Act 2011, Act No. 10.

[82] Section 3.2(c) Terrorism (Prevention) Act 2011, Act No. 10.

[83] Terrorism (Prevention) (Proscription Order) Notice 2013 Federal Republic of Nigeria Official Gazette No 34, Vol 100 24 May 2013.

[84] Section 9 Terrorism (Prevention) Act 2011, Act No. 10.

[85] Section 10, 12 Terrorism (Prevention) Act 2011, Act No. 10.

[86] Section 13 Terrorism (Prevention) Act 2011, Act No. 10.

[87] Section 15 Terrorism (Prevention) Act 2011, Act No. 10.

[88] Section 14 Terrorism (Prevention) Act 2011, Act No. 10.

up an elaborate mutual assistance and extradition process for the investigation and prosecution of terrorism related offences when there is a mutual treaty between the requesting and the requested state.[89] Regarding investigation of acts of terrorism, Part V addresses the issuance of warrant procedure, situations of urgency where search without warrant is permitted, intelligence gathering, the process of detention of property and persons reasonably suspected to have committed offences under the Act. It also provides for video recording admissible in evidence.[90] Part VI addresses prosecution of terrorism offences and designates the Attorney General of the Federation to institute and undertake criminal proceedings under the Act. However, this power may be delegated to any agency charged with investigating acts of terrorism addressed by the Act.[91] On witness protection, the Court may by application via a motion, exclude any person other than the parties and their legal representatives from terrorism related proceedings in the interest of public safety and order.[92] Under the Act, the Federal High Court is vested with the sole jurisdiction to try the offences therein. The maximum sentence prescribed is life imprisonment in the event that death occurs as a result of the act(s) of terrorism.[93] Additionally, on conviction, property forfeiture order may be made in addition to any of the prescribed penalties. The Act also provides for the domestic application of international counter-terrorism conventions when ratified.[94] It is, however, silent on the provision of Section 12 of the Constitution which prescribes an implementation procedure before international conventions may become applicable in Nigeria. The Terrorism Prevention Act represents the first broad-based criminalisation for the phenomenon of terrorism; however, it is only applicable to Boko Haram crimes committed after its coming into force in 2011. The violent crimes committed of Boko Haram committed between 2009 and 2011 are not covered by the provisions of the Act.

Barely two years after the enactment of the Act, twenty of its sections were substantially amended by the Terrorism (Prevention) (Amendment) Act, 2013. The amendment particularly provides for the extraterritorial application of the Act, and

[89] Sections 18–23 Terrorism (Prevention) Act 2011, Act No. 10.

[90] Sections 24–29 Terrorism (Prevention) Act 2011, Act No. 10.

[91] According to the interpretation section, such agencies include the Nigerian Police Force; the Economic and Financial Crimes Commission; the Department of State Security.

[92] Section 31 Terrorism (Prevention) Act 2011, Act No. 10.

[93] Section 33 Terrorism (Prevention) Act 2011, Act No. 10.

[94] The Conventions stated include the UN Convention on the Prevention and Punishment of Crimes against Internationally Protected Persons 1973, International Convention against the Taking of Hostages 1979, International Convention for the Suppression of Terrorist Bombing 1997, International Convention for the Suppression of the Financing of Terrorism 1999, Convention for the Offences and Certain Other Acts Committed on Board Aircraft 1969, Convention on the Suppression of the Unlawful Seizure of Aircraft 1971, Convention for the Suppression of Unlawful Acts Against the Safety of Civil Aviation 1971, Protocol for the Suppression of Unlawful Acts of Violence at Airports Serving International Civil Aviation 1988, Convention on the Making of Plastic Explosives for the Purpose of Detection 1991, Convention for the Suppression of Unlawful Acts against the Safety of Maritime Navigation 1992, Protocol for the Suppression of Unlawful Acts against the Safety of Maritime Navigation 2005, and Convention on the Physical Protection of Nuclear Material 1990 and any such convention assented by the Nigerian government.

an improvement of the provisions relating to terrorism financing offences. The Office of the National Security Adviser was designated as the national coordinating body for all security and enforcement issues relating to acts of terrorism. The amendment improved the responsibilities of law enforcement and security agencies for intelligence gathering, and investigation of offences under the Act.[95] It substituted Sections 3.3–3.8 of the 2011 Act addressing offences against internationally protected persons,[96] terrorist meetings, soliciting and giving support to terrorist groups for the commission of terrorist acts, harbouring of terrorist among other similar provisions. Membership of a terrorist group or a proscribed organisation attracts a liability of a term of imprisonment of not less than twenty years under the amendment.[97] Attempt to commit a terrorist offence is criminalised by Section 20 with a liability on conviction of life imprisonment. The Act permits proceedings *in camera* if the Court is satisfied that the life of a person or a witness is in danger.[98] The amendment Act additionally expands the jurisdiction of the Court to include terrorism offences committed outside Nigeria, by Nigerian citizens or by non-Nigerians ordinarily resident in Nigeria, or persons in transit or with a vital link to Nigeria.[99] Alongside deleting several provisions in the principal Act, it further expanded the definition of terrorist acts to include acts which constitute an offence under listed international agreements.[100] Collectively, the Terrorism Prevention Act and its 2013 Amendment apply to majority of the crimes committed by Boko Haram committed since 2011. Since its entry into force, both the principal Act and its subsequent amendment have remained the major law utilised as a response and for the prosecution of Boko Haram cases.[101]

---

[95] Section 3.2(3-4) Terrorism (Prevention) Amendment Act, 2013.

[96] The requirement of category of protected persons under international law is nebulous. It is not clear whether this refers to the categorization under international humanitarian law or whether it also includes the provision of Article 8(2) (a) of the Rome Statute. Under the Geneva Conventions I-III, protected persons may include the wounded, sick, shipwrecked soldiers and prisoners of war, members of the armed forces, the militia including volunteer corps. In non-international armed conflicts, Common Article 3 of the Geneva Conventions also extends protection to include persons taking no active part in hostilities, including members of the armed forces who have laid down their arms and those placed *hors de combats* by sickness, wounds, detention or any other cause. See generally, Werle and Jessberger 2020.

[97] Section 16 Terrorism (Prevention) Amendment Act 2013.

[98] Section 34 Terrorism (Prevention) Amendment Act 2013.

[99] The Federal High Court located in any part of Nigeria, regardless of the location where the offence is committed shall have jurisdiction to – (a) Try offences under this Act or any other related enactment; (b) Hear and determine proceedings arising under this Act; and (c) Whether or not the offence was committed in Nigeria and completed outside Nigeria and the victim is (i) a citizen or resident of Nigeria (ii) not a citizen of any country but ordinarily resident in Nigeria, (iii) in transit or has a link with Nigeria (iv) dealing with or on behalf of the Government of Nigeria, or a citizen of Nigeria or an entity registered in Nigeria, or (v) the alleged offender is in Nigeria and not extradited to any country for prosecution.

Section 32(1) Terrorism (Prevention) Amendment Act 2013.

[100] Section 19 (g) Terrorism (Prevention) Amendment Act 2013.

[101] By September 2017, according to the information available on the website of Nigeria's Federal Ministry of Justice, thirty-three cases instituted on the basis of the Terrorism Prevention Act were

3.3.5 Rome Statute Implementation

Nigeria is a founding member and the 39th State party of the Rome statute. It signed the Statute on 1 June 2000 and ratified on 27 September 2001. Although, the Rome Statute does not make the implementation of its provisions into domestic legislation mandatory, member states are required to have available procedures under their national laws for all forms of cooperation and legal assistance with the court.[102] Importantly, there is no obligation on the part of state parties to the Rome Statute to define crimes or alter the legal characterisation in its domestic legislations in accordance with the Rome Statute. There will be no complementarity gap as long as similar sets of conducts are covered.[103] Under the Statute, there is no obligation for state parties to criminalise genocide, war crimes, crimes against humanity and the crime of aggression in their domestic legislation.[104] States possess flexibility under the statute on its modes of incorporation of crimes and the test for admissibility prescribed by Article 17 of the Rome Statute is willingness and ability to genuinely prosecute irrespective of legal characterisation of offence.[105]

It is noteworthy that some of the crimes embodied in the Rome Statute have become generally recognised and have acquired the status of customary international law. There are clear treaty obligations to adopt necessary domestic legislation in this regard.[106] The Nigerian Constitution in Section 12 also creates a bar to the direct application of international treaties signed and/or ratified by Nigeria.[107] The obligation of domestic implementation of international treaties is vested in both the legislature and the executive arms of government.[108] For international treaties to be domestically applicable in Nigeria, the constitutionally required process of

ongoing at various Federal High Courts with 116 more charges filed and awaiting trial. See Federal Ministry of Justice 2017.

[102] Werle and Jessberger 2020. See also Article 88 Rome Statute.

[103] Gaddafi & Al-Senussi, ICC (PTC) 2013, paras 85 and 88.

[104] Nouwen 2013, p. 41.

[105] Werle and Jessberger 2020.

[106] See for example Article V of the 1948 Genocide Convention for Genocide. For War Crimes, Articles 49, 50, 129 and 146 of the four Geneva Conventions, Art 85–87 of the 1977 first additional protocol to the Geneva Convention, for crimes which committed as part of a widespread or systematic attack directed against a civilian population, qualifying as crimes against humanity; Art IV of the 1973 Apartheid Convention and Art 6 of the 1984 United Nations Convention against Torture. See also Kleffner 2003.

[107] Section 12 of the Constitution of the Federal Republic of Nigeria provides: '12(1) No treaty between the Federation and any other country shall have the force of law to the extent to which any such treaty has been enacted into law by the National Assembly. (2) The National Assembly may make laws for the Federation or any part thereof with respect to matters not included in the he Exclusive Legislative List for the purpose of implementing a treaty. (3) A bill for an Act of the National Assembly passed pursuant to the provisions of subsection (2) of this section shall not be presented to the President for assent, and shall not be enacted unless it is ratified by a majority of all the House of Assembly in the Federation.' See also African Reinsurance Corporation case 1986, 3NWLR pt. 31, p. 811.

[108] Okeke 1996, p. 337.

domestication must be undergone and a national corresponding enabling Act must be created. The domestication process for the Rome Statute was initiated by the Federal Ministry of Justice in 2001 when an Executive Bill, 'The Rome Statute of the International Criminal Court (Ratification and Jurisdiction) Bill 2001' was sent to the National Assembly. The Bill was eventually passed after four years in May 2005. Unfortunately, it failed to receive assent and was not signed into Law. In 2006, the Rome Statute (Ratification and Jurisdiction) Bill 2006 was once again passed before both the House of Senate and the House of Representatives, yet there was no presidential assent. Another failed attempt was instituted in 2012 with the drafting of the Crimes against Humanity, Genocide and Related Offences Bill 2012.[109] However, it only passed first reading at the senate. As it stands, the provisions of the Rome Statute cannot be applied before domestic courts in Nigeria.

A further challenge to the domestic application of the Rome Statute should the law be passed is a basic practical concern. By the nature of the federal system of Nigeria, Laws passed by the National Assembly is only applicable to the Federal Capital Territory (Abuja) and does not include the 36 states of the Federation.[110] It, therefore, becomes the responsibility of all the state assemblies to pass supporting legislation supplementing and extending the jurisdiction of the federal laws. In this instance, should the National Assembly pass domestic legislation implementing the regime of the Rome Statute in Nigeria at some point, all the other thirty-six states must also pass complementing legislation in order for equal applicability across the country.

3.3.6 Domestic Legal Framework for Crimes Committed Between 2009 and 2011

The question of the availability and the suitability of the legal characterisation and the legal framework generally that captures the severity of the acts in question under the domestic regime seem pertinent. This is due to some of the challenges highlighted with the definitions and characterisation available in the Criminal Code, the Penal Code, and the Economic and Financial Crimes Commission Act especially before 2011. Some of the violent acts committed by Boko Haram since 2009 may also constitute international crimes but can only be treated as simple crimes within the Criminal Code, Penal Code and the Economic and Financial Crimes Commission Act available between 2009 and 2011. If the acts in question have been prosecuted as simple crimes under the Criminal Code, Penal Code and the Economic and Financial Crimes Commission Act, does this have any effect on the fact that

[109] A Bill for an Act to Provide for the Enforcement and Punishment of Crimes against Humanity, War Crimes, Genocide and Related Offences and to give Effect to certain Provisions of the Rome Statute of the International Criminal Court in Nigeria 2013. 7th National Assembly, 2nd session Number 37.

[110] Olugbuo 2016.

some of these acts may also be categorised as international crimes? And should their characterisation as international crimes affect how they can be potentially prosecuted in the domestic sphere? Would domestic prosecution of the acts and conduct as simple crimes notwithstanding trigger the prohibition of double jeopardy, if the crimes in question are brought up at an international forum-court or tribunal? The law and practice of the ICTY and the ICTR is instructive in this regard.[111] It is clear that an individual may be tried by the Tribunals if the acts for which he was tried before national proceedings are categorised as ordinary crimes such that the defence of double jeopardy will not apply.[112] However, the approach of the International Criminal Court to this concern seems to vary from the ad-hoc tribunals. The ICC Statute refers to the conduct criminalised.[113] This differs from the legal categorisation approach and provides more flexibility with regards to prosecuting categories of crimes whose characteristics may overlap.[114]

That the rule against double jeopardy protects an individual who has been prosecuted for the same offence upon the same facts from future prosecution is clear. However, a salient question is whether the suitable domestic legal categorisation fitting to address the severity of the crimes committed affects the determination of the adequacy of a domestic process. If the answer is in the negative, would this be fatal for the cases that have or are being prosecuted, occasioning a complementarity gap? Additionally, since the ICC's approach relates to the criminalised conduct, is the legal categorisation generally completely meaningless and unnecessary? It is my view that the answer to this is in the affirmative due to the fact that it is acknowledged that the elements defining the international character of the crime may not be completely available under domestic law.[115] In this regard, the question of penalties accruing to domestic crimes is also pertinent. How do the penalties which naturally accrue to the acts categorised and criminalised under the domestic jurisdiction stand up to standards before the ICC for similar acts and conducts constituting international crimes? The Rome Statute in Article 20 is silent on whether penalties accruing have the potential to affect the rule of double jeopardy. Triffterer opines, however, that there are important fundamental criteria regarding the quality of criminal justice that must be fulfilled by national proceedings.[116] Such criteria should normally include, for instance, the severity or otherwise of the penalties accruing to the criminalised conduct. The ICC Statute also seem to suggest that member states should be willing and able, including through their available national legislation, to prosecute crimes

---

[111] Article 10(2)(a) of the ICTY Statute and Article 9(2)(a) of the ICTR Statute. See also Prosecutor v. Tadic IT -94-I-T, Decision on the Defense Motion on the Principle of Non bis in Idem, Trial Chamber, 14 November 1995 and Prosecutor v. Ntuyagha ICTR-98-40-T, Decision on the Prosecution's Motion to Withdraw the Indictment, Trial Chamber, 18 March 1999.

[112] Werle and Jessberger 2020.

[113] Article 20(3) ICC Statute.

[114] Triffterer and Ambos 2016.

[115] Ibid. 114.

[116] Ibid. 114.

within the jurisdiction of the court in a manner similar to the court.[117] According to Triffterer, substantial undercharging of conduct that is proscribed in Article 6, 7 and 8 of the Rome Statute as well as inadequacy of sentence may be regarded as falling under one of the exceptions of para 3.[118] Werle and Jessberger also opine that, a state whose criminal law provides for inadequate punishment for crimes under international law may have those prosecutions taken up if necessary by the ICC.[119] In the Boko Haram situation, should the persons most responsible for the crimes committed be captured and tried before the domestic courts for offences committed between 2009 and 2011, the provisions including the penalties of the Criminal Code, Penal Code and the Economic and Financial Crimes Commission Act may be ill-suited for the grave relentless acts, especially as it relates to sexual and gender-based violence committed before the Terrorism Prevention Act was passed into law. Among the few Boko Haram violence related cases that have been instituted, completed or ongoing in the Nigerian judicial system, none of them addresses any act of sexual and/or gender-based violence of Boko Haram in any form.[120] It is important to note that there are laws, protocols and treaty obligations that protect from sexual and gender-based violence including available means and mechanisms for the prosecution of violators.[121] However, prosecutions addressing acts of sexual violence and gender-based violence were not instituted.

3.4 Criminal Procedure

As earlier noted, before 1960, unwritten native law and custom including Islamic law of the Maliki School was applied as law and procedure in some of the Courts[122] of Northern Nigeria.[123] The Criminal Procedure Ordinance[124] established the law of criminal procedure in the High courts and the Magistrate courts. In preparation for

[117] Ibid. 112.

[118] Ibid. 114.

[119] Ibid. 112.

[120] See generally Council on Foreign Relations 2018.

[121] Nigeria has ratified the Convention on the Elimination of all forms of Discrimination against Women 1979 (CEDAW), the Protocol to the African Charter on Human and Peoples' Rights on the Rights of Women in Africa (Maputo Protocol) 2003, has enacted the Child Rights Act, a Violence against Persons'(Prohibition) Act (VAPP) 2015, and also created a National Action Plan (2017–2020) for the Implementation of UNSCR 1325 and related Resolutions for the protection against sexual and gender based violence. Regardless of all these measures, real- time practical protection against sexual and gender-based violence is almost non-existent.

[122] This specifically refers to the native courts, Alkali courts, and conciliar courts including non-Muslim courts.

[123] Williams 1966, p. 258.

[124] This ordinance became the Criminal Procedure Act Cap. 4B 1958 Laws of the Federation of Nigeria and Lagos.

Nigerian independence in October 1960, the Penal Code Law of 1959 was introduced alongside a Criminal Procedure Code Law of 1960. The Criminal Procedure (Northern States) Code[125] was in force in states in Northern Nigeria while the Criminal Procedure Act[126] applied in the southern states and throughout Nigeria for offences against federal laws.[127] The Criminal Procedure Code and Act continued to be applicable until the mid-2000s when a clamour for the renewal of the criminal procedure in Nigeria gathered steam. Consequently, the new Administration of Criminal Justice Act 2015 emerged in an attempt to modernise criminal procedure in Nigeria. This section examines the procedural challenges relating to the violent conflict of Boko Haram as it existed before and after the introduction of the Administration of Criminal Justice Law. It will further assess the specific provisions of the Criminal Procedure Act and the Criminal Procedure Code, the Current Administration of Criminal Justice Law, including a number of jurisdictional challenges with bail administration and imprisonment as related to the Boko Haram violence will also be addressed.

3.4.1 Criminal Procedure (Northern States) Act and the Criminal Procedure Code

The Nigerian criminal justice system is based on an intricate structure of institutions organised along the federal and state systems, lacking in cohesion and definitiveness.[128] The procedural system was similarly governed by differing legislations addressing different issues and regions including in particular the Criminal Procedure (Northern States) Act and the Criminal Procedure Code. The Administration of Criminal Justice Act is the current criminal procedure law in Nigeria. However, it has only been domesticated in a few states in the federation.[129] Its passing into law effectively repealed the Criminal Procedure (Northern States) Code and the Criminal Procedure Act (which was applicable in the South) including the Administration of Criminal Justice Commission Act in the federal regime. The preceding Criminal Procedure (Northern States) Act of 1960 provides for the jurisdiction, powers, practice and procedure of the Courts of the Northern state of Nigeria relative to offences contained in federal legislation. The Criminal Procedure Act pioneered an approach of equal application to all High Courts and Magistrate Courts while applying only in

[125] Criminal Procedure (Northern States) Code, Cap. 81, Laws of the Federation of Nigeria, 1990.

[126] Criminal Procedure Act Cap. 80, Laws of the Federation of Nigeria, 1990.

[127] Asein 2005, p. 308.

[128] These institutions are all involved in the various stages of the criminal justice system including; the arrest, prosecution and pre-trial stage, adjudication stage, sentencing stage, corrections and post-corrections stage. This is inclusive but not limited to the court system, the prisons system, the police force, the juvenile system among others. See generally, Saleh-Hanna and Ume in Saleh-Hanna 2008, 55–68. Otu 1999, and Dada, Dosumu and Oyedeji 2015.

[129] So far, only 11 out of the 36 States have domesticated the Act. They are; Kaduna, Ondo, Ekiti, Lagos, Oyo, Rivers, Anambra, Enugu, Cross-River, Abuja and Akwa-Ibom.

part to the Native Courts.[130] The drafting of charges which was previously carried out by the police in cases before the Magistrate court and the native court was vested in the court itself by the Act. The court is required to draft a charge only after a prima-facie case was established by oral evidence before it. While the previous system has undergone an overwhelming change, some of the crimes within the purview of this research were committed before the Administration of Criminal Justice Act was passed into law in 2015. Procedurally, crimes committed before 2015 will be addressed under the regime of the Criminal Procedure Act.

3.4.2 Administration of Criminal Justice Act 2015

Enacted by the National Assembly, the Administration of Criminal Justice Act became applicable in May 2015 in the courts of the Federal Capital Territory and federal courts in Nigeria regarding offences addressed by federal legislations.[131] The Act does not apply to court martial.[132] Its introduction effectively ended the dual application of the distinct criminal procedure regimes; the Criminal Procedure Act and the Criminal Procedure Code, creating a unified criminal procedure law for the country. The Administration of Criminal Justice Act is aimed to promote efficient management of criminal justice institutions and speedy dispensation of justice for the notoriously slow Nigerian court system.[133] It is geared towards bridging the existing gaps in the criminal justice system in Nigeria and addresses major aspects of the criminal procedure system in its 495 sections. It also features progressive innovations like an introduction of attributes of restorative justice with a victim-centred and rights-based approach. The Act represents a unified regime of criminal procedure for Nigeria as a whole. In its 49 parts, it is intended to pioneer the metamorphosis from punishment as a major goal but rather a focus on the restorative attributes of criminal justice and the interests of the defendants, victims, vulnerable persons and human dignity in general.[134] It is also envisioned to promote a speedy dispensation of justice, efficient management of the institutions involved in the criminal justice system, streamlining the criminal justice process, including due protection

[130] Under the Act, Native Courts were to be 'guided' by the remainder of the provisions that does not directly bind them. See Williams 1966, p. 259.

[131] Administration of Criminal Justice Act 2015, 2(1) although subject to interpretation of Section 3.2(1) and Section 86 of the Act it is unclear whether the Act can also be applied to offences within the jurisdiction of state courts. However, a number of states have begun the process of bringing their criminal legislation in line with the Administration of Criminal Justice Act and Lagos State has in fact enacted its own Administration of Criminal Justice Law 2011.

[132] Section 3.2(2) Administration of Criminal Justice Act 2015.

[133] Section 3.1(1) Administration of Criminal Justice Act 2015. The Nigerian judicial system's infamous slow nature has been a subject of spirited debates, articles and analysis over the past years. See generally Chatham House 2013, The Guardian 2017a, Punch Newspapers 2016, The Guardian 2016, Premium times 2014, Brems and Adekoya 2010 and Cocodia 2010.

[134] Section 3.1(1) Administration of Criminal Justice Act 2015.

of the rights of suspects, defendants and victims. Among the innovative provisions of the Administration of Criminal Justice Act is the prohibition of arrest in lieu of suspects,[135] prohibition of police arrest on a civil wrong or breach of contract,[136] the parole system,[137] the institution of a central criminal records registry to be maintained by the police,[138] procedure relating to recording of statements by suspects,[139] bail administration,[140] recognition of women as competent sureties for the purpose of securing bail,[141] including the introduction of the concept of plea bargaining in criminal matters among other innovations.[142] The Act represents a novelty in the Nigerian criminal justice system; the evolution of its innovative provisions and its positive and practical influence including the practice of criminal procedure in Nigeria as a whole continues to evolve in the long term. Although, it is currently applicable to criminal procedure law in Nigeria, it cannot apply to crimes committed before 2015 due to the prohibition of retroactivity. Additionally, efforts are ongoing by concerned organisations to provide critical training for practitioners including the police, prosecutors and judicial officers for the adequate utilisation of the provisions of the Act in the conduct of their duties. Efforts to support its adoption in the remaining twenty-five states of the federation are also ongoing.[143]

3.5 Justice Delivery Challenges

The institutions of the Police, the Judiciary and the Prison service are important pillars in the Nigerian justice system; however, they also represent the challenges that plague the system as a whole. According to the statistics relating to Boko Haram prosecutions provided by the Federal Ministry of Justice, as at 11 September 2017, only 13 cases have been concluded since the onset of the violence. As at May 2018, there were 33 ongoing trials, 116 cases awaiting trial, 1670 detainees awaiting judicial proceedings and 651 detainees remanded by the Federal High Court.[144]

As a gateway to the judicial system, the Nigerian Police Force represents the first port of call for a suspect. The Nigerian Police is tasked with the detection and the prevention of crime, apprehension of offenders, preservation of law and order, the protection of life and property, enforcement of all laws and regulations including

[135] Section 3.7 Administration of Criminal Justice Act 2015.

[136] Section 8(2) Administration of Criminal Justice Act 2015.

[137] Section 468 Administration of Criminal Justice Act 2015.

[138] Section 16 Administration of Criminal Justice Act 2015.

[139] Section 17 Administration of Criminal Justice Act 2015.

[140] Section 30 Administration of Criminal Justice Act 2015.

[141] Section 167 (3) Administration of Criminal Justice Act 2015.

[142] Section 270 Administration of Criminal Justice Act 2015.

[143] See for example Nigerian Bar Association (NBA) Administration of Criminal Justice Project.

[144] Data available on the website of the Federal Ministry of Justice.

performance of military duties when necessary.[145] Police officers are empowered, subject to the provisions of Sections 174 and 211 of the 1999 Constitution of the Federal Republic of Nigeria, to conduct prosecutions before any court in Nigeria. Additionally, the Nigerian Police is empowered to arrest without warrant and in the case of an available warrant, to arrest without said warrant in possession of the arresting officer.[146] The members of the Nigerian Police Force are similarly empowered to conduct searches of persons, premises and things,[147] to grant bail,[148] to interrogate and identify suspects, to prevent breach of peace, conduct criminal trials[149] among other powers. The Nigerian Police is one of the most widely criticised public institutions both domestically and internationally especially as it relates to its treatment of detainees and the carrying out its roles.[150] Alongside the police, in many instances, the Nigerian military have also carried out similar functions. Due to its prominent roles in the anti-terrorism efforts, military officers have often apprehended and detained offenders encountered in its operations. Some of these offenders have not been handed over to the police but have been held in military barracks and facilities. These facilities include the notorious 'Giwa Barracks' in Maiduguri Borno State, the Sector Alpha and the so-called Presidential Lodge managed by the military.[151] The handling of detainees and suspects including victims rescued by the military has regularly come under wide criticism since the Boko Haram crisis started.[152]

Although, part of the general aims of justice in Nigeria is retribution and deterrence, the Nigerian correctional service is tasked with ensuring the safe custody of legally interned persons and the rehabilitation of such persons.[153] The correctional service is, however, plagued with high death rate in custody, high rate of awaiting trial detainees, massively overcrowded prisons, and lack of basic amenities for the number of prisoners in the facilities.[154] In a 2016 report, the percentage of pre-trial or awaiting trial detainees relative to the general prison population was 71%.[155] Boko Haram detainees have been held in prisons across the country for years in abysmal conditions without cases instituted against them or progressing at the courts. Boko Haram as a group carried out a first of many successful jail breaks in 2010, freeing

[145] Section 4 Nigerian Police Act.

[146] Sections 24–25 Nigerian Police Act, Section 10 Criminal Procedure Act, and Section 35 Administration of Criminal Justice Act 2015.

[147] Section 6 Nigerian Police Act.

[148] Section 27 Nigerian Police Act.

[149] Section 23 Nigerian Police Act.

[150] The 2016 World Internal Security and Police Index (WISPI) in its index measuring the ability of the police to respond adequately to internal security challenges ranked the Nigerian Police as the worst in the world. See also Human Rights Watch Report 2010, and Amnesty International Report 2014.

[151] UK Home Office Country Policy and Information Note 2016.

[152] Amnesty International 2015, Amnesty International 2018, and Channelstv 2018.

[153] Aduba 1993, p. 185. See also Obioha 2011, p. 95.

[154] Obioha 2011, p. 99.

[155] UK Home Office Country Policy and Information Note 2016.

about 700 of its members.[156] In 2017, the Nigerian government began closed door mass trials for Boko Haram detainees. The courts were presided over by civilian judges but located in a military facility.[157] Concerns were raised, however, regarding the fundamental guarantees of the accused persons and the fairness of the process.[158] Additionally, a special internationalised court was also constituted in Niamey, Niger to try a cross-section of suspects from Nigeria, Niger and Chad.[159]

3.5.1 Prosecutions

The approach of the Nigerian prosecuting authorities to the Boko Haram cases since the crisis started is severely lacking in coherence and predictability. Before 2017, Boko Haram related cases were instituted within the normal court system in the Federal High Courts with the requisite jurisdiction to try terrorism offences. However, in 2017, when the Federal Ministry of Justice began syndicated undisclosed trials of Boko Haram suspects with judges sitting in a military facility in Kainji, it seemed to signal a change of strategy towards Boko Haram related cases. The trials involving **five hundred and seventy-five defendants were shrouded in secrecy, and many groups** including the United Nations High Commissioner on Human Rights raised massive concerns regarding the fair trial, due process and the respect of constitutional guarantees.[160] **The process seemed intended specifically to address the challenge of the** immense backlog of Boko Haram detainees held for years without trial. This approach also seemed distinct from the trial process in the normal court system. Consequent upon the concerns raised by members of the public, successive rounds of the proceedings were open to a few organisations to observe.[161] In an attempt to dispense expeditiously with the cases, ex-parte motions were instituted against as many as one hundred suspects on one charge sheet.[162] Regarding a two-day trial it observed, Human Rights Watch noted that over two hundred defendants were tried with one **hundred and thirteen convictions, five acquittals and ninety- seven discharges without** trial based on a no-case submission, nine cases struck-out due to error and nine more adjourned for further hearing in Abuja. The procedure was described as fraught with **errors by observing organisations including a lack of official interpreters, inadvertent** arraignment of persons purportedly discharged in previous trial rounds, short trials

[156] The Guardian 2010, Aljazeera 2012, The Telegraph 2013, and BBC 2014b.

[157] The Cable 2018.

[158] The Guardian 2017b, Deutsche Welle 2017, and VOA 2018.

[159] Reuters 2018. See also International Crisis Group Report 2017.

[160] **See United Nations Human Rights Office of the High Commissioner Press Briefing Notes on** Azerbaijan, Egypt and Indonesia/LGBT and Boko Haram Trials in Nigeria 2017.

[161] Human Rights Watch 2018.

[162] An example is the case with Motion No. FHC/KAINJI/CF/1/2017 an ex-parte motion Federal Republic of Nigeria versus Emmanuel Yakubu, Kamslim Abdullahi, Kefas Yusuf, Mohammed Garba and Ham Jangal and 95 others. Federal Ministry of Justice Press Release on ongoing trials.

including lack of defendant access to counsel until the day of trial among other fair trial and other clear due process challenges.[163] Some of the suspects released due to lack of sufficient evidence against them may have been held in custody after years without trial.[164] Within this process, Haruna Yahaya, the only major senior member of Boko Haram charged with participation in the infamous abduction of the Chibok girls was convicted and sentenced to a term of 15 years in prison and an additional 15 years term as a mastermind of the said abduction.[165]

Within the regular court system, cases were instituted principally at the Federal High Court Abuja.[166] Accused persons were for a variety of offences ranging from failure to disclose information relating to members of Boko Haram, conspiracy to commit terrorism, hostage taking, murder of internationally protected persons, membership of a terrorist group, giving support to a terrorist group, concealment of information about acts of terrorism, participation in acts of terrorism among others. According to Human Rights Watch, although, most of the defendants were charged with offences including the above, they were prosecuted for providing 'material and non-violent' support to Boko Haram including, for example, repairing their vehicles, laundering their clothes, or supplying them with food.[167]

The offences are charged under the Terrorism Prevention Act 2011 and the Terrorism Prevention (Amendment) Act 2013. There is no evidence that more specific terrorism offences inclusive of the egregious sexual and gender-based crimes and similar offences were charged in majority of the ongoing cases. Under Nigerian law, persons who may be charged with the commission of an offence include the principal perpetrator either by action or by omission, persons who aid the commission of an offence either by action or omission, persons who counsels or procures another to commit an offence, persons committing an offence jointly with others as part of a common purpose, and persons who provide assistance after the fact.[168] In the Boko Haram situation, this may include thousands of detainees in custody and potentially thousands more yet to be apprehended may have no real or direct impact on the entire conflict.

---

[163] See also Deutsche Welle 2017, and Human Rights Watch 2018.

[164] Federal Ministry of Justice Press Release.

[165] Federal Ministry of Justice Press Release.

[166] These include Federal Republic of Nigeria v. Mohammed Usman, Mohammed Sani, Abubakar Abdulrahman Habibu, Mohammed Bashir Saleh, Umar Mohammed Bello, Mohammed Salisu, Yakubu Nuhu and Halima Haliru Charge No: FHC/ABJ/CR/36/2017, Federal Republic of Nigeria v. Abubakar Barma Bukar Charge No: FHC/ABJ/CR/235/2015, Federal Republic of Nigeria v. Ibrahim Mohd Bello Charge No: FHC/ABJ/CR/227/2015 among others. However, some of these cases have been struck out either due to lack of diligent prosecution or absence of the accused persons.

[167] Human Rights Watch 2018.

[168] Chapter 2 Criminal Code Act Cap C38 Laws of the Federation of Nigeria 2004.

3.6 Victims Participation and Protection?

Generally, within the criminal system in Nigeria, the traditional role of victims is limited to that of complainant or witnesses.[169] Though unwritten, a so-called 'watching brief' may be granted for persons interested in a criminal trial, including victims to protect their interests in the proceedings.[170] In the Boko Haram situation, due to the specialised and protracted nature of the crisis and its impact on the communities, victims have been largely unable to participate in any form in the cases, victims interests have been left unprotected, no compensation for loss awarded against accused persons in the cases prosecuted and the role of complainant in the trials instituted have been undertaken exclusively by the federal government. The Administration of Criminal Justice Act 2015 empowers the court in criminal proceedings to order payment of expenses, costs, damages and or compensation against a defendant or convict within the proceedings or during judgement.[171] Although, this is an improvement from the earlier system, protection in this regard is extended only to 'any person injured by the offence' per Section 319. It is unclear whether this includes family members or dependents of the direct victims. The United Nations Declaration of Basic Principles of Justice for Victims of Crimes and Abuse of Power provides avenues for redress for victims of crimes including access to justice and fair treatment, restitution, compensation and assistance.[172] Additionally, the 2005 guidelines also make provisions relating to rights to remedy and reparation of victims.[173] It further extends protection to include the immediate family members or dependents of direct victims of crimes including persons who have suffered harm in intervening to assist the victim in distress.[174] The Rome Statute of the International Criminal Court also provides elaborately for the protection of victims and witnesses in proceedings before the court.[175] As a marked improvement on most domestic systems and the ad-hoc tribunals, victims are an integral part of proceedings before the ICC and their

[169] Sections 88–89 of the Administration of Criminal Justice Act 2015 prescribes the procedure for making complaint against a person alleged to have committed or committing an offence. This is similar to the provisions in Section 143(e) Criminal Procedure Code and Section 59(1) of the Criminal Procedure Act.

[170] See Federal Republic of Nigeria v. Abiola 1994, FHCLR 156, 160.

[171] Section 319 Administration of Criminal Justice Act 2015.

[172] G. A. Res. 40/34 United Nations Declaration of Basic Principles of Justice for Victims of Crimes and Abuse of Power U.N. Doc A/RES/40/34 (29 November 1985).

[173] G.A. Res. 60/147, Basic Principles and Guidelines on the Right to a Remedy and Reparation for Victims of Gross Violations of International Human Rights law and serious violations of International Humanitarian Law, U.N Doc. A/RES/60/147 (16 December 2005).

[174] Annex A (1) United Nations Declaration of Basic Principles of Justice for Victims of Crimes and Abuse of Power 29 November 1985 A/RES/40/34.

[175] Article 68 Rome Statute of the ICC and Rule 85 ICC Rules of Procedure and Evidence.

interests are well represented and taken into account seriously by the Court.[176] Additionally, a legal exception to the principle of public hearings prescribed in Article 67 is generally proceedings *in camera* for the protection of victims or witnesses. The ICC Pre-Trial Chamber and Trial Chamber in the DRC situation considered the notion of harm in the determination of which victims may participate in proceedings before the court.[177] Moffett advocates for what he describes as positive victim-orientated complementarity. He opines that there should be in place procedural and substantive rights, effective domestic institutions and mechanisms to achieve victims' rights and local political will to protect these rights.[178] The lack of provision for victims' participation in the domestic legal process and provisions for the protection of victims' rights should affect the determination of complementarity and whether gaps exist. In this vein, Osinuga advocates for compensation schemes to be created for victims of the Boko Haram violence.[179] Unfortunately, none of the cases so far prosecuted **have reflected any attempts at protecting or compensating any of the victims of the Boko Haram violence. Whether specific transitional justice mechanisms would be** utilised to respond to these concerns remain to be seen and will be further explored in the Chap. 5.

3.7 Summary and Conclusion

Domestic prosecutions have long been an important aspect of international criminal justice. Prosecution of crimes under international law during the period from the end of the Nuremberg and Tokyo trials and the creation of the ad-hoc tribunals were undertaken solely by domestic courts.[180] There were a plethora of prosecutions in domestic civil courts and military tribunals in post-World War II Germany.[181] There was also domestic prosecution of accused war criminals in the countries where the crimes in question were alleged to have been committed.[182] The role of the

[176] While the victims' protection regime of the ICC is a marked improvement from most common law systems, certain aspects of it have been widely criticised including the fact that recognition as victims is exclusively based on conviction of the accused person. See generally Van den Wyngaert 2011, p. 475. Mouthaan 2013, p. 619, and Bachvarova 2011, p. 11.

[177] Decision on the Applications for Participation 81, Situation in the Democratic Republic of the Congo, Decision on Victims' Participation, ICC-01/04-01/06-1119, 92 (Trial Chamber I, Jan. 18, 2008).

[178] Moffett 2014, p. 234.

[179] Osinuga 2013.

[180] See Werle and Jessberger 2020.

[181] See Lippman 1999–2000, p. 1.

[182] There were post-World War prosecutions in many countries utilizing different approaches and prosecutorial strategies. Australia, Canada, Britain, France, China and the United States favoured the utilization of Military Courts. The Netherlands for example utilized special criminal courts applying existing criminal code. Poland created special criminal courts for the purpose while Norway used the civilian courts and the existing criminal code. See generally Ibid. 181.

domestic legal regime is crucial to the overall success of international criminal law. The preamble of the Rome Statute in the sixth paragraph also recalls that 'it is the duty of every state to exercise its criminal jurisdiction over those responsible for international crimes.'

The International Criminal Court was not intended to have universal responsibility as a world criminal court, but rather as a stand-by court, hence the complementarity doctrine.[183] The complementarity model of the International Criminal Court operates on the thought that effective prosecution is to be 'ensured by taking measures at the national level and by enhancing international cooperation' and that it is primarily the duty of States to 'exercise its criminal jurisdiction over those responsible for international crimes'.[184] Even then, international jurisdiction was not intended to replace domestic jurisdiction, but rather to supplement it. Precedence is accorded to national prosecution as a rule unless the State in question is unwilling or unable to genuinely investigate or prosecute.[185] Domestic prosecutions have been utilised by states to respond to international crimes over which it possesses jurisdiction alongside recourse to an international mechanism.[186] Domestic mechanisms and prosecutions may also be implemented on its own or together with international criminal mechanisms such as special courts or prosecution at the ICC. It is clear that regarding the crimes committed by Boko Haram, primary jurisdiction to investigate and prosecute crimes committed by Boko Haram rest on Nigeria. However, regarding the domestic process completed and/or ongoing in Nigeria, the questions of adequacy of the available domestic legal framework and the effectiveness of criminal prosecutions arise. While the available legal regime is broad-based, there are some inherent gaps.

Under Nigeria's domestic legal regime, the acts of Boko Haram violence committed after the passing into law of the Terrorism Prevention Act of 2011are addressed by its provisions. However, none of its provisions address sexual and gender-based crimes. Before 2011, Boko Haram crimes committed in the other parts of the country except in Northern Nigeria were subject to the jurisdiction of the Criminal Code. In Northern Nigeria, the crimes committed were subject to the provisions of the Penal Code. The provisions of the Criminal Code also suffer from a number of major defects. For example, some of the offences addressed committed by Boko Haram were treated as simple offences and misdemeanours under the Code. The offence of unlawful assembly and breach of the peace was in reality intended to combat riots and thus is classified as a misdemeanour attracting a penalty upon conviction of one year imprisonment. However, this provision has been creatively interpreted to address egregious crimes committed by Boko Haram. Another defect of the Criminal Code is that while sexual and gender-based violence of Boko Haram are crucial parts of the conflict, the Code only criminalises the offence of rape,

183 Yarnold 1999.

184 Preamble Article 4 and 6 of the Rome Statute of the International Criminal Court.

185 Article 17 Rome Statute of the International Criminal Court.

186 In Rwanda for instance, while major offenders were tried by the International Criminal Tribunal for Rwanda (ICTR), lower-level offenders were tried through the national courts and a local mechanism known as the Gacaca Court system. See generally Wibabara 2014.

assault, kidnapping and deprivation of liberty. Other egregious forms of systematised violence against women and children for example were not addressed by the Criminal Code.[187]

The Penal Code also represents the legal framework for majority of the Boko Haram crimes committed in Northern Nigeria between 2009 and 2011. Majority of its provisions similarly suffer from defects and are inadequate to respond to the egregious crimes committed by Boko Haram. Its treatment of the violent crime of rape for example is grossly inadequate to respond to the Boko Haram violence. The potential for its provisions to be interpreted to not recognise rape and sexual abuse for women who were forcefully married by members of Boko Haram is troubling.

The Economic and Financial Crimes Prevention Act of 2004 which is the forerunner of the Terrorism Prevention Act contains one provision relating to the crime of terrorism, however, this only prohibits the financial aspects of the crime and not the acts of violent criminality. The Terrorism Prevention Act 2011 contains provisions which address the violent terrorism of Boko Haram; however, it can only address crimes committed after it passed into law in 2011. Although, on its own, its provisions criminalise majority of the crimes committed by Boko Haram, no acts of sexual and gender-based violence is criminalised as terrorism. The Act has been relied upon by the prosecuting authority in the majority of the cases concluded and pending before Nigerian courts, however, predictably, no act of sexual and gender-based crime has been prosecuted. The focus of Boko Haram on women and girls is a recognisable feature of the crisis and the lack of an adequate legal regime to address this showcases an inadequacy of the process.[188] Additionally, the recruitment and use of underage children (either as support or combatants or for the purpose of suicide bombing for example) is also not criminalised by the Terrorism Prevention Act. General acts committed in support of terrorism or to achieve a purpose of terror are strongly criminalised in the Terrorism Prevention Act. Nevertheless, the wide-ranging definitions particularly relating to the elements of the offences makes it a weak tool to adequately respond to terrorism.

Apart from the conviction and life sentence of Kabiru Dikko (Kabiru Sokoto) and his co-accused for the 2013 Christmas day bombing near Abuja, there is no evidence yet of other high-profile terrorist suspects successfully prosecuted under the Terrorism Prevention Act.[189] Despite the celebrated arrest of Mohammed Usman (also known as Khalid al-Barnawi, Abu Musab al-Barnawi) the erstwhile leader of the Boko Haram faction Ansaru in 2016, the case against him and his co-accused for the kidnap and subsequent murder of ten foreigners has not made much progress.[190] The case is stalled at the Court due to a number of investigative and prosecutorial defects and has been adjourned several times. Usman is one of the three Nigerians

[187] Such as sexual slavery, enforced pregnancy and other forms of sexual violence constituting a grave breach of the Geneva Conventions.

[188] See generally Attah 2016.

[189] See also Amnesty International Report 2018.

[190] The defendants include: Mohammed Usman, Mohammed Sani, Abubakar Habibu, Mohammed Saleh, Umar Bello (Abu Azzan), Mohammed Salisu and Yakubu Nuhu.

listed as 'specially designated global terrorists' by the government of the United States of America.[191] The arrest was heralded as a major milestone in the counter-terrorism fight by the Department of State Security and the case would have provided an opportunity for Nigeria to show its seriousness of investigating and prosecuting the Boko Haram related crimes. Unfortunately, the matter is still pending at the time of writing. Regardless, the charges in the cases are unrelated to what could potentially form the basis for a trial before the International Criminal Court.

The Terrorism Prevention Act has been criticised for containing provisions contrary to the Nigerian Constitution on fundamental guarantees such as the right of suspects to legal counsel, access their family members and independent medical treatment. The Nigerian Coalition for the International Criminal Court instituted a legal action against the Nigerian government to strike down provisions in the Terrorism Prevention Act which are incompatible with the Nigerian Constitution.[192]

Although, the relatively new Administration of Criminal Justice Law which passed into law in 2015 provides for some progressive procedural provisions, it is not yet applicable in all states of Northern Nigeria where majority of the Boko Haram crimes were committed. It, thus, suffers from lack of a real ability to provide protection in states where it has not yet been adopted and particularly relative to Boko Haram crimes committed before 2015. Another major defect of the domestic process is that in the trials that have been commenced including those concluded, victim's interests have not been taken into account and they have been completely shut out of the process. While some of the reforms in the Administration of Criminal Justice Act are great, they have not yet become impactful. Although, it may rightly be stated that the thousands of Boko Haram detainees who have been or are in government custody may not be those most responsible for the crimes of the group, however, even for the lower-level offenders, the quality of the trials is grossly inadequate. The sincerity of these prosecutions is in issue and it is unclear whether the Nigerian authorities are genuinely interested in a thorough process in which constitutional guarantees are respected.

In 2017, the Federal Ministry of Justice released a report on the status of terrorism cases. The first challenge noted with regards to the Boko Haram prosecutions was the inability to effectively investigate cases 'due to pressure during the peak of the crises.' Other challenges noted include 'over-reliance on confession based evidence, lack of forensic evidence, poor logistics, scarcity of skilled and trained forensic experts to handle investigation of complex cases, converting military intelligence to admissible evidence.'[193] These are errors that go to the root of the effectiveness of the process, however, it continues to arraign and prosecute hundreds of low-level suspects in a flawed process.[194] The legal regime available to respond to the egregious Boko Haram crimes is incoherent and inadequate and there is scant evidence that the Nigerian authorities are serious in properly investigating and prosecuting the Boko Haram

[191] See U.S. Department of State 2018.

[192] NCICC v Attorney General of the Federation.

[193] Federal Ministry of Justice Status of Terrorism Cases as at 11 September 2017.

[194] See generally Amnesty International 2018b.

related cases. There is also a general lack of relevant domestic proceedings which effectively address conduct which may fall within the jurisdiction of the International Criminal Court.

References

Adekoya P (2016) The Succession Dispute to the Throne of Lagos and the British Conquest and Occupation of Lagos. Vol. 10(3), An International Multi-Disciplinary Journal Ethiopia.

Adewoye O (1977) The Judicial System in Southern Nigeria: 1854-1954. Longman.

Aduba J (1993) 'Overcrowding' in Nigerian Prisons; A Critical Appraisal' 21, Journal of Criminal Justice.

Akpoghome T (2016) 'Analysis of the Domestic Legal Framework of Sexual Violence in Nigeria' Journal of Law and Criminal Justice.

Alemika E (2014) 'Criminal Victimization and Criminal Justice Administration in Nigeria' in Crime and Public Safety in Nigeria Etannibi Alemika (Ed) CLEEN Foundation.

Aljazeera (2012) 'Federal Prison Stormed in Nigeria' 17 February, 2012 available at https://www.aljazeera.com/news/africa/2012/02/201221614384989889.html.

Aljazeera Report (2013) 'Porous Borders and Boko Haram's Arms Smuggling Operations in Nigeria', 8 September 2013, Aljazeera Centre for Studies, available at http://studies.aljazeera.net/en/reports/2013/09/201398104245877469.html.

Amnesty International Report (2014) 'Welcome to hell-fire: Torture and other ill-treatment in Nigeria' 18 September 2014 available at https://www.amnesty.org/en/documents/AFR44/011/2014/en/

Amnesty International (2015) 'Nigeria: Senior Members of the Military Must be Investigated for War Crimes' 03 June 2015 available at https://www.amnesty.org/en/latest/news/2015/06/nigeria-senior-members-of-military-must-be-investigated-for-war-crimes/

Amnesty International (2018a) 'Nigeria: Boko Haram Survivors Raped and Starved by Military Rescuers' 24 May 2018 available at https://www.amnesty.org.uk/press-releases/nigeria-boko-haram-survivors-raped-and-starved-military-rescuers-new-report

Amnesty International Report (2018b) 'Willingly Unable: ICC Preliminary Examinations and Nigeria's Failure to Address Impunity for International Crimes' AFR 44/9481/2018 10 December 2018 Available at https://www.amnesty.org/download/Documents/AFR4494812018ENGLISH.PDF.

Asein J (2005) Introduction to Nigerian Legal System Ababa Press Lagos, 2nd edn.

Attah C (2016) 'Boko Haram and Sexual Terrorism: The Conspiracy of Silence of the Nigerian Anti-Terrorism Laws' 16, African Human Rights Law Journal.

Allott A (1962) Judicial and Legal Systems in Africa Butterworths.

Anderson J (1959) 'Conflict of Laws in Northern Nigeria: A New Start' Vol. 8, No. 3, the International and Comparative Law Quarterly.

Asein J (1998) Introduction to Nigerian Legal System, 2nd edn. Bookman.

Bachvarova T (2011) 'Victim's Eligibility before the International Criminal Court in Historical and Comparative Context' International Criminal Law Review.

BBC (2014a) 'Boko Haram to 'Sell' Nigerian Girls Abducted from Chibok', 5 May 2014. Available at https://www.bbc.com/news/world-africa-27283383.

BBC (2014b) 'Nigeria reveals wave of jailbreaks', 5 November 2014, available at https://www.bbc.com/news/world-africa-29924601.

Brems E, Adekoya C (2010) 'Human Rights enforcement by people living in poverty: access to justice in Nigeria' Journal of African Law.

Cable (2018) 'FG resumes mass trials of Boko Haram suspects' 12 February, 2018 available at https://www.thecable.ng/mass-trial-boko-haram-members-resume-monday.

Channels (2018) 'Boko Haram: Army Constructs New Detention Center in Maiduguri' 28 April 2018 available at https://www.channelstv.com/2018/04/28/boko-haram-army-constructs-new-detention-centre-in-maiduguri/.

CNN (2012) 'Boko Haram claims Responsibility for Nigeria Church Bombings' 18 June 2012 available at https://edition.cnn.com/2012/06/18/world/africa/nigeria-church-bombings/index.html.

Chatham House (2013) 'Too Many to Count? Human Rights, Justice and Accountability in Nigeria' (2013) Country Visit Report of the All-party Parliamentary Group.

Cocodia J (2010) 'Identifying causes for congestion in Nigeria's Courts via non-participant observation; a case study of Brass High Court, Bayelsa State Nigeria', Vol. 1(1) International Journal of Politics and Good Governance.

Council on Foreign Relations (2018) 'Boko Haram's Violence against Women and Girls Demand Justice' 11 May 2018 available at https://www.cfr.org/blog/boko-harams-violence-against-women-and-girls-demands-justice?sp_mid=56596864&sp_rid=c3I0MTJAY2FhLmNvbHVtYmlhLmVkdQS2.

Dailypost Nigeria (2017) 'Boko Haram destroyed over 900 Churches in the North-CAN' 29 January, 2017 available at http://dailypost.ng/2017/01/29/boko-haram-destroyed-900-churches-north-can/.

Dada A, Dosumu A, Oyedeji G (2015) 'Criminal Justice System; the Nigerian Scenarios Vol. 3(3) International Journal of Social Sciences and Humanities Research.

Deutsche Welle (2017) 'Trial of Boko Haram suspects poses legal nightmare' October 9, 2017 available at https://www.dw.com/en/trial-of-boko-haram-suspects-in-nigeria-poses-legal-nightmare/a-40867730.

De Tessieres S (2017) 'Measuring Illicit Arms Flow Niger' Small Arms Survey Briefing Paper March 2017.

Elias T (1963) The Nigerian Legal System, Routledge & Paul.

Essien V (1983) 'The Northern Nigerian Penal Code: A Reflection of Diverse Values in Penal Litigation' Vol 5 New York Law School Journal of International and Comparative Law.

Federal Ministry of Justice (2017) 'Status of Terrorism Cases as at 11th September 2017' Available at http://justice.gov.ng/images/Justice_doc/Status_of_Terrorism_Cases_.pdf.

Guardian (2010) 'More than 700 inmates escape during attack on Nigerian prison' 08 September, 2010 available at https://www.theguardian.com/world/2010/sep/08/muslim-extremists-escape-nigeria-prison.

Guardian (2014) 'Boko Haram abductees tell of forced marriages, rape, torture and forced abuse' 27 October 2014 available at https://www.theguardian.com/world/2014/oct/27/boko-haram-forced-marriage-rape-torture-abuse-hrw-report.

Guardian (2016) 'Osinbajo decries slow pace of criminal justice system' 30 October 2016 available at https://guardian.ng/news/osinbajo-decries-slow-pace-of-criminal-justice-system/.

Guardian (2017a)'Quick Justice Delivery and Burden of ACJ Act Implementation' 07 February 2017 available at https://guardian.ng/features/quick-justice-delivery-and-burden-of-acj-act-implementation/.

Guardian (2017b) 'Dozens of Boko Haram members convicted in mass secret trials in Nigeria' October 14, 2017 available at https://www.theguardian.com/world/2017/oct/14/dozens-of-boko-haram-members-convicted-in-mass-secret-trial-in-nigeria.

Guardian (2018) "'We are Soldiers, We Will Save You': How Boko Haram Tricked Dapchi Schoolgirls" March 8, 2018. Available at https://www.theguardian.com/global-development/2018/mar/08/nigeria-we-are-soldiers-we-will-save-you-how-boko-haram-tricked-dapchi-schoolgirls.

Human Rights Watch Report (2010) 'Everyone is in on the game: Corruption and Human Rights abuses by the Nigerian Police Force' 17 August 2010. Available at https://www.hrw.org/report/2010/08/17/everyones-game/corruption-and-human-rights-abuses-nigeria-police-force.

Human Rights Watch Report (2014) 'Those terrible weeks in their camp; Boko Haram violence against women and girls in Northeast Nigeria', 27 October 2014. Available at https://www.hrw.org/report/2014/10/27/those-terrible-weeks-their-camp/boko-haram-violence-against-women-and-girls

Human Rights Watch (2018) 'Nigeria: Flawed Trials of Boko Haram Suspects' 17 September 2018 available at https://www.hrw.org/news/2018/09/17/nigeria-flawed-trials-boko-haram-suspects

ICC Rules of Procedure and Evidence (2013) International Criminal Court, 2nd edn.

Ijaodola (1970) 'A Case for the Unification of Court Systems in Northern Nigeria' 4 Nigerian Law Journal.

ILGA Report (2007) 'State of Homophobia: A World Survey of Laws Prohibiting Same-Sex Activity between Consenting Adults' April 2007. Available at http://data.unaids.org/pub/manual/2007/070517_statehomophobia_ilga_en.pdf.

International Crisis Group Report (2017) 'Niger and Boko Haram: Beyond Counter–Insurgency' February 27, 2017 available at https://www.crisisgroup.org/africa/west-africa/niger/245-niger-and-boko-haram-beyond-counter-insurgency.

Inyang J (2013) 'Policing Nigeria: A case for Partnership between Formal and Informal Police Institutions' 1(4), Merit Research Journal of Art Social Sciences and Humanities.

Kleffner J (2003) 'The impact of Complementarity on National Implementation of Substantive International Criminal Law', Journal of International Criminal Justice, 1 Oxford University Press.

Lippman M (2000) 'Prosecution of Nazi War Criminals Before Post-World War II Domestic Tribunals' 8 U. Miami Int'l & Comp. L. Rev. 1.

Milner A (1969) 'Sentencing Patterns in Nigeria' African Penal Systems Routledge & Kegan Paul.

Mirror (2016) 'From age 15 Boko Haram forced me to wed three men, I had a child by each' 30 December 2016 available at https://www.mirror.co.uk/news/world-news/from-age-15-boko-haram-9537350.

Mouthaan S (2013) 'Victim Participation at the ICC for Victims of Gender-Based Crimes: A Conflict of Interest?' 21 Cardozo Journal of Internation and Comparative Law.

Nouwen S (2013) 'Complementarity in the line of Fire: The Catalysing Effect of the International Criminal Court in Uganda and Sudan'.

Obilade A O (1979) The Nigerian Legal System Spectrum Books.

Obilade A (2011) The Nigerian Legal System, Spectrum.

Obioha E (2011) 'Challenges and Reforms in the Nigerian Prisons System' 27-2, Journal of Social Sciences.

Okeke C (1996) 'International Law in the Nigerian Legal System' 27 California Western International Law Journal.

Okonkwo C, Naish M (1980) Criminal Law in Nigeria, Spectrum.

Olugbuo B (2016) 'Acceptance of International Criminal Justice in Nigeria; Legal Compliance, Myth or Reality?' 2 International Nuremberg Principles Academy Acceptance of International Criminal Justice Projects.

Otu N (1999) 'Colonialism and Criminal Justice System in Nigeria,' Vol. 23, (2), International Journal of Comparative and Applied Criminal Justice.

Osinuga O(2013) 'Nigeria, Boko Haram: Cutting Corners and the Illusion of Speedy Conflict Resolution' May 3, 2013 available at SSRN https://papers.ssrn.com/sol3/papers.cfm?abstract_id=2260446.

Ostien P (Ed.) (2007) Sharia Implementation in Northern Nigeria 1999-2006: A Source Book, Spectrum.

Punch Newspaper (2016) 'How delayed justice hobbles Nigeria's economy' 29 December 2016 available at http://www.punchng.com/delayed-justice-hobbles-nigerias-economic-growth/.

Premium times (2014) 'Fashola laments slow pace of justice in Nigeria' 24 September 2014 available at https://www.premiumtimesng.com/regional/nwest/168596-fashola-laments-slow-pace-of-justice-in-nigeria.html.

Reuters (2018) 'Boko Haram suspects go on public trials in Niger', 1 February 2018, available at https://www.reuters.com/article/us-nigeria-security-trial/boko-haram-suspects-go-on-public-trial-in-niger-idUSKBN1FL697.

Saleh-Hanna V, Ume C (2008) 'An Evolution of the Penal System; Criminal Justice in Nigeria' in Saleh-Hanna V (ed.) Colonial Systems of Control; Criminal Justice in Nigeria, University of Ottawa Press.

Smith R (1979) The Lagos Consulate: 1851-1861 University of California Press.

Telegraph (2013) 'Boko Haram Attacks Leaves Over Fifty Dead and Sees One Hundred Inmates Freed from Jail in Nigeria', 8 May 2013. Available at https://www.telegraph.co.uk/news/worldnews/africaandindianocean/nigeria/10043005/Boko-Haram-attack-leaves-over-50-dead-and-sees-100-inmates-freed-from-jail-in-Nigeria.html.

Telegraph (2015) 'Nigeria's Boko Haram isn't Just Kidnapping Girls, It's Enslaving Them' January 13, 2015. Available at https://www.telegraph.co.uk/women/womens-life/11342879/Nigerias-Boko-Haram-isnt-just-kidnapping-girls-its-enslaving-them.html.

Tobi N (1996) Sources of Nigerian Law MIJ Professional Publishers Ltd, Lagos.

Triffterer O, Ambos K (2016) 'Rome Statute of the International Criminal Court: A Commentary', 3rd edn.

Umozurike U (1962) International Law and Colonialism in Africa, Eastern Africa Law Review.

US Army Intelligence (2015) Report 'Threat Tactic Report: Boko Haram' March 2015. Available at https://info.publicintelligence.net/USArmy-BokoHaram.pdf.

U.S. Department of State (2018) 'State Department Terrorist Designations of ISIS Affiliates and Senior Leaders' February 27, 2018. Available at https://www.state.gov/r/pa/prs/ps/2018/02/278883.htm.

Van den Wyngaert C (2011) 'Victims before International Criminal Courts: Some Views and Concerns of an ICC Trial Judge' (2011) 44 Case W. Res. J. Int'l L. 475.

VOA (2018) 'Nigeria convicts 205 Boko Haram suspects in mass trials' February 19, 2018 available at https://www.voanews.com/a/nigeria-convicts-two-hundred-boko-haram-suspects-mass-trials/4261427.html.

Washington Post (2016) 'They were freed from Boko Haram's rape camps, but their nightmare is not over' 3 April 2016 available at https://www.washingtonpost.com/world/africa/they-were-freed-from-boko-harams-rape-camps-but-their-nightmare-isnt-over/2016/04/03/dbf2aab0-e54f-11e5-a9ce-681055c7a05f_story.html?utm_term=.74c351f3dd8e.

Weimann G (2010) 'Islamic Criminal Law in Northern Nigeria: Religion, Politics, Judicial Practice' Islamic Law and Society.

Werle G, Jessberger F (2020) 'Principles of International Criminal Law', 4th edn.

Whiteman K (2012) Lagos: A cultural and Historical Companion, Signal Books.

Wibabara C (2014) 'Gacaca Court versus the International Criminal Tribunal for Rwanda and National Courts: Lessons to Learn from the Rwandan Justice Approaches to Genocide' Nomos.

Williams T (1966) 'The Criminal Procedure Code of Northern Nigeria: The first five years' 29 Modern Law Review.

Yarnold B (1999) 'The Doctrinal Basis for the International Criminalization Process'. In: Bassiouni MC (ed) International Criminal Law, Vol. 1, (1999).

Cases

Bakare v. Inspector General of Police (1968) NMLR 99.

Bauchi v. Bauchi N.A. (1957) N.R.N.L.R 156.

Dawodu v. Danmole (1962) 1 W.L.R. 1053.

Decision on the Applications for Participation 81, Situation in the Democratic Republic of the Congo, Decision on Victims' Participation, ICC-01/04-01/06-1119, 92 (Trial Chamber I, Jan. 18, 2008).

Edet v. Essien (1932) 11 N.L.R. 47.
Federal Republic of Nigeria v. Abubakar Barma Bukar Charge No: FHC/ABJ/CR/235/2015.
Federal Republic of Nigeria versus Emmanuel Yakubu, Kamslim Abdullahi, Kefas Yusuf, Mohammed Garba and Ham Jangal and 95 others. Motion No. FHC/KAINJI/CF/1/2017 **Federal Ministry of Justice Press Release on ongoing trials available at file:** https://www.w7server/dfs/homedir/Downloads/Proceedings%20at%20the%20ongoing%20syndicated%20trial%20of%20suspected%20Boko%20Haram%20terrorists%20in%20Kainji.pdf.
Federal Republic of Nigeria v. Ibrahim Mohd Bello Charge No: FHC/ABJ/CR/227/2015.
Federal Republic of Nigeria v. Mohammed Usman, Mohammed Sani, Abubakar Abdulrahman Habibu, Mohammed Bashir Saleh, Umar Mohammed Bello, Mohammed Salisu, Yakubu Nuhu and Halima Haliru Charge No: FHC/ABJ/CR/36/2017.
Gaddafi & Al-Senussi, ICC (PTC), decision of 31 May 2013.
Gubba v. Gwandu Native Authority (1947) 12 West African Court of Appeal.
Lamidi Olukun v. Commissioner of Police (1974) NNLR III.
Modibbo v. Adamawa N.A. (1956) N.R.L.R. 101.
Moffett L (2014) Justice for Victims before the International Criminal Court. Routledge.
Odiai v. Commissioner of Police (1962) NNLR 9.
Ogoja v. Adamuwa, N. A. (1958) N.R.N. L.R.35.
Prosecutor v. Ntuyagha ICTR-98-40-T, Decision on the Prosecution's Motion to Withdraw the Indictment, Trial Chamber, 18 March 1999.
Prosecutor v. Tadic IT -94-I-T, Decision on the Defense Motion on the Principle of Non bis in Idem, Trial Chamber, 14 November 1995.
Re Native Court of Onitsha (1928)9 N.L.R. 65.
The State v. Ogwudiegwu (1968) NMLR.

Other Documents

Administration of Criminal Justice Act (2015).
Administration of Criminal Justice Law Lagos State (2011).
Bill for an Act to Provide for the Enforcement and Punishment of Crimes against Humanity, War Crimes, Genocide and Related Offences and to give Effect to certain Provisions of the Rome Statute of the International Criminal Court in Nigeria 2013· 7th National Assembly' 2nd session Number 37.
Convention on the Elimination of all forms of Discrimination against Women 1979.
Constitution of the Federal Republic of Nigeria 1999.
Convention for the Offences and Certain Other Acts Committed on Board Aircraft (1969).
Convention for the Suppression of Unlawful Acts Against the Safety of Civil Aviation (1971).
Convention on the Making of Plastic Explosives for the Purpose of Detection (1991).
Convention for the Suppression of Unlawful Acts against the Safety of Maritime Navigation (1992).
Convention on the Physical Protection of Nuclear Material (1990).
Convention on the Suppression of the Unlawful Seizure of Aircraft (1971).
Criminal Code Act Cap C38, Laws of the Federation of Nigeria, 2004.
Criminal Procedure Act Cap. 4B 1958, Laws of the Federation of Nigeria and Lagos.
Criminal Procedure Act Cap C41 Laws of the Federation of Nigeria, 2004.
Criminal Procedure (Northern States) Act 1960 Cap C42.
Criminal Procedure (Northern States) Code, Cap. 81, Laws of the Federation of Nigeria, 1990.
Economic and Financial Crimes Commission (Establishment) Act 2004.
Evidence Act Cap E14 Laws of the Federation of Nigeria 2004.
International Convention against the Taking of Hostages (1979).
International Convention for the Suppression of the Financing of Terrorism (1999).
International Convention for the Suppression of Terrorist Bombing (1997).

Nigerian Bar Association (NBA) Administration of Criminal Justice Project available at http://nba-acj.org.ng/index.php?option=com_content&view=article&id=477:training-manual-on-the-acja&catid=95:publication&Itemid=114.

Nigerian Police Act 2004.

Penal Code (Northern States) Federal Provisions Act (No. 25 of 1960) 30 September 1960.

Penal Code Law, Northern Nigeria Cap 89 Laws of the Federation of Nigeria 1963.

Protocol for the Suppression of Unlawful Acts of Violence at Airports Serving International Civil Aviation (1988).

Protocol for the Suppression of Unlawful Acts against the Safety of Maritime Navigation (2005).

Protocol to the African Charter on Human and Peoples' Rights on the Rights of Women in Africa (Maputo Protocol) 2003.

Report of concluded Boko Haram related cases. Available at http://www.justice.gov.ng/index.php/laws/law-report.

Rome Statute of the International Criminal Court 2002.

Terrorism (Prevention) Act 2011, Act No. 10.

Terrorism (Prevention) (Proscription Order) Notice 2013 Federal Republic of Nigeria Official Gazette, No. 34, Vol. 100, 24 May 2013.

UK Home Office Country Policy and Information Note' Nigeria: Prison Conditions' November 2016. Available at http://www.refworld.org/pdfid/5825c8044.pdf.

UN Convention on the Prevention and Punishment of Crimes against Internationally Protected Persons (1973).

United Nations Declaration of Basic Principles of Justice for Victims of Crimes and Abuse of Power U.N. Doc A/RES/40/34 G. A. (29 November 1985).

United Nations Human Rights Office of the High Commissioner Press Briefing Notes on Azerbaijan, Egypt and Indonesia/LGBT and Boko haram Trials in Nigeria 13 October 2017 available at https://www.ohchr.org/EN/NewsEvents/Pages/DisplayNews.aspx?NewsID=22232&LangID=E.

Violence against Persons (Prohibition) Act (VAPP) 2015.

World Internal Security and Police Index (WISPI) 2016 Report available at http://www.ipsa-police.org/images/uploaded/Pdf%20file/WISPI%20Report.pdf.

Chapter 4
The Boko Haram Crisis and the International Criminal Court

Contents

Abstract This chapter addresses the Boko Haram crisis and the intersection of international criminal law. It explores the conduct of Boko Haram and the requirements of war crimes and crimes against humanity within the contemplation of the Rome Statute.

Keywords Admissibility · Armed conflict · Complementarity · Core crimes · Crimes against humanity · Gross human rights violations · ICC elements of crime ·

V. Ojo-Adewuyi, *Criminal Justice Responses to the Boko Haram Crisis in Nigeria*, International Criminal Justice Series 34, https://doi.org/10.1007/978-94-6265-615-4_4

Inability to prosecute · Jurisdiction · Material elements · Sexual violence · Jurisdiction

4.1 Introductory Remarks

It is acknowledged that terrorism as a phenomenon particularly within the context of international law lacks a generally accepted definition.[1] While there are a number of approaches to dealing with terrorism, most of these approaches focus on norms of effective national prosecution. Nonetheless, the appropriate ways of responding to acts of terror is primarily through criminal law: domestic, transnational or international.[2] As noted in the preamble, the Rome Statute addresses grave crimes which threaten the peace, security and the well-being of the world and it is intended to put an end to impunity for the perpetrators of international crimes. The protected values of international criminal law cannot be separated and the norms of world peace and security are foundational to it.[3] Large-scale violation of human rights within one state can lead to a presumption of threat to world peace provided the central values of the international community have been attacked. This has the potential to change the character of the crimes in question from mere national crimes into crimes of international concern.[4] Strictly so-called international crimes are crimes within the jurisdiction of the Rome Statute of the International Criminal Court namely genocide, crimes against humanity, war crimes and the crime of aggression.[5] Additionally, every crime under international law possesses an international component which is usually a context of systematic or large-scale use of force.[6] This context varies depending on the crime in question. For genocide; the destruction of a protected group in whole or in part,[7] for crimes against humanity, it is the presence of a widespread or systematic attack against a civilian population,[8] regarding war crimes, it is the existence of an armed conflict whether of an internal, transnational or international character,[9] and relating to the crime of aggression, the contextual element is committing crimes against peace. Individual criminal responsibility is also a major cornerstone of international

[1] See generally a variety of opinions on the difficulty of arriving at a generally acceptable definition of terrorism. Margariti 2017, Ganor 2002, Weinberg et al. 2004, Van Krieken 2002, Young 2006, Scharf 2001, Guillaume 2004, and Konstantinov 1988.

[2] See generally, Cryer et al. 2014, p. 332, and Boister 2012, p. 62.

[3] Werle and Jessberger 2020, p. 35.

[4] Ibid. 3.

[5] Article 5(1) Rome Statute of the International Criminal Court 2002.

[6] Ibid. 3.

[7] Article 6 Rome Statute of the International Criminal Court 2002.

[8] Article 7 Rome Statute of the International Criminal Court 2002.

[9] Article 8 Rome Statute of the International Criminal Court 2002.

criminal law.[10] Moffett opines that international crimes can be distinguished from domestic crimes with five general features: mass victimisation, large-scale organised participation, ideologically driven nature, state involvement and the impact of crimes and impunity on the victims.[11] International crimes typically occur on an enormous scale, over a protracted period of time, with many perpetrators at various levels of command and resulting in large-scale victims.[12] Classifying a set of conduct as international crimes implies the possibility of prosecution at an international forum, an obligation by the state in question to prosecute or being subject to universal jurisdiction. Additionally, the lack of immunity before national courts and the lack of statute of limitation[13] are among the consequences of categorising certain criminal conduct as international crimes.[14] In the event that large-scale crimes have been committed by individuals on the territory or by citizens of a state party to the Rome Statute, once the other requirements are fulfilled, the crimes may be addressed as international crimes.

It is clear from the preceding chapters that the acts and conducts which are the subject of this book can be categorised as the crime of terrorism under the domestic jurisdiction in Nigeria. Additionally, the crime of terrorism has also been variously classified as a transnational or treaty crime in the international sphere. The analysis of whether the acts in question may also be prosecuted as crimes under international criminal law is relevant. It is settled that the same violent act or conduct may amount to terrorism if committed in peacetime and an act of warfare, whether legitimate or otherwise, if committed during an armed conflict. Additionally, such violent acts might also constitute war crimes should they violate the laws and customs of warfare.[15] In describing terrorism under international humanitarian law, the common elements include, fear, targeting of innocent civilians, and the existence of political aims.[16] While terrorism is not listed as a grave breach under international humanitarian law, it is expressly prohibited in the Geneva Conventions.[17] It is important to note the international humanitarian law only applies during armed conflict and thus may be used to address acts of terrorism committed during wartime; of an international character.[18] Due to the fact that the provisions can only be applied to situations

[10] On the recognition of the individual as a subject of international law, see generally for example, Greppi 1999, Werle and Jessberger 2020, and Werle 2007.

[11] Moffett 2014, p. 10.

[12] Fry 2015, p. 163.

[13] Article 29 Rome Statute of the International Criminal Court 2002.

[14] DeGuzman 2012, p. 21.

[15] Arnold 2004, p. 66.

[16] Arnold 2004, p. 80.

[17] Article 33, IV Geneva Convention Relative to the Protection of Civilian Persons in Time of War 12 August 1949. Article 51(2) Protocol Additional to the Geneva Conventions of 12 August 1949 and Relating to the Protection of Victims of International Armed Conflicts (Additional Protocol I). Articles 4, 13, Protocol Additional to the Geneva Conventions of 12 August 1949 and Relating to the Protection of Victims of Non-International Armed Conflicts (Additional Protocol II).

[18] Gasser 1986, p. 201.

of international conflict, they address only state terrorism against a civilian population and are binding on high contracting parties. When there are acts of terror and violence committed during an armed conflict, such acts may be legitimate if they are committed against combatants. However, such acts may become illegitimate when they are utilised to spread terror against civilian population and non-combatants.[19] Regarding non-state terrorism in non-international armed conflict, Article 4(2) (d) of the Additional Protocol II can be applied. Protection in this regard includes both non-combatants and civilians but also persons who have ceased to take part in hostilities.[20] The laws, rights and duties of war both of internal or international character, apply not only to armies but also to the so-called militia groups including volunteer corps.[21] Requirements for categorisation as a militia group includes, belonging to a party to the conflict, command by a person responsible for the subordinates; a distinctive and recognisable emblem; open carrying of arms; and the conduct of its operations according to the laws and customs of war. Some authors opined that the International Military Tribunal (the IMT) in Nuremberg seemed to recognised the use of terror as a means of warfare and the acts of so-called state terrorism utilised were identified as war crimes.[22] Although, the Statute of the International Criminal Tribunal for the Former Yugoslavia (the ICTY) did not have clear provisions regarding terrorism, it considered in some of its cases the use of terror as a method of warfare occasioning a war crime.[23] A major challenge with this viewpoint is that international humanitarian law requires the existence of an armed conflict and the determination whether acts of terrorism amount to an armed conflict or trigger the armed conflict may become crucial.[24] Additionally, there is also a potential challenge of distinguishing between the nature of the armed conflict, whether it is international or non-international subject to Common Article III of the Geneva Conventions. The armed conflict could also be mixed; an inter-state or transnational conflict which has taken an international character.[25] The classification of the acts whether as war crimes or crimes against humanity is important because this determines the categorisation of the parties, the jurisdiction to prosecute and the consequences accruing.[26]

---

[19] Arnold 2004, p. 74.

[20] Article 4, IV Geneva Convention Relative to the Protection of Civilian Persons in Time of War 12 August 1949. See also Greenwood 1989.

[21] Regulations Reflecting the Laws and Customs of War on Land Annex to the 1907 Hague Conventions on the Law and Customs of War on Land Article 1.

[22] Arnold 2004, p. 91.

[23] The Prosecutor v. Aleksovski TC, IT-95-14/1, Trial Judgement, 25 June 1999, Paras 241, 244. The accused was sentences in this case for a violation of the law and customs of war by enlisting the use of intimidation and terror. The Prosecutor v. Zdravko Mucic, Hazim Delic, Esad Landzo, Zejnil Delalic (Celebici case) IT-96-21, 20 February 2001. In this Case, the use of terror as a serious war crime was also addressed by the Court.

[24] Arnold 2004, p. 119.

[25] Werle and Jessberger 2020, p. 463.

[26] Acts of terrorism committed during peacetime 'terrorism out of wartime' is not subject to international humanitarian law and should normally be within the domestic legal regime barring other circumstances. However, the determination is usually very complicated depending on the factors

Arnold noted that while in recent times the shift has been to include other categories of combatants, including civilians engaged in hostilities, for example suicide bombers, the traditional notion is that international humanitarian law was intended to regulate the conduct of warfare between members of the armed forces of states.[27] The International Criminal Tribunal for Rwanda (the ICTR) in Akayesu[28] noted that the determination of persons bound by the provisions of Common Article III and Additional Protocol II should not be too restrictive. Additionally, once there is a link or connection to a party to the conflict, civilians might become subject to individual criminal liability for war crimes.[29] The nexus criterion is now only relative to the act in question and the armed conflict situation and no longer has to include a party to the conflict.[30] In the determination of the nature of the armed conflict, an evaluation of the acts and its context is crucial.[31] Regarding acts amounting to terrorism, provided the threshold requirements for an armed conflict are present, the law of war may be applied in the territory of the state party and the territory of the non-state party (in this case the terrorist group) which has established a quasi-military infrastructure.[32]

Regarding the prosecution of acts of terrorism as crimes against humanity, the contextual including the mental elements need to be present for the requirements to be fulfilled. This implies that once the acts have been committed as a part of a widespread or systematic attack, against a civilian population, with knowledge of the broader context, the acts in question whether it amounts to acts of terror may also be prosecuted as crimes against humanity. The Trial Court in the Akayesu case noted that the 1919 Commission on the Responsibility of the Authors of the War and on the Enforcement of Penalties found that 'systematic terrorism' was considered a crime against humanity.[33] Although, the differences between the treatment of war crimes and crimes against humanity by the IMT were not thoroughly clear, the terrorisation of civilians was treated both as a war crime and crime against humanity.[34] The IMT judgement, while addressing crimes against humanity, also referred to 'a policy of

involved. The example of the September 11 attacks on the World Trade Center is instructive in this regard. Although there was no subsisting armed conflict between the United States of America and Afghanistan at the time of the attack, questions arise whether the subsequent American use of force in Afghanistan were reprisal attacks and it is unclear whether the acts in question may be prosecuted under Article 33 of the IV Geneva Convention. See further Arnold 2004, pp. 120–124. See generally Byers 2002.

[27] Arnold 2004, p. 125.

[28] Prosecutor v. Akayesu, ICTR-96-4-T, Trial Judgment, 2 September 1998 paras 640–644. Although this finding has been repealed on appeal, the reasoning has been reconfirmed by subsequent trial judgements judgement including Prosecutor v. Clement Kayishema and Obed Ruzindana ICTR-95-1-T, Trial Judgement, 21 May 1999, para 175.

[29] Prosecutor v. Alfred Musema ICTR-96-13-A, Judgment and Sentence, 27 January 2000, paras 274–275.

[30] See Arnold 2004, p. 136. See also Werle and Jessberger 2020, pp. 473–476.

[31] Ibid. 30.

[32] Werle and Jessberger 2020, p. 472.

[33] Prosecutor v. Akayesu, ICTR-96-4-T, Trial Judgment, 2 September 1998, para 585.

[34] Arnold 2004, p. 237.

terror' carried out on a vast scale.[35] In the ICTY), the so-called policy of terror was charged as different crimes amounting to crimes against humanity including under-persecution or inhumane act.[36] The ICTR in Kayishema and Ruzindana noted also that the use of terror tactics has the potential of serious mental or physical harm.[37]

The ICC both in its Article 5 Report on Nigeria[38] and the portion of its 2017 Preliminary Examination Report[39] on the Nigerian situation did not address the violent crimes of Boko Haram as crimes amounting to terrorism under the domestic sphere for obvious reasons, but rather as international crimes. Alongside exploring the preconditions for the ICC to open cases against the perpetrators of the crimes within the purview of this research provided for in Article 53(1) (a)–(c), this chapter will also address the possible modes of prosecution by the ICC; as war crimes and crimes against humanity. Due to the nature of the case study, the statutory criteria to be explored include, broadly, jurisdiction; temporal, territorial or personal and subject matter jurisdiction. Additionally, the important consideration of the admissibility requirements particularly as it relates to complementarity, interests of justice and the particular Boko Harm conducts which are contrary to the Rome Statute will be addressed.

4.2 Jurisdictional Requirements

The jurisdiction of the international criminal court is broadly limited to the 'most serious crimes of international concern'; crime of genocide, war crimes, crimes against humanity and the crime of aggression.[40] Regarding the scope of the powers of the court, the Rome Statute broadly addresses the jurisdiction question in a number of Articles.[41] The Rome Statute makes provision for the major forms of jurisdiction relating to cases before it. Jurisdiction *ratione temporis* or temporal jurisdiction is addressed by the Statute in Article 11(1), jurisdiction *ratione personae* (personal jurisdiction) is also largely provided for in Article 12(2) (b). Territorial jurisdiction (jurisdiction *ratione loci)* is addressed in Article 12(2) (a) and jurisdiction *rationae materia*e, (subject matter jurisdiction) as a major principle undergirding the exercise

---

[35] Arnold 2004, pp. 244–245.

[36] Prosecutor v. Blaskic, IT-95-14, Trial Judgement, 03 March 2000, para 205. See also Prosecutor v. Slobodan Milosevic et al. IT-99-37-PT Second Amended Indictment 29 October 2001.

[37] Prosecutor v. Clement Kayishema and Obed Ruzindana ICTR-95-1-T, Trial Judgement, 21 May 1999, paras 107–110.

[38] Situation in Nigeria, Article 5 Report, Office of the Prosecutor 2013.

[39] Office of the Prosecutor Report on Preliminary Examination Activities 2017.

[40] Article 5(1) Rome Statute of the International Criminal Court 2002.

[41] Article 5 addresses crimes within the jurisdiction of the court, Article 11 discusses temporal jurisdiction, Article 12 addresses the precondition to the exercise of jurisdiction particularly territorial and personal jurisdiction, Article 13 addresses the criteria for the exercise of jurisdiction and Article 19 deals with challenges to the jurisdiction of the court on a case. See also Schabas 2011, p. 62.

of jurisdiction of the Rome Statute is expressed in Article 5. Regarding temporal jurisdiction, Article 11(1) provides clearly that the jurisdiction of the court may only be exercised regarding crimes which were committed after the entry into force of the Statute. On personal jurisdiction, the court may exercise its power if the accused person is a national of a state party to the Rome Statute or a national of a state that has accepted the jurisdiction of the court subject to the exceptions in Article 13 of the Rome Statute. The court also has powers to exercise jurisdiction based on the membership of the State on whose territory the crime in question was committed. Article 26 of the statute provides a major exception to the general principle of jurisdiction regarding persons under the age of eighteen.[42] In this section, temporal jurisdiction, territorial or personal jurisdiction and subject matter jurisdiction will be discussed specifically as it relates to the Boko Haram situation.

4.2.1 Jurisdiction Ratione Temporis

The preamble of the Rome Statute re-states the duty of states 'to exercise its criminal jurisdiction over those responsible for international crimes'. The temporal jurisdiction of the International Criminal Court is limited to crimes committed after its entry into force on 01 July 2002 as provided for in Article 11 of the Rome Statute. The Statute clearly prohibits *ex post facto* prosecutions in accordance with the principle of non-retroactivity in Article 24.[43] Crimes committed before the entry into force of the statute cannot be included in the temporal jurisdiction.[44] The notion of the temporal threshold of the court is also alluded to in the *nullum crimen sine lege* principle established in Article 22(1).[45] The temporal jurisdiction of the International Criminal Court may be subject to some preconditions. When an investigation has been instituted on the basis of a self-referral by a state or the investigation was commenced by the prosecutor *proprio motu*,[46] the court may exercise jurisdiction if the state on whose territory the crime was committed or the state of nationality of the accused person; is a party to the statute or has made a declaration accepting the jurisdiction of the court regarding the crimes in question.[47] However, this does not apply to the

[42] 'The court shall have no jurisdiction over any person who was under the age of eighteen at the time of the alleged commission of a crime'. Article 26 Rome Statute of the international Criminal Court 2002.

[43] The principle of non-retroactivity is an established and generally recognized of international law codified in the 1969 Vienna Convention on the Law of Treaties 1155 UNTS 331.

[44] Bourgon 2002, p. 549.

[45] 'A person shall not be criminally responsible under this statute unless the conduct in question constitutes, at the time it takes place, *a crime within the jurisdiction of the court*' (emphasis mine). Although temporal jurisdiction is distinct from the *nullum crimen sine lege* principle, the provision referring to crimes within the jurisdiction of the court includes the temporal scope of the court provided for in Article 11. See Rastan and Badar in Triffterer and Ambos 2016, p. 658.

[46] Article 13(a), (c) Rome Statute of the International Criminal Court 2002.

[47] Article 12(2), (3) Rome Statute of the International Criminal Court 2002.

temporal jurisdiction of the court emanating from an investigation by the prosecutor based on a United Nations Security Council referral under Chapter VII of the UN Charter.[48] Generally, the temporal jurisdiction of the court is not absolute as it may be extended, limited or barred. It may be extended by a declaration of a state party to cover crimes committed before the entry into force of the statute for that state.[49] Temporal jurisdiction may be limited or barred by a state party with respect to war crimes committed by nationals or on the territory of such state by opting out under the transition provision in Article 124 of the statute.[50] Controversially, UN Security Council may also limit temporal jurisdiction by requesting a deferral of investigation or prosecution.[51]

Regarding the temporal jurisdiction of the Boko Haram crimes, Nigeria signed the Rome Statute on 1 June 2000 and deposited its instrument of ratification on 27 September 2001 without reservation. Therefore, the temporal threshold of the court will apply from the date of entry into force of the Rome Statute. This implies broadly that international crimes committed in Nigeria after 1 July 2002 may be investigated and/or prosecuted by the International Criminal Court. The egregious crimes of Boko Haram first came to the forefront of national discourse in Nigeria with an uprising of July 2009.[52] Since then, the group has held and lost territory, utilised and changed tactics and committed large-scale violent domestic and international crimes affecting millions of Nigerians. The Nigerian military has also been engaged in a sustained offensive against the group for about a decade. In the Boko Haram situation, Nigeria has not made a declaration limiting the jurisdiction of the ICC subject to prescribed procedure. Thus, the ICC possesses the temporal jurisdiction to investigate and prosecute war crimes and crimes against humanity committed by Nigerian nationals and on the territory of Nigeria since becoming a member state at inception in 2002.

4.2.2 Jurisdiction Rationae Materiae

Article 5 of the Rome Statute reiterates the provision in the preamble and acts to limit the jurisdiction of the court to this category of the most serious crimes of international concern expressly mentioned in (a)–(d). Membership of the Rome Statute practically

[48] Article 12(2), 13(b) Rome Statute of the International Criminal Court 2002.

[49] Article 11(2) Rome Statute of the International Criminal Court 2002.

[50] Article 124 is one of the provisions of the Rome Statute subject to a mandatory review process. In 2015, Norway submitted a proposal for the amendment of Article 124. In November 2015, a resolution for the deletion of Article 124 was adopted by consensus. Per Article 121(4) the 'amendment shall enter into force one year after the instruments of ratification have been with the Secretary General of the United Nations by seven-eighths of them' See generally, UN 2015. ICC-ASP Resolution on Article 124 Resolution 2015. See also Zimmermann 2016, pp. 505–514.

[51] Article 16 Rome Statute of the Rome Statute of the International Criminal Court 2002. See also Bourgon 2002, p. 554.

[52] CNN 2018a, b, c.

implies the acceptance of the jurisdiction of the court relating to crimes stated in Article 5 of the Statute namely: genocide, crimes against humanity, war crimes and the crime of aggression.[53] The subject matter jurisdiction is confined to the provisions in Article 5 of the Rome Statute. There may also be the possibility of the future inclusion of further crimes such as terrorism and drug related offences into the material jurisdiction of the court.[54] In the determination of whether there is a reasonable basis to proceed with an investigation by the prosecutor,[55] the provisions of Article 5 may serve as a general tool for consideration.[56] Regarding crimes against humanity, the chapeau of Article 7 para 1 requires that the acts in question are committed as part of a widespread or systematic attack directed against a civilian population.[57] As provided for in Article 8, the jurisdiction regarding war crimes shall be exercised 'in particular' when the crimes in question have been 'committed as part of a plan or policy or as part of a large scale commission of such crimes'. This suggests that isolated crimes of individual members of the armed forces or singular civilians may not be eligible to be tried by the International Criminal Court.[58] The jurisdiction relating to war crimes is not limited only to the grave breaches of the Geneva Conventions and those of the Additional Protocol I, it also includes serious violation of the law and customs of war in international armed conflict, Common Article III of the four Geneva Conventions including the serious violations of the laws and customs of war applicable in internal armed conflicts.[59] The Office of the Prosecutor in its preliminary examination report found a reasonable basis to believe that specific conduct amounting to crimes against humanity and war crimes have been committed in the Nigerian situation within the context of the Boko Haram crisis.[60]

4.2.3 Jurisdiction Ratione Loci and Ratione Personae

Territorial jurisdiction may arise where the crime in question has been committed in whole or in part in the territory of a state.[61] Arising out of the notion of state sovereignty is the principle of jurisdiction *ratione loci* or territorial jurisdiction. This implies, for instance, that if an international crime was committed on the territory

---

[53] Regarding the crime of aggression, a distinct jurisdictional regime applies based on agreement of states parties in 2010. An acceptance or ratification of the Kampala agreement or lodging a declaration with the registrar might exclude the jurisdiction of the court with regards to a state party. See generally Kreß and von Holtzendorff 2010, Clark 2010.

[54] See Final Act of the United Nations Diplomatic Conference of Plenipotentiaries on the Establishment of an International Criminal Court 1998. See also Van der Vyver 2000, p. 1.

[55] Article 15(3) Rome Statute of the International Criminal Court 2002.

[56] Zimmermann 2016, p. 117.

[57] Article 7(1) Rome Statute of the International Criminal Court 2002.

[58] Bothe 2002, p. 380.

[59] Zimmermann 2016, p. 118.

[60] The Office of the Prosecutor Report on Preliminary Examination Activities 2018.

[61] Akehurst 1999, p. 32. See also the first Lotus Principle as established in the SS Lotus Case 1927.

of a first state, by a national of a second state (which may or may not be a member state of the Rome Statute), the Rome Statute may be empowered based on its territorial jurisdiction to investigate and prosecute vis-à-vis states parties. The loci of the commission of the crimes in this instance make the alleged perpetrator amenable to the jurisdiction of the ICC. Article 12(2) (a) (b) of the Rome Statute provides specifically for territorial jurisdiction and jurisdiction by nationality or personal jurisdiction.[62] The jurisdictional nexus of the Rome Statute is that the territorial state or the state of nationality of the accused are states parties to the statute. Membership of the Rome Statute by states parties is symbolic of a voluntary delegation of its sovereign ability to prosecute international crimes to the ICC.[63] Although, there is no express provision regarding this in the statute, state's party may choose to make a declaration regarding the scope of jurisdiction *ratione loci.*[64] Generally, a state also has unlimited jurisdiction over crimes committed by its nationals.[65]

Regarding the nationality of the perpetrator, Article 12(2) (b) governs the scope of jurisdiction in international criminal law. The practical implications of the application of territorial jurisdiction and/or personal jurisdiction with regards to the Boko Haram crimes are all encompassing. Some of the crimes in issue alleged to have been committed by Nigerian nationals, amenable to jurisdiction *ratione personae* based on Nigeria's membership of the Rome Statute, in the territories of another state which may or may not be a state's party to the Rome Statute. It is, thus, useful that there are differing categorisations through which jurisdiction may be exercised under the international criminal justice system. The preconditions required for the exercise of jurisdiction is either of the two. This implies that the presence of either territorial jurisdiction or personal jurisdiction will suffice for the International Criminal Court to exercise its rights to investigate and/or prosecute.[66] The preconditions in Article 12 do not apply in the instance of a United Nations Security Council referral.[67] In Nigeria, a large percentage of the crimes in issue are alleged to have been committed

[62] 'In the case of article 13, paragraph (a) or (c), the court may exercise its jurisdiction if one or more of the following states are parties to this statute or have accepted the jurisdiction of the court in accordance with paragraph 3: (a) *the state on the territory of which the conduct in question occurred* or, if the crime was committed on board a vessel or aircraft, the state of registration of that vessel or aircraft; (b) *the state of which the person accused of the crime is a national.*' (emphasis mine) Article 12(2) (a) (b) Rome Statute of the International Criminal Court 2002.

[63] Schabas and Pecorella, p. 682. However, Scheffer argues that such delegation is illegal. See generally Scheffer 1999.

[64] A number of states have entered such interpretative declarations. The Netherlands made a declaration that the Rome Statute also applies to Dutch Antilles and Aruba. Denmark also made a declaration that the Rome Statute would not apply to the Faroe Islands and Greenland. This was withdrawn in 2006. New Zealand also entered a declaration in relation to Tokelau. See generally UN Treaties 1998.

[65] Akehurst in Reisman 1999, p. 36.

[66] '... the court may exercise its jurisdiction if one or more of the following states are parties to this statute or have accepted the jurisdiction of the court in accordance with paragraph 3: (a) the state on the territory of which the conduct in question occurred... (b) the state of which the person accused of the crime is a national.' Article 12 (2) Rome Statute of the International Criminal Court 2002.

[67] Bergsmo 1998, p. 347.

by Nigerian nationals within the territorial borders of Nigeria, the jurisdiction of the ICC in this regard should largely be uncontested. Regarding crimes committed in third states, among the neighbouring states where Boko Haram crimes have been committed, only Cameroon is not a state party to the Rome Statute.[68]However, a majority of the perpetrators may, notwithstanding, be within the jurisdiction of the ICC based on jurisdiction *ratione personae*.

4.3 Admissibility Requirements

The determination of admissibility of cases before the ICC is guided by paragraph 10 of the preamble, Articles 1 and 17 of the Rome Statute. To determine the subject matter jurisdiction of the Court, the Prosecutor relies on the standards provided in Article 17(1) of the Rome Statute. In its case selection in situations under investigation, the Prosecutor considers complementarity as provided in Article 17(1) (a–c) and gravity of the crimes committed as provided in Article 17(1) (d) as principal criteria.[69] The preconditions for determining a case inadmissible as provided for by Article 17 include the following: investigation and prosecution of the case by a state with jurisdiction over it,[70] investigation by a state with jurisdiction with a decision not to prosecute,[71] and a domestic trial by a court of competent jurisdiction for the same conduct triggering the rule against double jeopardy.[72] With regards to domestic investigations and prosecutions generally, the determination of whether the state is willing or able to genuinely carry out investigations and/or prosecutions is crucial. Article 17(1) (a–c) represents the principle of complementarity. The existence of the four criteria in Article 17(1) must be ascertained by the court before a determination on admissibility is made; 'that the state which has jurisdiction is investigating or prosecuting the case, that the state has investigated or prosecuted and concluded that there is no reasonable basis to prosecute, that the person has been tried for the conduct forming the basis of the complaint, and that the case is of insufficient gravity to proceed before the court'.

In determining unwillingness, the consideration of the court should also include principles of due process recognised by international law, including whether the proceedings are or were being undertaken to shield persons concerned from criminal responsibility, where there is an unjustified delay in the proceedings which might be inconsistent with bringing persons concerned to justice and where proceedings

[68] Cameroon signed the Rome Statute in 1998 but failed to ratify it. It is not a state party to the Rome Statute.

[69] International Criminal Court Office of the Prosecutor Policy Paper on Case Selection and Prioritization 15 September 2016, p. 4.

[70] Article 17(1) (a) Rome Statute of the International Criminal Court 2002.

[71] Article 17(1) (b) Rome Statute of the International Criminal Court 2002.

[72] A subsequent trial is not permitted here under the rule prohibiting double jeopardy as provided for in Article 20, paragraph 3 of the Rome Statute of the International Criminal Court. Article 17(1) (c) Rome Statute of the International Criminal Court 2002.

were not conducted independently and impartially or being conducted in a manner inconsistent with an intent to bring the persons concerned to justice.[73] Should a case be inadmissible under Article 17, the Court cannot exercise jurisdiction. It is the duty of the Court to determine its own jurisdiction and admissibility regarding cases before it. The provisions of Article 17 reflect the principle of international law that it is the duty of every state to exercise its jurisdiction over those responsible for international crimes.[74] Should the states fail to fulfil this duty, there can be recourse to the International Criminal Court in order to eliminate an impunity gap.

The admissibility of the cases before the International Criminal Court may also be challenged on the grounds of gravity per Article 17(1) (d).[75] The notion of gravity is crucial to the purpose of the ICC and its application is an integral part of the work of the Court.[76] Gravity as a case selection criterion before the ICC is critical because the Court, according to its Statute, is tasked with the responsibility of making its own determination regarding the admissibility of cases before it.[77] It is the duty of the prosecutor in the preliminary examination of a situation to 'analyze the seriousness of the information received' regardless of the trigger mechanism.[78] While gravity serves as an important threshold requirement below which the Court should not exercise its jurisdiction, deGuzman opines that additionally, the Prosecutor possesses discretion to select situations and cases among those above the statutory gravity threshold (relative gravity).[79] According to the Office of the Prosecutor, the gravity criterion comprises of both quantitative and qualitative considerations which includes the scale, nature, manner of commission and impacts of the crimes committed.[80]

Under this section, both the requirements of the Court as it relates to complementarity and gravity to warrant ICC intervention in the Boko Haram crisis will be explored. The considerations for the assessment of both complementarity and gravity by the Office of the Prosecutor in its case selection process will be assessed vis-à-vis the Boko Haram crimes.

---

[73] Article 17(2) Rome Statute of the International Criminal Court.

[74] Schabas and El Zeidy 2016, p. 786.

[75] See Prosecutor v. Francis Kirimi Muthaura, Uhuru Muigai Kenyatta and Mohammed Hussein Ali 2012.

[76] De Guzman 2009, p. 1400.

[77] Article 17(1) (d) Rome Statute of the International Criminal Court. The gravity of the crime may also be taken into account in the determination of the sentence of the convicted person before the ICC. See Article 78(1) Rome Statute of the International Criminal Court 2002. See further, De Guzman 2009, Murphy 2006, and El Zeidy 2008.

[78] Article 15 Rome Statute of the International Criminal Court 2002, Rule 104 Rules of Procedure and Evidence.

[79] De Guzman 2009, p. 1403.

[80] International Criminal Court Office of the Prosecutor Policy Paper on Case Selection and Prioritization 2016, p. 13.

4.3.1 Complementarity

The tenth paragraph of the preamble and Article 1 of the Rome Statute noted that the ICC shall be 'complementary to national criminal jurisdictions.' The Statute itself did not plainly use the term 'complementarity'; however, the term has become accepted as representing the standards that govern the relationship between the International Criminal Court and national jurisdictions.[81] Not only is the principle of complementarity based on respect for the primary jurisdiction of states, but also on the practicality of conducting effective prosecutions and the access of states to witnesses, evidence and resources.[82] It is a major element in determining the relationship between the International Criminal Court and national accountability mechanisms.[83] The practice of complementarity is intended to strike a balance between the right of a state to exercise its sovereignty through its domestic proceedings and the interest of the mechanisms of international criminal justice.[84] A core premise of the complementarity regime is that the International Criminal Court does not interfere in domestic investigations and prosecutions. A finding on complementarity does not affect the existence or otherwise of jurisdiction of the court, but rather, it regulates the exercise of jurisdiction by the court.[85] The complementarity regime of the International Criminal Court is governed by Article 17(1) (a–c). Article 17(1) (a) requires that 'a case is being investigated or prosecuted by a state with jurisdiction over it, unless the state is unwilling or unable to genuinely carry-out investigation or prosecution'. The first finding then would be for the court to determine the existence of domestic investigations or prosecution. The Pre-Trial Chamber in Lubanga noted that it is a '*conditio sine qua non* that the national proceedings encompass both the person and the conduct which is subject of the case before the court.'[86] In the event that there are no domestic investigation or prosecutions as envisaged under Article 17(1), examining the criterion of 'unwillingness' or 'inability' under Article 17(2) and (3) would be unnecessary. Where there are domestic investigations and prosecutions, the genuineness and effectiveness of the national proceedings may then be assessed.[87]

Regarding Article 17(1) (a), a determination of inadmissibility may be made where the case is being investigated or prosecuted by a state which has jurisdiction over it, unless the state is unwilling or unable to genuinely carry out investigation or prosecution. What the Court considers to be sufficient to constitute 'investigation' or 'prosecution' is determined by recourse to national practice and the practice of the ad-hoc tribunals. Nouwen opines that an investigation as envisaged by Article 17 does not seem to cover investigations by commissions of enquiry existing without a

[81] Benzing 2003, p. 592.

[82] Olugbuo 2011, p. 251.

[83] Zawati 2016, p. 210.

[84] Nsereko 2013, p. 427.

[85] Benzing 2003, p. 594.

[86] Prosecutor v. Thomas Lubanga Dyilo 2006, para 38.

[87] Ibid. 87.

direct view to prosecution.[88] The Appeal Chamber also agreed with the reasoning of the Trial Chambers that the State must show, 'concrete investigative steps' with relation to the cases.[89]

The element of a state's jurisdiction is also important in the determination of admissibility. According to Benzing, the claim of a state that a case would be inadmissible before the court should fail if that states' jurisdiction under the domestic legal regime is not established.[90] The exception to inadmissibility provided for by Article 17(1) (a) is the criteria of 'unwillingness' or 'inability'. The existence of these criteria suggests that not only is the International Criminal Court interested in the exercise of jurisdiction by the domestic legal regime, such domestic processes must be of the appropriate quality and standard. A further qualification for these criteria is the notion of 'genuineness' of the domestic investigation or prosecution. Should the State exercise of domestic investigation and/or prosecution be found to be genuine and effective, further proceedings before the ICC may be unnecessary.[91] Issues relating to admissibility may be raised by the Court,[92] the Prosecutor,[93] a State with jurisdiction over the case on the ground of its domestic activities, or a state from which acceptance of jurisdiction is required under Article 12,[94] or an accused or person subject to Article 58.[95] Complementarity activities have become a core part of the functions of the ICC and the court not only seeks to prosecute perpetrators of mass atrocities, but also to support and facilitate domestic prosecution of cases within the jurisdiction of the court.[96] Burke-White envisions a more direct participation by the ICC encouraging and supporting national proceedings, so-called 'proactive complementarity'. This includes utilising measures such as cooperation and political leverage to motivate the domestic prosecution of international crimes.[97] The complementarity principle has evolved and the ICC now seems to embrace the practice of the so-called positive complementarity in other to strengthen domestic capacity to genuinely investigate and/or prosecute.[98] The so-called positive complementarity activities might also have the 'unintended consequences of

88 Nouwen 2013, p. 60.

89 The Prosecutor v. Francis Kirimi Muthaura, Uhuru Muigai Kenyatta and Mohammed Hussein Alli 2011.

90 Benzing 2003, p. 602.

91 Nsereko 2013, p. 429.

92 Article 19 (1) Rome Statute of the International Criminal Court 2002.

93 Article 19(3) Rome Statute of the International Criminal Court 2002.

94 Article 19(2) (b)–(c) Rome Statute of the International Criminal Court 2002.

95 Article 19(2) (a) Rome Statute of the International Criminal Court 2002.

96 Olugbuo 2011, p. 254.

97 See generally Burke-White 2008. The approach was also supported by El-Zeidy 2008.

98 See Marshall 2010.

increasing domestic prosecution of international crimes'.[99] The notion of 'negative complementarity' was also posited by some commentators.[100]

4.3.1.1 Determination of 'Inability' and 'Unwillingness'

The criterion provided by the Rome Statute for the determination of inability in a particular case is not clearly defined. Article 17(3) provides that 'in order to determine inability in a particular case, the court shall consider whether, due to a total or substantial collapse or unavailability of its national judicial system, the state is unable to obtain the accused or the necessary evidence and testimony or otherwise unable to carry-out its proceedings'. As stated, in the determination of inability, situations where the judicial system has been unable to function due to a breakdown or inability and the difficulty of carrying out investigations shall be considered. Article 17 may also address circumstances where states are unable to conduct trials that meet international human rights standards.[101] This determination will require an assessment on the available mechanisms to obtain the accused and the necessary evidence.[102] These may include investigatory capabilities including the availability of the judicial system as a whole to properly adjudicate. The decision of inability may also result from the absence or inadequate substantive legislation. The conduct punishable under the Rome Statute should be effectively criminalised in the domestic legislation in order to avoid legislative gaps which enable perpetrators to escape justice[103] Under Article 17(2) and (3); the nature and quality of the available domestic proceedings are in issue.[104] This suggests that availability of adequate substantive legislation matter, not necessarily that a crime must be defined the same way but similar sets of conducts should be covered and that the domestic process are required to meet international human rights standards.

In the Nigerian domestic process, as noted, there is a major lack of the legal framework to address crimes within the jurisdiction of the International Criminal Court. Majority of the completed trials were based on charges for conducts which are not within the jurisdiction of the International Criminal Court; such as membership of terrorist organisation, support towards achieving a terrorist purpose or failure to disclose information about a terrorist act leaving serious international crimes without recourse.[105] This is a major challenge to the assessment of admissibility and the determination of the criterion of inability. In the mass trials, only two major cases

[99] See generally Dancy and Montal 2017.

[100] This implies that the prosecutor of the ICC should decline to investigate and or prosecute except the state with jurisdiction has failed to do so. See generally, Heller 2006, Schabas 2008a, b, and Greenawalt 2009.

[101] McNeal 2006, p. 327.

[102] McNeal 2006, p. 329.

[103] Kleffner 2003, p. 89.

[104] Brighton 2012, p. 636.

[105] The Office of the Prosecutor Report on Preliminary Examination Activities 2018.

were tried on charges which may be the subject of a case before the International Criminal Court.[106] Should an individual already be tried by the domestic legal regime, a prosecution may only be opened by the International Criminal Court subject to the provisions of Article 20(3) of the Rome Statute.

Article 17(2) regulates the determination of a finding of unwillingness.[107] The criterion of unwillingness in the Statute addresses circumstances where domestic proceedings might have been carried out in order for the accused to escape justice. Most especially, where domestic proceedings have been undertaken: (a) for the purpose of shielding the accused from criminal responsibility; (b) present an unjustified delay; (c) are not conducted independently or impartially. The determination of unwillingness will be made by the court 'having regard to the principles of due process recognized by international law'. The Appeals Chamber in the Al-Senussi case noted that while human rights standards may assist the court in the determination of admissibility, the violation of due process rights to the detriment of the accused, unless egregious, should not be sufficient to satisfy the criterion of unwillingness under the statute.[108] A state's unwillingness may also be inferred from an 'objective departure from standard practice applicable in similar cases such as the inadequate allocation of resources to investigations, the appointment of a special investigator who is politically close to the accused, the transfer of a case to secret or special tribunals, the general lack of support and cooperation with investigative authorities, or the granting of blanket amnesties and immunities.'[109] Concerning Article 17(2) (b), a second sub-category in the determination of unwillingness is unjustified delay. There must have been a delay in the domestic proceedings, the said delay must have been unjustified and such unjustified delay must be inconsistent with an intention to bring the person concerned to justice. Long delays may be exempted by provisions of valid considerations and the assessment of unjustified delay will be conducted by considering comparable situations under established domestic law.[110] The third sub-category in the determination of the unwillingness criterion refers to lack of

[106] The trial of Haruna Yahaya for his participation in the abduction of the so-called Chibok girls for which he was sentenced to fifteen years imprisonment and the case of Abba Umar, a low-level Boko haram commander, sentenced to sixty years imprisonment.

[107] 'In order to determine unwillingness in a particular case, the court shall consider having regard to the principles of due process recognized by international law, whether one or more of the following exist, as applicable: (a) the proceedings were or are being undertaken or the national decision was made for the purpose of shielding the person concerned from criminal responsibility for crimes within the jurisdiction of the court referred to in Article 5; (b) there have been an unjustified delay in the proceedings which in the circumstances is inconsistent with an intent to bring the person concerned to justice; (c) the proceedings were not or are not being conducted independently or impartially, and they were or are being conducted in a manner which, in the circumstances, is inconsistent with an intent to bring the person concerned to justice'. Article 17(2) Rome Statute of the International Criminal Court 2002.

[108] Prosecutor v. Saif al-Islam Gaddafi and Abdullah Al-Senussi 2014, paras 219–220 and 230.

[109] See Dalpe 2017, p. 58. See also Prosecutor v. Germain Katanga and Mathieu Ngudjolo Chui 2009, para 90 and Prosecutor v. William Somei Ruto, Henry Kiprono Kosgey and Joshua Arap Sang 2011, para 17.

[110] Dalpe 2017, p. 59.

independence and impartiality in the domestic proceeding as provided for in Article 17(2) (c). In the determination of a lack of independence, the court will examine, 'the manner of appointment of the members and their term of office, the existence of guarantees against outside pressures, including the question of whether the body presents an appearance of independence.'[111] Although, non-egregious violation of due process rights may not be enough to fulfil the criterion towards the determination of unwillingness, a departure from standard practice such as in the case of Boko Haram trials may be crucial in this determination.[112] The quality of national proceedings is an important consideration based on the laid down requirements of Article 20(3) (b) of the Rome Statute. The provisions of Article 17(1) (c) must be applied in line with Article 20(3) of the Rome Statute which provides for the *ne bis in idem* principle.

A further distinction of Article 17(1) includes circumstances where: (a) domestic investigation or prosecution have not yet been closed; (b) a case has been investigated, but the state decided not to prosecute the person concerned; (c) the person concerned has already been tried before the domestic courts. When there are domestic proceedings, the test of the court includes a requirement for the same person and the same conduct being investigated and/or prosecuted at the domestic venue and the International Criminal Court.

It is clear that domestic investigations and prosecutions are not an automatic bar to the admissibility of a case before the International Criminal Court. Although, a state may have already investigated or prosecuted, proceedings may still be instituted at the International Criminal Court. This would require addressing the domestic process using the standards established in Article 17 of the Rome Statute: that is, the state's willingness and ability to genuinely investigate and prosecute. The second stage of the Boko Haram prosecutions was not conducted within the normal court system departing from standard procedure. The entire process was fraught with major defects including lack of adequate legal defence, lack of interpreters, lack of prosecutable evidence and a heavy reliance on confessional statements -which may have been obtained through torture.[113] The trials were characterised by a lack of coherence; and there are several concerns regarding fair trial; also, there are due process challenges that have the potentials to mar the process.[114] The rushed nature of the second phase of the trials also raised credibility questions. The governing legislation for the second phase trials lacked clarity as it was technically not part of the normal court processes,

[111] Dalpe 2017, p. 60.

[112] In the mass Boko Haram related trials which held in October 2017, February 2018 and July 2018, in a departure from standard practice, the government set up courts in military facilities with civilian judges, prosecuting a high volume of cases behind closed doors. The process has been criticized not only for the major due process challenges but also a massive lack of protection for fundamental guarantees, fair trial and human rights concerns. See generally United Nations Human Rights Office of the High Commissioner 2017, Amnesty International Report 2018, Human Rights Watch 2018, and Daily Trust 2018.

[113] See Human Rights Watch 2005 and New York Times 2015.

[114] See generally, Human Rights Watch release 2018. See also The Guardian 2017, Deutsche Welle 2017.

neither was it a court martial although civilian judges sat in a special court in a military facility. The model chosen by the government failed to be seen as a true and thorough exercise of accessing justice for all the parties concerned. According to the Office of the Prosecutor in its 2018 Preliminary Examination Report, the domestic process was 'rather scarce in quantity and often lacking in progression compared to the quantity of allegations and the numbers of persons in detention. Files provided to the Office of the Prosecutor further suggest that some of the proceedings considered by the authorities as relevant to the admissibility assessment may be affected by procedural and substantive issues.'[115]

The determination of willingness and inability to genuinely investigate and prosecute those most responsible for the Boko Haram crimes in Nigeria is crucial. It does not appear that the government has in their custody any major senior Boko Haram commander. A few have been announced as killed while majority are still engaging in an active operation against the members of the Nigerian military. Additionally, for the cases involving mid to senior level Boko Haram officials, only two have been prosecuted on charges similar to crimes within the jurisdiction of the International Criminal Court. In the determination of ability, particularly regarding the lack of domestic legal frameworks for conduct criminalised under the Rome Statute, the potential for a gap is present. These include specifically certain conduct amounting to sexual and gender-based crimes such as 'forced marriages, rapes, sexual slavery and sexual violence, use of women and girls for operational tasks such as suicide attacks.' Other prohibited acts include 'targeting of females including of student girls for attending public schools, the use of girls as suicide bombers and the targeting of males including student boys by means of forced conscription to fight for the group and through the selective execution of men of fighting age constituting acts of persecution on gender grounds' under article 7(1) (h) of the Statute. 'From the available facts and the standards of the court's admissibility determination, Nigeria may be determined as unable based on the lack of adequate domestic legal framework and the lack of prosecutions conducts constituting crimes within the jurisdiction of the court particularly, occasioning a complementarity gap.

4.3.2 Gravity Determination of Boko Haram Violence

The seriousness of the crimes within the jurisdiction of the court alleged to have been committed affect the determination of whether they meet the gravity threshold as a criterion for admissibility. The Rome Statute affirms that 'the most serious crimes of concern to the international community as a whole must not go unpunished…'[116]

[115] The Office of the Prosecutor Report on Preliminary Examination Activities 2018.

[116] Preamble, Article 5 of the Rome Statute of the International Criminal Court 2002. This section focuses on the seriousness of the crimes (gravity determination) and does not dwell on a determination of whether the crimes are crimes of concern to the international community as a whole.

This is implying that the seriousness of the crimes in issue matter. Gravity is a separate admissibility criterion, not a part of the standards for the determination of complementarity.[117] Also, distinct from the jurisdictional requirements, Article 17(1) (d) of the Rome Statute imposes a further threshold to guide the selection of situations and cases by the prosecutor.[118] Concerning the language of the chapeau of Article 17(1) '…the Court shall determine that a case is inadmissible…' the evaluation of gravity is important and an obligatory part of the admissibility assessment.[119] El-Zeidy also describes it as a 'mandatory test, not subject to derogation.'[120] Article 53(1) (b) provides for an assessment of gravity for the initiation of an investigation.[121] Evaluating the gravity requirement is crucial both for the procedural stage of initiating an investigation and the assessment of individual cases.[122] The preliminary examination of the situation on the registered vessel of the Union of Comoros was closed on the basis of a finding of insufficient gravity.[123]

The Pre-Trial Chamber 1 in the Lubanga case developed factors for the determination of gravity including; the large-scale or systematic nature of the crimes and the social alarm caused to the international community.[124] Additionally, the perpetrator of the alleged conduct within the jurisdiction of the court should be the 'most senior leaders suspected of being the most responsible for the crimes within the jurisdiction of the court.'[125] Although, the Appeal Chamber overturned the Pre-Trial Chambers approach, it did not develop a new model for the determination of the threshold of gravity. Statutorily, the notion of admissibility-related gravity is outlined under Article 17(1) (d) and Article 53(1) (b) (referring to gravity of a case) while gravity as a case selection mechanism is provided for in Article 53(1) (c) and 2(c) (referring to gravity of the crime) of the Rome Statute.[126] While there is no clear outline for the determination of gravity, the approach of the Office of the Prosecutor and scholarly literature include a consideration of the scale and nature of the crimes committed, the

[117] Article 17(1) (d) Rome Statute of the International Criminal Court.

[118] Sacuoto and Cleary 2008.

[119] Stegmiller, p. 550. See also Prosecutor v. Lubanga, Decision on the Prosecutor's application for warrant of arrest, Article 58, para. 29; Prosecutor v. Ntaganda, Annex II, Decision on the Prosecutor's application for warrants of arrest 2008, para 29.

[120] El Zeidy 2008, p. 39.

[121] 'The Prosecutor shall, having evaluated the information made available to him or her, initiate an investigation unless he or she determines that there is no reasonable basis to proceed under this Statute. In deciding whether to initiate an investigation, the Prosecutor shall consider whether: (b) the case is or would be admissible under Article 17'.

[122] Stegmiller 2009, p. 550.

[123] See Pre-Trial Chamber I Situation on the Registered Vessels of the Union of Comoros, the Hellenic Republic and the Kingdom of Cambodia 'Decision on the Request of the Union of the Comoros to Review the Prosecutor's Decision not to initiate an Investigation' 16 July 2015. See also Statement of the ICC Prosecutor Fatou Bensouda, on the Situation of the Registered Vessel of the Union of Comoros et al. 2017.

[124] Prosecutor v. Lubanga, Decision on the Prosecutor's application for warrant of arrest 2006, para 29.

[125] Stegmiller 2009, p. 551.

[126] Stegmiller 2009, p. 563 examines the potential differences between the two scenarios.

manner of commission and the impacts of the crimes on the victims and the affected populations.[127] The Office of the Prosecutor addressed the four specific factors for the purpose of determining gravity in situations and cases in its first activities report.[128]

The scale of the crimes committed is an important criterion in the assessment of gravity. The Prosecutor evaluates the scale from the perspective of 'the number of direct and indirect victims, the extent of the damage caused by the crimes, the bodily and psychological harm to the victims and their families, and the geographical and temporal spread of the crimes committed.'[129] Regarding the nature of crimes committed, the 'factual elements of each offence such as killings, rapes, other sexual or gender-based crimes, crimes committed against or affecting children, persecution, or the imposition of conditions of life on a group calculated to bring about its destruction' is specifically addressed.[130] The manner of commission which contributes to the assessment of gravity include: 'the means employed to execute the crime, the extent to which the crimes were systematic or resulted from a plan or organised policy or otherwise resulted from the abuse of power or official capacity, the existence of elements of particular cruelty, including the vulnerability of the victims, any motives involving discrimination held by the direct perpetrators of the crimes, the use of rape and other sexual or gender-based violence or crimes committed by means of, or resulting in, the destruction of the environment or of protected objects.'[131] The Prosecutor assesses the impact of the crimes committed from the perspective of 'the increased vulnerability of victims, the terror subsequently instilled, or the social, economic and environmental damage inflicted on the affected communities…' Priority will also be given to 'prosecuting Rome Statute crimes that are committed by means of, or that result in, inter alia, the destruction of the environment, the illegal exploitation of natural resources or the illegal dispossession of land'.[132] It is important to note

[127] See Regulation 29(2), International Criminal Court Regulations of the Office of the Prosecutor ICC-BD/05-01-09 23 April 2009. See also The Prosecutor v. Bahar Idriss Abu GardaICC-02/05-02/09-243-Red, Decision on the confirmation of charges, 8 February 2010, para 31. Murphy also noted that the degree of participation in the prohibited conduct should be considered. See Murphy 2006, p. 283. The restrictive approach of the Pre-Trial Chamber particularly relative to the consideration of the 'most senior leaders' was overturned by the Appeal Chambers in Situation in DRC, Judgment on the Prosecutor's appeal against the decision of Pre-Trial Chamber I Decision on the Prosecutor's application for warrants of arrest, Article 5, ICC-01-04-169, 13 July 2006, reclassified as public on 23.9.2008 pursuant to Decision on the unsealing of judgment of the Appeals Chamber issued on 13 July 2006, 22.9.2008 (ICC-01-04-538-PUB-Exp). Regarding differing perspectives and criticisms of the Pre-Trial Chamber's approach on the determination of gravity see also El Zeidy 2008, p. 44, who opined that other factor should be considered such as: '(1) the degree of participation in committing the crime which reflects those who bear the greatest responsibility for the crimes; (2) impact on ICC investigations; (3) other aggravating factors.' See also Schabas 2008a, b, and De Guzman 2009.

[128] The Office of the Prosecutor Report of the Activities Performed During the First Three Years June 2003–June 2006, 2006.

[129] International Criminal Court Office of the Prosecutor Policy Paper on Case Selection and Prioritization 2016, p. 13.

[130] Office of the Prosecutor Policy Paper on Case Selection and Prioritization 2016.

[131] Office of the Prosecutor Policy Paper on Case Selection and Prioritization 2016.

[132] Office of the Prosecutor Policy Paper on Case Selection and Prioritization 2016.

that the Office of the Prosecutor recognised that 'sexual and gender-based crimes are amongst the gravest under the statute.'[133]

Regarding the scale of the crimes committed in the Boko Haram situation, the crisis has led to killing of over twenty thousand people, the displacement of about 2.4 Million people in Northeast Nigeria, Cameroon, Niger and Chad. It has also resulted in food-insecurity that affected about 7.2 million people.[134] According to the United Nations, more than 4000 women and girls have been abducted by Boko Haram with over ten million people requiring humanitarian assistance as at March 2018.[135] The crisis was characterised by reported and unreported incidences of rape, sexual slavery, forced marriages and other acts of sexual violence. About 30 percent of women in Northeast Nigeria experienced varying forms of sexual and gender-based violence since 2013 according to a baseline survey.[136] These statistics often change based on an increase or decrease in the ferocity of attacks. The activities of Boko Haram led to the degradation of infrastructure, the destruction of educational facilities, critically required health facilities, destroying communities and stunted economic growth. The crisis is often quoted to have led to the loss of about nine billion dollars as a result of damages in Northeast Nigeria.[137] The activities of Boko Haram also led to the bodily and psychological harm to thousands of Nigerians. Although, the most frequent attacks of Boko Haram were particularly carried out in Borno, Yobe and Adamawa states, the impacts of the group's violence spread across large swathes of North-eastern Nigeria in different frequencies. Their violent attacks also spread into northern Cameroon, Niger and Chad.[138]

Regarding the nature of the activities of Boko Haram, the crimes committed have resulted in killings of thousands of people, abduction, rapes, forced marriages and forced pregnancy, crimes against children and persecution among other criminal conducts contrary to the Rome Statute of the International Criminal Court. Generally, the crimes were committed using violence and the perpetuation of terror, including massive use of improvised explosive devices and suicide bombings. The crimes were committed in a systematic manner and in many instances, communities received letters of an impending Boko Haram attack,[139] with operatives attacking in a coordinated nature across different locations with sophisticated weapons at the same time.[140] Victims and survivors of Boko Haram attacks and activities generally in the North-East were subjected to an increased state of vulnerability in many internally displaced camps. Attacks on such camps also became frequent and occupants became sitting targets for varying forms of violence both within and outside

[133] Office of the Prosecutor Policy Paper on Sexual and Gender-Based Crimes 2014.

[134] Council of Foreign Relations Nigeria Security Tracker.

[135] United Nations Secretary General 2018.

[136] Results from Baseline Survey on Gender-Based Violence in Borno State Nigeria. A Report from Women Protection and Empowerment International Rescue Committee 2017.

[137] Aljazeera Centre for Studies Report 2018.

[138] See generally Botha et al. 2017.

[139] See for example Daily Post 2014.

[140] See generally Torbjörnsson and Jonsson 2017.

Nigeria.[141] Schools, hospitals, churches and other religious worship centres have been destroyed by Boko Haram. Most importantly, the use of rape and other acts of gender-based violence were widespread. The scale of the Boko Haram violence and the nature and manner of commission of the crimes have resulted in a high vulnerability of the victims, instilled a climate of terror in the North-East Nigeria and the Lake Chad Basin region as a whole and led to massive social, economic and environmental damage. The crimes of Boko Haram are egregious and should fulfil the gravity determination for the assessment of admissibility.

4.4 Interests of Justice

The Rome Statute in Article 53(1) (c) makes provision for another hurdle for the Prosecutor's decision regarding the initiation of an investigation. The Prosecutor must assess potential reasons to believe an investigation would not serve the interests of justice in specific situations. Additionally, for the initiation of a prosecution after investigations, the Prosecutor must also consider whether a potential case is not in the interest of justice, considering particularly, the gravity of the crimes, interests of the victims, age and infirmity of the alleged perpetrator, and his or her role in the alleged crime.[142] While this determination is a policy requirement by the Office of the Prosecutor for its case selection,[143] there is a statutory oversight to be exercised by the Pre-Trial Chamber in this regard.[144] The practice of the determination of the criterion in Article 17 and 53 of the Rome Statute is rooted in the exercise of prosecutorial discretion. Counterbalancing the obligation to prosecute the most serious crimes of international concern and exercising the discretion for the determination of interests of justice is potentially an exercise that may be fraught with tension and requires a clear structure.[145] While there is no statutory definition of what constitutes interest of justice, non-governmental organisations previously provided varying perspectives of potential approaches to its application.[146] Additionally, the wording of Article 53(1) (c) suggests a link of interests of justice to 'gravity of the crime' and the 'interests of the victims'. The Office of the Prosecutor in a 2007 policy paper also gave an idea of its standards for determination of interests of justice.[147] Situations or cases which otherwise qualify for selection based on jurisdictional and admissibility requirements but were not pursued solely pursuant to a determination on the 'interests of justice'

[141] See for example United Nations 2018a, b, and Norwegian Refugee Council 2017.

[142] Article 53(2) (c) Rome Statute of the International Criminal Court 2002.

[143] Office of the Prosecutor Policy Paper on Case Selection and Prioritization 2016.

[144] Article 53(1), 2(c) and 53(3) Rome Statute of the International Criminal Court 2002.

[145] Webb 2005, p. 316.

[146] See generally Human Rights Watch Policy Paper 2005, and Amnesty International 2005. Both opine that there was a need for clarity and the development of objective standards regarding Article 53.

[147] Office of the Prosecutor Policy Paper on the Interests of Justice 2007.

was described as 'exceptional'. It also opines that generally, such application of interest of justice is exceptional in nature and that there was a presumption favouring investigation or prosecution should the criterion in Article 53(1) (a) and (b) or Article 53(2) (a) and (b) be met. It stressed that the objects and purposes of the ICC should guide its determination of interests of justice and that its approach will depend on the facts and circumstances of specific cases or situations. The policy paper's distinction of the notion of 'interests of peace' and 'interests of justice' has been criticised as questionable.[148] Commentators opine on whether the determination of interests of justice should additionally take into account non-prosecutorial transitional justice mechanisms such as amnesties and truth commissions particularly for crimes within the mandate of the ICC.[149] Davis similarly argued that political considerations should be taken into account in the determination of interests of justice.[150] The controversial decision of the Pre-Trial Chamber II that there is no reasonable basis to proceed with an investigation in the situation in the Islamic Republic of Afghanistan appears to support this position.[151] This decision further muddled the already murky waters of the interest of justice criterion by utilising non-legal factors such as the chances of success of an investigation including the likelihood of obtaining evidence due to the political climate, and financial and human resource concerns to arrive at a determination in the negative while admitting that the legal requirements of jurisdiction and admissibility were met.[152]

In 2015, the Office of the Prosecutor identified eight potential cases in relation to the Boko Haram crisis. Nigerian government's amnesties project relating to 'repentant' low-level offenders and Boko Haram members in its ongoing de-radicalisation programme may also factor into the determination of interests of justice. As a whole, should the previous approach to the criterion (before the Afghanistan decision) be utilised, a positive finding for the senior members of Boko Haram might be made. However, with the new approach utilised by the Court, there is no longer clarity regarding the factors that the court may take into account in its finding. A negative finding on the interest of justice criterion in the Boko Haram crisis would be regrettable because conducts such as acts of sexual and gender-based crimes, which lack a sufficient legal framework and have not been adequately addressed by the domestic

---

[148] See Schabas 2008a, b, p. 749.

[149] See generally Lovat 2007, p. 276, Robinson 2003, Stahn 2005, Goldstone and Fritz 2000, and Clarke 2005.

[150] See generally Davis 2015.

[151] See Situation in the Islamic Republic of Afghanistan, Decision Pursuant to Article 15 of the Rome Statute on the Authorization of an Investigation into the Situation in the Islamic Republic of Afghanistan 2019. In this decision, the Pre-Trial Chamber II declined the request of the Prosecutor to open formal investigations on war crimes and crimes against humanity committed in Afghanistan. This decision was made on the basis that such investigations were contrary to the interests of justice requirement. Although the Chamber noted that 'relevant requirements regarding jurisdiction and admissibility are met,' 'the prospects for a successful investigation and prosecution are extremely limited'.

[152] Situation in the Islamic Republic of Afghanistan, Decision Pursuant to Article 15 of the Rome Statute on the Authorization of an Investigation into the Situation in the Islamic Republic of Afghanistan 2019.

legal regime could potentially come before the court. This is crucial to prevent impunity or a perception of impunity for grave crimes, such as those committed in Nigeria and has not and cannot be addressed by the domestic framework. Whether a finding that the crimes in question are of sufficient gravity and a consideration of the interests of the victims may influence a positive finding regarding the interest of justice criterion lacks immediate clarity. Therefore, since there no longer appears to be clear and fixed criteria for the determination of the norm of interests of justice in specific situations or cases, the determination in the Nigerian situation and potential cases remain within the discretion of the Prosecutor subject to an article 15 decision by the Pre-Trial Chamber. In 2020, the Office of the Prosecutor concluded preliminary examination and announced that the statutory criteria for opening investigations into Nigeria's situation, inclusive of the Boko Haram crisis have been met.[153] The Office of the Prosecutor determined that there was a reasonable basis to believe that acts constituting war crimes and crimes against humanity had been committed by Boko Haram and its splinter groups. It also stated that it did not identify substantial reasons why an investigation would not serve the interests of justice.

4.5 Boko Haram Crimes Within the Jurisdiction of the ICC

As noted, the jurisdiction of the International Criminal Court is restricted to the 'most serious crimes of concern to the international community as a whole' and the subject-matter jurisdiction of the Rome Statute is limited to the crime of genocide, crimes against humanity, war crimes and the crime of aggression.[154] Within the Boko Haram crisis, it is clear that conducts amounting to genocide and the crime of aggression have not been committed and the requirements, according to Article 6 of the Rome Statute for genocide and Article 8 *bis* for the crime of aggression, have not been met.[155] Therefore, there will be no elaborate discussion on the requirements of the crimes of genocide and aggression and why they have not been met. This is because such exercise is unlikely to be useful. However, egregious acts amounting to crimes against humanity and war crimes have been variously committed by the Boko Haram group.[156] In this section, individual acts which fulfil the requirements of crimes against humanity and war crimes will be assessed including the elements of the crimes in question.

---

[153] See Statement of the prosecutor, Fatou Bensouda, on the conclusion of the preliminary examination of the situation in Nigeria 2020.

[154] Article 5 Rome Statute of the International Criminal Court 2002.

[155] From the criteria for the fulfilment of the stringent conditions amounting to the crime of Genocide, and the crime of Aggression in the Kampala review conference amendments, no conduct amounting to both crimes have been committed in Nigeria within the purview of the Boko Haram crisis. See generally Article 5, 8, 8 bis and 15 bis Rome Statute of the International Criminal Court 2002.

[156] See generally, Office of the Prosecutor 'Report on Preliminary Examination Activities 2018' 05 December 2018, pp. 56–58.

4.5.1 Conducts Amounting to Crimes against Humanity

Fundamental human rights, particularly life, health, freedom and dignity are protected by the prohibition of crimes against humanity.[157] Article 7(1) of the Rome Statute address crimes against humanity with a provision for the material elements of the crime to be the commission of any of the individual acts listed, when committed as part of a widespread or systematic attack against a civilian population. The civilian population as the object of the attack directly relates to groups of people sharing similar characteristics which make them a target of the attack.[158] The nature and context of crimes before the ICC seeks to distinguish the crimes from 'ordinary crimes' that should typically be dealt with by domestic law (except the crime of aggression).[159] For crimes against humanity, this distinction is crucial in order to differentiate the acts from other common crimes which may not fulfil the requirements under international law.[160] The chapeau requirement of widespread or systematic has been interpreted to mean either widespread or systematic and the presence of both, although usually present in practice, is unnecessary.[161] The determination whether an attack is widespread may be inferred from the geographical areas covered or the number of victims affected.[162] The systematic criterion may be inferred from the degree of organisation and planning involved and the pattern that the violations adhere to. The requirement that the attack be 'pursuant to or in furtherance of a state or organizational policy' is also an important component of crimes against humanity.[163] The ICC Pre-Trial Chamber II found that proving an 'established hierarchy', an existing 'military wing', an 'effective system of communication', 'a chain of command', 'the means and capacity to carry-out military operations' is sufficient for a finding of organisational policy.[164] The policy element may also be inferred from the circumstances and events including political platforms or writings, public statements or propaganda, including the creation of political or administrative structures.[165] A state may be understood in a functional sense and an organisation could be interpreted to include groups that have the potential to commit crimes of a widespread

[157] Werle and Jessberger 2020, p. 374

[158] Ibid. 162.

[159] For example, the crime of genocide comes with a requirement of 'an intent to destroy in whole or in part' Article 6, crimes against humanity relates to one or more of the stated acts 'committed as part of a widespread or systematic attack' against a civilian population Article 7, while war crimes relate to crimes committed 'as part of a plan or policy or as part of a large-scale commission of such crimes Article 8. Additionally, war crimes also require a contextual element of an armed conflict whether of an international or internal character. See deGuzman 2009.

[160] Hall and Ambos 2016, p. 167.

[161] Ibid. 165, see also Ibid. 162.

[162] See for example the decision in Prosecutor v. Germain Katanga and Mathieu Ngudjolo Chui 2008, para 395.

[163] Article 7(2) (a) Rome Statute of the International Criminal Court 2002.

[164] The Prosecutor v. Bosco Ntaganda ICC-01/04-02/06 Decision Pursuant to Article 61(7) (a) and (b) of the Rome Statute on the Charges of the Prosecutor Against Bosco Ntaganda 2014, para 14.

[165] Ibid. 162.

or systematic nature on a civilian population. In the dissenting opinion of Judge Kaul in the Kenyan Decision,[166] he stated that within the contemplation of Article 7(2) (a) of the Rome Statute, an organisation must 'partake of some characteristics of a State. Those characteristics could involve the following: (a) a collectivity of persons; (b) which was established and acts for a common purpose; (c) over a prolonged period of time; (d) which is under responsible command or adopted a certain degree of hierarchical structure, including, as a minimum, some kind of policy level; (e) with the capacity to impose the policy on its members and to sanction them; and (f) which has the capacity and means available to attack any civilian population on a large scale'.[167] All these requirements have been fulfilled by Boko Haram. Boko Haram has been found to have an established hierarchy, a chain of command with the clear means and capacity to carry out military operations over a prolonged period of time, functionally for over a decade. The prosecutor of the ICC agrees with this view and stated, 'the available information appears sufficient to establish that Boko Haram could be considered as an "organization" capable of defining and implementing a policy of committing crimes against humanity…the group appears to be under a responsible command, namely the leadership exerted by Abubakar Shekau.'[168]

For acts to constitute crimes against humanity there is no required nexus to an armed conflict.[169] The context in which the crime in question has been committed is crucial because the same set of conducts may amount to a war crime or a crime against humanity, depending on the context. It is unnecessary that each prohibited act in question be widespread or systematic as long as it forms a part of attacks which have these characteristics.[170] In this vein, a singular conduct such as murder may constitute a crime against humanity when committed with sufficient nexus to the conflict and within the relevant context. The specific prohibited acts need not be widespread or systematic as this requirement is limited to the attacks and not the individual acts of the accused. For crimes against humanity, the attacks must have been directed against a civilian population and it is unnecessary to prove the membership of specific groups.[171] Article 30 provide for the mental element of crimes against humanity as intent and knowledge. The prohibited act must have been committed with awareness, as part of a widespread or systematic attack on a civilian population. Knowledge in this instance does not imply the provision of proof that the perpetrator had knowledge of all the characteristics and finer details of the plan, however, the perpetrator must be aware that their acts form part of the

[166] Situation in the Republic of Kenya, The Prosecutor v. William Samoei Ruto, Henry Kiprono Kosgey and Joshua Arap Sang. Decision Pursuant to Article 15 of the Rome Statute on the Authorization of an Investigation into the Situation in the Republic of Kenya 2010. See also Dissenting Opinion by Judge Hans-Peter Kaul to Pre-Trial Chamber II's Decision on the Prosecutor's Application for Summons to Appear for William Samoei Ruto, Henry Kiprono Kosgey and Joshua Arap Sang 2011.

[167] See also Kress 2010, p. 23.

[168] Situation in Nigeria: International Criminal Court Article 5 Report, p. 22. 5 August 2013.

[169] Gaeta 2014, p. 755.

[170] Hall and Ambos 2016, p. 166.

[171] De Guzman 2000, p. 362. Hall and Ambos 2016, p. 173.

attacks.[172] Not only could the acts in question constitute a part of a widespread or systematic attacks, it could also amount to the attack itself.[173] To constitute an attack as a crime against humanity, an act of violence must have been committed.[174] Any of the enumerated acts in Article 7(1) alone is sufficient to constitute crimes against humanity.[175] Generally, the provision of crimes against humanity has the potential to address a higher range of conducts than war crimes. This is because of its focus on civilians generally, and the lack of a nexus to an armed conflict. Prohibited acts may be committed not only by members of a state or organisation, but may include individuals acting to implement or provide support for the policy of the state or organisation.[176] To constitute crimes against humanity, the crimes in question must be 'particularly odious, constituting a serious attack on human dignity, or a grave humiliation or degradation of one or more human beings.'[177]

As provided for by the Rome Statute, acts constituting crimes against humanity when committed as part of a widespread or systematic attack against a civilian population with knowledge of the attack include murder, extermination, enslavement, deportation or forcible transfer of population, imprisonment or severe deprivation of liberty, torture, rape, sexual slavery, enforced prostitution, forced pregnancy, enforced sterilisation or any other forms of sexual violence of comparable gravity, persecution, enforced disappearance of persons, apartheid and other inhumane acts of similar character.[178]

4.5.1.1 Murder

Article 7(1) of the Rome Statute prohibits murder when committed as part of a widespread or systematic attack directed against a civilian population, with knowledge of the attack. The attack refers to 'a course of conduct involving multiple commissions against any civilian population, pursuant to or in furtherance of a state or organisational policy to commit such attack.'[179] For the crime against humanity of murder; (a) the perpetrator must have killed or caused the death of one or more persons; (b) the act in question must have been committed as part of a widespread or systematic attack directed against a civilian population; (c) the perpetrator knew that the conduct was part of or intended the conduct to be part of a widespread or systematic attack against a civilian population.[180] In order to constitute murder as a crime against humanity, the victim must have died, and the death must have 'resulted

[172] Cassese 2002, p. 353. See also Article 7(2) Element of Crimes 2011.

[173] Ibid. 175.

[174] Werle and Jessberger 2020, p. 379.

[175] Ibid. 175.

[176] Werle and Jessberger 2020, p. 380.

[177] Ibid. 177.

[178] Article 7(1) (a)–(k) Rome Statute of the International Criminal Law 2002.

[179] Article 7(2) (a) Rome Statute of the International Criminal Court 2002.

[180] Article 7(1) (a) Elements of Crimes International Criminal Court 2011.

from an unlawful act or omission of the accused or his subordinate'.[181] The conduct or omission by the perpetrator must have resulted in death for the material element to be fulfilled. For the mental elements of murder amounting to crime against humanity, Article 30 of the Rome Statute applies. The perpetrator must have 'meant to cause death or was aware that death "will occur in the ordinary course of events."'[182] Since 2009 when the Boko Haram crisis came to the fore in Nigeria, the group has killed thousands of civilians in large and small attacks through explosions, suicide bombings, and indiscriminate massive shootings. For example, in 2011, about 20 people were killed, with over a hundred injured, in a car bomb attack on the United Nation's Building in Nigeria's Capital city.[183] In the so-called 'Baga massacre' perpetrated by Boko Haram in the once-bustling town of Baga and sixteen surrounding villages in January 2015, between one hundred to two thousand people were reportedly killed over the course of four days.[184] Boko Haram intentionally killed and maimed civilians in attacks throughout Borno State and in parts of Adamawa and Yobe states. According to the United Nations High Commissioner for Human Rights, 'many witnesses reported that Boko Haram shot civilians that attempted to escape during attacks in Askira Uba, Baga, Bama, Damasak, Gombi, Gwoza, Kwajafa, Madagali, Maiduguri, Michika, and Mubi. Those who refused to join were killed, and their bodies often left to rot in streets, wells or riverbeds.'[185]

Boko Haram attacks were directed at civilians in public spaces such as schools, markets, places of worship, motor-parks with large-scale attacks intended to maximise casualties. Boko Haram murders have been conducted in a widespread and systematic manner directed against the civilian population in Northeast Nigeria, Northern Cameroon, Niger and Chad. From the conduct of the Boko Haram members who perpetrated the various attacks, the knowledge that their conduct would result into the deaths of people and intended that death results from the attacks may be inferred. The attacks were widespread, large-scale and occurred over an extended period of time. The widespread attacks were also typically carried out with a great degree of organisation.[186] Murders are a part of the policy of Boko Haram and this was clearly communicated through a variety of the group's writings, public statements and propaganda materials.[187] The Office of the Prosecutor in its preliminary

[181] Prosecutor v. Akayesu ICTR 96-4-T, Trial Judgement, 2 September 1998, para 589.

[182] The Prosecutor v. Jean Pierre Bemba Gombo, Decision Pursuant to Article 61(7) (a) and (b) of the Rome Statute on the Charges of the Prosecutor Against Jean-Pierre Bemba Gombo 2009, paras 135, 138.

[183] BBC 2011, and Reuters 2011.

[184] A survivor was reported to have stated that 'No one stayed back to count bodies.' The area was within the stronghold of Boko Haram until it was retaken by the Nigerian security forces. The accurate figures of that particular incident remain unclear. See generally Muscati 2015, Segun 2015, Amnesty International 2015a, and UN News 2015.

[185] Human Rights Council 2015, p. 6.

[186] Stanford University Mapping Militant Project 2016.

[187] See generally, Mahmood 2017.

examination found a reasonable basis to believe that murder that may amount to crimes against humanity has been committed by Boko Haram.[188]

4.5.1.2 Extermination

Extermination by its definition in Article 7(2) (b) refers to the intentional infliction of conditions of life such as the deprivation of access to food or medicine, calculated to bring about the destruction of a part of the population. As a crime against humanity, such acts of extermination must have been committed in a widespread or systematic manner against a civilian population with the requisite mental element. The act of extermination similarly addresses large-scale killings.[189] The perpetrator must have knowledge that his individual act was part of a context of mass killings. In this vein, an individual killing within the context of mass or large-scale killings may be prosecuted as extermination which may amount to crimes against humanity. Members of Boko Haram carried out large-scale attacks which seem calculated to lead to the destruction of a part of the population in North-eastern Nigeria. Large-scale attacks were carried out which led to the death of twenties and hundreds of civilians at a time. The group succeeded in ridding villages of people through mass killings, with survivors fleeing, lucky to escape with their lives.[190] In November 2011, at least 100 people were believed killed in gun and bomb attacks in Yobe state when members of Boko Haram attacked three police stations, including the state police headquarters, two banks and about six church buildings. Such large-scale and widespread attacks became the norm. According to Amnesty International, 'in 2013 Boko Haram conducted more than 100 deadly attacks, killing more than 1,350 civilians. In 2014, there were at least 230 raids and bomb attacks against civilians, killing more than 4,000 civilians.'[191] The pattern created and the regular repetition of the acts in question suggests a systematic occurrence. The mental element for extermination is also governed by Article 30 of the Rome Statute.

4.5.1.3 Enslavement

Conducts amounting to enslavement, constituting crimes against humanity were committed by Boko Haram. Article 7(2) (c) describes enslavement to mean the 'exercise of any or all of the powers attaching to the rights of ownership over a person. Other forms of enslavement include purchasing, selling, lending, or bartering a person or persons.[192] The mental element of this crime is governed by Article 30 of the Rome Statute. Within the context of a widespread or systematic attack, Boko

---

[188] Office of the Prosecutor Report on Preliminary Examination Activities 2018.

[189] Article 7(1) (b) Elements of Crimes International Criminal Court 2011.

[190] See for example, Guardian 2015 and BBC 2015.

[191] Amnesty International 2015b.

[192] Article 7 (1) (c) Elements of Crimes, International Criminal Court 2011.

Haram members abducted and exercised ownership over civilians in North-eastern Nigeria and the Lake Chad Basin region, most especially women and children. In 2014, Boko Haram' leader, Abubakar Shekau, threatened to 'sell' some of the so-called abducted 'Chibok girls.' According to a statement, 'God instructed me to sell them, they are his properties and I will carry out his instructions'.[193] The ICTY) in Kunarac expanded the notion of enslavement from the traditional viewpoint of classic slavery to include; 'elements of control and ownership, restriction or control of individual's autonomy, freedom of choice or freedom of movement; and often, the accruing of some gain to the perpetrator…'[194] According to the reasoning in Kunarac, the exercise of control over groups of civilians, such as the Chibok girls, where the threat or use of force or other forms of violence, and the absence of freewill of the victims within the context may be sufficient to fulfil the requirement of enslavement as a crime against humanity. The Appeal Chamber in Kunarac noted that there is no specific required length of time and the opposition of the victim is unnecessary. The Pre-Trial Chamber in Ntaganda also found that exercising ownership may be shown by a 'combination of factors' such as the detention or captivity in which the victim was held and its duration, the limitation to the victim's free movement, measures taken to prevent or deter escape, the use of force, threat of force or coercion, and the personal circumstances of the victims including their vulnerability.'[195]

Boko Haram's focus on exerting 'ownership' over women and children was documented in a number of its propaganda documents indicating that its importance as a policy bedrock of the group.[196] Majority of the women and children kidnapped by Boko Haram since the inception of the crisis are still believed to be within the control of the group almost a decade later. The capture and the subsequent enslavement of people by Boko Haram was carried out in a methodical and organised manner and has been widespread since the inception of the conflict.

4.5.1.4 Imprisonment and Other Severe Deprivation of Liberty

Imprisonment and severe deprivation of liberty in violation of fundamental rules of law is expressly prohibited in Article 7(1) (e) of the Rome Statute and may amount to crimes against humanity when committed as part of a widespread or systematic attack against a civilian population with knowledge of the attack. The action amounting to the crime against humanity of imprisonment and other severe deprivation of liberty include, the perpetrator must have imprisoned 'one or more persons, or otherwise severely deprived one or more persons of their liberty', and 'the conduct was committed as part of a widespread or systematic attack directed

[193] See generally, The Telegraph 2015, BBC 2014, and Globe and Mail 2018.

[194] The Prosecutor v. Dragoljub Kunarac, Radomir Kovac and Zoran Vukovic 2001, para 120.

[195] Prosecutor v. Bosco Ntaganda. Decision Pursuant to Article 61(7) (a) and (b) of the Rome Statute on the Charges of the Prosecutor against Bosco Ntaganda, Pre-Trial Chamber II) 2014, para 209.

[196] UNICEF 2018, United Nations human Rights Council 2015, and Washington Post 2018.

against a civilian population'.[197] The mental element governed by Article 30 of the Rome Statute include an awareness by the perpetrator of the factual circumstances establishing the gravity of the conduct and a knowledge that the conduct was part of or intended to be part of a widespread or systematic attack directed against a civilian population.

The length of time of the imprisonment and deprivation is crucial in the determination whether the deprivation of liberty is 'severe' in terms of Article 7(1) (e). Additionally, other factors to be taken into account for the determination of severity may include an assessment of the conditions under which the detainees were imprisoned. Imprisonment and any acts amounting to other severe deprivation of liberty are essentially prohibited because it violates fundamental rules of human rights treaties and standards, international legal regime and international humanitarian law.[198] The ICTY) in Kordic and Cerkez noted that imprisonment connotes 'arbitrary imprisonment, that is to say, the derivation of liberty of the individual without the due process of law, as part of a widespread or systematic attack against a civilian population.'[199] Within the context of the widespread and systematic attacks against the civilian population in North-eastern Nigeria and the Lake Chad Basin region, Boko Haram has severely deprived numerous civilians of their liberty contrary to Article 7(1) (e) of the Rome Statute. In its occupation of a number of large towns, Boko Haram held civilians in these areas without their consent. Thousands of civilians in camps and in towns under its control, detained in large houses and under armed guard in prison-like conditions. Civilians caught in an attempt to leave were often flogged or execute.[200] The Office of the Prosecutor also found a reasonable basis to believe that conduct constituting crimes against humanity of imprisonment and other severe deprivation of physical liberty in violation of the fundamental rules of law pursuant to Article 7(1) (e) were committed by Boko Haram.[201]

4.5.1.5 Torture

The use of torture as a crime against humanity connotes the 'intentional infliction of severe pain or suffering, whether physical or mental, upon a person in custody or under the control of the accused...'[202] The prohibition against torture is a *jus cogens* obligation and violations amount to a violation of customary international law. Under the Rome Statute, causing pain without desiring to achieve a particular purpose may also amount to torture. According to the Elements of Crimes, the physical elements of torture includes: that the perpetrator must have 'inflicted severe physical or mental pain or suffering upon one or more persons,' the presence of the victims in

[197] Article 7(1) (e), Elements of Crimes, International Criminal Court 2011.

[198] Prosecutor v. Dario Kordic & Mario Cerkez, Judgment, 2001, para 302.

[199] Prosecutor v. Dario Kordic & Mario Cerkez, Judgment, 2001, para 302.

[200] Amnesty International 2015b.

[201] Office of the Prosecutor Report on Preliminary Examination Activities 2018, p. 56.

[202] Article 7(2) (e) Rome Statute of the International Criminal Court 2002.

'the custody or under the control of the perpetrator', The 'pain or suffering did not arise only from, and was not inherent in or incidental to, lawful sanctions' and the commission of the conduct in question 'as part of a widespread or systematic attack directed against a civilian population'. The mental element governed by Article 30 is knowledge.[203] In the determination of torture as a crime against humanity, the duration of abuse including its physical and mental effects in the individual case should be considered. Torture carried out by non-state organisations or private individuals is also covered by the provisions in Article 7(2) (e) of the Rome Statute. According to a 2015 Report of the UNHCHR, Boko Haram subjected civilians living in its controlled areas, villages and abductees to various forms of torture and other cruel, inhuman or degrading treatment, including repeated beatings when they were unable or unwilling to walk to different strongholds, vicious punishment for inability to recite the Quran, or refusal to adopt the groups' beliefs, deprivation of food for general breaches, cutting off hands for infractions such as stealing, including burying up to the neck and stoning to death for the offence of adultery.[204] Any act of torture committed within the context of a widespread or systematic attack against a civilian population would fulfil the requirement as a crime against humanity. The activities of Boko Haram in this regard were organised and exhibited a pattern with the potential to fulfil the widespread or systematic requirement.

4.5.1.6 Acts of Sexual Violence

Article 7(1) (g) of the Rome Statute directly addresses rape, sexual slavery, enforced prostitution, forced pregnancy, enforced sterilisation, or any other form of sexual violence of comparable gravity. Acts of sexual violence may be prosecuted as an underlying act for the crime against humanity of torture, persecution or under the category of other inhumane acts. The provisions in the Rome Statute addressing acts of sexual violence are gender neutral and may apply both to men and women.

In commission of rape amounting to a crime against humanity, 'the perpetrator invaded the body of a person by conduct resulting in penetration, however slight, of any part of the body of the victim or of the perpetrator with a sexual organ, or of the anal or genital opening of the victim with any object or any other part of the body.' The invasion was committed by force, or by threat of force or coercion, such as that caused by fear of violence, duress, detention, psychological oppression or abuse of power, against such person or another person, or by taking advantage of a coercive environment, or the invasion was committed against a person incapable of giving genuine consent.'[205] The twin elements of perpetration and coercion are crucial to

[203] 'The perpetrator knew that the conduct was part of or intended the conduct to be part of a widespread or systematic attack directed against a civilian population.' Article 7 (1) (f) Elements of Crimes, International Criminal Court 2011.

[204] Human Rights Council 'Report of the United Nations High Commissioner for Human Rights on violations and abuses committed by Boko Haram and the impact on human rights in the affected countries' 2015, p. 8.

[205] Article 7 (1) (g)-1 Elements of Crimes, International Criminal Court 2011.

prove the existence of rape. Regarding coercion, proving one of the conditions (that is force, threat of force or coercion, fear of violence, duress, detention, psychological oppression or abuse of power, or by taking advantage of a coercive environment) is necessary under Article 7(1) (g). Consent cannot be inferred from any word or conduct of the victim in the instances where any of the elements of coercion have been used.[206] The acts in question must have been committed as part of a widespread or systematic attack directed against a civilian population. The mental element for rape as a crime against humanity is knowledge-governed by Article 30 of the Rome Statute. The ICTR in Akayesu[207] recognised rape as an instrument and defined it as a physical invasion of a sexual nature, accompanied by coercion.[208] The Trial Chamber adopted a broad-based approach in its definition of the crime of rape and sexual violence, inclusive of other related acts with an important focus on the notion of violation.[209] The Trial Chamber in Katanga also included situations where women and girls were forced to 'share' their lives with individuals with whom they had to perform sexual acts.[210]

Sexual slavery may fulfil some of the requirements of enslavement under Article 7; however, the perpetrator must cause the victim to engage in sexual acts. The perpetrator in relation to sexual slavery 'exercised any or all of the powers attaching to the right of ownership over one or more persons, such as by purchasing, selling, lending or bartering such a person or persons, or by imposing on them a similar deprivation of liberty' and 'the perpetrator caused such person or persons to engage in one or more acts of a sexual nature.'[211] Sexual slavery also encompasses circumstances where women and girls were forced into 'marriages', domestic servitude, forced labour involving sexual activity including rape by their captor (s).[212] According to the Katanga Trial Chamber, the exercise of powers of ownership within the context of sexual slavery may take any form and the listed forms were not intended to be exhaustive. The context of a widespread or systematic attack directed against a civilian population is paramount. The mental element is also provided for by Article 30.

Enforced prostitution includes a number of different elements; elements of sexual slavery, including the pecuniary advantage for the acts gained by the perpetrator. According to the Elements of Crimes, the elements of the crime are:

---

[206] Rule 70 (a) Rules of Procedure and Evidence International Criminal Court 2013.

[207] Prosecutor v. Jean-Paul Akayesu, Trial Judgement 2001.

[208] Other forms of sexual and gender-based violence have been prosecuted in a number of cases including by the ICTY and the ICTR in Prosecutor v. Dragoljub Kunarac, Radomir Kovac and Zoran Vukovic, Judgement, 2001. Prosecutor v. Zejnil Delalic, Zdravko Mucic, Hazim Delic & Esad Landzo (Celebici case) 2001. In the Celebici case, superiors in the camp were convicted for sexual violence against men. Prosecutor v. Anto Furundzija, 1998, and Prosecutor v. Kvocka 2001 represent the shifting position that acts of sexual violence will no longer be treated a natural consequence of armed conflict but rather as serious violations deserving punishment.

[209] Bensouda 2007, p. 406.

[210] Prosecutor v. Germain Katanga, Judgment Pursuant to Article 74 of the Statute, 2014, para 978.

[211] Article 7 (1) (g)-2 Elements of Crimes, International Criminal Court 2011.

[212] Ibid. 221.

> The perpetrator caused one or more persons to engage in one or more acts of a sexual nature by force, or by threat of force or coercion, such as that caused by fear of violence, duress, detention, psychological oppression or abuse of power, against such person or persons or another person, or by taking advantage of a coercive environment or such person's or persons' incapacity to give genuine consent. The perpetrator or another person obtained or expected to obtain pecuniary or other advantage in exchange for or in connection with the acts of a sexual nature.[213]

The conduct must have been committed as part of a widespread or systematic attack against a civilian population and the mental element is provided for by Article 30. Enforced prostitution may amount to a continuing offence of sexual slavery, rape and other forms of sexual violence or a separate act in itself, as a form of 'sexual violence of comparable gravity'.[214]

The provision addressing forced pregnancy under the statute provides for 'the unlawful confinement of a woman forcibly made pregnant, with the intent of affecting the ethnic composition of any population or carrying out other grave violations of international law…'[215] when committed as part of a widespread or systematic attack against a civilian population to be a crime against humanity. The non-contextual elements particularly address the confinement, and the intent of affecting the ethnic of a population or, carrying out other grave violations of international law.[216]

The category of 'other forms of sexual violence of comparable gravity' is also provided for in Article 7(1) (g). This may address other acts of violence carried out through sexual means. It may also include acts that do not involve penetration or physical contact, but with a sexual motive or targeting sexuality and may include psychological attacks. The Elements of Crimes of the factual elements of the crime include: the commission of 'an act of a sexual nature against one or more persons or caused such person or persons to engage in an act of a sexual nature by force, or by threat of force or coercion, such as that caused by fear of violence, duress, detention, psychological oppression or abuse of power, against such person or persons or another person, or by taking advantage of a coercive environment or such person's or persons' incapacity to give genuine consent.'[217] Regarding threshold, the prohibited conduct in question must be of comparable gravity to other offences amounting to a crimes against humanity and the conduct must have been committed as part of a widespread or systematic attack against a civilian population. The mental element is governed by Article 30 of the Rome Statute.

Acts amounting to gender-based and sexual violence committed by Boko Haram received some of the largest research interests and was the subject of a number of reports by international non-governmental organisations since the inception of the crisis. This is due to the large-scale nature and widespread perspectives of the

---

213 Article 7 (1) (g)-3 Elements of Crimes, International Criminal Court 2011.

214 Ibid. 221.

215 Article 7(2) (f) Rome Statute of the International Criminal Court 2002.

216 Article 7 (1) (g)-4 Elements of Crimes, International Criminal Court 2011.

217 Article 7(1) (g)-6 Elements of Crimes, International Criminal Court 2011.

crimes committed in this regard.[218] Since 2009, women and girls were subjected to widespread abuses. These abuses include sexual slavery, sexual violence, forced marriages, forced pregnancies and forced conversions, rapes of women and children as young as fifteen years old.[219] Although, this category of crime by Boko Haram has received a major attention and visibility internationally, it is widely believed that the true extent of the crimes was grossly under-reported due to stigma, cultural and religious norms and gender stereotypes.[220] The Office of the Prosecutor found a reasonable basis to believe that rape, sexual slavery and other forms of sexual violence pursuant to article 7(1) (g) was committed by Boko Haram.[221]

4.5.1.7 Persecution

As a crime against humanity, the Rome Statute addresses persecution in Article 7(1) (h). Persecution under the statute refers to 'the intentional and severe deprivation of fundamental rights contrary to international law by reason of the identity of the group or collectivity.'[222] In order for the requirements to be fulfilled, the object of the persecution must be an identifiable group or community. This also covers acts against individuals as representatives of the group. The prohibited acts in question may be committed on the basis of 'political, racial, national, ethnic, cultural, religious or gender' identity of the victim, or other grounds that are universally recognised as impermissible under international law.[223] Other grounds universally recognised as impermissible under international law refers to customary international law. There is a required connection to any other act amounting to crimes against humanity or any other crime within the jurisdiction of the court. The conduct in question must have been committed as part of a widespread or systematic attack against a civilian population, and the mental element is governed by Article 30 of the Rome Statute. The mental element for persecution as a crime against humanity is intent and knowledge under Article 30 of the Rome Statute. The language of the statute is not only limited to female victims, and persecution as a crime against humanity also encompasses the targeting of men and women in different ways based on their gender.[224] The early targeting of Christians, perceived 'un-devoted' Muslims and targeted destruction of religious and worship centres and the inherent crimes committed may amount to persecution on religious basis as a crime against humanity. Boko Haram's utilisation

---

218 A number of research papers on the focus of Boko Haram on women and children have been published. These include a number of books devoting sections to Boko Haram's treatment of women and girls. See generally, Iyi and Strydom 2018, and Amnesty International 2015a, b.

219 Human Rights Council 2015, p. 9.

220 UNHCR 2017.

221 Office of the Prosecutor Report on Preliminary Examination Activities 2018, p. 56.

222 Article 7(2) (g) Rome Statute of the International Criminal Court 2002.

223 Article 7(1) (h) Elements of Crimes, International Criminal Court 2011.

224 Prosecutor V. Callixte Mbarushimana, Prosecution's Application under Article 58, Pre-Trial Chamber I, 2011, Para 4.7.

of abducted girls for suicide bombing, targeting women for abduction and other purposes, selective execution of men and forced conscription within the context may also amount to persecution as a crime against humanity.

4.5.1.8 Other Inhumane Acts

The Rome Statute also makes provision for a residual clause in Article 7(1) (k) intended to address inhumane acts not expressly prohibited under Article 7. The character of the acts in question must be of similar character to other acts amounting to crimes against humanity under Article 7(1) and the perpetrator must have 'inflicted great suffering, or serious injury to body or to mental or physical health, by means of an inhumane act.'[225] Not every human rights violation would fit the requirement as 'other inhumane acts.' The violations in questions must be 'serious violations of international customary law and the basic rights pertaining to human beings drawn from the norms of international human rights law which are of a similar nature and gravity to the acts referred to in Article 7(1)'.[226] The circumstances of the individual cases must be taken into account in the determination of the severity requirement. The perpetrator must be aware of the factual circumstances establishing the nature and gravity of the acts[227] and the acts must have been committed as part of a widespread or systematic attack directed against a civilian population. Within the conduct of the Boko Haram violence, specific acts committed against children, committed within the appropriate context, with capacity to meet the severity threshold may be charged under the heading of 'other inhumane acts.' According to the OHCHR, the recruitment and use of boys and girls for different purposes were widespread, 'Some boys were forced to attack their own families to demonstrate loyalty to Boko Haram, whilst girls were forced to marry, clean, cook and carry equipment and weapons. OHCHR received consistent reports that some boys and girls were increasingly used as human shields and to detonate bombs.'[228] These acts were widespread, systematic and may be similar in character to the acts addressed in Article 7.

4.5.2 Existence of and Legal Qualification of the Armed Conflict

Identifying the character and legal qualification of a conflict is central to the determination of the applicable framework.[229] Generally, the rules regarding international

[225] Article 7(1) (k) Elements of Crimes, International Criminal Court 2011.

[226] Prosecutor v. Germain Katanga and Mathieu Ngudjolo Chui, 2008, para 448.

[227] Article 7 (1) (k) Elements of Crimes, International Criminal Court 2011.

[228] Human Rights Council 2015, p. 10.

[229] Zimmermann and Greiß 2016, p. 531. See also Prosecutor v. Thomas Lubanga Dyilo, Judgement Pursuant to Article 74 of the Statute, 2012, para 539.

armed conflict are broader than those addressing internal armed conflict. Characterising the Boko Haram violence, whether as an international armed conflict or armed conflict not of an international character, is crucial in order to determine the applicable provisions of the Rome Statute and the material jurisdiction of the ICC in the specific potential cases. Article 8(2) (a) and (b) apply to international armed conflict while (c)–(f) make provision for acts amounting to serious violations in an armed conflict not of an international character. Article 8(2) (d) and (f) apply to non-international armed conflicts to the exclusion of 'internal disturbances and tensions, such as riots, isolated and sporadic acts of violence or other acts of similar nature.'[230] The provisions of Common Article 3 of the 1949 Geneva Conventions apply generally to internal armed conflicts with a threshold for such determination.[231]

Zimmermann and Greiß highlighted four circumstances where the distinction regarding the nature of the conflict must be made namely: (a) armed conflict which occur exclusively between two or more states, (b)armed conflict occurring within the territory of one state without the involvement of a third state, (c) armed conflict governmental armed forces on one side and organized armed groups on the other with the involvement of third states, (d) armed conflict between a states armed forces and transnational non-state armed group which do not occur within the territory of the respective states.[232] The Boko Haram violence does not seem to fall neatly into any of the highlighted categories, albeit, it is more closely related to the third scenario. A classic non-international armed conflict may become internationalised pursuant to the involvement of third states. However, if the third states intervention is on the side of the governmental armed forces, the characterisation of the armed conflict will not be altered.[233] Should a third states' direct intervention be on the side of the armed group, the classification of the armed conflict might be affected.[234] The ICJ decision in the Nicaragua case found that if a third state exercises 'effective control' over the armed group, the character of the conflict may change into an international one.[235] Although, the Nicaragua standard has been applied variously,[236] the Appeals Chamber in the Tadic case found it to be of little persuasion.[237] The Tadic decision established a standard of 'overall control' and this reasoning was adopted by the

[230] Werle and Jessberger 2020, p. 470.

[231] Whitelaw 2016, p. 32.

[232] Zimmermann and Greiß 2016, p. 532.

[233] Zimmermann and Greiß 2016, p. 535.

[234] Prosecutor v. Dusko Tadic, Judgement, Appeal Chamber, 1999, para 84.

[235] Military and Paramilitary Activities in and against Nicaragua (Nicaragua v. United States of America) (Merits), ICJ Reports 1986, para 109. Judge McDonalds in his separate and dissenting opinion applied a 'dependency and control' test and found that the 'effective control' test is not required to internationalize the conflict.

[236] See generally, Prosecutor v. Rajic, Review of the Indictment Pursuant to Rule 61 of the Rules of Procedure and Evidence, Trial Chamber, 1996, para 13. Prosecutor v. Alekssovski, Joint Operation of the Majority, Judge Vohrah and Judge Nieto-Navia, 1999, para 10. Prosecutor v. Delalic et al., Judgement, Trial Chamber, 1998, para 204.

[237] Prosecutor v. Dusko Tadic No., Judgement, Appeals Chamber, 1999.

Pre-Trial Chamber I in the Lubanga decision.[238] According to the authority of the Tadic appeal decision, in other for an armed conflict to be regarded as one not of an international character: (a) the conflict in question must take place between governmental authorities and organised armed groups or between such groups with a degree of organisation; and (b) the conflict must be protracted, as an indication of its intensity.[239]

Internal disturbances, tensions and sporadic acts of violence and other acts of similar nature may develop into what may amount to an internal armed conflict. While the Provisions of the Protocol II Additional to the Geneva Conventions addressing internal armed conflict do not address internal disturbances, it is not clear which threshold must be reached before an internal disturbance rises up to fulfil the criterion of an armed conflict not of an internal character.[240] According to the ICTY) in the Tadic case, 'in an armed conflict of an internal or mixed character, those closely related criteria are used solely for the purpose, as a minimum, of distinguishing an armed conflict from banditry, unorganised or short-lived insurrections, or terrorist activities, which are not subject to international humanitarian law.' 'A determination should be made on a case-by-case basis with a factual evaluation of the level of organisation of the parties to the conflict and the intensity of the hostilities.[241] The Delalic case also prescribes a threshold of 'protracted degree of the armed violence and the extent of the organization of the parties involved.'[242] The determination of the existence of an internal armed conflict must be made on the basis of an objective criterion and not a subjective determination of the parties.[243] Zimmermann and Greiß opine that for the purposes of the Rome Statute, the character of an armed conflict will not change on the basis of the presence of the United Nations Peacekeeping forces.[244] The fourth categorisation relating to the existence of a transnational armed conflict is also of interest. This directly addresses conflict between states armed forces and a transnational non-state armed group which do not occur within the territory of the respective state. This categorisation has been applied variously in relation to anti-terror activities in third states, for example, Kenya's operations against al-Shabab in the territory of Somalia or the United States' military operations against Al-Qaeda in third states. While this category possesses an extraterritorial character,

[238] Prosecutor v. Thomas Lubanga Dyilo, Decision on the Confirmation of Charges, Pre-Trial Chamber I, 2007, para 211.

[239] Prosecutor v. Dusko Tadic, Decision on the Defense Motion for Interlocutory Appeal on Jurisdiction, Appeals Chamber, 1995. The Court in the Lubanga case also provided criteria for determining the intensity of a conflict. See Prosecutor v. Thomas Lubanga Dyilo, Judgment pursuant to Article 74 of the Statute, Trial Chamber I, 2012, para 538.

[240] See for further discussions, Ibanga and Archibong 2018, p. 138.

[241] Prosecutor v. Dusko Tadic IT-94-T, Judgement, Trial Chamber, 7 May 1997, para 562.

[242] Prosecutor v. Zejnil Delalic, Zdravko Mucic, Hazim Delic & Esad Landzo (Celebici case), 20 February 2001, para 184.

[243] Dörmann 2003, p. 442.

[244] Zimmermann and Greiß 2016, p. 539.

it may only be described as a 'transnational armed conflict'.[245] Werle and Jessberger opine that transnational armed conflicts are to be classified from a legal perspective as non-international armed conflict if the minimum threshold requirements are met. A critical look at the Boko Haram crisis reveals that while the egregious crimes committed by a so-called terrorist group or a non-state armed group is at the centre of the conflict, it does not conform to the criterion of transnational armed conflict, and there is no involvement of third states armed forces in the form envisaged.

Legally, an armed conflict may also fulfil the requirements to be regarded as both international and non-international in nature;[246] however, this is not applicable to the Boko Haram crisis. The major parties involved in the conflict are the Boko Haram group itself and the Nigerian security forces. However, from time to time, there was the involvement of external military forces (not third states) which may be capable of turning the crisis into an internationalised one. For example, the African Union Multinational Joint Task Force consisting of troops from the Lake Chad Basin Region countries and Benin intervened in the crisis in 2015, providing assistance to the Nigerian security forces.[247] Additionally, the security forces of Niger, Chad and Cameroon routinely joined the efforts of the Nigerian security forces in their fight against Boko Haram. However, due to the nature of such interventions and the fact that they were designed to assist the Nigerian security forces, such interventions do not have the capacity to alter the characterisation of the armed conflict. Additionally, the presence of an African Union Joint Task Force cannot alter the legal character of the conflict from an internal armed conflict since the presence of UN Peacekeeping forces is incapable of doing so. A cross-border element in an armed conflict is also not sufficient to alter the characterisation of such conflict as Common Article 2 of the Geneva Convention requires states ('high contracting parties') on both sides of the conflict for a character of international armed conflict.[248] For categorisation as an internal armed conflict, the requirement of high intensity of hostility or protracted violence and a degree of organisation on the part of the non-state armed group must be met.[249] The armed group should possess the ability to plan and carry out sustained military operations.[250] The Pre-Trial Chamber II in the Bemba decision found that

[245] The authors also opine that counter-terrorist operations in some cases may not constitute an armed conflict according to the Geneva Convention or the Rome Statute, but in some instances may be treated as domestic law enforcement missions to repress severe crimes. However, this determination may be made on a case-by-case basis.

[246] Prosecutor v. Lubanga Dyilo, Judgement Pursuant to Article 74 of the Statute, Trial Chamber I, 14 March 2012, para 540.

[247] See generally Assanvo et al. 2016.

[248] Zimmermann and Greiß 2016, p. 541. This has been supported by the ICTY decision in the Tadic decision and the ICC in the Bemba decision. See, Prosecutor v. Dusko Tadic, Decision on the Defense Motion for Interlocutory Appeal, Appeals Chamber 1995, para 70. Prosecutor v. Jean Pierre Bemba, Pre-Trial Chamber II, Decision Pursuant to Article 61(7) (a) and (b) of the Rome Statute on the Charges of the Prosecutor, 2009, para 231.

[249] Prosecutor v. Jean Pierre Bemba, Pre-Trial Chamber II, Decision Pursuant to Article 61(7) (a) and (b) of the Rome Statute on the Charges of the Prosecutor, 2009, para 225.

[250] Prosecutor v. Thomas Lubanga, Decision on the Confirmation of charges, Pre-Trial Chamber I, 2007, para 233.

the armed group must be under a responsible command, and there must be a degree of organisation, including the possibility to discipline and the ability to plan and carry out military operations. These criteria are necessary for the fulfilment of the requirements under Article 8(2) (f) of the Rome Statute.[251] The Boko Haram group is more suited as an armed group under a responsible command with the ability to carry out sustained operations.[252] Legally, major aspect of the crisis is more appropriately regarded as an internal armed conflict. The Prosecutor in the preliminary examination reports agrees with this characterisation and addresses the crisis as an internal armed conflict.[253] The provisions relating to internal armed conflicts protect a category of victims as similar to those protected in the circumstance of an international armed conflict, that is, persons taking no active part in hostilities, including members of the armed forces who have laid down their arms and those placed *hors de combat* by sickness, wounds, detention or any other cause.[254] Possible perpetrators of war crimes in an internal armed conflict are typically limited to 'commanders, combatants and other members of the armed forces.'[255]

4.5.2.1 Conducts Amounting to War Crimes Committed by Boko Haram

The law of war crimes may only be triggered in the context of an armed conflict.[256] A war crime is a violation of a rule of international humanitarian law in the context of an armed conflict resulting in criminal responsibility under international law. The existence of an armed conflict may be established when there is a 'resort to armed force between states or protracted armed violence between governmental authorities and organised armed groups or between such groups within a state.'[257] Article 8 of the Rome Statute provides the framework for war crimes as a whole. Jurisdiction in relation to war crimes should be exercised 'in particular when committed as part of a plan or policy or as part of a large scale commission of such crimes.'[258] This implies that individual acts which are isolated, committed by members of the armed forces or even by individual civilians may not be tried as a war crime by

[251] Zimmermann and Greiß 2016, p. 545.

[252] The group has carried out consistent, sustained and concerted military operations since 2009 in North-eastern Nigeria, Northern Cameroon, Niger and Chad attacking civilians and conducting active hostilities against military and security forces. They are driven by the ideology of Salafi Jihadism, have exercised control over a portion of the territory and meet the minimum characterisation as an organisation. See also Ibanga and Archibong 2018, p. 145.

[253] Office of the Prosecutor Report on Preliminary Examination Activities 2018.

[254] Article 8(2) (c) Rome Statute of the International Criminal Court 2002.

[255] Dörmann 2003, p. 391.

[256] Clapham and Gaeta 2014, p. 745.

[257] Prosecutor v. Dusko Tadic, Decision on the Defense Motion for Interlocutory Appeal on Jurisdiction, Appeals Chamber, 1995, para 70.

[258] Article 8(1) Rome Statute of the International Criminal Court 2002.

the court without the necessary nexus requirement.[259] Prohibited acts highlighted in Article 8 are categorised by referring to conduct prohibited by the Geneva Conventions [in paragraph 2(a) and (c)] excluding the additional protocols and paragraph 2(b) and (e) relating to conducts violating international humanitarian law generally including the additional protocols. This addresses serious crimes committed in violation of international humanitarian law, regarded as grave breaches, some of which also constitute crimes within the jurisdiction of the ICC and are contrary to the four Geneva Conventions and Additional Protocol I.[260] The classification of certain conducts constituting grave breaches of the Geneva Convention as war crimes under the provisions of Article 8 requires that the stringent qualification for grave breaches must be fulfilled in the event of an international armed conflict. Additionally, the acts in question must have been directed at protected persons or properties under the Geneva Conventions. The so-called Tadic test highlights four applicable criteria for the determination of war crimes in non-international armed conflict. They include: (a) the war crime must constitute a breach of international humanitarian law; (b) the rule must be a customary law rule or an applicable treaty law; (c) the violation must be serious and result in grave consequences for the victims; and (d) the violation must include, either under custom or treaty law, individual criminal responsibility.[261] The Court in Tadic also found that many of the rules in the Additional Protocol II relating to non-international armed conflict also reflect customary international law.[262] The decision led to the notion that serious violations of international humanitarian law of non-international armed conflict may amount to war crimes if the conduct in question is criminalised by international law.[263]

For a conduct to constitute a war crime, it must have been committed in the context of or associated with an armed conflict whether of an international or non-international character, the determination of which should be factually established.[264] In the Boko Haram crisis, it has been established that the conflict may be largely construed as one of a non-international character. Article 8(2) (c)–(f) addresses violations of the law applicable in time of armed conflict not of an international character, serious violations of common Article 3 of the Geneva Conventions including crimes committed against certain protected persons.[265] In general, persons protected in an internal armed conflict are, 'persons taking no active part in the hostilities, including

[259] Bothe 2002, p. 380, Dörmann 2016, p. 322 opine that a singular act may amount to a war crime without a plan, policy or large-scale commission and that the provisions of Article 8(1) is a practical guideline for the ICC in its case selection.

[260] Cassese et al. 2011, p. 118.

[261] Prosecutor v. Dusko Tadic, Decision on the Defense Motion for Interlocutory Appeal on Jurisdiction, Appeals Chamber, 1995.

[262] Kolb and Del Mar 2014, p. 58.

[263] Gaeta 2014, p. 746.

[264] Bothe 2002, p. 388. See also Prosecutor v. Clement Kayishema and Obed Ruzindana, Trial Judgement, 1999, paras 185–188.

[265] 'Persons taking no active part in the hostilities, including members of the armed forces who have laid down their arms, and those placed *hors de combat* by sickness, wounds, detention or any other cause' Article 8(2) (c) Rome Statute of the International Criminal Court 2002.

members of the armed forces who have laid down their arms and those placed *hors de combat* by sickness, wounds, detention, or any other cause'.[266] For acts constituting a war crime within the definition of the Rome Statute, a sufficient nexus to the armed conflict is crucial. The act must be 'closely' and 'obviously' related to the armed conflict. It is unnecessary, however, to prove that the armed conflict is the cause of the commission of the crime.[267] The nexus is essential to link the armed conflict to the crime and not the criminal.[268]

The application of Article 8(2) (c) is limited to internal armed conflicts to the exclusion of internal disturbances, tensions, riots, isolated and sporadic violence and similar acts.[269] Until the threshold of internal armed conflict is reached, internal conducts within a country may not be examined by the Court as possible war crimes.[270] 'Acts of terrorism' and 'acts of threats of violence the primary purpose of which Is to spread terror among the civilian population' is prohibited by the Geneva Convention. These may be committed during an international or non-international armed conflict.[271] However, these were not included as grave breaches or in the first Additional Protocol. The ICTR Statute included 'acts of terrorism' as war crimes in non-international armed conflict and the Special Court for Sierra Leone also list terrorism as a war crime. While this categorisation is not expressly provided for in the Rome Statute, conducts which may also amount to terrorism are criminalised in its provisions. Thus, such conducts may be prosecuted as war crimes. The mental element for war crimes under the statute is intent and knowledge-provided for in Article 30. The requirement for knowledge is in relation to the facts and may not relate to a legal estimation of the classification of the armed conflict.[272] All conducts prohibited under Article 8(2) (c) must have taken place 'in the context of, or associated with an armed conflict not of an international character'. In the Boko Haram crisis, egregious crimes with the potential of amounting to war crimes were committed. Therefore, the provision of the Rome Statute particularly Article 8(2) (c)–(f) addressing war crimes committed in a non-international armed conflict may be applied.

---

[266] Common Article 3(1) of the Geneva Conventions

[267] Zimmermann and Greiß 2016, p. 531.

[268] Clapham and Gaeta 2014, p. 751.

[269] Article 8(2) (d) Rome Statute of the International Criminal Court 2002.

[270] Dörmann 2003, p. 382.

[271] Article 33(1) IV Geneva Convention, Article 4(2) (d) and 13(2) Additional Protocol II, Article 51(2) Additional Protocol I. Article 51(2) of Additional Protocol I and 13(2) of the Additional Protocol II have been recognized as customary international law. See also Bianchi and Naqvi 2014, p. 593.

[272] Bothe 2002, p. 389.

4.6 Serious Violations of Common Article 3 Article 8(2) (i)–(iv)

In other for Article 8(2) (c) of the Rome Statute to be applicable to a conflict, conduct regarded as 'serious violations of Common Article 3' must have taken place. For a conflict to qualify as armed conflict under Article 3 common to the Geneva Conventions, it must have 'led to combat and the use of armed forces.'[273] It has also been established that an objective requirement relating to the intensity of the conduct of hostilities and the degree of organisation of the armed group must be met for the situation of an internal armed conflict. The Pre-Trial Chamber in the Bemba case found that an armed conflict not of an international character must reach 'a certain level of intensity exceeding that of internal disturbances and tensions, such as riots, sporadic acts of violence or any other acts of a similar nature.'[274] In the determination of intensity, the Trial Chamber of the ICTY) utilised criteria such as gravity and recurrence of attacks, number of victims, temporal and territorial spread of the attacks, the increase in the number of the government forces, whether the conflict led to a large displacement of people, whether parties operated from territories under their control, whether the UN Security Council specifically addressed the conflict, among other factors.[275] Regarding the terminology 'serious', Zimmermann and Greiß opine that since the crimes within the jurisdiction of the court are so-called serious 'crimes of concern to the international community as a whole' and that the threshold requirement relating to 'serious violations' are usually easily met by conduct violating Article 8(2) (c) (i)–(iv).[276] The provisions of Article 8(2) (c) of the Rome Statute are subject to the limitations in Article 8(2) (d),[277] and they protect 'persons taking no active part in the hostilities, including members of the armed forces who have laid down their arms and those placed *hors de combat* by sickness, wounds, detention or any other cause.'[278] The protected persons include civilians and those who may have been combatants, but for the stated reasons or any other cause, no longer possess combatant status.[279] The ICTY) in the Tadic case noted that the protection under Common Article 3 may also extend to persons covered by the grave breaches regime in an international armed conflict.[280]

[273] Zimmermann and Greiß 2016, p. 543.

[274] Prosecutor V. Bemba, Pre-Trial Chamber II, Decision Pursuant to Article 61(7) (a) and (b) of the Rome Statute on the Charges of the Prosecutor, 2009, para 225.

[275] See further discussions on these standards in Zimmermann and Greiß 2016, p. 544.

[276] Zimmermann and Greiß 2016, p. 546.

[277] Article 8(2) (c) of the Rome Statute applies to armed conflict not of an international character, to the exclusion of situations of internal disturbances and tensions such as riots, isolated and sporadic acts, of violence or other acts of a similar nature. Article 8(2) (d) Rome Statute of the International Criminal Court 2002.

[278] Article 8(2) (c) Rome Statute of the International Criminal Law 2002.

[279] Ibid. 290.

[280] Prosecutor v. Dusko Tadic, Judgement, Trial Chamber, 1997, para 615.

4.6.1 Violence to Life and Person

Article 8(2) (c) (i) of the Rome Statute addresses war crime of violence to life and person particularly murder, mutilation, cruel treatment and torture within the context of an internal armed conflict committed against persons taking no active part in hostilities, including members of the armed forces who have laid down their arms, and those placed *hors de combat* by sickness, wounds, detention or any other cause. This is based on the provisions of Common Article 3 of the Geneva Conventions. The list of crimes is non-exhaustive and this is evidenced by the use of the words 'in particular'.[281]

Acts of violence against life, such as killing of civilians and non-combatants in the conduct of the conflict is prohibited as murder in Article 8(2) (c) (i). Regarding the war crime of murder, the perpetrator in question must have 'killed one or more persons' not actively taking part in hostilities, with an awareness of the factual circumstances establishing the status and the existence of an armed conflict, and the conduct was committed in the context of and was associated with an armed conflict not of an international character.[282] The elements of murder as a crime against humanity and murder as a war crime are similar. However, the contexts are markedly distinct.[283] The Elements of Crimes extend the protection to include 'civilians, medical personnel, or religious personnel, (including non-confessional, non-combatant military personnel carrying out a similar function) taking no active part in the hostilities. Within the context of Article 8(2) (c) (i), murder refers to the intentional killing of one or more persons protected under the provisions without lawful justification. A causal link must be established between the conduct (or the omission) and the resulting death of the victim(s).[284] Circumstantial evidence, including factors such as pattern of mistreatment or disappearance of victims, general climate of lawlessness, including the length of time in which the alleged victim has not been in contact, may be sufficient to prove death.[285]

Mutilation is specifically mentioned in Article 8(2) (c) (i) as violence to life and person. The Elements of Crimes describe mutilation as the subjection of 'one or more persons to mutilation, in particular by permanently disfiguring the person or persons, or by permanently disabling or removing an organ or appendage.' The conduct in question 'was neither justified by the medical, dental or hospital treatment of the person or persons concerned nor carried out in such person's or persons' interests.'[286]

---

[281] Dörmann 2003, p. 394.

[282] Article 8(2) (c) (i)-1 Elements of Crimes, International Criminal Court 2011.

[283] The context of murder as a crime against humanity is the commission as part of a widespread of systematic commission of the attack against a civilian population. Other criteria for the requirement of crimes against humanity of murder have been discussed in the relevant section.

[284] Prosecutor v. Bemba, Pre-Trial Chamber II, Decision Pursuant to Article 61(7) (a) and (b) of the Rome Statute on the Charges of the Prosecutor, 2009, para 274.

[285] Prosecutor v. Krnojelac, Judgement, Trial Chamber II, 2002, para 327.

[286] Article 8(2) (c) (i)-2, Elements of Crimes, International Criminal Court 2011.

It is unnecessary that the act of mutilation neither cause death nor seriously endanger the physical or mental health of the victim.[287]

Cruel treatment as an act of violence to life and persons is similar to the notion of 'inhuman treatment' under the grave breaches provisions. The perpetrator in this regard must have 'inflicted severe physical or mental pain or suffering upon one or more persons.'[288] The determination of whether a conduct amounts to cruel treatment may be made on a case-by-case basis.[289] For cruel treatment, the perpetrator committed 'an intentional act or omission, that is an act which when judged objectively, is deliberate and not accidental, which causes serious mental or physical suffering or injury or constitutes a serious attack on human dignity.'[290]

In a non-international armed conflict, torture as a form of violence to life and person is also prohibited under Article 8(2) (c) (i). In the commission of torture, 'the perpetrator inflicted severe physical or mental pain or suffering upon one or more persons, for such purposes as: obtaining information or a confession, punishment, intimidation or coercion or for any reason based on discrimination of any kind.'[291] There are no material differences between the treatment of torture in the context of an international armed conflict and an internal armed conflict.[292] According to the ICTY) in Furundzija, the elements of torture in an armed conflict include; (i) the infliction by act or omission, of severe pain or suffering, whether physical or mental; in addition (ii) the act or omission must be intentional; (iii) aimed at obtaining information or a confession or at punishing, intimidating, humiliating or coercing the victim or a third person; on any ground, against the victim or a third person; (iv) linked to an armed conflict; (v) at least one of the persons involved in the torture process must be a public official or at any rate act in a non-private capacity.[293] For the requirement of official capacity, particularly with respect to non-international armed conflicts, the provisions can also be interpreted to include officials of non-state parties to a conflict.[294] Rape and other acts of sexual violence may also constitute torture within the context of an internal armed conflict under Article 8(2) (c) (i).[295]

For all acts of violence to life and persons, it is necessary that 'the perpetrator was aware of the factual circumstances that established the status, the conduct must have taken place in the context of and was associated with an armed conflict not

---

[287] Zimmermann and Greiß 2016, p. 551.

[288] Article 8(2) (c) (i)-3, Elements of Crimes, International Criminal Court 2011.

[289] Prosecutor v. Limaj, Judgement, Trial Chamber, 2005, para 232.

[290] Prosecutor v. Zejnil Delalic, Zdravko Mucic, Hazim Delic & Esad Landzo (Celebici case), 2001, para 552.

[291] Article 8(2) (c) (i)-4, Elements of Crimes, International Criminal Court 2011.

[292] Prosecutor v. Zejnil Delalic, Zdravko Mucic, Hazim Delic & Esad Landzo (Celebici case), 2001, para 443.

[293] Prosecutor v. Anto Furundzija, 1998, para 162.

[294] Prosecutor v. Zejnil Delalic, Zdravko Mucic, Hazim Delic & Esad Landzo (Celebici case) 2001, para 473.

[295] Prosecutor v. Akayesu ICTR-96-4-T, Judgment, Trial Chamber, 2 September 1998, para 597.

of an international character and the perpetrator must have been aware of factual circumstances that established the existence of an armed conflict.'

Within the context of the internal armed conflict in Nigeria, Boko Haram directly killed and caused the death of civilians, medical personnel, religious personnel and other persons not taking active part in the hostilities.[296] They also mutilated and inflicted severe physical pain and suffering[297] on civilians and persons taking no active part in hostilities. Within the context and with the requisite awareness of the relevant factual circumstances, a finding of a reasonable basis to believe that violence to life and persons have been committed is logical.

4.6.2 Outrages Upon Personal Dignity

Acts amounting to outrages upon personal dignity are prohibited in Article 8(2) (c) (ii) of the Rome Statute. It also criminalises particularly humiliating and degrading treatments. The elements of crime noted that the perpetrator must have 'humiliated, degraded or otherwise violated the dignity of one or more persons', including dead persons, and the humiliation, degradation or violation must have been of a severe degree as to be generally recognised as an outrage.[298] This decision will be made by an objective standard. Awareness by the victim of the humiliation or degradation is irrelevant and the cultural background of the victim may be taken into account in the determination of what constitutes humiliation and degradation. The conduct constituting outrages upon personal dignity must have taken place within the context of, or associated with an internal armed conflict. It must also be proven that the perpetrator had an awareness of the factual circumstances establishing the status of the victims and the existence of an internal armed conflict. The general mental element is governed by Article 30 of the Rome Statute with no requirement for a specific intent to humiliate. Rape was prosecuted in the Bemba case as outrages upon personal dignity.[299] The Trial Chamber of the Special Tribunal for Sierra Leone found, however, that acts of sexual violence are 'humiliating and degrading to victims, and constitute a serious attack on human dignity, falling within the scope of outrages upon personal dignity'.[300] Varying acts and conducts may be prosecuted as outrages upon personal dignity because the right protected may be understood broadly to include 'all rights inseparable from human existence, especially the rights to physical, moral and intellectual integrity'. Acts of sexual violence committed by Boko Haram

[296] See generally, United Nations General Assembly 2015.

[297] See United Nations Security Council Resolution 2349, 2017.

[298] Article 8(2) (c) (ii), Elements of Crimes, International Criminal Court 2011.

[299] The Pre-Trial Chamber in the case rejected the category of humiliating and degrading treatment. Although, all the requirements were met, in favour of the conduct being fully covered by the crime of rape. See Prosecutor v. Bemba, Pre-Trial Chamber II, Decision Pursuant to Article 61(7) (a) and (b) of the Rome Statute on the Charges of the Prosecutor, 2009, paras 310–312.

[300] Prosecutor v. Charles Taylor, Judgement, Trial Chamber II, 18 May 2012, para 432.

since the inception of the conflict are well documented. These acts may be prosecuted as acts amounting to outrages upon personal dignity based on the cultural and deeply religious climate of Northeast Nigeria where majority of the crimes were committed. The Prosecutor in the 2018 Preliminary Examination Report also found a reasonable basis to believe that Boko Haram committed war crimes of outrages upon personal dignity pursuant to Article 8(2) (c) (ii).[301]

4.6.3 *Hostage Taking*

Article 8(2) (c) (iii) of the Rome Statute prohibits taking any protected person hostage within the context of a non-international armed conflict. To fulfil the requirements of the war crime of taking hostage, the perpetrator seized, detained or otherwise held hostage one or more protected persons including dead persons, with a threat to kill, injure or continue to detain such persons.[302] The conduct must have been intended to compel certain concessions as a condition for the safety of the detainees. According to Werle and Jessberger, it is unnecessary that the conduct was against the will of the hostage. In addition to the provisions of Article 30 governing the mental elements, the Elements of Crimes also makes provision for a specific criterion of an intention 'to compel a State, an international organisation, a natural or legal person or a group of persons to act or refrain from acting as an explicit or implicit condition for the safety or the release of such person or persons.'[303] The prosecution in Kordic and Cerkez identified elements of the war crime of hostage taking to include; (i) the occurrence of the acts or omissions causing a person(s) to be seized, detained or otherwise held unlawfully as a hostage; (ii) the act or omission involved a threat to injure, kill or continue to detain such person in order to compel a state, military force, international organisation, natural person or groups of persons to act or refrain from acting, as an explicit or implicit condition for the safe release of the hostage; (iii) the act or omission was committed wilfully.[304]

Since the Boko Haram crisis started, the group has taken a record number of Nigerians hostage, infamously abducted girls in the 'Chibok and the Dapchi' Schoolgirls,[305] taken women and children hostage, including two aid workers who were subsequently executed.[306] The group utilised threats of harm against some of its hostages to negotiate for the release of its members from government custody. Among the abducted 113 Dapchi schoolgirls, 107 were released as a result of successful negotiations, five reportedly died during the abductions and the lone Christian girl

[301] Office of the Prosecutor Report on Preliminary Examination Activities 2018.

[302] Article 8(2) (c) (iii), Elements of Crimes, International Criminal Court 2011.

[303] Article 8(2) (c) (iii), Elements of Crimes, International Criminal Court 2011.

[304] Prosecutor v. Dario Kordic & Mario Cerkez, Prosecutor's Pre-Trial Brief, p. 48. See also Dörmann 2003, p. 407.

[305] See CNN 2016a, b.

[306] CNN 2018a, b, c, and CNN 2018a, b, c.

remain captive.[307] Majority of the Chibok girls captured in 2014 also remain captive four years after the infamous abduction. In an attack on Rann in Borno state on 1 March 2018, Boko Haram members, among other acts, abducted three female health workers, two working for the International Committee of the Red Cross (ICRC) and one for UNICEF. Both ICRC health workers were executed in September and October 2018. Within the context of the internal armed conflict, the taking of hostages of these protected persons, may be sufficient for a finding of hostage taking as war crime in an internal armed conflict contrary to the provisions of the Rome Statute.

4.7 Other Serious Violations of the Law and Customs in Armed Conflict Not of an International Character

Within the provisions of the Rome Statute, conducts amounting to other serious violations of the laws and customs of war are also prohibited alongside violations of Common Article 3 of the Geneva Conventions in an internal armed conflict. Serious violations of the laws and customs of war amount to crimes within the framework of international law and are prohibited both during an international armed conflict and an armed conflict not of an international character. These conducts are specifically prohibited in Article 8(2) (e) of the Rome Statute and subject to the limitations in Article 8(2) (f). During the Boko Haram crisis, prohibited conducts of interest under this category include: intentional attacks directed against civilian populations, attacks against installations and personnel using the distinctive emblem, attacks against United Nations and associated personnel, intentional attacks directed against cultural objects, places of worship and similar institutions, intentional attacks against humanitarian and protected personnel, pillaging, rape and other forms of sexual violence, conscripting and enlisting of children when committed within the context of an internal armed conflict.

4.7.1 Intentional Attacks Against Civilian Population

Attacks intentionally directed against a civilian population not taking direct part in hostilities are expressly prohibited in Article 8(2) (e) (i) of the Rome Statute. The perpetrator in question must have directed the attack at a civilian population or an individual civilian not taking direct part in hostilities, with an intention that the civilian population or such individual civilians be the object of the attacks.[308] The provision protects the civilian population as a whole, and individual civilians from attacks. It is unnecessary that the civilian population or the particular civilian in

[307] Office of the Prosecutor Report on Preliminary Examination Activities 2018.

[308] Article 8(2) (e) (i), Elements of Crimes, International Criminal Court 2011.

question be the only target of the attack.[309] The notion of civilians not taking direct part in hostilities was interpreted in line with the ICRC guideline[310] and the protection of a civilian may be lost when such civilian 'uses weapons or other means to commit violence against human or material enemy forces, unless in self-defense'.[311] The prohibited conduct must have taken place within the context of or associated with an internal armed conflict. The mental element is governed by Article 30 of the Rome Statute. The prohibition against intentional attack against civilian populations was interpreted to extend to non-international armed conflicts.[312] Within the Boko Haram crisis, the group has intentionally directed its attacks against civilian populations generally in Northeast Nigeria and individual civilians with guns, explosives and other weapons. Thousands of men, women and children not taking part in hostilities have been attacked, killed, or displaced by Boko Haram since 2009.[313] These attacks were committed within the context of an internal armed conflict as earlier addressed in this work.

4.7.2 Attacks Against Installation and Personnel Using the Distinctive Emblem

The Rome Statute in Article 8(2) (e) (ii) prohibits 'intentionally directing attacks against buildings, material, medical, units and transport, and personnel using the distinctive emblems of the Geneva Conventions in conformity with international law'. According to the elements of the crimes, the perpetrator must have attacked one or more persons or building and other protected objects and intended such persons, buildings or objects to be the recipient of the attacks.[314] A war crime under the statute is committed when the objects of the attack are protected and the distinctive emblem is used in accordance with international law.[315] Protection in this regard covers those authorised to bear the distinctive emblems under the Geneva Conventions including employees of aid organisations, and other personnel that may be identified by the emblems.

The prohibited conduct must have taken place within the context of or associated with an internal armed conflict and the perpetrator must be aware of the

309 Prosecutor V. Callixte Mbarushimana Decision on the Confirmation of Charges, Pre-Trial Chamber I, 2008, para 142.

310 ICRC Interpretative Guideline on the Notion of Direct Participation in Hostilities under International Humanitarian Law 2009, p. 27.

311 Prosecutor v. Germain Katanga and Mathieu Ngudjolo Chui, Decision on the Confirmation of Charges, Pre-Trial Chamber I, 2008, paras 272–273.

312 See Dörmann 2003, p. 445.

313 See generally for example, United Nations Security Council 2017, International Centre for Investigative Reporting 2019, Reuters 2014, and VOA 2014.

314 Article 8(2) (e) (ii), Elements of Crimes, International Criminal Court 2011.

315 Dörmann 2003, p. 451.

factual circumstances of the existence of such armed conflict. The mental element is governed by Article 30 of the Rome Statute. Since the conflict started, Boko Haram members attacked personnel of the International Committee of the Red Cross (ICRC) in an attack in Rann, killed at least three members of personnel and infamously abducted and subsequently killed two of its health workers in 2018.[316]

4.7.3 Attacks Against United Nations and Associated Personnel

Article 8(2) (e) (iii) prohibits intentionally directing attacks against persons and installations involved in humanitarian assistance or peacekeeping according to the UN Charter entitled to protection as civilians and civilian objects under international law. The attack in question must have been directed by the perpetrator with the intent of the object and an awareness of the factual circumstances establishing the protection subject to international law of armed conflict.[317] In the determination of what constitutes a peacekeeping mission without a specific legal basis in the UN Charter, the Pre-Trial Chamber I mentioned three characteristics: (i) consent of the parties, (ii) impartiality and (iii) the non-use of force except in self-defense.[318] The court found that there is no specific definition for what constitutes peacekeeping and 'UN peacekeeping has evolved to meet the demands of different conflicts and a changing political landscape'.[319] This reasoning was utilised in the Decision on the Confirmation of Charges in Nourain and Jamus.[320] The Court in the Garda case also found that 'installations, materials, units or vehicles involved in peacekeeping missions in the context of an armed conflict not of an international character shall not be considered military objectives.'[321] As long as installations for humanitarian assistants and peacekeeping missions have not been utilised for acts of hostility outside their normal functions, they shall be sufficiently protected under the statute.[322] Alongside the standard *mens rea* requirement in Article 30 of the Rome Statute, this conduct must be intentional, 'encompassing *dolus directus* in the first degree'.[323] In an attack in March 2018, Boko Haram repeatedly attacked and killed humanitarian workers and attacked UN

316 See generally, CNN 2018a, b, c, and BBC 2018. See also, IRIN 2018. Report on Preliminary Examination Activities 2018, 05 December 2018, Office of the Prosecutor, International Criminal Court, para 229.

317 Article 8(2) (e) (iii), Elements of Crimes, International Criminal Court 2011.

318 Prosecutor v. Bahar Idriss Abu Garda, Decision on the Confirmation of Charges (Public Redacted Version) Pre-Trial Chamber I, 2010, para 71.

319 Ibid., paras 69–70.

320 Prosecutor v. Abdallah Banda Abakaer Nourain and Saleh Mohammed Jerbo Jamus, Corrigendum of the Decision on the Confirmation of Charges (Public Redacted Version) Pre-Trial Chamber I, 2011, para 61.

321 Ibid. 853, para 89.

322 Dörmann 2003, p. 457.

323 Zimmermann and Greiß 2016, p. 560.

aid convoys.[324] Additionally, public executions of captured humanitarian workers have since been staged periodically throughout the crisis, most notably in 2019[325] and 2020. These attacks committed within the context or associated with the internal armed conflict have the potential of meeting the requirements as war crimes under the Statute.

4.7.4 Attacks Against Protected Objects

Article 8(2) (e) (iv) of the Rome Statute provides protection for buildings dedicated to religion, education, arts, science or charitable purposes, historic monuments and hospitals so long as that they are not military objectives within the context or associated with an internal armed conflict. The attacks in question must have been directed by the perpetrator, with an intention that the protected buildings be the object of the attack. An awareness of the factual circumstances establishing the armed conflict is also crucial.[326] The mental element of this war crime is governed by Article 30 of the Rome Statute. Article 16 of the Additional Protocol II also protects cultural objects and places of worship within the context of an internal armed conflict.[327] Cultural properties, religious objects and objects dedicated to education and science and other protected objects retain their protection provided that they are not military objectives.[328]

At the inception of the Boko Haram crisis, attacks against religious buildings such as churches and so-called moderate mosques were a common feature of the crisis. At this point, it was not yet clear that there was in existence an internal armed conflict. As the crisis progressed and reached its first peak in 2014, the status of an internal armed conflict became clearer and the focus of the group on schools, hospitals and religious buildings also exponentially increased. Educational buildings were attacked for a number of reasons including for the recruitment or execution of boys, abduction of girls and to further the group's ideology against western education and civilisation.[329] Hospitals and clinics were attacked to facilitate the abduction of medical personnel and obtain critically required medication for the group and churches and mosques were attacked to create a climate of terror and force the Boko Haram sanctioned version of Islam on the populace.[330] According to a report, social infrastructure in

---

324 See generally UNOCHA 2017, UN News 2017, and Reuters 2018.

325 Aljazeera 2019.

326 Article 8(2) (e) (iv), Elements of Crimes, International Criminal Court 2011.

327 International Committee of the Red Cross (ICRC), Protocol Additional to the Geneva Conventions of 12 August 1949, and relating to the Protection of Victims of Non-International Armed Conflicts (Protocol II), 1977.

328 Dörmann 2003, p. 462.

329 See generally for example, Reuters 2014, Human Rights Watch 2016, and Global Coalition to Protect Education from Attack 2018.

330 See for example, Premium Times 2017.

most villages recaptured by the Nigerian military was completely destroyed. Attacks by improvised explosive devices, suicide bombs attacks and shooting attacks on churches and mosques was also rife.[331] These attacks were committed within the context of or connected with the internal armed conflict in Northeast Nigeria contrary to the Rome Statute.

4.7.5 Pillaging

The war crime of pillaging within the context of or associated with an armed conflict of an internal character is prohibited by Article 8(2) (c) (v) of the Rome Statute. Pillaging is expressly prohibited even when the town or village in question was taken by force. To fulfil the requirements of the war crime of pillaging, the perpetrator must have appropriated the property for private and personal use, with an intention to deprive the owner of it. The conduct must have taken place without the consent of the owner and within the context of an internal armed conflict.[332] The Elements of Crimes notes that appropriation justified by military necessity cannot fulfil the requirement of the war crime of pillaging. The mental element is governed by Article 30 of the Rome Statute. According to the Bemba decision, pillaging within its definition in an internal armed conflict 'entails a somewhat large-scale appropriation of all types of property, such as public or private, movable or immovable property, which goes beyond mere sporadic acts of violation of property rights.'[333] It is prohibited when committed against 'persons taking no direct part in hostilities or who have ceased to take part in hostilities, whether or not their liberty has been restricted'.[334] The seriousness of the particular violation must be examined on a case-by-case basis.[335] The Special Court for Sierra Leone noted that 'both organized or systematic appropriation and isolated acts of individuals' are covered by the prohibition of pillaging.[336] Additionally, according to the jurisprudence of the ICC, ICTY) and the SCSL, there seems to be a consensus that private and publicly owned properties are protected against the crime of pillaging.[337]

Characterising major Boko Haram attacks was systematic appropriation and looting of properties.[338] In its attacks, a pattern of killings, looting and arson

[331] Human Rights Council 2015, p. 10.

[332] Article 8(2) (e) (v), Elements of Crimes, International Criminal Court 2011.

[333] Prosecutor v. Jean Pierre Bemba, Pre-Trial Chamber II, Decision Pursuant to Article 61(7) (a) and (b) of the Rome Statute on the Charges of the Prosecutor, 2009, para 317.

[334] Article 4(2) (g), Protocol Additional to the Geneva Conventions of 12 August 1949 and Relating to the Protection of Victims of Non-International Armed Conflicts (Additional Protocol II).

[335] Zimmermann and Greiß 2016, p. 561.

[336] Prosecutor v. Charles Taylor, Judgement, Trial Chamber II, 2012, para 453.

[337] See generally, Prosecutor v. Jean Pierre Bemba, ICC (PTC) 2009, para 319. Prosecutor v. Kordic and Cerkez, ICTY (AC), 2004, para 79. Prosecutor v. Aliu Fofana and Kondewa, 2007, para 159.

[338] Human Rights Council 2015, p. 11.

emerged.[339] The pattern of looting was not limited to private homes alone, public institutions such as banks were also systematically looted including shops and markets. A report by the Financial Action Task Force details methods of fundraising by Boko Haram and other ISIL affiliates in West Africa. This is done through extortion, robbing and looting banks, businesses, cattle rustling and other sophisticated forms of cross-border organised crime.[340] These systematic looting and pillaging were carried out with an intention to permanently deprive the owners of their properties, without their consent and to be utilised for the purposes of Boko Haram.

4.7.6 *Rape and Other Forms of Sexual Violence*

Rape, sexual slavery, enforced prostitution among other conducts are specifically prohibited in Article 8(2) (c) (vi) of the Rome Statute as acts of sexual violence. The invasion, by a member of any gender, of the body of a victim resulting in penetration, however slight, by force, threat of force or coercion or against a person incapable of giving consent constitutes rape.[341] Regarding sexual slavery, the exercise of powers of ownership over a person or persons 'such as by purchasing, selling, lending or bartering such a person or persons, or by imposing on them a similar deprivation of liberty' is prohibited.[342] The perpetrator must have also caused the victim to engage in acts of a sexual nature. The war crime of sexual violence includes the commission of acts of a sexual nature against one or more persons, in an environment of coercion or against persons incapable of giving consent.[343] The acts in question must be comparable in gravity to conduct constituting serious violations of Common Article 3. All prohibited conducts relating to sexual violence must have been committed in the context of or associated with the armed conflict of an internal character. The perpetrator in question must have been aware of the factual circumstances establishing the existence of the armed conflict. There is in existence a clear prohibition of rape and other forms of sexual assault under international humanitarian law.[344] The treatment of rape and sexual violence as other serious violations of the law and customs of internal armed conflict is similar in nature to their treatments as serious violations of Common Article 3. The wording of para 4.2(e) (vi) may also be interpreted to suggest that all the specific acts listed in the provision constitute serious violations of Common Article 3.[345] The egregious acts of sexual violence committed by Boko Haram are well documented and they are an integral part of the strategy

339 See generally, Amnesty International 2015a, b, p. 40.

340 See generally, FATF 2016.

341 Article 8(2) (e) (vi)-1, Elements of Crimes, International Criminal Court 2011.

342 Article 8(2) (e) (vi)-2, Elements of Crimes, International Criminal Court 2011.

343 Article 8(2) (e) (vi)-6, Elements of Crimes, International Criminal Court 2011.

344 See Dörmann 2003, p. 469.

345 Zimmermann and Greiß 2016, p. 562.

of Boko Haram.[346] The prohibited conducts were committed within the context of or associated with the internal armed conflict in Northeast Nigeria contrary to the Rome Statute.

4.7.7 Using, Conscripting and Enlisting of Children

Article 8(2) (c) (vii) of the Rome Statute prohibits the use, conscripting or enlisting of children under the age of fifteen to participate in armed forces or groups or armed hostilities. To constitute a crime, the perpetrator must have conscripted or enlisted one or more persons under the age of fifteen years or used one or more of such persons to participate actively in hostilities. Voluntary participation of a child in active hostilities is also prohibited and the consent of the child cannot be raised as a valid defence. The perpetrator in question knew or should have known the age of the child.[347] An awareness of the factual circumstances establishing the armed conflict is essential and the conduct in question must have been carried out in the context of and associated with an internal armed conflict. The mental element is governed by Article 30 of the Rome Statute. The prohibition of conscripting or enlisting of children within the pendency of an internal armed conflict extends to all armed groups or armed forces.[348] What constitutes a group within the provision of Article 8(2) (c) (vii) is limited to armed groups possessing a level of organisation. The group must be under a responsible command, with a degree of organisation to enable the planning and carrying out of concerted military operations and the imposition of discipline within the group.[349] The notion of 'active participation in hostilities' may be interpreted widely to include, not only front-line activities, but also utilising children for supporting roles.[350] This may include any activities as long as there is a link to armed combat operations.

Boko Haram recruited, conscripted and used children in the conduct of hostilities in North-eastern Nigeria. According to a UN Secretary General's Report, between 2013 and 2015, 'incidents of child recruitment and use, abductions and sexual violence increased and Boko Haram continued to be the main perpetrator of grave violations.'[351] The 2017 Report estimated that 'at least 8,000 children have been recruited and used by Boko Haram since 2009 including children as young as four years old.' According to the Report, 'Children were used in direct hostilities, for

[346] See generally, Report of the United Nations Secretary General on Conflict Related Sexual Violence 2018.

[347] Article 8(2) (e) (vii), Elements of Crimes, International Criminal Court 2011.

[348] Zimmermann and Greiß 2016, p. 562.

[349] Prosecutor v. Alex Tamba Brima, Brima Bazzy Kamara & Santigie Borbor Kanu, Judgment, 2007, para 738.

[350] Zimmermann and Greiß 2016, pp. 564–565. See generally Zimmermann and Greiß's convincing argument. See also Prosecutor v. Lubanga Dyilo, Judgment Pursuant to Article 74 of the Statute, Trial Chamber I, 2012, para 627.

[351] United Nations Security Council 2017, p. 6.

planting improvised explosive devices and burning schools and houses and in support roles such as cooks, messengers and lookouts. Children were also reportedly used as human shields to protect Boko Haram elements during military operations. Many children were also subjected to forceful religious conversions and forced marriage and used for sexual purposes. According to the Security Council, predominately from mid-2014 to 2017, children, including girls as young as 10, were used by Boko Haram in suicide bombings.'[352] The use, conscripting or enlistment of children under the age of fifteen by Boko Haram within the context of and associated with the internal armed conflict in North-eastern Nigeria, is a war crime within the contemplation of the Rome Statute.

4.8 The Need for Accountability

The Office of the Prosecutor addressed the Boko Haram crisis in its 2012 Preliminary Examination Report highlighting alleged conduct amounting to war crimes and crimes against humanity by the group. The investigation was advanced to phase 3, for an assessment of admissibility according to Article 17 of the Statute.[353] In its 2013 report, the office detailed its examination of jurisdictional issues, including a determination on the existence of a non-international armed conflict, and whether Boko Haram met the requirement as an armed group under the statute among other criteria. It was concluded that Boko Haram fulfil the requirements as an armed group with the capability of planning and carrying out sustained military activities in the estimation of the prosecutor.[354] In 2015, the Office of the Prosecutor concluded its subject-matter assessment and identified six potential cases for conducts amounting to war crimes and crimes against humanity by Boko Haram.[355] In the 2018 Report, the office noted concerning domestic processes in Nigeria that majority of the proceedings were 'unrelated' to the potential cases before the ICC, and that only a few cases prosecuted in Nigeria against low-level Boko Haram members may be related to potential cases by the OTP.[356] At the conclusion of the preliminary examination in 2020, the prosecutor in a statement noted that 'my Office has concluded that there is a reasonable basis to believe that members of Boko Haram and its splinter groups have committed the following acts constituting crimes against humanity and war crimes: murder; rape, sexual slavery, including forced pregnancy and forced marriage; enslavement; torture; cruel treatment; outrages upon personal dignity; taking of hostages; intentionally directing attacks against the civilian population or against individual civilians not taking direct part in hostilities; intentionally directing attacks against personnel,

[352] United Nations Security Council 2017, p. 7.

[353] Office of the Prosecutor, Report on Preliminary Examination Activities 2012.

[354] Office of the Prosecutor, Report of Preliminary Examination Activities 2013.

[355] Office of the Prosecutor, Report on Preliminary Examination Activities 2015.

[356] Office of the Prosecutor, Report on Preliminary Examination Activities 2018.

installations, material, units or vehicles involved in a humanitarian assistance; intentionally directing attacks against buildings dedicated to education and to places of worship and similar institutions; conscripting and enlisting children under the age of fifteen years into armed groups and using them to participate actively in hostilities; persecution on gender and religious grounds; and other inhumane acts.'[357]

It is clear that specific conducts amounting to international crimes under the Rome Statute were committed by Boko Haram in Nigeria. There is clarity that the court possesses temporal, material, territorial and personal jurisdiction regarding the prohibited conducts amounting to war crimes and crimes against humanity. It is also sufficiently clear that, based on the requirements of complementarity and gravity according to the provisions of Article 17, Boko Haram related cases could be potentially admissible before the ICC.

The exercise of the *pro prio motu* powers of the prosecutor for the selection of situations to investigate is discretionary.[358] The prosecutor is not obligated to prosecute all allegations of serious and potential crimes falling within its jurisdiction, but rather to select the so-called representative cases amounting to the gravest crimes.[359] The discretion in choosing cases among serious crimes that may have been committed is also mostly unregulated and rest on the Office of the Prosecutor.[360] A 2016 policy paper of the Office of the Prosecutor addresses the Office's practice of case selection and prioritisation.[361] Alongside the consideration of the legal criteria of jurisdiction, admissibility and interests of justice, the Prosecutor also considers the gravity of the crime(s), the degree of responsibility of the alleged perpetrators and the inherent charges as a representative sample of the main types of crimes committed. Additionally, crimes that have been under-prosecuted such as sexual or gender-based crimes, crimes affecting children, rape, crimes against cultural, religious, historical and protected objects including crimes against humanitarian and peacekeeping personnel may receive particular attention.[362] In other to meet the requirement for effective investigation and prosecution of crimes as provided for in Article 54(1)(b), the prosecutor may consider (i) a comparative assessment across the selected cases; (ii) whether the accused has been subject to investigation or prosecution by the office or by a state for another serious crime; (iii) the potential impact of investigation and prosecutions on victims and affected communities; (iv) whether ICC's investigation has the potential of affecting ongoing criminality or may contribute to the prevention of crimes; and (v) whether the office of the prosecutor is able to pursue

[357] Statement of the Prosecutor, Fatou Bensouda, on the Conclusion of the Preliminary Examination of the Situation in Nigeria 2020.

[358] The word 'may' is used in Article 13 regarding the exercise of jurisdiction and Article 15 relating to *proprio motu* initiation of investigations by the prosecutor. See also Schabas in Cassese (Ed.) 2012, pp. 256–257. Schabas 2008a, b, p. 753.

[359] Aptel 2012, p. 1359.

[360] See Regulation 29 Regulations of the Office of the Prosecutor International Criminal Court.

[361] Office of the Prosecutor Policy Paper on Case Selection and Prioritization 2016.

[362] Office of the Prosecutor Policy Paper on Case Selection and Prioritization 2016, p. 15.

cases involving opposing parties to a conflict in whichever form.[363] In the selection of factual allegations to make up the charges, illustrative and representative events may be designated to the exclusion of the majority of other similarly serious allegations.[364] Additionally, the decision relating to the legal characterisation of conduct, which may fulfil the requirement either as war crimes and crimes against humanity or one conduct fulfilling the requirements as different types of either war crime or crime against humanity, may also be largely discretionary.[365] The Prosecutor is not obliged to take the interest of the victims into account in its selection of situations and cases with the exception of circumstances when the personal interests of the victim have been affected subject to the provisions of Article 68(3) of the Statute.[366]

Due to the nature of international criminal justice and the fact that the consent of states parties is required for the successful investigation and prosecution of cases before the court, non-legal and political considerations may also play into the prosecutor's decision in the selection of situations and cases including playing into the consideration of the interests of justice criterion or for general selection.[367] With the prosecutor acting as a 'gatekeeper' for the ICC and the notion of international criminal justice, such determinations become extremely crucial.[368] Although, the Office of the Prosecutor does not acknowledge the influence of non-legal considerations in its selection of situations and cases, the statutory criteria lacks sufficient clarity.[369]

The interests of the prosecutor in the Boko Haram crisis may be inferred with the progress of the preliminary examination up to the latest identification of specific potential cases. However, it must be noted that major suspected perpetrators of the egregious crimes within the jurisdiction of the Court have not been captured by the Nigerian authorities and hostilities are still engaged as at the time of writing. Regarding cases that have been instituted, most relate to conduct that are not within the purview of the Rome Statute and it is doubtful that any of them address acts of sexual and/or gender based violence of Boko Haram in any form.[370] It is important to note that there are laws, protocols and treaty obligations that protect from sexual

---

[363] Office of the Prosecutor Policy Paper on Case Selection and Prioritization 2016, p. 16.

[364] Aptel 2012, p. 1362.

[365] For example, the choice between a charge under Article 8(2) (c) (ii) and Article 8(2) (e) (vi) of the Rome Statute of the International Criminal Court 2002.

[366] See Situation in the Republic of Congo, Public Redacted Version Decision on the Applications for Participation in the Proceedings of VPRS 1, VPRS 2, VPRS 3, VPRS 4, VPRS 5 and VPRS 6, Pre-Trial Chamber I, 2006, paras 23–76.

[367] Further on political considerations, see generally, Davis 2015. See also in this regard the controversial decision in Situation in the Islamic Republic of Afghanistan, Decision Pursuant to Article 15 of the Rome Statute on the Authorization of an Investigation into the Situation in the Islamic Republic of Afghanistan. ICC-02/17, 2019.

[368] Olasolo 2003, p. 89, See also Schabas 2009, pp. 542–549.

[369] See Davis 2015, pp. 174–175.

[370] See generally Council on Foreign Relations 2018. See also the report of concluded Boko Haram related cases.

and gender-based violence including available means and mechanisms for the prosecution of violators.[371] However, sexual and gender-based crimes, including crimes involving children, have not been prioritised in Nigeria for effective prosecution. The role of the Court in the Boko Haram crisis is also symbolic due to the fact that should cases be instituted, crimes that may amount to terrorism will be subject to the jurisdiction of the Court as war crimes and crimes against humanity.[372] Going forward, whether the prosecutor makes a choice to take decisive action regarding senior members of Boko Haram connected to the identified cases, or whether the Pre-Trial Chamber allows full investigations or not, challenges are inherent. For example, should the court decide to issue arrest warrants, unintentional consequences may include the inability of the crisis to be potentially resolved by negotiations. This is crucial because the Nigerian government has shown in many instances that it is open to a negotiated settlement with Boko Haram and this may be truncated by issuance of ICC arrest warrants.[373] Other challenges might include the major problems with potentially executing such warrants.[374] Regardless of the inherent challenges, a decision to indict by the ICC has the potential of representing zero tolerance for impunity by the international community and sending a strong message that conducts constituting crimes that threaten the peace, security and well-being of the world will not be ignored. While a decision on interests of justice has not been made, prosecuting Boko Haram related cases may ultimately be in the interest of justice in other to prevent identified impunity gaps especially for sexual and gender-based crimes and crimes affecting children unaddressed by the Nigerian legal system.

References

Aljazeera Centre for Studies Report (2018) 'Anatomy of Boko Haram: The Rise and Decline of a Violent Group in Nigeria' 22 April 2018 available at http://studies.aljazeera.net/en/reports/2018/04/anatomy-boko-haram-rise-decline-violent-group-nigeria-180422110920231.html#e2.

Aljazeera (2019) 'Nigeria: Abducted Aid Worker Killed by ISIL Affiliate' 25 September 2019. Available at https://www.aljazeera.com/news/2019/09/nigeria-aid-worker-abducted-isil-affiliate-july-executed-190925144357367.html.

[371] Nigeria has ratified the Convention on the Elimination of all forms of Discrimination against Women in 1979 (CEDAW); the Protocol to the African Charter on Human and Peoples' Rights on the Rights of Women in Africa (Maputo Protocol) 2003; has enacted the Child Rights Act, a Violence against Persons' (Prohibition) Act (VAPP) 2015; and also created a National Action Plan (2017–2020) for the Implementation of UNSCR 1325 and related Resolutions for the protection against sexual and gender based violence. Regardless of all these measures, real- time practical protection against sexual and gender-based violence is almost non-existent.

[372] On the utilisation of the ICC to respond to terrorism, see generally, Arnold 2004.

[373] Part of the criticism for the ICC issuance of arrest warrant for LRA commanders in the Ugandan situation was that it supposedly contributed to close the door to negotiation and peaceful resolution. See generally, Apuuli 2006, and Kriksciun 2007. Similar criticisms were also raised concerning the Omar Al Bashir arrest warrant and arrest warrants issued in for Abdullah Al-Senusi in the Libyan situation.

[374] See generally, Banteka 2016, and Dtubak 2012.

Ambos K (2000) 'Individual Criminal Responsibility in International Criminal Law-From Nuremberg to the Hague' In MacDonald G. K. (Ed), Substantive and procedural aspects of international criminal Law. The experience of international and national courts, (2000), Vol. 1, Commentary. Nijhoff, The Hague.

Amnesty International (2005) 'Open Letter to the Chief Prosecutor of the International Criminal Court on the Concept of Interests of Justice' 17 June 2005 AI Index: IOR 40/023/2005. Available at https://www.amnesty.org/download/Documents/84000/ior400232005en.pdf.

Amnesty International (2015a) 'Nigeria: Satellite Image Show Horrific Scale of Boko Haram Attack on Baga' 15 January 2015. Available at https://www.amnesty.org/en/latest/news/2015/01/nigeria-satellite-images-show-horrific-scale-boko-haram-attack-baga/.

Amnesty International (2015b) '"Our Job is to Shoot, Slaughter and Kill": Boko Haram's Reign of Terror in Northeast Nigeria' April 2015. Available at https://www.amnesty.be/IMG/pdf/nigeria_full_report_webv3.pdf.

Amnesty International Report (2018) 'Willingly Unable: ICC Preliminary Examinations and Nigeria's Failure to Address Impunity for International Crimes' AFR 44/9481/2018. Available at https://www.amnesty.org/download/Documents/AFR4494812018ENGLISH.PDF.

Aptel C (2012) 'Prosecutorial Discretion at the ICC and Victims' Right to Remedy: Narrowing the Impunity Gap' Journal of International Criminal Justice.

Apuuli K (2006) 'ICC Arrest Warrants for the Lords' Resistance Army Leaders and Peace Prospects for Northern Uganda', 4, Journal of International Criminal Justice.

Arnold R (2004) The ICC as a New Instrument for Repressing Terrorism, Transnational Publishers.

Assanvo W, Abatan J and Sawadago W (2016) 'Assessing the Multinational Joint Task Force against Boko Haram', 19, Institute for Security Studies West Africa Report, September 2016.

Banteka N (2016) 'Mind the Gap: A Systematic Approach to the International Criminal Court's Arrest Warrant Enforcement Problem', 49, Cornell International Law Journal.

BBC (2011) 'Abuja Attack: Car Bomb Hits Nigeria's U.N. Building' 27 August 2011. Available at https://www.bbc.com/news/world-africa-14677957.

BBC (2014) 'Boko Haram 'to Sell' Nigerian Girls Abducted from Chibok' 05 May 2014. Available at https://www.bbc.com/news/world-africa-27283383.

BBC (2015) '"Boko Haram" Kills Dozen in Raid on Nigerian Village' 06 March 2015. Available at https://www.bbc.com/news/world-africa-31757272.

BBC (2018) 'Boko Haram Faction Kills Second Aid Worker in Nigeria' 16 October 2018. Available at https://www.bbc.com/news/world-africa-45871361.

Benzing M (2003) 'The Complementarity Regime of the International Criminal Court: International Criminal Justice Between State Sovereignty and the Fight against Impunity', 7, Max Planck Yearbook of United Nations Law.

Bergsmo M (1998) 'The Jurisdictional Regime of the International Criminal Court (Part II Articles 11–19)', 6, European Journal of Crime, Criminal Law and Criminal Justice.

Bianchi A, Naqvi Y (2014) 'Terrorism'. In: Clapham A, Gaeta P (eds). The Oxford Handbook of International Law in Armed Conflict. Oxford University Press.

Boister N (2012) An Introduction to Transnational Criminal Law, 2nd edn. Oxford University Press.

Botha A, Ewi M et al. (2017) 'Understanding Nigerian Citizens' Perspectives on Boko Haram' Institute for Security Studies Monograph.

Bothe M (2002) 'War Crimes'. In: Cassese A, Gaeta P, Jones J (eds). The Rome Statute of the International Criminal Court: A Commentary.

Bourgon S (2002) Jurisdiction Ratione Temporis. In: Cassese A et al. (eds) The Rome Statute of the International Criminal Court: A Commentary. Oxford University Press.

Brighton C (2012) 'Avoiding Unwillingness: Addressing the Political Pitfalls Inherent in the Complementarity Regime of the International Criminal Court', 12 International Criminal Law Review.

Burke-White W (2008) 'Proactive Complementarity: The International Criminal Court and National Courts in the Rome System of International Justice', 19, (1), Harvard International Law Journal.

Byers M (2002) 'Terrorism, the Use of Force and International Law after 11 September', 51, International and Comparative Law Quarterly.

Cassese A (ed) (2012) Realizing Utopia: The Future of International Law. Oxford University Press.

Cassese A, Acquaviva G, Fan M, Whiting A (2011) International Criminal Law: Cases and Commentary, Oxford University Press.

Cassese A (2002) The Rome Statute of the International Criminal Court: A Commentary. Oxford University Press.

Clapham A, Gaeta P (eds) (2014) Oxford Handbook on International Law in Hand Conflict Oxford University Press.

Clark R (2010) 'Negotiating provisions defining the crime of aggression, its elements and conditions for ICC exercise of jurisdiction over it', 20(4), The European Journal of International Law.

Clarke T (2005) 'The Prosecutor of International Criminal Court, Amnesties and the Interests of Justice: Striking a Delicate Balance', 4 Washington University Global Studies Law Review.

CNN (2016a) 'Nigeria's Missing Girls: A Glimpse of the Stolen' 14 April 2016. Available at https://edition.cnn.com/2016/04/13/africa/chibok-girls-new-proof-of-life-video/index.html.

CNN (2016b) 'Kidnapped to Kill: How Boko Haram is Turning Girls into Weapons' 13 April 2016. Available at https://edition.cnn.com/2016/04/12/africa/cameroon-boko-haram-child-bombers/index.html.

CNN (2018a) 'Kidnapped International Red Cross Aid Worker Killed in Nigeria' 17 September 2018. Available at https://edition.cnn.com/2018/09/17/africa/nigerian-female-aid-worker-killed/index.html.

CNN (2018b) 'Second Aid Worker Held by Boko Haram Executed as Negotiation Deadline Expires' 16 October 2018. Available at https://edition.cnn.com/2018/10/16/africa/second-nigerian-aid-worker-killed-intl/index.html.

CNN (2018c) 'Boko Haram Fast Facts' 19 October, 2018 available at https://edition.cnn.com/2014/06/09/world/boko-haram-fast-facts/index.html

Council of Foreign Relations (2018) 'Boko Haram's Violence against Women and Girls Demand Justice' 11 May 2018 available at https://www.cfr.org/blog/boko-harams-violence-against-women-and-girls-demands-justice?sp_mid=56596864&sp_rid=c3I0MTJAY2FhLmNvbHVtYmlhLmVkdQS2

Cryer R, Friman H, Robinson D, and Wilmshurst E (2014) An Introduction to International Criminal Law and Procedure, Cambridge University Press.

Daily Post (2014) 'Scores Flee Garkida as Boko Haram Sends Threat Letter' 3 August 2014, available at http://dailypost.ng/2014/08/03/scores-flee-garkida-boko-haram-sends-threat-letter/.

Daily Trust (2018) 'Remove Discharged 475 Boko Haram Suspects from Military Facilities, Rights Commission tells FG' 5 March 2018. Available at https://www.dailytrust.com.ng/remove-discharged-475-boko-haram-suspects-from-military-facilities-rights-commission-tells-fg.html.

Dalpe V (2017) 'On the Difficult Case for a Functional Interpretation of the Unwillingness Criterion before the International Criminal Court', 13 (2), Journal of International Law and International Relations.

Dancy G and Montal F (2017) 'Unintended Positive Complementarity: Why International Criminal Court Investigations May Increase Domestic Human Rights Prosecutions', The American Journal of International Law.

Davis C (2015) 'Political Considerations in Prosecutorial Discretions at the International Criminal Court', 15 International Criminal Law Review.

DeGuzman M (2000) 'The Road from Rome: The Developing Law of Crimes Against Humanity', 22 Human Rights Quarterly.

DeGuzman M (2009) 'Gravity and the Legitimacy of the International Criminal Court', 32, Fordham International Law Journal.

DeGuzman M (2012) 'How serious are International Crimes-The Gravity Problem in International Criminal Law', 51 Columbia Journal of Transnational Law.

Deutsche Welle (2017) 'Trial of Boko Haram Suspects pose Legal Nightmare' 09 October 2017 available at https://www.dw.com/en/trial-of-boko-haram-suspects-in-nigeria-poses-legal-nightmare/a-40867730
Dörmann K (2003) Elements of War Crimes under the Rome Statute of the International Criminal Court: Sources and Commentary, Cambridge University Press.
Dtubak A (2012) 'Problems Surrounding Arrest Warrants Issued by the International Criminal Court: A Decade of Judicial Practice', 32 Polish Yearbook of International Law.
El-Zeidy M (2008) Principle of Complementarity in International Law: Origin, Development and Practice, Martinus Nijhoff Publishers.
El Zeidy M (2008) 'The Gravity Threshold Under the Statute of the International Criminal Court', 19 Criminal Law Forum.
FATF (2016) 'Terrorism Financing in West and Central Africa', October 2016. Available at https://www.fatf-gafi.org/media/fatf/documents/reports/Terrorist-Financing-West-Central-Africa.pdf.
Fry E (2015) 'International Crimes and Case Demarcation: What are we trying to prove?' 27 Florida Journal of International Law.
Ganor B (2002) 'Defining Terrorism: Is One Man's Terrorist another Man's Freedom Fighter?' Police Practice and Research.
Gasser H (1986) 'Prohibition of Terrorist Acts in International Humanitarian Law', International Review of the Red Cross.
Globe and Mail (2018) 'Nigeria's Modern Slave Raiders' 02 March 2018. Available at https://www.theglobeandmail.com/opinion/nigerias-modern-slave-raiders/article38179797/.
Goldstone R, Fritz N (2000) 'In the Interest of Justice and Independent Referral: The ICC Prosecutor's Unprecedented Powers', 13 Leiden Journal of International Law.
Guardian (2015) 'Boko Haram Massacre: I Walked through Five Villages and Each One Was Empty Except for Dead Bodies' 14 January 2015. Available at https://www.theguardian.com/world/2015/jan/14/boko-haram-deadliest-attack-baga-nigeria-politics-insurgency.
Guardian (2017) 'Secret Trial of Thousands of Boko Haram Suspects to start in Nigeria' 09 October 2017 available at https://www.theguardian.com/world/2017/oct/09/nigeria-begin-secret-trials-thousands-boko-haram-suspects.
Guillaume G (2004) 'Terrorism and International Law', International and Comparative Law Quarterly.
Greenawalt A (2009) 'Complementarity in Crisis: Uganda, Alternative Justice, and the International Criminal Court', 50, Virginia Journal of International Law.
Greenwood C (1989) 'Terrorism and Humanitarian Law-The Debate over Additional Protocol I', 19, Israel Yearbook of Human Rights.
Greppi E (1999) 'The Evolution of Individual Criminal Responsibility Under International Criminal Law', Revue Internationale de la croix Rouge/International Review of the Red Cross.
Heller J (2006) 'The Shadow Side of Complementarity: The Effect of Article 17 of the Rome Statute on National Due Process', 17, Criminal Law Forum.
Human Rights Council (2015) Report of the United Nations High Commissioner for Human Rights on violations and abuses committed by Boko Haram and the impact on human rights in the affected countries. 29 September 2015 A/HRC/30/67.
Human Rights Watch Policy Paper (2005) 'The Meaning of "the Interests of Justice" in Article 53 of the Rome Statute' 1 June 2005. Available at https://www.hrw.org/news/2005/06/01/meaning-interests-justice-article-53-rome-statute.
Human Rights Watch (2005b) 'Rest in Pieces: Police Torture and Deaths in Custody in Nigeria' 27 July 2005. Available at https://www.hrw.org/report/2005/07/27/rest-pieces/police-torture-and-deaths-custody-nigeria.
Human Rights Watch (2016) 'They Set Classrooms on Fire: Attacks on Education in Northeast Nigeria' April 2016. Available at https://www.hrw.org/sites/default/files/report_pdf/nigeria0416web.pdf.

Human Rights Watch (2018) 'Nigeria: Flawed Trials of Boko Haram Suspects: Ensure Due Process, Victim Participation' 17 September 2018. Available at https://www.hrw.org/news/2018/09/17/nigeria-flawed-trials-boko-haram-suspects

Ibanga M, Archibong J (2018) The Boko Haram Insurgency: Characterisation and Implications under Municipal and International Laws. In: Iyi J, Strydom H (eds) Boko Haram and International Law. Springer.

International Centre for Investigative Reporting (2019) 'Thousands of Civilians Paying Heavy Price over Boko Haram Attacks' 04 February 2019. Available at https://www.icirnigeria.org/thousands-of-civilians-paying-heavy-price-over-boko-haram-attacks-icrc/

International Criminal Court Office of the Prosecutor (2016) Policy Paper on Case Selection and Prioritization, 15 September 2016. Available at https://www.icc-cpi.int/itemsdocuments/20160915_otp-policy_case-selection_eng.pdf.

IRIN (2018) Aid Under Attack, 19 October 2018. Available at https://www.irinnews.org/news/2018/10/19/boko-haram-humanitarian-access-aid-attack.

Iyi J and Strydom H (2018) Boko Haram and International Law, Springer.

Kleffner J (2003) The Impact of Complementarity on National Implementation of Substantive International Criminal Law. 1 Journal of International Criminal Law.

Konstantinov E (1988) 'International Terrorism and International Law', 31 German Yearbook of International Law.

Kress C (2010) 'On the Outer Limits of Crimes Against Humanity: The Concept of Organization within the Policy Requirement: Some Reflection on the March 2010 ICC Kenya Decision', 23 Leiden Journal of International Law.

Kreß C and von Holtzendorff L (2010) 'The Kampala Compromise on the Crime of Aggression', 8 Journal of International Criminal Justice.

Kriksciun A (2007) 'Uganda's Response to International Criminal Court Arrest Warrants: A Misguided Approach?' 16 Tulane Journal of International & Comparative Law.

Lovat H (2007) 'Delineating the interests of Justice' 35 Denver Journal of International Law and Policy.

Mahmood O (2017) 'More than Propaganda: A Review of Boko Haram's Public Messages' Institute for Security Studies West Africa Report, March 2017. Available at https://issafrica.s3.amazonaws.com/site/uploads/war20.pdf.

Margariti S (2017) Defining International Terrorism: Between State Sovereignty and Cosmopolitanism. T.M.C. Asser Press.

Marshall K (2010) 'Prevention and Complementarity in the International Criminal Court', 17, Human Rights Brief.

McNeal G (2006) 'ICC Inability Determinations in Light of the Dujail Case' 39 Case Western Reserve Journal of International Law.

Moffett L (2014) Justice for Victims before the International Criminal Court, Routledge.

Murphy R (2006)'Gravity Issues and the International Criminal Court', 17 Criminal Law Forum.

Murungu C, Biegon J (eds) (2011) Prosecuting International Crimes in Africa, Pretoria University Law Press.

Muscati S (2015) 'Anatomy of A Boko Haram Massacre' Human Rights Watch 10 June 2015. Available at https://www.hrw.org/news/2015/06/10/anatomy-boko-haram-massacre.

New York Times (2015) 'Abuse by Nigeria's Military Found to be Rampant in its War against Boko Haram' 03 June 2015. Available at https://www.nytimes.com/2015/06/04/world/africa/abuses-nigeria-military-boko-haram-war-report.html.

Norwegian Refugee Council (2017) 'Attacks Increasingly Targeting Displaced People in Northeast Nigeria' 16 August 2017. Available at https://www.nrc.no/attacks-increasingly-targeting-displaced-people-in-northeast-nigeria.

Nouwen S (2013) Complementarity in the line of fire; The Catalysing effect of the International Criminal Court in Uganda and Sudan. Cambridge University Press.

Nsereko D (2013) 'The ICC and Complementarity in Practice', Leiden Journal of International Law, (2013).

Office of the Prosecutor (2006) 'Report of the Activities Performed During the First Three Years June 2003–June 2006)' 12 September 2006.

Office of the Prosecutor (2007) 'Policy Paper on the Interests of Justice' September 2007.

Office of the Prosecutor (2012) Report on Preliminary Examination Activities November 2012. Available at https://www.icc-cpi.int/NR/rdonlyres/C433C462-7C4E-4358-8A72-8D99FD00E8CD/285209/OTP2012ReportonPreliminaryExaminations22Nov2012.pdf.

Office of the Prosecutor (2013) Report of Preliminary Examination Activities November 2013.

Office of the Prosecutor (2014) 'Policy Paper on Sexual and Gender-Based Crimes' June 2014.

Office of the Prosecutor (2015) Report on Preliminary Examination Activities November 2015.

Office of the Prosecutor (2017) Report on Preliminary Examination Activities, 4 December 2017.

Office of the Prosecutor (2018) Report on Preliminary Examination Activities 5 December 2018. Available at https://www.icc-cpi.int/itemsDocuments/181205-rep-otp-PE-ENG.pdf.

Olasolo H (2003) 'The Prosecutor of the ICC Before the Initiation of Investigations: A Quasi-Judicial or a Political Body?', 3, International Criminal Law Review.

Olugbuo B (2011) Acceptance of International Criminal Justice in Nigeria: Legal Compliance, Myth or Reality. International Nuremberg Principles Academy.

Premium Times (2017) 'Boko Haram Destroyed 267 Hospitals, Clinics in Borno-Commissioner' 10 August 2017. Available at https://www.premiumtimesng.com/health/health-news/239869-boko-haram-destroyed-267-hospitals-clinics-borno-commissioner.html.

Pulse (2014) 'Terrorists Write Warning Letter to Borno Residents' 27 November 2014. Available at https://www.pulse.ng/boko-haram-terrorists-write-warning-letter-to-borno-residents/nq4rh3w.

Reisman W (1999) Jurisdiction in International Law, Ashgate /Dartmouth, Aldershot, Hants, England.

Reliefweb (2018) Global Coalition to Protect Education from Attack 'I Will Never Go Back To School: The Impact of Attack on Education for Nigerian Women and Girls' October 2018. Available at https://reliefweb.int/sites/reliefweb.int/files/resources/attacks_on_nigerian_women_and_girls.pdf.

Reuters (2011) 'Islamic Sect Boko Haram Claim Nigeria's U.N. Bombing' 29 August 2011. Available at https://www.reuters.com/article/us-nigeria-bombing-claim-idUSTRE77S3ZO20110829.

Reuters (2014) 'Nigerian Islamists Kill 59 Pupils in Boarding School Attack' 26 February 2014. Available at https://www.reuters.com/article/us-nigeria-violence/nigerian-islamists-kill-59-pupils-in-boarding-school-attack-idUSBREA1P10M20140226.

Reuters (2018) 'Suspected Boko Haram Militants Kill 11 Including Three Aid Workers in Nigeria' 02 March 2018. Available at https://www.reuters.com/article/us-nigeria-security/suspected-boko-haram-militants-kill-11-including-three-aid-workers-in-nigeria-idUSKCN1GE14Z.

Robinson D (2003) 'Serving the Interests of Justice: Amnesties, Truth Commissions and the International Criminal Court', 14 European Journal of International Law.

Sacuoto S and Cleary K (2008) 'The Gravity Threshold of the International Criminal Court' 23 American University International Law Review.

Schabas W (2008) 'Complementarity in Practice: Some Uncomplimentary Thoughts' 19, Criminal Law Forum.

Schabas W (2008) 'Prosecutorial Discretion v. Judicial Activism at the International Criminal Court', (2008), Journal of International Criminal Justice.

Schabas W (2009) 'Victor's Justice: Selecting 'situations' at the International Criminal Court', 43, John Marshall Law Review.

Schabas W (2011) An Introduction to the International Criminal Court, Cambridge University Press

Scharf M (2001) 'Defining Terrorism as the Peacetime Equivalent of War crimes: A Case of Too Much Convergence between International Humanitarian Law and International Criminal Law' (2001), 7, ILSA, Journal of International and Comparative Law.

Scheffer D (1999) 'U.S. Policy and the International Criminal Court', 32, Cornell International Law Journal.

Segun M (2015) Dispatches: What Really Happened in Baga, Nigeria? Human Rights Watch 14 January 2015. Available at https://www.hrw.org/news/2015/01/14/dispatches-what-really-happened-baga-nigeria.

Stahn C (2005) 'Complementarity, Amnesties and Alternative Forms of Justice: Some Interpretative Guidelines for the International Criminal Court', Journal of International Criminal Justice.

Stanford University Mapping Militant Project (2016) 'Boko Haram' 26 August 2016. Available at http://web.stanford.edu/group/mappingmilitants/cgi-bin/groups/view/553?highlight=boko+haram.

Stegmiller I (2009) 'The Gravity Threshold Under the ICC Statute: Gravity Back and Forth in Lubanga and Ntaganda', International Criminal Law Review.

Telegraph (2015) 'Nigeria's Boko Haram isn't Just Kidnapping Girls: It's Enslaving Them' 13 January 2015. Available at https://www.telegraph.co.uk/women/womens-life/11342879/Nigerias-Boko-Haram-isnt-just-kidnapping-girls-its-enslaving-them.html.

Torbjörnsson D, Jonsson M (2017) 'Boko Haram: On the Verge of a Defeat or a Long-Term Threat?' November 2017, FOI-R-4488-SE.

Triffterer O, Ambos K (2016) The Rome Statute of the International Criminal Court: A Commentary. Nomos Publishers.

UNHCR (2017) 'Nigeria Situation 2017' July 2017. Available at https://www.unhcr.org/597704b87.pdf.

UNICEF (2018) 'More than 1000 Children in Northeastern Nigeria Abducted by Boko Haram since 2012' 13 April 2018. Available at https://www.unicef.org/wca/press-releases/more-1000-children-northeastern-nigeria-abducted-boko-haram-2013.

United Nations Human Rights Council (2015) 'Boko Haram' Available at https://www.ohchr.org/EN/HRBodies/HRC/Pages/NewsDetail.aspx?NewsID=16176&LangID=R.

United Nations Security Council (2017) 'Report of the Secretary-General on Children and Armed Conflict in Nigeria' S/2017/304 10 April 2017.

UN News (2015) 'UN Rights Chief Urges Concerted Action to Tackle Boko Haram's "Extensive and Far-Reaching Abuses"' 01 July 2015. Available at https://news.un.org/en/story/2015/07/503282-un-rights-chief-urges-concerted-action-tackle-boko-harams-extensive-and-far.

UN News (2017) 'Attack on Aid Convoy in North-East Nigeria Leaves Four Civilians Dead-UN Relief Official' 18 December 2017. Available at https://news.un.org/en/story/2017/12/639742-attack-aid-convoy-north-east-nigeria-leaves-four-civilians-dead-un-relief.

UN (2018) 'Norway Proposal of Amendment' C.N.439.2015.TREATIES-XVIII.10 available at https://treaties.un.org/doc/Publication/CN/2015/CN.439.2015-Eng.pdf (accessed 22 October 2018) ICC-ASP Resolution on Article 124 Resolution ICC-ASP/14/Res.2 available at https://treaties.un.org/doc/source/docs/ICC-ASP-14-Res2-ENG.pdf.

United Nations General Assembly (2015) 'Atrocities committed by the terrorist group Boko Haram and its effects on human rights in the affected States' A/HRC/RES/S-23/1. 21 May 2015.

United Nations Human Rights Office of the High Commissioner (2017) 'Press Briefing Notes on Azerbaijan, Egypt and Indonesia/LGBT and Boko Haram Trials in Nigeria' 13 October 2017. Available at https://www.ohchr.org/EN/NewsEvents/Pages/DisplayNews.aspx?NewsID=22232&LangID=E.

United Nations (2018) 'Report of the United Nations Secretary General on Conflict Related Sexual Violence' 16 April 2018 S/2018/250. Available at https://www.un.org/sexualviolenceinconflict/wp-content/uploads/report/s-2018-250/SG-REPORT-2017-CRSV-SPREAD.pdf.

United Nations Secretary General (2018) 'Deputy Secretary General's Briefing to the Security Council on the Activities of Boko Haram and the Situation in the Lake Chad Basin Region (as prepared for delivery) 22 March 2018. Available at https://www.un.org/sg/en/content/dsg/statement/2018-03-22/deputy-secretary-generals-briefing-security-council-activities-boko.

United Nations (2018) 'UN Humanitarian Coordinator in Nigeria Condemns Deadly Attacks on IDP Camps, North-East Nigeria' 1 November 2018. Available at https://reliefweb.int/sites/reliefweb.int/files/resources/HC%20Statement%201%20November%202018_Final.pdf.

UNOCHA (2017) 'UN Humanitarian Coordinator in Nigeria Gravely Concerned by Ambush on Convoy Carrying Humanitarian Items in Borno State' 18 December 2017. Available at https://reliefweb.int/sites/reliefweb.int/files/resources/Press%20Release%20Attacks%20on%20Convoy%2018%20Dec%202017.pdf.

Van der Vyver J (2000) 'Personal and Territorial Jurisdiction of the International Criminal Court', 14 Emory International law Review.

Van Krieken P (2002) (ed.) Terrorism and the International Legal Order. Springer.

Vienna Convention on the Law of Treaties 1969 1155UNTS.

VOA (2014) 'Boko Haram Increases Deadly Attacks on Civilians in Northern Nigeria' 24 March 2014. Available at https://www.voanews.com/a/boko-haram-increases-deadly-attacks-on-civilians-in-northern-nigeria/1878156.html.

Washington Post (2018) 'Boko Haram Has Kidnapped More Girls: Here's What We Know' Hilary Matfes, 8 March 2018. Available at https://www.washingtonpost.com/news/monkey-cage/wp/2018/03/08/boko-haram-has-kidnapped-more-girls-heres-what-we-know/?noredirect=on&utm_term=.befa2af4f30d.

Webb P (2005) 'The ICC Prosecutor's Discretion Not to Prosecute in the Interests of Justice', 50 Criminal Law Quarterly.

Weinberg L et al. (2004) The Challenges of Conceptualizing Terrorism. Vol 16 Terrorism and Political Violence.

Werle G (2007) 'Individual Criminal Responsibility in Article 5 ICC Statute', 5 Journal of International Criminal Justice.

Werle G and Jessberger F (2020) Principles of International Criminal Law. 4th edn. Oxford University Press.

Whitelaw I (2016) 'Internationalization of Non-International Armed Conflict', 30, Perth International Law Journal.

Young R (2006) 'Defining Terrorism: The Evolution of Terrorism as a Legal Concept in International Law and its Influence on Definitions in Domestic Legislations' Boston College International and Comparative Law Review.

Zawati H (2016) 'The International Criminal Court and Complementarity', 12, Journal of International Law and International Relations.

Zimmermann A (2016) 'Finally…. Or Would Rather Less Have Been More?', (2016), 14, Journal of International Criminal Justice.

Cases

Dissenting Opinion by Judge Hans-Peter Kaul to Pre-Trial Chamber II's "Decision on the Prosecutor's Application for Summons to Appear for William Samoei Ruto, Henry Kiprono Kosgey and Joshua Arap Sang" ICC-01/09-01/11-2 16 March 2011.

Pre-Trial Chamber I Situation on the Registered Vessels of the Union of Comoros, the Hellenic Republic and the Kingdom of Cambodia 'Decision on the Request of the Union of the Comoros to Review the Prosecutor's Decision not to initiate an Investigation' 16 July 2015.

Prosecutor v. Abdallah Banda Abakaer Nourain and Saleh Mohammed Jerbo Jamus ICC-02/05-03/09, Corrigendum of the Decision on the Confirmation of Charges (Public Redacted Version) Pre-Trial Chamber I, 07 March 2011.

Prosecutor v. Akayesu, ICTR-96-4-T, Trial Judgment, 2 September 1998

Prosecutor v. Alfred Musema ICTR-96-13-A, Judgment and Sentence, 27 January 2000.

Prosecutor v. Alekssovski IT-95-14/I-T, Joint Operation of the Majority, Judge Vohrah and Judge Nieto-Navia, 25 June 1999.

Prosecutor v. Bahar Idriss Abu GardaICC-02/05- 02/09-243-Red, Decision on the confirmation of charges, 8 February 2010.

Prosecutor v. Bahar Idriss Abu Garda ICC-02/05-02/09, Decision on the Confirmation of Charges (Public Redacted Version) Pre-Trial Chamber I, 08 February 2010.
Prosecutor v. Blaskic, IT-95-14, Trial Judgement, 03 March 2000.
Prosecutor v. Bosco Ntaganda, Annex II, Decision on the Prosecutor's application for warrants of arrest, Article 58 of 10.2.2006, incorporated in the record of the case pursuant to decision ICC-01/04-520, 21.7.2008 (ICC-01-04-02-06-20-Anx2).
Prosecutor v. Bosco Ntaganda ICC-01/04-02/06 (Decision Pursuant to Article 61(7) (a) and (b) of the Rome Statute on the Charges of the Prosecutor Against Bosco Ntaganda) para 14, 9 June 2014. Available at https://www.icc-cpi.int/CourtRecords/CR2014_04750.PDF.
Prosecutor v. Bosco Ntaganda ICC-01/04-02/06-309, Decision Pursuant to Article 61(7) (a) and (b) of the Rome Statute on the Charges of the Prosecutor against Bosco Ntaganda, Pre-Trial Chamber II,) June 2014.
Prosecutor V. Callixte Mbarushimana ICC-01/04-01/07 Decision on the Confirmation of Charges, Pre-Trial Chamber I, 26 September 2008.
Prosecutor V. Callixte Mbarushimana ICC-01/04-01/10-11, Prosecution's Application under Article 58, Pre-Trial Chamber I, 27 January 2011.
Prosecutor v. Charles Taylor SCSL-03-01-T, Judgement, Trial Chamber II, 18 May 2012.
Prosecutor v. Clement Kayishema and Obed Ruzindana ICTR-95-1-T, Trial Judgement, 21 May 1999.
Prosecutor v. Dario Kordic & Mario Cerkez IT-95-14/2-T, Judgment, 26 February 2001.
Prosecutor v. Delalic et.al. IT-96-21-T, Judgement, Trial Chamber, 16 November 1998.
Prosecutor v. Dusko Tadic IT-94-I-A, Judgement, Appeal Chamber, 15 July 1999.
Prosecutor v. Dragoljub Kunarac, Radomir Kovac and Zoran Vukovic, IT-96-23-T& IT-96-23/1-T, Judgement, 22 February 2001.
Prosecutor v. Francis Kirimi Muthaura, Uhuru Muigai Kenyatta and Mohammed Hussein Ali, ICC-01/09-02/11-382-Red, Decision on the Confirmation of Charges Pursuant to Article 61(7) (a) and (b) of the Rome Statute 29 January 2012 | Pre-Trial Chamber II. Available at https://www.icc-cpi.int/CourtRecords/CR2012_01006.PDF.
Prosecutor v. Germain Katanga and Mathieu Ngudjolo Chui ICC-01/04-01/07-717, 30 September 2008.
Prosecutor v. Germain Katanga and Mathieu Ngudjolo Chui, ICC-01/04-01/07 Decision on the Confirmation of Charges, Pre Trial-Chamber I, 16 September 2008
Prosecutor v. Germain Katanga ICC-01/04-01/07-3436, Judgment Pursuant to Article 74 of the Statute, 7 March 2014.
Prosecutor v. Jean Pierre Bemba Gombo ICC-01/04-01/07, Decision Pursuant to Article 61(7)(a) and (b) of the Rome Statute on the Charges of the Prosecutor Against Jean-Pierre Bemba Gombo, 15 June 2009.
Prosecutor v. Jean- Paul Akayesu ICTR-96-4-T, Trial Judgement, 1 June 2001.
Prosecutor v. Krnojelac IT-97-25-T, Judgement, Trial Chamber II, 15 March 2002.
Prosecutor v. Limaj IT-03-66-T, Judgement, Trial Chamber, 30 November 2005.
Prosecutor v. Rajic IT-95-12, Review of the Indictment Pursuant to Rule 61 of the Rules of Procedure and Evidence, Trial Chamber, 13 September 1996.
Prosecutor v. Saif al-Islam Gaddafi and Abdullah Al-Senussi ICC-01/11-01/11 OA4, Judgment on the Appeal of Mr Abdullah Al-Senussi against the Decision of Pre-Trial Chamber I of 11 October Entitled 'Decision on the Admissibility of the Case against Abdullah Al-Senussi", 24 July 2014.
Prosecutor v. Slobodan Milosevic et al. IT-99-37-PT Second Amended Indictment 29 October 2001.
Prosecutor v. Thomas Lubanga Dyilo ICC-01/04-01/06, Decision on the Prosecutions Application for a Warrant of Arrest Article 58, Pre-Trial Chamber, 24 February 2006.
Prosecutor v. Thomas Lubanga Dyilo ICC-01/04-01/06, Decision on the Confirmation of charges, Pre-Trial Chamber I, 29 January 2007.
Prosecutor v. William Somei Ruto, Henry Kiprono Kosgey and Joshua Arap Sang ICC-01/09-01/11, 30 May 2011.

Prosecutor v. Zdravko Mucic, Hazim Delic, Esad Landzo, Zejnil Delalic (Celebici case) IT-96-21, 20 February 2001.
Prosecutor v. Zejnil Delalic, Zdravko Mucic, Hazim Delic & Esad Landzo (Celebici case) IT-96-21, 20 February 2001.
SS Lotus Case (France v. Turkey), (1927) P.C.I.J. (ser. A) No. 10 (Sept. 7).
Statement of the ICC Prosecutor Fatou Bensouda, on the Situation of the Registered Vessel of the Union of Comoros et al. 30 November 2017. Available at https://www.icc-cpi.int/Pages/item.aspx?name=171130_OTP_Comoros.

Other Documents

Baseline Survey on Gender-Based Violence in Borno State Nigeria. A Report from Women Protection and Empowerment International Rescue Committee. 17 December 2017. Available at https://reliefweb.int/sites/reliefweb.int/files/resources/borno_state_-_women_protection_and_empowerment_baseline_survey.pdf.
Council of Foreign Relations Nigeria Security Tracker available at https://www.cfr.org/nigeria/nigeria-security-tracker/p29483.
Convention on the Elimination of all forms of Discrimination against Women 1979.
Final Act of the United Nations Diplomatic Conference of Plenipotentiaries on the Establishment of an International Criminal Court, Resolution E, U.N. Doc. A/CONF.183/C.1/L.76/Add.14 (July 16, 1998).
Fourth Geneva Convention Relative to the Protection of Civilian Persons in Time of War 12 August 1949
ICRC Interpretative Guideline on the Notion of Direct Participation in Hostilities under International Humanitarian Law (2009).
International Committee of the Red Cross (ICRC), Protocol Additional to the Geneva Conventions of 12 August 1949, and relating to the Protection of Victims of Non-International Armed Conflicts (Protocol II), 8 June 1977, 1125 UNTS 609. Available at https://www.refworld.org/docid/3ae6b37f40.html.
Military and Paramilitary Activities in and against Nicaragua (Nicaragua v. United States of America) (Merits), ICJ Reports, 1986.
Protocol Additional to the Geneva Conventions of 12 August 1949 and Relating to the Protection of Victims of International Armed Conflicts (Additional Protocol I).
Protocol Additional to the Geneva Conventions of 12 August 1949 and Relating to the Protection of Victims of Non-International Armed Conflicts (Additional Protocol II).
Protocol to the African Charter on Human and Peoples' Rights on the Rights of Women in Africa (Maputo Protocol) 2003.
Regulation 29 (2), International Criminal Court Regulations of the Office of the Prosecutor ICC-BD/05-01-09 23 April 2009.
Regulations Reflecting the Laws and Customs of War on Land Annex to the 1907 Hague Conventions on the Law and Customs of War on Land.
Rome Statute of the International Criminal Court (2002).
Rules of Procedure and Evidence International Criminal Court as amended on 22 May 2013.
Situation in the Islamic Republic of Afghanistan, Decision Pursuant to Article 15 of the Rome Statute on the Authorization of an Investigation into the Situation in the Islamic Republic of Afghanistan. ICC-02/17 12 April 2019. Available at https://www.icc-cpi.int/CourtRecords/CR2019_02068.PDF.
Situation in Nigeria, Article 5 Report, Office of the Prosecutor 5 August 2013.
Situation in the Republic of Congo ICC-01/04-101-tEN-Corr, Public Redacted Version Decision on the Applications for Participation in the Proceedings of VPRS 1, VPRS 2, VPRS 3, VPRS 4, VPRS 5 and VPRS 6, Pre-Trial Chamber I, 17 January 2006.

Situation in the Republic of Kenya, (the Prosecutor v. William Samoei Ruto, Henry Kiprono Kosgey and Joshua Arap Sang) Decision Pursuant to Article 15 of the Rome Statute on the Authorization of an Investigation into the Situation in the Republic of Kenya, ICC-01/09, 31 March 2010.

UN Treaties 'Status of the Rome Statute of the International Criminal Court Rome 17th July 1998' available at https://treaties.un.org/Pages/ShowMTDSGDetails.aspx?src=UNTSONLINE&tabid=2&mtdsg_no=XVIII-10&chapter=18&lang=en.

Chapter 5
Beyond Criminal Prosecutions: Alternatives and Adjuncts

Contents

Abstract This chapter broadens the discourse by exploring the possible alternatives to domestic and international criminal prosecutions to the Boko Haram crisis discussed in previous chapters.

Keywords Deradicalization · Deradicalization Rehabilitation and Reintegration (DRR) · Hybrid (or internationalized) courts · Operation Safe Corridor · Restorative justice · Transitional justice

5.1 Introductory Remarks

Nigeria's handling of the investigation and prosecution of cases regarding the perpetrators of the Boko Haram crimes at the domestic level has been examined in previous chapters. Nevertheless, the decision and action of the ICC, particularly the next stage at the Pre-Trial Chamber concerning opening full investigations on the identified potential cases in Nigeria, is still unfolding. Within the domestic regime, a variety of crimes within the jurisdiction of the ICC, including egregious crimes of sexual violence and crimes against children, have not been effectively prosecuted. Thus, this has occasioned a potential complementarity gap. Although, a positive decision on opening proper investigations regarding the Boko Haram crisis has been made at the ICC, it is imperative to note that due to its limited scope, the cases that could

V. Ojo-Adewuyi, *Criminal Justice Responses to the Boko Haram Crisis in Nigeria*, International Criminal Justice Series 34, https://doi.org/10.1007/978-94-6265-615-4_5

potentially end up at the Court would be a few of the so-called representative cases.[1] The crisis has been multifaceted and has directly affected hundreds of thousands of civilians and indirectly affected millions more. Additionally, a large percentage of the ripple effect of the crisis may not be effectively resolved by prosecutions either at the ICC or in Nigerian courts. With the handling of the cases before Nigerian courts and the inherent challenges, assessing non-prosecutorial measures to achieve peace and potential reconciliation therefore seems pertinent. Alongside the prosecution of perpetrators of these heinous crimes, at the eventual end of the crisis, a full range of mechanisms may prove necessary, populations who have been displaced would need support to return, the Salafi-Jihadist ideology would require specific address by both the religious and political leadership and the entire society would require healing from the crisis.[2]

Due to the nature of the crisis, some non-judicial efforts have been explored alongside judicial ones. Still, political attempts of resolution and efforts to negotiate have not fared well since the crisis started.[3] True to Nigeria's constant attempt to solve problems by committees, the government in 2011 constituted a seven-member committee on the security challenges in the Northeast, particularly the Boko Haram violence.[4] Headed by Ambassador Usman Galtimari, it was touted as the committee that will 'solve' the Boko Haram crisis. Its report identified levels of responsibilities of all parties to the conflict and made a number of recommendations. Its recommendations were not utilised for any specific purpose. In 2013, another twenty-six-member committee was inaugurated to explore dialogue and ways of achieving a peaceful resolution to the conflict.[5] The activities of both committees failed to make a dent in the crisis and were unable to achieve their aims and contribute to a lasting resolution of the Boko Haram crisis.

In 2015, the Nigerian government inaugurated a multi-agency De-radicalisation, Rehabilitation and Reintegration (DRR) programme for 'repentant' Boko Haram members under the Office of the National Security Adviser. The programme was intended to serve as a conduit for Boko Haram defectors and former members including those convicted upon the conclusion of their sentences to be de-radicalised and reintegrated into the society. The programme utilises three major points of focus: concentrating on religious ideology, structural and political grievances including post-conflict trauma.[6] Working with locally respected religious leaders on the religious component of the programme, the participants are also provided therapy to deal

[1] On the limited scope of international prosecutions, see generally Aptel 2012, and Badagard and Klamberg 2017, p. 639.

[2] Hasan and Tyvoll 2018.

[3] The Nigerian government alongside a number of international players have at various times attempted to negotiate with the Boko Haram group, a few times, these efforts led to swapping of Boko Haram detainees with some hostages, however, such negotiations have not been successful in the sense of ending hostilities. See generally, Nwankpa 2016, and Obamamoye 2018.

[4] Presidential Committee on the Security Challenges in the North East.

[5] Presidential Committee on Dialogue and Peaceful Resolution of Security Challenges in the North.

[6] See generally VON 2019.

with trauma. Useful vocational skills and trainings are offered as well.[7] Although, the so-called 'Operation Safe Corridor' has arguably achieved relative success, reactions to the process have also been rightly varied.[8] The programme has graduated sets of the so-called former Boko Haram members now equipped with varying technical skills; part of its criticisms is that these former perpetrators were receiving a better treatment than the actual victims. The attention of the government has so far been paid more to the former perpetrators, treated as needing rehabilitation, while the victims appear to be ignored. There have also been allegations of forced labour and unlawful detention tainting the otherwise seemingly successful legacy of the programme.[9]

The conversations around other potential transitional justice mechanisms within the Boko Haram crisis therefore began as an offshoot of the general handling of the crisis by the government, a perception of inadequacy and the insufficiency of prosecutorial mechanisms, the fluidity of categorisation as perpetrators,[10] in addition to a lack of a perception of an efficient recourse for the victims and the larger society. Traditional notions of conflict resolution have also been touted as possible options by commentators.[11] In 2017, all previously inaugurated initiatives were consolidated under the North East Development Commission (NEDC) to harmonise the entirety of the intervention programmes.[12] The commission was intended as a victim-facing organisation designed to pioneer reconstruction and the development of the North East by harmonising the duties of previous initiatives such as the Victims Support Funds (VSF), Presidential Committee on the North East Initiative (PCNI), the Presidential Initiative on the North East (PINE), including the NGOs working in the region. Despite these and other military and non-military efforts, as of August 2018, about 1.7 million people remained displaced and the indices of the crisis failed to improve significantly.[13] A high percentage of those affected by the Boko Haram violence continue to live in internally displaced persons' camps without access to basic necessities.[14]

---

[7] See Bukarti and Bryson 2019.

[8] See further in Felbab-Brown 2018, and Bukarti 2019.

[9] Amnesty International 2020.

[10] For instance, a high percentage of some of the so-called Boko Haram detainees and some prosecuted were those who are not members of the group, but who provided forms of non-violent support for the group. See further discussion in Section 5.3.4.1 and Human Right Watch 2018.

[11] See Hasan and Tyvoll 2018.

[12] See https://nedc.gov.ng/.

[13] Reliefweb 2018.

[14] See for example UNHCR Nigeria Emergency. Aljazeera 2018.

5.2 Why Does Transitional Justice Matter in the Boko Haram Discourse?

The borders of transitional justice were initially advanced as 'a conception of justice associated with periods of political change, characterised by legal responses to confront the wrongdoings of repressive predecessor regimes'.[15] The 'transition' process has, however, come to be described more liberally to include 'political and socio-cultural change taking place in a society following a dramatic upheaval.'[16] Generally, transitional justice no longer refers only to periods of political change; rather it is now understood to include changes from periods of war to peace as well as additional forms of post-conflict transitions.[17] Some commentators have also embraced a wider range of transition to include, economic transitions/crimes alongside political transitions traditional to the field.[18] Regardless of the type of transition envisaged, transitional justice may be utilised to respond to large-scale past abuses and at its heart are the goals of 'accountability and fairness in the protection and vindication of rights and the prevention and the punishment of wrongs'.[19] Its measures may include both retributive and restorative justice mechanisms, in order to achieve various aims including truth-telling, peace and reconciliation.[20] Effective transitional justice measures should ideally take into account the rights of the victims, the rights of the perpetrators and the larger society.[21] Generally, transitional justice mechanisms seem to continue to evolve from strictly legal tools into veritable tools for the achievement of political and social goals.[22] While prosecutions are an integral aspect of transitional justice, its mechanisms are not limited to prosecutions alone and it typically involves both judicial and non-judicial measures.[23] It is granted that investigations and prosecutions are a fundamental part of the transitional justice discourse. However, within this chapter, references to transitional justice will directly relate to other available mechanisms apart from investigation and prosecution which have been copiously addressed in earlier chapters.[24]

---

[15] See Teitel 2003.

[16] See Szablewska and Bachmann 2015, p. 340.

[17] See generally Ainley et al. 2015, Bassiouni 2002, and Aolain and Campbell 2005.

[18] See Posner and Vermeule 2004, p. 763. See also Carranza 2008.

[19] See Ambos 2009, p. 22, and Lambourne 2009.

[20] See generally, Sriram 2007, and Mani 2008.

[21] Clamp 2014, p. 11.

[22] Clamp 2014, p. 3.

[23] Transitional justice in this section is understood as a 'full-range of mechanisms with which a society deals with large scale past abuse, for the aims of accountability, justice and reconciliation'. These mechanisms may include prosecutions, amnesties, truth commissions, lustrations, public acknowledgement of wrongdoing, reparations, truth seeking, vetting, etc. See generally, Ambos in Ambos, Large and Wierda 2009, p. 21, and Turner 2017.

[24] A detailed assessment of both domestic investigatory and prosecutorial mechanisms, including potential international criminal legal responses have been done in the second to fourth chapters.

The duty to prosecute crimes under international law is a crucial backdrop for the application of transitional justice mechanisms.[25] This duty typically sets the scene for states to respond (whether in a judicial or non-judicial nature) to crimes-domestic or international committed within its territory or by its citizens. For conducts amounting to core crimes in the Rome Statute, there is sufficient clarity on the obligation of state parties and their responsibilities generally under the prescriptions of the Statute and under principles such as complementarity.[26] Within the Nigerian system, the legal basis to deal with the past can be deduced first from the duty to guarantee and protect constitutionally granted fundamental rights and seek redress in the court of Law,[27] including its obligations under specific international treaties.[28]

In many conflict/post-conflict or transitional states, the feasibility of utilising prosecution alone to respond to an extended period of conflict like the Boko Haram crisis may be impractical and ineffective for a variety of reasons.[29] Countless factors may also contribute to the challenges with mass prosecution and incarceration including widespread and varying levels of offenders, the ages of some of the perpetrators, peculiarities of the local context and the nature of the crimes committed.[30] Additionally, an insistent focus on trials and criminal accountability alone has been variously noted

---

[25] The existence of such duty, while initially controversial, has become generally recognised in customary international law. This duty also sets the scene for states to take decisive action for conduct amounting to crimes under international law within their territory. See generally, Bassiouni 1996a, b, Cassese 1998, Edelenbos 1994, and Jessberger 2007.

[26] The principle of complementarity has been elsewhere discussed in this work. See also on the duty to prosecute in the Rome Statute, Preamble (4), and (6) Rome Statute of the ICC (2002). Werle and Jessberger 2020. Ambos 2009, p. 29, Newman 2004–2005.

[27] Fundamental human rights are expressly provided for in Chapter four of the Nigerian Constitution. The chapter includes all the classic rights including an option of redress before the courts should the rights be violated. This might be interpreted to include a constitutional obligation to prosecute. See Section 46(1) Constitution of the Federal Republic of Nigeria 1999.

[28] These include the Geneva Conventions-Articles 50, 51, 130 and 147 of the Geneva Convention for the Amelioration of the Condition of the Wounded and Sick in Armed Forces in the Field (Geneva Convention I), Geneva Convention for the Amelioration of the Condition of the Wounded, Sick and Shipwrecked Members of Armed Forces at the Sea (Geneva Convention II), Geneva Convention Relative to the Treatment of Prisoners of War (Geneva Convention III), Geneva Convention Relative to the protection of Civilian Persons in Time of War (Geneva Convention IV) of 12 August 1949. Article 7 of the Convention Against Torture and Other Cruel Inhuman or Degrading Treatment or Punishment of 10 December 1984 (ratified in 2001), Article 2(1) of the International Covenant on Civil and Political Rights of 16 December 1966. Articles IV-VI of the Convention on the Prevention and Punishment of the Crime of Genocide of 9 December 1948 for the crime of genocide, and Article 2(1) of the European Convention for the Protection of Human Rights and Fundamental Freedom of 4 November 1950 and Article 26 of the African Charter on Human and Peoples' Rights 1981.

[29] In some instances, aside from overcoming the challenges of the past, a number of transitional or post-conflict societies also have the additional challenge of weak institutions, inadequate legal regime, large scale and widespread offenders including lack of government cooperation. See for example some of these challenges addressed in, Balint 2014, p. 13, Benvenuti 2014, p. 119, and Call 2004.

[30] See for example varying viewpoints in Villa-Vicencio 2000, Seibert-Fohr 2003, and Grossman 2007.

to be grossly insufficient for the purposes of post-conflict transformation.[31] Some of the inherent challenges are present within the Nigerian context and a number of them bedevil accountability for perpetrators in the Boko Haram crisis both at the domestic level and from the perspective of the ICC have been highlighted in previous chapters.

This section is, therefore, focused on an assessment of potential alternatives and adjuncts to prosecutions, the appropriateness of the transitional justice discourse within the pendency of the Boko Haram crisis, and whether such de-radicalisation as a transitional justice mechanism would be useful within the Nigerian context. Potential mechanisms that may be utilised in Nigeria particularly to achieve the aims of transitional justice are also explored. Lessons are also drawn from Nigeria's misadventures in transitional justice in the past, with particular focus on the Human Rights Violations Investigation Commission (HRVIC) also known as the Oputa Panel, and the Niger Delta Amnesty Programme. Additionally, the ongoing de-radicalisation, rehabilitation and reintegration programme (Operation Safe Corridor) of the Nigerian government is explored for its current contribution, whether it can indeed be regarded as transitional justice mechanisms including its potential to contribute towards the overall aims of justice. This chapter closes on exploring the possibility of utilising specific conflict resolution methods indigenous to North-Eastern Nigeria.

5.3 Transitional Justice for Boko Haram: Problems Arising

By its very nature, simplistically, the existence of a form of transition in a society should be the basic foundation for the utilisation of transitional justice mechanisms.[32] However, the discourse of transitional justice seems to have become expanded and variously applied to societies without or before any indication of any form of transition.[33] Due to the central nature of the existence of some form of 'transition', the application of transitional mechanisms to conflict situations before an apparent transition has the potential to raise a number of challenges.[34] Generally, discourse on transitional justice mechanisms usually fall between majority of dual perspectives. First, commentators who view the mechanisms through the lens of utilising them to usher in a form of transition-a form of pre-transitional justice,[35] and those employing transitional justice mechanisms post-transition for the ends of justice and

[31] See Teitel 2014, p. 29.

[32] See generally, Kritz and Wilson 2010, and Quinn 2014–15, p. 64.

[33] The application of transitional justice mechanisms to the so-called pre-transitional societies seems to have become an integral part of the field with lack of clarity particularly regarding societies where there has been no apparent transition. See for example further discussion on this in Quinn 2014–15, p. 64.

[34] A veritable example is the pre-transition process in Uganda, which has been underway for at least two decades. See generally, Quinn 2014–15, p. 72, and Posner and Vermeule 2004, p. 763.

[35] See generally, Mihai 2010, David and Holliday 2006, p. 93, and Teitel 2005.

other symbolic purposes.[36] In a sense, regardless of whether transition is a precursor of the utilisation of transitional justice mechanisms or a goal of the process, there is a lack of abundant clarity and a worrying tendency for over-exertion of the mechanisms particularly in societies where it appears premature.[37] Without critiquing the validity of both scenarios, the approaches have received varying level of assessment and analysis.[38] In any case, it is acknowledged that no two 'transitions are the same' and that the process of transition itself might be a continuum, with regime transition only as an endpoint.[39] To be abundantly clear, societies where transition has already taken place, the so-called post-transitional societies, are quite distinct from the so-called pre-transitional societies. Quinn in this vein describes the so-called pre-transitional justice states in terms of the lack of a 'move from neither conflict to peace nor an apparent regime change, where conflict is ongoing and citizens live in suspended animation.'[40] It begs the question then why mechanisms which seem to be designed for post-transitional states would be utilised in such pre-transitional states?

Another inherent challenge is the recent tendency to treat transitional justice mechanisms as a toolbox or a checklist to be thrown at every crisis situation without a careful consideration of its appropriateness for the local context.[41] The current format of transitional justice mechanisms has also been rightly criticised for other reasons such as its purported rigidity in application,[42] including the impracticality of some of its mechanisms when applied in any and every crisis state.[43] As rightly noted by Ambos, this tendency to 'templatize' transitional justice mechanisms may prove counterproductive.[44]

The first question should then be whether transitional justice mechanisms are suitable for any and every crisis situation? After the determination of suitability, the question of timing is also crucial. At what point in the crisis should the transitional justice discourse arise? Regarding the first question, the answer would depend on which definition of transitional justice is being adopted and what mechanisms are being imagined. Criminal prosecutions are an integral part of most legal regimes; however, other restorative justice mechanisms such as amnesties, truth commissions may not be. On the second question, assuming mechanisms other than prosecutions are being explored, the appropriateness of the discourse in all crisis situations especially within the pendency of the conflict may be in question.

---

[36] For example, mechanisms utilized for a variety of goals in post-genocide Rwanda, post-apartheid South Africa and post-conflict Sierra-Leone. See generally, Dyzenhaus 2003, Teitel 2006, Weinstein 2014, and Layus 2010.

[37] See Muvingi 2011.

[38] For example, David and Holliday examined the utilisation of mechanisms such as amnesties and prosecutions as part of a national policy option, to facilitate the transition process. See generally, David and Holliday 2006, see also Posner and Vermeule 2004.

[39] See Posner and Vermeule 2004, p. 763.

[40] Quinn 2014–15, p. 72.

[41] See Ojo and Filbert 2020.

[42] See for example, Nagy 2008.

[43] See Mendeloff 2004.

[44] See Ambos 2015.

In the context of the Boko Haram crisis and generally in North-East Nigeria, there has been no apparent transition. The crisis is still ongoing as at the time of writing: more than a decade after they started. Displaced persons are still mostly unable to return home, abductions are still rife, large swaths of the region still lay within the control of Boko Haram and there is an active military offensive against the group. Due to these and other factors, the reintegration programme of the Nigerian government targeted at the so-called repentant Boko Haram has been largely negatively perceived by the general populace. While the discourse around transitional justice mechanisms other than prosecutions generally may be commendable, it appears to be premature within the context. There is also an apparent lack of clarity as to how these mechanisms will usher in peace and eventual justice.[45] Should the crisis eventually terminate and the discourse around the mechanisms in my view become timely, utilising the classic mechanisms may prove ineffective without a thorough design of domestic and context-sensitive mechanisms with a higher chances of success.[46] **Utilising specific transitional justice mechanisms should not be a one-size-fits-all approach without** a thorough assessment of the local context. Should transitional justice mechanisms become necessary for North-East Nigeria, a more bespoke outlook has the potential to create a higher likelihood of legitimacy, a better chance of success and an enhanced usefulness for the victims and the larger society.[47] In its current form, some of the mechanisms appear to be overambitious, promising much but realistically seeming to achieve very little.[48] Its traditional aims seem to have become too wide-ranging and include varying goals typically geared towards achieving the ends of justice. Peacebuilding,[49] truth-telling,[50] reparations for victims,[51] for the purposes of recognition of victims and perpetrators,[52] restorative justice,[53] all of which seem extremely **difficult if not impossible to achieve within the process in Nigeria.**

Another critical question is whether the mechanisms of transitional justice which were developed to be utilised after major upheavals such as regime changes or armed **conflict may also be utilised as a response to non-state terror acts.**[54]

The utilisation of 'the carrot approach' as a response to terrorism is not novel and has been practiced successfully and otherwise in a number of societies. This will also be examined in greater detail in the next section. To achieve clarity on this point,

---

45 See similar concerns raised in Ambos 2015, pp. 46–48. See also Leebaw 2008.

46 See further on these, Hasan and Tyvoll 2018, and Vinck and Pham 2008.

47 The idea of adapted transitional justice mechanisms is not new, and a number of commentators have recommended this for a variety of situations and in a variety of formats. See for example, Ramji-Nogales 2010, Duong and Ear 2010, Gready and Robins 2014, Aolain 2008, and Ambos 2015, p. 46.

48 **See for example varying opinions on the efficacy of transitional justice in Mutua** 2015, Balasco 2013, and Bonacker and Buckley-Zistel 2013.

49 On peacebuilding see generally, Laplante 2008.

50 Brants and Klep 2013.

51 See Garcia-Godos 2008.

52 See for example, Haldemann 2008.

53 See Doak and O'Mahony 2012.

54 This perspective was extensively explored by Renner and Spencer 2011.

however, it appears crucial to draw a distinction on whether any acts of engagement, negotiation or amnesty (which I refer to as 'the carrot approach') extended to the so-called repentant or defected terrorists, borrowing from classic transitional justice prescriptions may be regarded as transitional justice mechanisms *stricto sensu*. Once clarity is reached on this, it may clarify whether the mere borrowing of ideas from transitional justice mechanisms lend itself to be regarded as such. If terrorism is not one of the conflicts within the contemplation of classic transitional justice, it may be unwise to have such high standards and expectation in the event of an overextension of its prescriptions to terrorism or acts that may also be prosecuted as terrorism. Again, programmes designed to respond to terrorism that focus merely on the terrorist perpetrator without a commensurate attention for the victims and survivors only have a form of transitional justice mechanisms but are missing an important component of it. While the evolution of classic transitional justice mechanisms did not include terrorism (of the non-state variety) as a focus area, its extended interpretation as a response to a multiplicity of crisis situations mean that there have been varied calls for its prescriptions to be utilised to respond to terrorism.[55]

A further relevant question is whether we can refer to attempts to put an end to acts of violence and maintaining peace by non-state groups if no end of justice is being pursued as transitional justice? Or should it rather be viewed in the lens of what Teitel terms as trading justice for peace?[56] While the peace vs justice debate is noted,[57] Teitel, in discussing the genealogy of transitional justice, centralises the role of justice pursued.[58] As rightly noted by the author, the overextension of transitional justice mechanisms to respond to terrorism is problematic for a number of good reasons including the fact that the state of terrorism, war and political crisis are quite distinct and over extending transitional justice mechanisms may be inadequate.[59]

It is my view that the ongoing programme which is being utilised as a response to the Boko Haram crisis in the Lake Chad Basin region cannot be regarded as transitional justice mechanism as it fails to fulfil some basic characteristics as such. It does not aim to prosecute perpetrators, neither does it illuminate the truth on the crimes committed, it does not seek to provide state or institutional reform nor provide some form of reparations for victims and survivors of the crimes committed. Additionally, as have been noted, it is not generally accepted that the utilisation of transitional justice mechanisms is rightly suited for situations of terrorism, nor were its prescriptions intended for such scenario, and such an overextension of its mechanisms for terrorism is bound to lead into confusion.

However, whether Nigeria's response to the crisis fulfils the requirement as transitional justice mechanism or not, an assessment of the programme will be done in order to provide a general overview and an understanding of the government's responses. The programme will be examined in greater detail in the next section.

---

[55] See for example Sciandra 2017.

[56] See Teitel 2003, p. 81.

[57] See, generally, Baker and Obradovic-Wochnik 2016, and Lekha Sriram 2007.

[58] See Teitel 2003, p. 69.

[59] Teitel 2003, p. 92.

5.4 A Closer Look at Nigeria's De-radicalisation, Rehabilitation and Reintegration Programme

It is abundantly clear that de-radicalisation programmes are not transitional justice mechanisms in the classic sense. However, there seems to be a consensus that such programmes may exist alongside transitional justice mechanisms and perform complementary functions.[60] While de-radicalisation programmes are not regarded as part of transitional justice mechanisms, they may be an accompanying partner for conflict societies, and may funnel candidates to other classic transitional justice mechanisms such as truth commissions or amnesties and vice versa. They have also been long used by countries dealing with some form of terrorism.[61] Additionally, transitional justice as a concept consists of elements of both retributive and restorative justice,[62] and therefore, it is not far-fetched to imagine de-radicalisation programmes as feeding into its restorative justice elements. Classic de-radicalisation programmes typically begin with a legal framework, formal agreements or peace treaties.[63] Others also emerge as a result of a more informal approach or a private sector initiative.[64] According to the United Nations, preconditions for effective deradicalisation programmes should include 'the signing of a negotiated peace agreement that provide a legal framework for the process, trust in the peace process, willingness of the parties to the conflict to engage in the process, including a minimum guarantee of security'.[65] In recent times, more generous, flexible and innovative approaches are being utilised to set up de-radicalisation programmes particularly with a focus on the encouragement of voluntary defections from terror groups.[66] While some commentators laud these forms of de-radicalisation programmes as truly novel approaches to counter-terrorism,[67] others are concerned about a lack of clarity,[68] and some rightly note the high rate of terrorist recidivism inherent in these de-radicalisation programmes especially without commitments and formal agreements between combatants, armed groups and government functionaries or peace keepers.[69] Some scholars also propose that de-radicalisation mechanisms should form a part of a holistic peacebuilding process helping to encourage an environment

[60] See Sriram and Herman 2009.

[61] See generally Horgan and Braddock 2010, El-Said 2015, Horgan and Altier 2012, and Aslam et al. 2016.

[62] Mühlhausen 2016/17, p. 263.

[63] See for example Parrin 2016.

[64] Parrin 2016.

[65] UN 2006.

[66] See for example the disengagement, disassociation, reintegration and reconciliation program for Boko Haram associates in Niger. Morier 2019, p. 118.

[67] See El-Said 2015.

[68] See for example, Horgan 2009, and Pettinger 2017.

[69] See for example Horgan and Altier 2012, p. 84.

of security and confidence, and ideally be utilised along with other restorative justice mechanisms.[70]

De-radicalisation, broadly, has been described as a process of rejection of the radical beliefs and ideology which may lead to disengagement and a change in behaviour.[71] Scholars have highlighted the importance of opening the lines of communication with radical groups,[72] particularly due to an understanding that some groups resorted to violent acts due to the fact that they were unable to have their voices heard peacefully. Speckhard and Akhmedova[73] argue that terror groups have become savvy users of the media to pass across their messages. Initially, the attention of the world was commanded through traditional media by these groups when major acts of terror were committed, while the group responsible takes swift responsibility and uses the medium to pass across its demands. However, social media has also now become a veritable tool in the hands of these groups and it is being used to pass across demands, spread ideologies through preaching broadcasts on social media including pronouncing opinions and fatwah on topical issues. In this vein, the authors opine that it might make a difference for government and authorities to take control of the communication and the information flow. Others argue that cutting off communication with terror groups and preventing them access to the public sphere might be beneficial since 'terrorism itself is a communication strategy'.[74] Another perspective is that, while negotiations may not lead to an immediate end to the conflict, such negotiations may be instrumental to collecting information 'about group leaders, individuals and especially group dynamics for splintering and ending the terrorist organization.'[75] Negotiating with terrorists and terror groups in itself is a profoundly complicated and sore subject which many governments shy away from appearing to be utilising the so-called 'no-concessions doctrine',[76] as they do not want to appear as legitimising the terror groups and their agitations.[77] While the propriety or otherwise of communicating with terrorists and terror groups is not the focus of this section, the argument that de-radicalisation programmes provides an in-road for understanding, receiving intelligence and critical information on terrorist groups through giving concessions to 'defected' or 'repentant' former members merits a closer look.[78]

[70] See Mühlhausen 2016/17.

[71] See Doosje et al. 2016, p. 82.

[72] See generally, Powel 2014, Goerzig 2010.

[73] Speckhard and Akhmedova 2005.

[74] See Goerzig 2010, See also, Cordes 1987.

[75] Mühlhausen 2016/17, p. 263. See also Neumann 2007.

[76] Haspeslagh 2020.

[77] See generally Gross 2010, and Duhart 2019.

[78] See for example Cronin 2011.

Differing forms of de-radicalisation programmes as a response to terrorism became more attractive in the 2000s and had been utilised by a number of countries. Such programmes had been used in Saudi Arabia,[79] Singapore,[80] Indonesia,[81] Yemen,[82] Egypt,[83] Malaysia,[84] Morocco[85] with varying and mixed results.

In theory, de-radicalisation programmes for terrorism sounds highly novel, a tidy solution to a thorny problem. However, the high rate of recidivism, among other factors, are a particular blight on the otherwise promising outlook.[86] Again, whether de-radicalisation programmes are actually successful is not the concern of this section, but rather, whether the Nigerian programme actually fits as a response to the Boko Haram crisis.

The DRR programme in Nigeria was designed for low-risk Boko Haram defectors: some of whom claim to be unwilling conscript. There are three major components of the programme. The first component is the Prison Programme designed for Boko Haram detainees already in custody, including inmates who were convicted fighters primarily in the Kuje Prison in the Federal Capital Territory in Abuja.[87] The programme includes modules in religious training by respected imams coupled with a vocational training. The second component is the Yellow Ribbon Initiative. The initiative is coordinated by the Neem Foundation,[88] supporting reintegration and peacebuilding efforts including psycho-social care particularly for women and children associated with Boko Haram and survivors of sexual and gender-based violence. In reality, this component appears limited in scope and is focused on communities only in Borno, Adamawa and Yobe states. It is also important to note that of the three components of the programme, the Yellow Ribbon Initiative which directly interfaces with a small number of victims is the only part not fully funded by the Nigerian government. The not-for-profit organisation relies solely on donor funding to carry out its activities.

Operation Safe Corridor is the more famous component of the programme. Established in 2016, it was created to respond directly to the needs of surrendered and repentant Boko Haram members and combatants. It includes courses on dealing with religious ideology and extremism, trauma support and counselling, including vocational training.[89] The programme was meant to serve as a pipeline for the so-called

[79] See Capstack 2015. See also European Eye on Radicalization 2019.

[80] See Jayakumar 2020.

[81] See Muhammad et al. 2021.

[82] McDonnell 2017.

[83] Kaya 2016.

[84] See Aslam et al. 2016.

[85] See Dalhoum et al. 2020, see also Carnegie Endowment for International Peace 2019.

[86] See for example Horgan and Altier 2012.

[87] See Council on Foreign Relations 2020.

[88] Neem Foundation, website https://neemfoundation.org.ng/projects/yri-hop/.

[89] See ICIR Nigeria 2020.

low-level Boko Haram terrorists to rejoin society. By the end of 2020, over 2000 men have been enrolled in the Operation Safe Corridor programme.[90]

The programme was instituted and has continued to run without a legal basis. Under Nigerian law, the President is empowered to grant clemency under Section 175 (1)–(3) of the Constitution. Persons 'concerned with or convicted of' any offence within the contemplation of Nigerian law may enjoy the exercise of this prerogative of mercy. In support of the exercise of these powers, as provided for in Section 153 of the Constitution, the president is to consult with the Council of State, a committee made up of eminent elder statespersons, to make the decision on a case-by-case basis. And as such, decisions on prerogative of mercy, amnesties or pardon while remaining within the discretion of the president should generally not be a blanket decision.

In 2009, the President (Former President Shehu Musa Yar Adua) granted amnesty and unconditional pardon to the Niger Delta militants. It must be noted that it is on the basis of that history that many began to also call for amnesty for the Boko Haram fighters. However, a crucial distinction must be drawn between the two scenarios. First, although the means and methods utilised by the Niger Delta militants were illegitimate, the crisis was a legitimate call for resource control including a call for intervention in the damaging environmental practices of the oil exploration companies directly suffered by the indigenous communities in the Niger Delta.[91] Before the amnesty was to take effect, the militants were required to surrender arms and ammunition in their possession and to publicly denounce the use of such tactics going forward. Pardon was available and any militant who came forward within a stipulated 60-day deadline received it. This approach proved to be hugely successful and there was an immediate sharp decline in the use of violence in the region. Those who surrendered and renounced militancy went through the demobilisation and disarmament process and received vocational and educational training including monthly stipends for five years. While the programme had its flaws, it led to the end of the crisis in the region and it forced the government to create systems and structures to provide lasting solution to the systemic problems in the region.

In the case of Boko Haram, the means, method and the agitation of Boko Haram are clearly illegitimate. The sectarian aspiration to create an Islamic caliphate is manifestly illegal within the contemplation of Nigerian law. Additionally, the group has made it clear that it is not interested in any offer of amnesty, has rebuffed the attempts to be drawn out to sit at a table and negotiate a possible resolution of the crisis, and has continued to increase the tempo and tactics of its acts of violence. It is, therefore, mind boggling, why, despite the insensitivity of the offer of amnesty particularly for the victims of Boko Haram crimes, the government still went ahead with the amnesty policy and has not designed a robust response for the victims of the crisis. Rather, it has focused primarily on the offer of amnesty and DRR programme which appear dead on arrival.

---

[90] See Bukarti and Bryson 2019.

[91] See for example Nwankpa 2014, and Oluduro and Oluduro 2012.

The DRR process does not enjoy full support even among the lawmakers as a Bill introduced in 2020 to harmonise all processes and create an Act for the establishment of a National Agency for De-radicalisation, Rehabilitation and Reintegration of repentant Boko Haram members was unsuccessful. The Bill was roundly condemned by majority of the members of the Senate, and one of the members termed it 'a stupid piece of legislation'.[92]

In April 2017, the then President Goodluck Jonathan announced that he was setting up a committee to assess the option of amnesties for repentant combatants as a response to the crisis. The presidency made this major policy decision after it was prevailed upon by the Northern Nigeria Elders Forum and the Northern Nigerian Emirs.[93] After the inauguration of the committee was announced, Boko Haram famously rejected any conversations around amnesty and claimed that it was 'the Nigerian government that was committing atrocities against Muslims'.[94] The amnesty idea appeared to enjoy legitimacy and interest at the beginning especially in Northern Nigeria as many were desperate for any sort of improvement in the intensity of the crisis and the Boko Haram attacks. However, any such legitimacy appeared to wane early as it became apparent that the amnesty offer did not draw out the fighters and seem not to make a dent in the intensity of the crisis. This was not surprising since the classification of who the programme will serve versus who it served in reality were very much different. Those the programme catered for and tagged 'repentant' Boko Haram members and low-grade offenders were in reality former abductees and hostages that were previously taken by the group.[95] Many of these people had no choice and had in most cases committed no crimes. Most had also not subscribed to the terrorist ideology of Boko Haram and as such, de-radicalisation and rehabilitation did not seem necessary. Investing in an elaborate programme for defectors who had little to no influence on the policies, plans and actions of the group has not proven a successful approach. In Nigeria, the DRR process has not led wholly to large groups of combatants abandoning violence and embracing peace and cannot be seen as making any major improvement in the crisis.

The DRR process also did not make provisions for public acknowledgement of guilt, public denunciation of violence including efforts towards recognition, truth or reconciliation. Most of its activities appear only to be for the benefit and the reintegration of the so-called former combatants. As a whole, although aggrieved communities should be a central part of the reintegration component of a DRR process, the Nigerian programme is being conducted far away, both physically and ideologically, from the victim groups and the communities where majority of the crimes were perpetrated.

---

92 See Guardian Newspaper 2020a, b.

93 See the Guardian 2018.

94 BBC 2013a, b.

95 See ICIR Nigeria 2020.

5.5 Reconciliation and Restorative Justice: Problematic Concerns

Reconciliation, while typically idealistic, has been variously expressed as an important goal of the transitional justice process, a logical end of the transitional justice process and a way to prevent the use of the past as a seed for renewed conflict.[96] Reconciliation, while laudable, is a contentious component of transitional justice because in many instances, it may suggest pressure on victims for a forceful forgiveness and collective amnesia.[97] What reconciliation in itself actually entails seems to be subject to vigorous debate, and as a concept of transitional justice, some scholars opine that it may include religious, moral or political components.[98] Skaar describes a dual level of reconciliation, at the individual level between victim and perpetrator and at the societal or national level, as a social process towards sustainable peace.[99] Other authors alternatively describe these ideas in terms of micro or macro levels of reconciliation.[100] Reconciliation has been expressed to include, but not limited to efforts to return to normalcy,[101] reconstruction, an opportunity of reckoning with the past by both victim and perpetrator, acknowledgement of responsibility, some efforts at restitution, including promotion of a social consensus potentially geared towards political change.[102] While the centrality of truth to reconciliation is also oft-cited,[103] some commentators question the basis of such assertions.[104] Although, reconciliation is typically prescribed for post-conflict societies, in the Boko Haram crisis, the central question of concern is: Who needs reconciliation? The necessity of conflict resolution measures for the Boko Haram crisis also requires more scrutiny. Is there a conflict to be resolved? And for what category of people? The problematic concern of the lack of actual transition in the crisis situation which is the subject matter of this work has been addressed elsewhere in this chapter. It is, therefore, important to define the borders of the category of persons for whom programmes improving reconciliation may be designed. This is due to the fact that speaking of reconciliation regarding a crisis that has not ended and for terrorists who have refused to lay down their arms and embrace peace seems inappropriate. A tainted category of people for which the reconciliation discourse might be appropriate include those who were abducted by the group and forced to carry out different (perhaps non-violent) domestic activities. Some of these people include in particular, women, children and

---

[96] Doorn 2021, p. 4.

[97] Van Zyl 2003, p. 8.

[98] Skaar 2013.

[99] Skaar 2013, p. 66.

[100] See for example Janoff-Bulmann 2007, and Hovland 2003.

[101] Sarkin and Daly 2004.

[102] See Anderlini et al. 2004.

[103] See Bassiouni 1996a, b, p. 23, and Gibson 2004, p. 201.

[104] Clark 2011, p. 253.

the elderly. Some of these women were repeatedly raped and they gave birth to children for the members of Boko Haram. In a sense, these individuals are victims of the actions of the group and in some other perspective, may be regarded as perpetrators. Over the years, a number of people in this category have managed to escape or have been rescued. However, many have found it difficult to reintegrate into their former communities as they bear the stigma of their association, however brief, with Boko Haram. Alongside the so-called repentant former terrorists, rescued or escaped victims, including lower-level perpetrators, are also an important category of people for which reconciliation efforts might be useful.

In the discourse around restorative justice, the acclaimed TARR model (truth, accountability, reconciliation and reparation) gained recognition as a veritable approach to post-conflict justice.[105] The authors describe the components of the model as the building blocks of post-conflict justice, truth, accountability, reparation and reconciliation. While the pursuit or finding of truth is generally accepted as a herculean task, truth itself is a nebulous and complex concept.[106] Unearthing truth in its many notions as shown by the report of the South African truth and reconciliation commission has proven to be valuable.[107] Truth is an important component of effective reconciliation and while some commentators opine that the pursuit of such truth should be as a result of or emanating from a judicial process,[108] as long as some notion of truth is being offered, the process retains some legitimacy. Accountability as a component of the model is equally challenging. In cases of widespread criminality usually typifying crisis situations, the ability of the system to handle extensive prosecution despite a clear duty to prosecute is often not practical. And so, there is usually a need to maintain a balance between justice concerns, due process and non-prosecutorial activities that promote a type of accountability without compromising the new state of order or contribute towards improving it. Reparation is also an integral component of the TARR model and it is understood as more broad-based and inclusive of both individual and collective measures incorporating 'restitution of goods, financial compensation, rehabilitation, symbolic measures and guarantees of non-repetition'. Reparation itself is hardly a simple component of the model. Questions on what would be regarded as adequate reparations, the centralised nature of financial compensation in effective reparations, and who bears the burden of the payment? Other more practical concerns include delineating the borders of persons to be considered for reparations-victims, survivors, their dependant, persons affected by the conflict? However, despite the obvious challenges, reparations, understood in a broader sense, should potentially work towards promoting the rights of the victims and survivors. Reconciliation as the fourth building block of the model is a crucial way of reckoning with the past and improving social cohesion after a crisis. The South African TRC report highlights four levels: the individual, the interpersonal

[105] See Parmentier 2003.

[106] See, for example, van der Merwe et al. 2009. See also Lambourne 2009.

[107] Truth and Reconciliation Commission of South Africa 1998.

[108] Zyberi and Černič 2015.

between victims and perpetrators, the community level and the national level.[109] Reconciliation at these different levels comprise of various factors, at the individual level, families receiving information on the death and burial places of their loved ones including exhumations and reburial in the necessary cases are crucial to provide a form of closure. At the interpersonal level, reconciling between specific victim and perpetrators are no less fraught with tension and concerns, at the community level and at the national level. Reconciliation as a component of post-conflict justice is not a hard-liner approach as the victim, the perpetrator and the community should ideally benefit from the process. Reconciliation becomes problematic when it feels forced or when the victim is not considered as an important part of the equation at all. In the processes being employed for the so-called Boko Haram defectors and low-level offenders, there is no obvious requirement for truth that prioritises the requirement of the victims, it is unclear what measures of accountability has been sought or extended, a structured process of reparations has not been afforded to victims, survivors or their dependents and efforts to reconcile victims and perpetrators whether at the interpersonal, community or societal level do not appear centralised in the process. On the centralised nature of truth to the process of reconciliation, the question whether truth qualifies a recipient for reconciliation is well-debated and oft-cited.[110] Unlike in the programmes designed to respond to the Boko Haram crisis, truth not told privately should be centralised, the victims should be an integral part of the transitional justice process where they are also privy to the versions and notions of truths told for cathartic purposes. So, because this has not been done, the transitional justice process appears to be focused more on reintegration than reconciliation and does not prioritise the needs of the victims and the affected communities.

5.6 Lessons from Nigeria's Past Adventure and Misadventure with Transitional Justice Mechanisms

Previous sections have concluded that the ongoing DRR programme cannot be regarded as transitional justice mechanisms for a multiplicity of reasons. It is, therefore, useful to examine Nigeria's past relationship with the utilisation of transitional justice prescriptions. As previously noted, references to transitional justice mechanism within this section will not include investigations and prosecutions, which has been dealt with in greater detail in previous chapters. Emphasis will be placed on other mechanisms such as public apology, symbolic reparation, civil litigation, lustration including particularly truth commissions and amnesties which were previously utilised by the Nigerian government to respond to past large-scale abuses. Although, it may be inaccurate to categorically state that transitional justice mechanisms have

[109] Truth and Reconciliation Commission of South Africa 1998.

[110] See Truth and Reconciliation Commission of South Africa 1998. See also Asmal 1996.

never achieved its aims in Nigeria, the impacts of the mechanisms employed have been severely limited.[111]

Nigeria's history with transitional justice mechanisms is short and uninspiring. Since independence from British hegemony in 1960, Nigeria has experienced a total of 30 years military rule. The first civilian administration was unceremoniously disrupted by a coup d'état on 15 January 1966. The armed forces took over with the General Officer Commanding of the Armed Forces, Major General Johnson Aguiyi-Ironsi at the helm of affairs. A decree was issued immediately suspending the major provisions of the Constitution including those relating to fundamental human rights, the legislature, regional government and the executive council.[112] Under the Ironsi regime, Nigeria ceased to be a federation, and important functions of state were centralised in the National Military Government.[113] Law making powers were also vested in the Military government which continued to promulgate different decrees affecting varying facets of national life without consultation and its decrees were not subject to judicial review. The Supreme Military Council-composed of the head of the military government, the head of the Nigerian army, the Nigerian Navy, the Air Force, the Chief of Staff of the Armed Forces and the Nigerian Army, the Military Governors of the Northern Nigeria, Eastern Nigeria, Western Nigeria and the Mid-West region-acted as the highest policy making body.[114]

Although, the military takeover was presented to the citizenry as a voluntary transfer of power from the Federal Council of Ministers to the armed forces, the process was unconstitutional, lacked legitimacy and marked a truncation of Nigeria's fledgling democracy. Barely six months after the first coup d'état, on 26 July 1966, the Ironsi regime was overthrown, and Lieutenant Colonel Yakubu Gowon took over power. Between 1966 and 1999, Nigeria grappled with a state of continued and gross state-sponsored violation of human rights and civil liberties among other egregious acts perpetuated by successive military regimes.[115] Following military regimes enacted different criminal laws which made provisions contrary to the fundamental rights existing under the erstwhile suspended constitution. In 1976, under the military regime of the then General Olusegun Obasanjo, the Public Officers (Protection against False Accusation) Decree No. 11 was passed. Although, the Decree was repealed, it was re-enacted as Decree No. 4 in 1984 by the Buhari regime. Characterising the successive military regimes were a high rate of repression, arrests,

[111] The limited impact of transitional justice mechanisms in Nigeria have been interpreted in a variety of ways by commentators. See for example, Yusuf 2018.

[112] Eweluka 1967, p. 3.

[113] See generally, Constitution (Suspension and Modification) (No. 5) Decree 24 May 1966.

[114] The body was established under Section 8 of the Constitution (Suspension and Modification) Decree of 17 January 1966. The Attorney General was originally a member, but his membership was terminated shortly under Decree No. 4 on the 1st of April 1966.

[115] Nigeria's short-lived post-independence democracy was halted on January 15, 1966, ushering in successive military regimes. The period between 1966 and1999 marked a turbulent and dark time for human rights in Nigeria as power changed hands from one military regime to the other in 1966-1979, a short-lived democracy between 1979 and 1983 and an unbroken military dictatorship from 1983 until a return to democracy in 1999.

indefinite detention and in many cases, subsequent murder of dissident voices by the state, long jail terms for human rights activists, a high rate of political detainees, the editor of a newspaper who allegedly had incriminating documents of the Babangida regime received and died of a parcel bomb.[116] Environmental activists in the Niger Delta were executed after sham trials by Abacha's regime despite massive international outcry.[117] High-profile pro-democracy activists and government critics were hounded, some into exile and some assassinated. Unlawful arrests, disappearances, large-scale use of torture, including murders were rife. Due to many factors including the length of the period of repression, the nature, ethnic and religious makeup of the Nigerian society including the recent establishment of the South African truth and reconciliation commission, truth commissions began to appear as an attractive option for the Nigerian situation.

After Nigeria's eventual return to democracy in 1999, the federal government of Nigeria under the Presidency of Olusegun Obasanjo instituted the Human Rights Violations Investigation Commission chaired by the very respected Justice Chukwudifu Oputa, a retired justice of the Nigerian Supreme Court. Serving as the secretary of the Commission was a Catholic Priest, Rev. Father Matthew Hassan Kukah. The Tribunal of Enquiry Act Cap 447, alongside the Nigerian Constitution provided the legal basis for instituting the commission. The panel was given a wide mandate to investigate the massive human right abuses which occurred in Nigeria between 1966 and 1999. The panel was empowered to call and examine witnesses, make factual and legal findings and make useful recommendations to be implemented by the government.[118] The panel was intended to improve reconciliation and help establish the new and fledgling democracy.[119] The members were also described as seeing themselves as 'serving on a cathartic body, which would emotionally heal wounds for those who have suffered unjustly under the military regimes'.[120] About 10,000 petitions were submitted to the Panel, with only about 1–2% of those petitions heard. Several special hearings were held for agencies critical to the functioning of the federal government, including the police and the prison service.[121] At the end of its activities, the panel produced an eight-volume report of over 15,000 pages of its administrative, judicial,

[116] Dele Giwa was a journalist and the Editor of the Newswatch publication whose mainstay was investigative journalism. He was a virulent critic of the administration of General Ibrahim Babangida. He was killed by a parcel bomb on 19 October 1986 after an invitation by the State Security Services two days earlier. The Oputa Panel asked the democratic government to investigate the murder. However, nothing was done. Till date, the case remains unsolved. See generally, The Guardian 2020a, b. See also Egwu and Wogu 2019.

[117] The execution of Ken Saro-Wiwa and eight other Niger Delta environmental activists is well documented. See for example, Campbell 2002, Narr 1997, Tam-George 2010, and Deutsche Welle 2015.

[118] See generally Yusuf 2007.

[119] Zwanbim 2017.

[120] Krishnan and Ajagbe 2018, p. 229.

[121] See Yusuf 2008, p. 209.

legislative and institutional findings including policy recommendations. Interestingly, some members of the former military junta sued members of the panel.[122] Among the arguments raised was that the federal government lacked the jurisdiction to impose the recommendation of the panel on successive state governments since they had not been involved in the panel's establishment nor consented to its powers. The Nigerian Supreme Court agreed with this reasoning and in its judgement ruled that the panel and its actions were unconstitutional. Eventually, in 2003, President Olusegun Obasanjo dismantled the commission and proscribed the public release of its report. The entire exercise appeared like a giant waste of time, public resources and the emotions of Nigerians. It cannot be categorically said that mass public recognition or reconciliation in any form was achieved through the exercise. The commission also suffered budgetary challenges as the government appeared to starve it of funds and the commission was forced to end its activities after hearing only two hundred of over ten thousand petitions.[123] The process did not result in massive public acknowledgement of the plight of the victims, majority of perpetrators did not seek nor was granted forgiveness, some high-ranking military officers including the current Nigerian president shunned the invitation and subsequent subpoena of the panel,[124] and there were no significant lustration efforts particularly in the military, the police, the judiciary[125] and in the core civil service.[126] Neither retributive nor restorative justice measures were afforded the victims. The same government that set up the commission failed to properly fund it, and after it folded up, did not publish nor implement its report.

The more successful utilisation of amnesty as a transitional justice mechanism was by the government of the late Shehu Umaru Yar Adua during whose regime oil terrorism assumed frightening dimensions in Nigeria. The people of the Niger Delta, from where majority of Nigeria's oil come, had long agitated for basic amenities in their communities, including a respect for and protection of the human rights of their people and agitators. To draw attention to their cause, large-scale attacks and destruction of oil infrastructure, oil bunkering, kidnapping for ransom including piracy became common. Several militant groups operated in the region, unleashing massive violence on government infrastructure including those belonging to private companies operating in the region. Between 2004 and 2008, the Niger Delta became a

---

[122] See generally Chukwudifu Oputa (Rtd.) and Human Rights Violations Investigation Commission and Gani Fawehinmi v. General Ibrahim Babangida, Brigadier Halilu Akilu and Brigadier Kunle Togun, [2003] M.J.S.C. 63 (Nigeria).

[123] See Human Rights Watch Report 2002.

[124] Gen Ibrahim Babangida and General Abdulsalam Abubakar and the current president Muhamadu Buhari were indicted and failed to honour subpoenas by the commission. See generally, The New Humanitarian 2005, and BBC News 2001.

[125] On the apparent lack of judicial accountability during Nigeria's military era see, Yusuf 2013.

[126] Some senior military officials were retired by the President as a result of some revelations by the panel. However, these officials were not prohibited from subsequent involvement in politics. Most of them simply rebranded and became strong political players who sought and won important positions including becoming so-called godfathers. See generally Agbese and Udogu 2005, and Folarin 2013.

theatre of crisis and violence and there was a marked proliferation of arms particularly in the hands of the militants in the region.

When the crisis could no longer be ignored, the government constituted a technical committee in September 2008 to investigate and give recommendations on the crisis in the region.[127] The chair of the technical committee (Ledum Mitee) was one of the original Ogoni environmental activists who escaped execution following their death sentence during Abacha's military regime in 1995. The committee's report was presented to the president in December 2008 and it included many recommendations, topmost of which was the amnesty idea. It gave recommendations on a Disarmament, Decommission and Reintegration (DRR) programme for the militants including key findings and recommendations on governance and rule of law in the region, infrastructural development, institutional mechanisms, resource management, stakeholders engagement including human capital development.[128] The report called for an increase in oil and gas revenue allocated to the region to 25% including an implementation of the DRR process within 6 months of the submission of the committee's report. Additionally, it also called for the release of the leader of one of the militant groups, Movement for the Emancipation of the Niger Delta (MEND), Mr. Henry Okah, who was in government custody. The Amnesty programme was to be implemented in three stages. First, militants were invited to surrender their arms and ammunition and renounce the utilisation of violence, then deserving militants were granted amnesty and lastly made to go through the rehabilitation process which ended in a five-year salary for successful participants. The amnesty policy was officially approved by the Federal Government in June 2009 and the 60-day programme started in August of the same year. The power of the President for prerogative of mercy under Section 175 of the Constitution of the Federal Republic of Nigeria was invoked as the legal basis for the grant of the conditional amnesty.[129] Again, there was no specific amnesty law outlining the borders of the legal framework for the programme.

At a public ceremony in August 2009 at the Isaac Boro Peace Park, militants in Bayelsa State formally began to surrender their weapons.[130] Such public surrender of weapons happened many more times within the provided 60-day deadline. A

[127] Unrepresented Nations and Peoples Organisation 2008.

[128] Expressed in Technical Committee of the Niger Delta 2008.

[129] (1) The President may—(a) grant any person concerned with or convicted of any offence created by an Act of the National Assembly a pardon, either free or subject to lawful conditions; (b) grant to any person a respite, either for an indefinite or for a specified period, of the execution of any punishment imposed on that person for such an offence; (c) substitute a less severe form of punishment for any punishment imposed on that person for such an offence; or (d) remit the whole or any part of any punishment imposed on that person for such an offence or of any penalty or forfeiture otherwise due to the State on account of such an offence. (2) The powers of the President under subsection (1) of this section shall be exercised by him after consultation with the Council of State. (3) The President, acting in accordance with the advice of the Council of State, may exercise his powers under subsection (1) of this section in relation to persons concerned with offences against the army, naval or air-force law or convicted or sentenced by a court-martial. Section 175 CFRN 1999.

[130] See Reuters 2009, and Reliefweb 2009.

Presidential Amnesty Implementation Committee chaired by the minister of defence was instituted to oversee the process. The militants were demobilised and placed in military camps within the region where they acquired skills acquisition and vocational training. Participants received a monthly salary including a daily fee for the period spent in the de-radicalisation and reintegration camp.

The amnesty process was a two-sided approach. Militants who failed to surrender after the 60-day expiration were expected to face the full weight of the law. The government also appeared to stage a psychological warfare by increasing military checkpoints in the region, acquiring sophisticated military weaponry including trailers carrying gunboats appearing in some of the communities.[131] This served to place additional pressure on some of the militants that had not surrendered and by the 4th October 2009 deadline, majority of the militants had surrendered their weapons and accepted the offer of amnesty.

In the Niger Delta situation, the offer of amnesty to get the militants to cease acts of violence proved to be largely successful. The programme empowered the former militants, who were required to surrender their arms and ammunitions including disavow the use of violence and militancy. The militants were in turn provided with vocational training and placed on a salary for five years. While there was widespread concern on whether this approach was a sustainable one,[132] the reality is that violence has become a thing of the past in the region and there has been relative peace since the programme was fully implemented. The programme was far from perfect and was rightly criticised as appearing as an archetype of a cash-for-peace programme.[133]

While the Niger Delta amnesty programme appears to make a compelling case for the utilisation of transitional justice mechanisms in Nigeria, the earlier discussed failure of the so-called Oputa Panel suggests otherwise. The question would then be that what can be learnt from these two scenarios, particularly for the benefit and that may be applied with the ongoing Boko Haram crisis.

The first point to note is the central nature of political will to the success of any transitional justice process. Political will is a crucial component of the realisation of the goals of the process. While there is no permanent state of will, as the stance of the government may change depending on the government of the day, it is crucial that there is a genuine intention to support transitional justice measures.[134] The lack of political will was the death knell for the process in Egypt[135] and in Afghanistan.[136] In South Africa, due to the imminent change in government and in the era, a negotiated mechanism was preferred and the government was invested in the process. With the earlier Nigerian example of the Human Rights Investigations Commission, it was clear that the government was not devoted to a successful outcome. Rather, it became quickly apparent that the exercise was a sham. The government did not fully support

131 See Albert 2019, p. 662.

132 See generally Albert 2019.

133 See Ushie 2013, BBC 2013a, b, Forbes 2018, and Reliefweb 2020.

134 Pham et al. 2019.

135 Abou-El-Fadl 2012.

136 Nadery 2007.

the process to take-off and the committee had to beg foreign donors for funds to commence its activities. Influential Nigerians disregarded the invitations, summons and eventual subpoena of the commission with no consequences. When it faced legal challenges, the federal government quietly asked the committee to wind down its activities, did not publish or implement the report. There were no large-scale lustrations and major policy recommendations for the civil service and the military were ignored. On the contrary, the Niger Delta Amnesty programme appeared to enjoy full support of the federal government and it provided the funds to execute the programme. The result was that the Niger Delta process presented a more successful outcome.

The centrality of transition is also crucial because this supposes that the parties who understand their precarious situation will be more inclined to appear at a negotiation table. While the crucial nature of transition to the utilisation of transitional justice mechanisms has been addressed in earlier sections, it is my view that an obvious shift ensures that none of the partners will be inclined to maintain status quo, if it becomes apparent that there will be no status quo to maintain. In the case of South Africa, widespread violence, sustained international outcry and chaos in the country had forced the government into a position to negotiate with the African National Congress (ANC), South African Communist Party (SACP) and South-West Africa People's Organisation (SWAPO) and their armed factions. The freedom fighter groups were also in the position where they could no longer go on fighting for an unending period as they had also suffered massive casualties, heavy repression, including large-scale imprisonment and exile of key members. Due to this peculiar state of transition, what ensued was negotiation which resulted among others to the famed transitional justice process in South Africa.[137] As I have argued elsewhere in this work, the utilisation of transitional justice prescriptions should be in the aftermath of a crisis not within the pendency of the conflict. If the Boko Haram crisis had already ended or the strength of the group had been significantly militarily reduced, it would have been much easier to have an open invitation to specified categories of its members for a transitional justice process to aid peacebuilding, and to reintegrate former offenders. This was the process with the Niger Delta militants with relative success.

A third necessary lesson is the importance of a legal framework specifying the borders of the programme. The existence of legal specified guidelines for the transitional justice process is crucial because a lack of such suggests a dearth of seriousness and preparedness by the authority regarding the process. In the same vein, without a solid legal background, if the process is tested in court, it may fall under its own hubris. This is not far-fetched as that was exactly what happened with the previously addressed Oputa Panel that led to the eventual end of the truth and reconciliation efforts. The more famed and somewhat successful transitional justice examples have a solid legal backing and unlike the case of the Oputa Panel including the Boko Haram DRR process, they have the borders and framework of the programme legally certain. Unfortunately, the ongoing DRR process for the Boko Haram crisis is legally uncertain and its legal basis lacks clarity.

[137] See Johnson and Schlemmer 1996, p. 5.

A successful transitional justice programme includes among its necessary ingredients, a sustained political will to see the process to fruition, an apparent transition including the willingness of parties to come to the negotiation table including clarity of its legal basis and legal certainty. Without these, the DRR process for the Boko Haram crisis is a mere farce that with time, will possibly end up like its predecessor programmes.

5.7 Concluding Remarks

This chapter has assessed Nigeria's response to the Boko Haram crisis beyond criminal prosecutions. For all intent and purpose, the process taking place within the **pendency of the conflict and being referred to as transitional justice has been shown** clearly as a misnomer that fails to meet even the loose requirements of transitional justice mechanisms. With a cursory and in-depth look at the predecessor programmes which are being emulated by the Boko Haram response, it becomes immensely clear that these programmes, even from their names are merely intended as a pipeline to transition the perpetrators back into society, that is, reintegration programmes as opposed to reparations or reconciliation programmes. The curious approach of an excessive focus on the perpetrator at the expense of the victims clearly shows that the 'justice' aspect of restorative justice has not been taken into account and the goal is to end violence at all costs, even at the cost of the victims. Unfortunately, this approach has failed to produce the required results, and a rethinking of the response is therefore necessary.

References

Abou-El-Fadl R (2012) 'Beyond Conventional Transitional Justice: Egypt's 2011 Revolution and the Absence of Political Will' International Journal of Transitional Justice.

Agbese P, Udogu E (2005) Taming of the Shrew: Civil-Military Politics in the Fourth Republic. Nigeria in the Twenty-First Century,Strategies for Political Stability and Peaceful Coexistence Africa World Press.

Aggestam K, Björkdahl A (eds) (2012) Rethinking Peace-building Routledge.

Ainley K, Friedman R, Mahony C (eds) (2015) Evaluating Transitional Justice: Accountability and **Peace-building in Post-Conflict Sierra Leone. Palgrave Macmillan.**

Albert I (2019) 'Hazy Agenda, Multiple Interests: Stakeholders Engagement with the First Phase of the Niger Delta Amnesty Deal in Nigeria', Beijing Law Review.

Aljazeera (2018) 'Thousands Displaced by Boko Haram Languish in Abuja IDP Camps' Available at https://www.aljazeera.com/indepth/features/thousands-displaced-boko-haram-languish-abuja-idp-camps-180325070133915.html.

Ambos K, Large J, Wierda M (2009a) Building a Future on Peace and Justice: Studies on Transitional Justice, Peace and Development: The Nuremberg Declaration of Transitional Justice, Springer.

Ambos K (2009b) 'The Legal Framework of Transitional Justice: A Systematic Study with a Special Focus on the Role of the ICC'. In: Ambos K, Large J, Wierda M (eds) 'Building a Future on Peace and Justice: Studies on Transitional Justice, Peace and Development' Springer.

Ambos K (2015) 'Assessing the Efficiency of Transitional Justice', Yonsei Law Journal
Amnesty International (2020) 'We dried our tears-Addressing the toll on Children of Northeast Nigeria's Conflict' Amnesty International Index AFR 44/2322/2020. Available at https://www.amnestyusa.org/wp-content/uploads/2020/05/We-dried-our-tears-AFR-44.2322.2020.pdf.
Anderlini S, Conaway C, Kays L (2004) 'Transitional Justice and Reconciliation'. Inclusive Security, Sustainable Peace: A Toolkit for Action and Advocacy Justice, Governance and Civil Society.
Aolain F (2008) 'Expanding the Boundaries of Transitional Justice' Ethics and International Affairs.
Aolain F, Campbell C (2005) 'The Paradox of Transition in Conflicted Democracies', Human Rights Quarterly.
Aslam M, Othman I, Rosili N (2016) 'Deradicalization Programs in Southeast Asia: A Comparative Study of Rehabilitation Programs in Malaysia, Thailand, Indonesia and Singapore' Journal of Education and Social Sciences.
Asmal K (1996) 'Reconciliation through Truth: A Reckoning of Apartheid's Criminal Governance' Mayibuye History and Literature, Series No. 74. Claremont, South Africa: David Phillip and University of the Western Cape.
Badagard L, Klamberg M (2017) 'The Gatekeeper of the ICC: Prosecutorial Strategies for Selecting Situations and Cases at the International Criminal Court', 48, Georgetown Journal of International Law.
Baker C, Obradovic-Wochnik J (2016) 'Mapping the Nexus of Transitional Justice and Peace-Building', Journal of Intervention and State-building.
Balasco L (2013) 'The Transitions of Transitional Justice: Mapping the Waves from Promise to Practice', Journal of Human Rights.
Balint J (2014) 'Transitional Justice and State Crime', 13, Macquarie Law Journal.
Bassiouni C (1996a) 'International Crimes: Jus Cogens and Obligatio Erga Omnes' 59 Law and Contemporary Problems.
Bassiouni C (1996b) 'Searching for Peace and Achieving Justice: The Need for Accountability', 59, Law and Contemporary Problems.
Bassiouni C (ed) (2002) Post-Conflict Justice, Brill Nijhoff.
BBC News (2001) 'Generals Evade Nigeria Rights Panel' 01 November 2001. Available at http://news.bbc.co.uk/2/hi/africa/1632714.stm.
BBC (2013a) 'Nigeria's Boko Haram reject Jonathan's Amnesty Idea' 11 April 2013. Available at https://www.bbc.com/news/world-africa-22105476.
BBC (2013b) 'Has Nigeria's Niger Delta Managed to Buy Peace?' 01 May 2013. Available at https://www.bbc.com/news/world-africa-22357597.
Benvenuti P (2014) 'Transitional justice and Impunity', 11, International Studies Journal.
Bonacker T, Buckley-Zistel S (2013) 'Introduction: Transitions from Violence-Analyzing the Effects of Transitional Justice', 7(1), International Journal of Conflict and Violence.
Brants C, Klep K (2013) Transitional Justice: History Telling, Collective Memory, and the Victim Witnesses. 7(1), International Journal of Conflict and Violence.
Bukarti A, Bryson R (2019) 'Dealing with Boko Haram Defectors in the Lake Chad Basin: Lessons from Nigeria' Tony Blair institute for Global Change April 2019.
Bukarti B (2019) 'Making Peace with Enemies: Nigeria's Re-integration of Boko Haram Fighters' 27 March 2019. Available at https://warontherocks.com/2019/03/making-peace-with-enemies-nigerias-reintegration-of-boko-haram-fighters/.
Call C (2004) 'Is Transitional Justice Really Just', 11, Brown Journal of World Affairs.
Campbell M (2002) 'Witnessing Death: Ken Saro-Wiwa and the Ogoni Crisis', Postcolonial Studies: Culture Politics, Economy.
Capstack A (2015) 'Deradicalization Programs in Saudi Arabia: A Case Study' in Understanding Deradicalization: Pathway to Enhance Transatlantic Common Perception and Practices available at https://www.mei.edu/publications/deradicalization-programs-saudi-arabia-case-study
Carnegie Endowment for International Peace (2019) Morocco's Failure to Reintegrate Former Jihadis, 6 February 2019. Available at https://carnegieendowment.org/sada/78313.

Carranza R (2008) 'Plunder and Pain: Should Transitional Justice Engage with Corruption and Economic Crimes?', 2(3), International Journal of Transitional Justice.

Cassese A (1998) 'On the current Trend towards Criminal Prosecution and Punishment of Breaches of International Humanitarian Law', 9(1), European Journal of International Law.

Clamp K (2014) 'Restorative Justice in Transition' Routledge.

Clark J (2011) 'Transitional Justice, Truth and Reconciliation: An Under-Explored Relationship', International Criminal Law Review.

Council on Foreign Relations (2020) 'Nigeria Considers National DRR Agency Amid Boko Haram Setbacks' 18 March 2020. Available at https://www.cfr.org/blog/nigeria-considers-national-drr-agency-amid-boko-haram-setbacks.

Cordes B (1987) 'When Terrorists do the Talking: Reflections on Terrorist Literature', 10(4), Journal of Strategic Studies.

Cronin A (2011) How Terrorism Ends: Understanding the Decline and Demise of Terrorist Campaigns, Princeton University Press.

Czarnota A, Parmentier S (eds) (2013) Transitional Justice and Rule of Law: Institutional Design and the Changing Normative Structure of Post: Authoritarian Societies. Intersentia Belgium.

Dalhoum M et al (2020) Deradicalization of Returnees to Jordan and Morocco: Limitations, Strengths and Lessons for the Region. IMES Capstone Paper Series. Available at https://cpb-us-e1.wpmucdn.com/blogs.gwu.edu/dist/6/1613/files/2020/05/Deradicalization-of-Returnees-to-Jordan-and-Morocco.pdf

David R, Holliday I (2006) 'Set the Junta Free: Pre-Transitional Justice in Myanmar's Democratization', Australian Journal of Political Sciences.

Deutsche Welle (2015) 'Why Nigerian Activist Ken Saro-Wiwa was Executed' 09 November 2015. Available at https://www.dw.com/en/why-nigerian-activist-ken-saro-wiwa-was-executed/a-18837442.

Doak J, O'Mahony D (2012) 'Transitional Justice and Restorative Justice', International Criminal Law Review.

Doorn N (2021) 'Forgiveness and Reconciliation in Transitional Justice Practices' Radboud Repository.

Doosje B et al. (2016) 'Terrorism, Radicalization and Deradicalization', Current Opinion in Psychology.

Duhart P (2019) 'Talking with Terrorists, Talking with governments: Insurgent Perspectives on Legitimization and Engagement', 12(3), Critical Studies on Terrorism.

Duong V, Ear S (2010) 'Transitional Justice Dilemma: The Case of Cambodia', 2, Peace and Conflict Review.

Dyzenhaus D (2003) 'Transitional Justice', 1, International Journal of Constitutional Law.

Edelenbos C (1994) 'Human Rights Violations: A Duty to Prosecute?', Leiden Journal of International Law.

Egwu P, Wogu J (2019) 'Doing Investigative Journalism in Nigeria: Challenges, Impacts and Strategies', Academic Track Reader.

El-Said H (2015) New Approaches to Countering Terrorism: Designing and Evaluating Counter-Radicalisation and De-Radicalisation Programs, Palgrave Macmillan.

European Eye on Radicalization (2019) Why Saudi Arabia's Deradicalization Program is Successful, 10 June 2019. Available at https://eeradicalization.com/why-saudi-arabias-deradicalization-program-is-successful/e

Ewald U, Turković K (2006) Large Scale Victimization as a Potential Source of Terrorist Activities. NATO Security Through Science series.

Eweluka D (1967) 'The Constitutional Aspects of Military Takeover in Nigeria', 2(1), Nigeria Law Journal.

Felbab-Brown B (2018) 'In Nigeria we don't want them back: Amnesty, Defectors Program, Leniency Measure, Informal Reconciliation, and Punitive Responses to Boko Haram' United Nations University. Available at https://www.brookings.edu/research/in-nigeria-we-dont-want-them-back/.

Folarin S (2013) Africa's leadership challenges in the 21st century: A Nigerian perspective., 7(1) African Journal of Political Science and International Relations.

Forbes (2018) 'Amnesty and the New Violence in the Niger Delta' 20 March 2018. Available at https://www.forbes.com/sites/uhenergy/2018/03/20/amnesty-and-new-violence-in-the-niger-delta/.

Garcia-Godos J (2008) 'Victim Reparations in Transitional Justice, What Is at Stake and Why?' 26, Nordisk Tidsskrift for Menneskerettigheter.

Gibson J (2004) 'Does Truth Lead to Reconciliation? Testing the Causal Assumptions of the South African Truth and Reconciliation Process', 48 American Journal of Political Science.

Goerzig C (2010) Talking to Terrorists, Concessions and Renunciation of Violence, Routledge.

Gready P, Robins S (2014) 'From Transitional to Transformative Justice: A New Agenda for Practice', 8(3) International Journal of Transitional Justice.

Gross J (2010) 'Talking with Terrorists: Terrorist Groups and the Challenge of Legitimization', Princeton University Journal of Public and International Affairs.

Grossman N (2007) 'Rehabilitation or Revenge: Prosecuting Child Soldiers for Human Rights Violations', 38 Georgetown Journal of International Law.

Guardian (2018) 'Amnesty for Boko Haram' 20 April 2018. Available at https://guardian.ng/opinion/amnesty-for-boko-haram/.

Guardian (2020a) 'Opposition Voices Knock Gaidam over Bill on Boko Haram' 03 March 2020. Available at https://guardian.ng/politics/opposition-voices-knock-gaidam-over-bill-on-boko-haram/

Guardian (2020b) '34 Years after Murder, Dele Giwa's Family seeks Justice; Colleague insists on government Investigation' 20 October 2020. Available at https://guardian.ng/features/media/34-years-after-murder-dele-giwas-family-seeks-justice-colleague-insists-on-govt-investigation/.

Haldemann F (2008) 'Another Kind of Justice: Transitional Justice as Recognition', 41 Cornell International Law Journal.

Hasan I, Tyvoll J (2018) 'After Boko Haram: Prospects for Transitional Justice in North East Nigeria' Center for Democracy and Development.

Haspeslagh S (2020) 'The Mediation Dilemma of (Not) Talking to Terrorists', Swiss Political Science Review.

Horgan J (2009) 'Deradicalization or Disengagement: A Process in need of Clarity and a Counter Terrorism Initiative in need of Evaluation', 4(24) Revista de Psicología Social.

Horgan J, Altier M (2012) 'The Future of Terrorist De-Radicalisation Programs', 13(2) Georgetown Journal of International Affairs.

Horgan J, Braddock K (2010) 'Rehabilitating the Terrorist? Challenges in Assessing the Effectiveness of De-radicalisation Programs', 22(2) Terrorism and Political Violence.

Hovland I (2003) 'Macro/Micro Dynamics in South Africa: Why the Reconciliation Process Will Not Reduce Violence', Journal of Peace-Building and Development.

Human Rights Watch (2002) Human Rights Watch Report 2002-Nigeria 17 January 2002. Available at https://www.refworld.org/docid/3c46e92a2.html.

Human Right Watch (2018) 'Nigeria: Flawed Trials of Boko Harm Suspects' 17 September 2018 available at https://www.hrw.org/news/2018/09/17/nigeria-flawed-trials-boko-haram-suspects.

ICIR Nigeria (2020) 'Repentant Boko Haram': A Look at Operation Safe Corridor Deradicalization and Rehabilitation Camp' 01 November 2020. Available at https://www.icirnigeria.org/repentant-boko-haram-a-look-at-operation-safe-corridor-deradicalisation-and-rehabilitation-camp/.

Janoff-Bulmann R (2007) 'Macro versus Micro Justice and Perceived Fairness of Truth and Reconciliation Commissions', 13 Peace and Conflict Journal of Peace Psychology.

Jayakumar S (2020) 'Deradicalization in Singapore: Past, Present and Future' International Center for Study of Radicalization. Available at https://icsr.info/wp-content/uploads/2020/08/ICSR-Report-Deradicalisation-in-Singapore-Past-Present-and-Future.pdf

Jessberger F (2007) 'Universality, Complementarity and the Duty to Prosecute Crimes under International Law in Germany'. In: Kaleck W et al (eds) International Prosecution of Human Rights Crimes, Springer.

Johnson R, Schlemmer L (eds) (1996) Launching Democracy in South Africa: The First Open Election, April 1994, Yale University Press.

Kaleck W et al (eds) (2007) International Prosecution of Human Rights Crimes, Springer.

Kaya Z (2016) 'Letting Go: Deradicalization in Egypt', Journal for Deradicalization.

Krishnan J, Ajagbe K (2018) 'Legal Activism in the Face of Political Challenges: The Nigerian Case', 42(2) The Journal of the Legal Profession.

Kritz B, Wilson J (2010) 'No Transitional Justice Without transition: Darfur, A Case Study', Michigan State Journal of International Law.

Lambourne W (2009) 'Transitional Justice and Peacebuilding after Mass Violence', 3(1) International Journal of Transitional Justice.

Laplante L (2008) 'Transitional Justice and Peacebuilding: Diagnosing and Addressing the Socioeconomic Roots of Violence through a Human Rights Framework', 2(3) International Journal of Transitional Justice.

Layus R (2010) The Role of Transitional Justice in the Midst of Ongoing Armed Conflict: The Case of Colombia, Potsdam Universitätsverlag.

Leebaw B (2008) 'The Irreconcilable Goals of Transitional Justice', 30 Human Rights Quarterly.

Lekha S (2007) Justice as Peace? Liberal Peace-building and Strategies of Transitional Justice. Global Society.

Mani R (20089 'Dilemmas of Expanding Transitional Justice or Forging the Nexus between Transitional Justice and Development', 2 International Journal of Transitional Justice.

McDonnell A, Burbridge H, Salloum Y (2017) 'Addressing Jihadi Salafism in Yemen: The Role of Religion and Community in the Middle of Civil War' International Center for Religion and Diplomacy.

Mendeloff D (2004) 'Truth-Seeking, Truth-Telling, and Post-Conflict Peacebuilding: Curb the Enthusiasm', 6(3) International Studies Review.

Mihai M (2010) 'Transitional Justice and the Quest for Democracy: A Contribution to a Political Theory of Democratic Transitions', International Journal of Jurisprudence and the Philosophy of Law.

Morier F (2019) 'Program Insight: The Screening Process of Disengaged Boko Haram Associates in Niger', 21 Journal of Deradicalization.

Muhammad A, Hiariej E, Boateng J (2021) 'Deradicalization Programs in Indonesia Radicalizing the Radicals', 7(1) Cogent Social Sciences.

Mühlhausen A (2016/17) 'Conflict Management, Transitional Justice and De-radicalization- Different, but common goals', 9 Journal for Deradicalization.

Mutua M (2015) 'What is the Future of Transitional Justice', 9(1) International Journal of Transitional Justice.

Muvingi I (2011) 'Transitional Justice and Political Pre-transition in Zimbabwe', 1 Conflict Trends.

Nadery A (2007) 'Peace or Justice? Transitional Justice in Afghanistan', 1(1), International Journal of Transitional Justice.

Nagy R (2008) 'Transitional Justice as a Global Project: Critical Reflections', Third World Quarterly.

Narr W (1997) 'Ken Saro-Wiwa and the Global Irresponsibility for Human Life', 22 Dialectical Anthropology.

Neumann P (2007) 'Negotiating with Terrorists', 86 Foreign Affairs.

New Humanitarian (2005) 'Rights Panel wanted three Ex-Military Rulers Probed for Killings' 12 January 2005. Available at https://www.thenewhumanitarian.org/report/52654/nigeria-rights-panel-wanted-three-ex-military-rulers-probed-killings.

Newman D (2004–2005) 'The Rome Statute, Some Reservations Concerning Amnesties and A Distributive Problem', 20 American University International Law Review.

Nwankpa M (2014) 'The Politics of Amnesty in Nigeria: A Comparative Analysis of the Boko Haram and Niger Delta Insurgencies', (2014), 5 Journal of Terrorism Research.

Nwankpa M (2016) 'Dialoguing and Negotiating with Terrorists: Any Prospects for Boko Haram?', Journal of Behavioral Sciences of Terrorism and Political Aggression.

Obamamoye B (2018) 'Navigating the Enigma of Negotiating with a Jihadist Terrorist Group', Journal of African Security.

Ojo V, Filbert N (2020) 'Too Much of a Good Thing: When Transitional Justice Prescriptions May Not Work', 33 South African Journal of Criminal Justice.

Oluduro O, Oluduro F (2012) 'Nigeria: In Search of Sustainable Peace Through the Amnesty Program', Journal of Sustainable Development.

Parmentier S (2003) 'Global Justice in the Aftermath of Mass Violence: The Role of the International Criminal Court in Dealing with Political Crimes', International Annals of Criminology.

Parrin A (2016) 'Creating a Legal Framework for Terrorism Defectors and Detainees in Somalia', Columbia Journal of Transnational Law.

Pettinger T (2017) 'De-Radicalization and Counter-Radicalization: Valuable Tools Combating Violent Extremism or Harmful Methods of Subjugation?', Journal for Deradicalization.

Pham P, Gibbons N, Vinck P (2019) 'A Framework for Assessing Political Will in Transitional Justice Contexts', 23 The International Journal of Human Rights.

Posner E, Vermeule A (2004) 'Transitional Justice as Ordinary Justice', 117 Harvard International Law Review.

Powel J (2014) Talking to Terrorists: How to End Armed Conflicts, Penguin Random House.

Quinn J (2014–15) 'Whither the 'Transition' of Transitional Justice?', Interdisciplinary Journal of Human Rights Law.

Ramji-Nogales J (2010) 'Designing Bespoke Transitional Justice: A Pluralist Process Approach' 32 Michigan Journal of International Law.

Reliefweb (2009) 'Nigerian Militant Groups Surrender More Arms in Bayelsa State' 01 September 2009. Available at https://reliefweb.int/report/nigeria/nigerian-militant-groups-surrender-more-arms-bayelsa-state.

Reliefweb (2018) 'Nigeria: A Critical Humanitarian Situation is Unfolding among Internally Displaced People in Bama Borno State', 17 August 2018. Available at https://reliefweb.int/report/nigeria/nigeria-critical-humanitarian-situation-unfolding-among-internally-displaced-people.

Reliefweb (2020) 'Assessment of the Presidential Amnesty Program' August 2020. Available at https://reliefweb.int/sites/reliefweb.int/files/resources/Presidential-Amnesty-Programme-Report-Policy-Brief.pdf.

Renner J, Spencer A (2011) Reconciliation after Terrorism: Strategy, Possibility or Absurdity? Routledge.

Reuters (2009) 'Hundreds of Nigerian Oil Militants Surrender Arms' 22 August 2009. Available at https://www.reuters.com/article/idUSLM105574.

Sarkin J, Daly E (2004) 'Too many questions, too few answers: Reconciliation in Transitional Societies', 35 Columbia Human Rights Law Review.

Sciandra E (2017) Facing the State of Fear: The Emerging Issues of Terrorism and Counterterrorism in Transitional Justice, Palgrave Handbook of Global Counterterrorism Policy.

Seibert-Fohr A (2003) 'The Relevance of the Rome Statute of the International Criminal Court for Amnesties and Truth Commissions', 7(1) Max Planck Yearbook of United Nations Law Online.

Skaar E (2013) 'Reconciliation in a Transitional Justice Perspective', 1 Transitional Justice Review.

Speckhard A, Akhmedova K (2005) 'Talking to Terrorists', 33 Journal of Psychohistory.

Sriram C (2007) Justice as Peace? Liberal Peacebuilding and Strategies of Transitional Justice. Global Society.

Sriram C, Herman J (2009) DDR and Transitional Justice: Bridging the Divide. 9(4) Conflict, Security and Development.

Szablewska N, Bachmann S (eds) (2015) Current Issues in Transitional Justice: Towards a more Holistic Approach, Springer.

Tam-George A (2010) 'Ken Saro-Wiwa, The Ogoni Struggle and the Aesthetics of Spectacle', Canadian Review of Comparative Literature.

Technical Committee of the Niger Delta (2008) Report of the Technical Committee of the Niger Delta November 2008. Available at http://www.mosop.org/Nigeria_Niger_Delta_Technical_Committee_Report_2008.pdf

Teitel R (2003) 'Transitional Justice Genealogy', Harvard Human Rights Journal.

Teitel R (2005) 'The Law and Politics of Contemporary Transitional Justice', 38 Cornell International Law Journal.

Teitel R (2006) 'Transitional Justice: Post War Legacies', 27, Cardozo Law Review.

Teitel R (2014) Globalizing Transitional Justice: Contemporary Essays, Oxford University Press.

Tellidis I, Toros H (2015) Researching Terrorism, Peace and Conflict Studies: Interaction, Synthesis and Opposition. Routledge.

Truth and Reconciliation Commission of South Africa (1998) Truth and Reconciliation Commission of South Africa Report Volume Four 29 October 1998. Available at https://www.justice.gov.za/trc/report/finalreport/Volume%204.pdf.

Turner C (2017) 'Violence, Law and the Impossibility of Transitional Justice' Taylor and Francis.

UN (2006) Integrated Disarmament, Demobilization and Reintegration Standards: The UN Approach to DDR. August 2006.

UNPO (2008) 'Ogoni: Technical Committee Crucial to Delta Security' 09 October 2008. Available at https://unpo.org/article/8762

Ushie V (2013) 'Nigeria's Amnesty Program as a Peacebuilding Infrastructure: A Silver Bullet?', 8 Journal of Peacebuilding and Development.

van der Merwe H, Baxter V, Chapman A (eds) (2009) Assessing the Impact of Transitional Justice: Challenges for Empirical Research. United States Institute of Peace Press.

Vanfraechem I, Pemberton A, Ndahinda F (eds) (2014) Justice for Victims, Perspectives on Rights, Transition and Reconciliation. Routledge.

Van Zyl P (2003) 'Transitional Justice: Conflict Closure and Sustainable Peace' (2003) 9 Dispute Resolution Magazine.

Villa-Vicencio C (2000) 'Why Perpetrators Should not always be Prosecuted: Where the International Criminal Court and Truth Commissions Meet' 49 Emory Law Journal.

Vinck P, Pham P (2008) 'Ownership and Participation in Transitional Justice Mechanisms: A Sustainable Human Development Perspective for Eastern DRC' International Journal of Transitional Justice.

VON (2019) 'Operation Safe Corridor De-radicalizes Convicted Boko Haram Members' 12 October 2019.

Weinstein H (2014) 'Victims, Transitional Justice and Social Reconstruction: Who is setting the Agenda?' In: Vanfraechem I et al (eds) Justice for Victims, Perspectives on Rights, Transition and Reconciliation. Routledge.

Yusuf H (2007) 'Travails of Truth: Achieving Justice for Victims of Impunity in Nigeria', International Journal of Transitional Justice.

Yusuf H (2008) 'Calling the Judiciary to Account for the Past: Transitional Justice and Judicial Accountability in Nigeria', 30(2), Law and Policy.

Yusuf H (2013) 'Chequered Accounts: Truth, Justice and the Judiciary in Post Authoritarian Nigeria'. In: Czarnota A, Parmentier S (eds) Transitional Justice and Rule of Law: Institutional Design and the Changing Normative Structure of Post Authoritarian Societies. Intersentia Belgium.

Yusuf H (2018) 'Colonialism and the Dilemmas of Transitional Justice in Nigeria', 12 International Journal of Transitional Justice in Nigeria.

Zwanbim E (2017) 'The Challenge of Transitional Justice in Nigeria: Echoes from the Oputa Panel' Journal of Language, Technology and Entrepreneurship in Africa.

Zyberi G, **Černič J (2015) 'Transitional Justice Processes and Reconciliation in the Former** Yugoslavia: Challenges and Prospects', 33(2) Nordic Journal of Human Rights.

Cases

Chukwudifu Oputa (Rtd.) and Human Rights Violations Investigation Commission and Gani Fawehinmi v. General Ibrahim Babangida, Brigadier Halilu Akilu and Brigadier Kunle Togun (2003) M.J.S.C 63 Nigeria.

Other Documents

African Charter on Human and Peoples' Rights 1981.
Constitution of the Federal Republic of Nigeria 1999.
Convention Against Torture and Other Cruel Inhuman or Degrading Treatment or Punishment of 10 December 1984.
Convention on the Prevention and Punishment of the Crime of Genocide of 9 December 1948
European Convention for the Protection of Human Rights and Fundamental Freedom of 4 November 1950.
Geneva Convention for the Amelioration of the Condition of the Wounded and Sick in Armed Forces in the Field (Geneva Convention I) 1949.
Geneva Convention for the Amelioration of the Condition of the Wounded, Sick and Shipwrecked Members of Armed Forces at the Sea (Geneva Convention II) 1949.
Geneva Convention Relative to the Protection of Civilian Persons in Time of War (Geneva Convention IV) 1949.
Geneva Convention Relative to the Treatment of Prisoners of War (Geneva Convention III) 1949.
International Covenant on Civil and Political Rights of 16 December 1966.

Chapter 6
Concluding Remarks: Towards a Victim-Centred Approach

Contents

Abstract This chapter concludes the book and represents the recommendations of the author regarding the domestic and international criminal perspectives to the Boko Haram crisis in Nigeria.

Keywords Al-Qaeda · UN Counter Terrorism Committee · Nigeria · Political will · Operation Safe Corridor · Victims

6.1 Concluding Remarks

An alleged terrorist financier and owner of a bank—Al Taqwa, accused of managing money for Al-Qaedawas a man with massive business interests in Nigeria, the Middle East and Europe. His bank and financial management firms were accused of helping Al-Qaeda place, layer and integrate money across the world. Consequently, the assets of the bank were frozen by US President George Bush in a public declaration in the aftermath of the September 11 attacks in 2001.[1] He was also specifically named in a letter to the United Nations pursuant to resolution 1373 (2001) by Nigeria's representative to the Chairman of the UN Counter-Terrorism Committee.[2] However, as a result of many factors including a sanctions regime allegedly not properly implemented,[3] alleged deals made with the American government via his corporation in

[1] See White House Archive 2001.

[2] United Nations Security Council Resolution 1373, 2001. See also United Nations Security Council Letter dated 7 February 2007 from the Chairman of the Security Council Committee established pursuant to resolution 1373 (2001) concerning counter-terrorism addressed to the President of the Security Council 08 February 2007.

[3] NBC News 2005, and Los Angeles Times 2007.

V. Ojo-Adewuyi, *Criminal Justice Responses to the Boko Haram Crisis in Nigeria*, International Criminal Justice Series 34, https://doi.org/10.1007/978-94-6265-615-4_6

Nigeria headquartered in Jos, a town which is a boiling point of tribal and religious tensions in Nigeria, continued to operate as usual.

In 2012, President Goodluck Jonathan in his speech described his government as being overrun by terrorist sympathisers who favoured the ideology of Boko Haram and were quietly supporting the group.[4] Similarly, in 2018, a former Nigerian Chief of Army Staff and Minister of Defence, Lt Gen Danjuma, also accused certain top military officials of complicity in some of the killings attributed to the herdsmen and Boko Haram in Northern Nigeria. He claimed that the military was no longer neutral in the war against terror.[5]

In 2019, six Nigerians were sentenced to various terms including life imprisonment by the Abu Dhabi Federal Court of Appeal after being found guilty of providing critical financial support for Boko Haram between 2015 and 2016. The funds in question totalling nearly a million US dollars were transferred from Dubai to Nigeria by the accused persons for the benefit of the terror group.[6] The decision of the lower court was upheld on appeal at the Federal Supreme Court and the six Nigerians were further added to a terror watch-list by the UAE cabinet via its Ministerial Resolution No. 83 of 2021.[7] While the list itself was not without controversy, as it was alleged that some human rights activists—four members of the UAE94—were included,[8] the inclusion of the six Nigerians was incontrovertible, they were indeed convicted of terrorism financing by the highest court in the UAE.

In 2021, Nigeria's minister of Communication and Digital Economy, Dr Isa Pantami, became embroiled in controversy when statements he made in earlier sermons resurfaced.[9] In these sermons, he shared extremist rhetoric, using similar language to Al-Qaeda and the Taliban against Christians and the west. He preached his support of Jihad in Nigeria and held public debates with the erstwhile leader of Boko Haram, Mohammed Yusuf. Although, he claimed not to approve of the means of Boko Haram, he appeared to support the goal of the group. He believed in the extreme form of Salafi ideology and, as the Chief Imam of Abubakar Tafawa Balewa University Mosque, he taught radical Salafism to his impressionable student members and declared fatwas on so-called unbelievers. His inflammatory rhetoric led to the gruesome murder of a Christian student who was preaching on the campus.[10] He publicly mourned the death of Abu Musab Al-Zarqawi, the former Al-Qaeda fighter in Afghanistan, whose protégé, Abu Bakr al-Baghdadi, was one of the founders of the Islamic State. He once stated in a sermon that he considered Osama bin Laden a better Muslim than himself and that Boko Haram fighters were 'our Muslim brothers' who do not deserve to be 'killed like pigs'.[11] All the allegations and facts were not denied

[4] Deutsche Welle 2012, and The Guardian 2012.

[5] Thisday Live 2018, and Vanguard 2019.

[6] VOA 2020, and The Guardian 2021a.

[7] See UAE Government undated; National News 2021.

[8] See MENA Rights 2021.

[9] BBC 2021.

[10] ICIR Nigeria 2021a.

[11] BBC 2021.

by the minister, but rather he claimed to have repented of his extremist views. Amidst pressure mounted on him to resign, the presidency rose strongly in his support and a motion at the lower legislative house calling for his sack was not heard.[12] While the minister remains in power, the Nigerian public is concerned whether there are more influential Nigerians in government who share these views, including closet terrorist sympathisers in the Nigerian government, and the implications of this for the unsuccessful war against terror so far.[13]

The so-called war on terror cannot be described as a success since the Boko Haram crisis started. The modest gains of the military against the group were soon reversed as Boko Haram became increasingly sophisticated, gained territory and has continued to be a major factor in Nigeria's national security crisis for over a decade. Nigeria's military strategy to combat the activities of the group often lacked cohesion and its legal strategy has also not fared better. The body language of the current Nigerian government and its war against terror is very disturbing to say the least. Mr. Lai Mohammed, the information and culture minister, at different fora accused western countries of refusing to provide support and sell weapons to Nigeria for the fight against Boko Haram.[14] Indeed, the American government placed an embargo at different times on the sale of military hardware to Nigeria over human rights concerns.[15] However, when the American government offered to provide more material support including naming funders of Boko Haram, the Nigerian government did not seem ready to take up the offer.[16] At the same time, the increasing incidences of Boko Haram fighters high-jacking high tech hardware from the Nigerian military has raised concerns of poor training, low morale including the possibility of internal subversion.[17]

6.2 Towards a Victim-Centred Approach

While a few cases against suspected Boko Haram fighters have been prosecuted, the majority of the high-level perpetrators have not been apprehended. Surrendered low-level offenders are funnelled back into society, through programmes such as Operation Safe Corridor, often with government stipends, skills and a better financial means. However, the sole programme for the victims relies on donor funding, and major victim groups continue to live in internally displaced camps, existing in a state of limbo, having lost nearly everything, most unable to return home to a meaningful life. These victims are able to juxtapose government's treatment of the perpetrators and their neglect. Additionally, since the ICC's preliminary examination ended, the

[12] Vanguard 2021, and ICIR Nigeria 2021b.

[13] Africa Report 2021a.

[14] Vanguard 2020b, and Vanguard 2020a.

[15] Africa Report 2021b.

[16] The Guardian 2021b.

[17] Council of Foreign Relations 2021, and Daily Trust 2021.

façade of serious prosecution of Boko Haram crimes is no longer maintained by the authorities.

Under Nigerian law, the role of the victim in a trial process is merely that of an observer, or at best a witness. Generally, the focus of the Nigerian criminal justice system is principally on the accused persons, with a view to meting punishment for the crime committed, and the State standing as the complainant. The excessive focus on punishment without balancing the injury suffered by the victims translates into the fact that they are completely side-lined in the justice process, only invited as witnesses or observers of the process, but not as beneficiaries of the justice sought. In criminal trials in Nigeria, another way a victim or victim's representatives may be involved in the process is that the law allows a person or persons with necessary interest in a trial to apply to the court for 'watching brief' within the case. This may be granted by the Judge upon determination that the interest in question may be jeopardised. When granted, although the person is technically not a party to the case, they will be allowed to enter an appearance, take note of the proceedings and assist the prosecutor with facts within their purview.[18] However, no restorative justice determination such as compensation may be made for the benefit of the party watching brief. The movement seeking to centre victims in the criminal justice process in Nigeria is not recent. Justice Chukwudifu Oputa of the Nigerian Supreme Court, in *Godwin Josiah v. The State,* in 1985 famously described justice as a three-way traffic, including justice for the accused, for the victims of the crime and for the society.[19] While the Criminal Procedure Code and the Criminal Procedure Act—predecessors of the Administration of Criminal Justice Law—both makes provisions for some compensation in certain criminal proceedings, such compensation is only consequent upon conviction of the accused and the value is determined by the court to the exclusion of the victim showing evidence of damage suffered.[20] Another approach may be for the victims to institute a civil action for compensation after the completion of the criminal process. This is often impractical, the wheels of justice grind very slowly in Nigeria, cases take an inordinate length of time and many victims may not have the financial wherewithal to pursue an action against a convict years after they suffered the loss.[21]

Although, the Administration of Criminal Justice Act of 2015 introduced elements of restorative justice, its provisions are not progressive enough and it has also not been adopted by all the thirty-six states of the federation.[22] In practice, the Nigerian criminal justice system is still mainly slanted towards retribution without a major focus on a restorative aspect. This attitude to justice, although initially common in many legal systems, is now obsolete, and many have moved away from this antiquated

[18] See Federal Republic of Nigeria v. Abiola (1994) FHCLR 156, 160.

[19] Godwin Josiah v. The State (1985) 1 NWLR 125.

[20] See Sections 255–262 and 435 (2) of the Criminal Procedure Act and Sections 78, 356 and 357 of the Criminal Procedure Code.

[21] Worika and Ozuru 2018.

[22] At the time of writing, thirty out of Nigeria's thirty-six states have adopted a form of the Administration of Criminal Justice Act/Law.

approach to justice.[23] Ideally, the justice system is for the benefit of citizens and if they become victims of crimes, they should be entitled to be properly aided by the justice system. The victim should be nearer to the centre of the justice process in modern justice perspective.

Under international criminal law, the victim's role in the justice process is much more robust. The victim occupies a centralised role with specific provisions relating to restitution, rehabilitation and compensation to be made for the benefit of the victims. The Rome Statute recognises the suffering of victims and survivors. It also makes specific provisions for compensation upon conviction of the accused person.[24] Inherent in the idea of individual responsibility for criminal conduct is also the notion of perpetrators responsibility for redressing the harm suffered by the victims. The Rome Statute of the ICC utilises a two-pronged approach to respond to the needs of the victims. In the first instance, the Court is empowered to make reparations order against convicted persons for the benefit of the recognised victims.[25] Additionally, as provided for in Article 79 of the Statute, the Trust Fund for the Victims also provides assistance for victims. The trust fund is empowered to provide broad-based support including 'physical, psychological rehabilitation and/or material support.'[26] This includes implementing court-ordered reparations.[27] While the response of the ICC to victims is far from perfect and often criticised,[28] the reality is that in comparison to Nigeria's non-existent domestic law and practices for the benefit of the victims, there exists a clear gap with regards to victims' redress. Victim justice in the Boko Haram situation is crucial for a number of reasons: on the restorative justice front, rethinking Nigeria's approach to the conflict is necessary due to the lack of an actual justice component of the so-called restorative justice programmes being embarked upon as shown in the previous chapter. It is also clear that there is a dearth of political will in investing in a robust response to the suffering of the victims of the Boko Haram crisis. At the same time, decisive prosecutorial action does not appear to be taken actively against the perpetrators. While the Boko Haram crisis continues, although it no longer grabs the headlines, it is imperative that the victims of the crisis are placed where they belong, that is in the centre of the discourse.

References

Africa Report (2021a) 'Nigeria: After Pantami, are there more closet extremists in government?' 20 July 2021. Available at https://www.theafricareport.com/83029/nigeria-after-pantami-are-there-more-closet-extremists-in-government/.

---

[23] Cardenas 1986.

[24] See Garkawe 2003.

[25] Article 75 Rome Statute of the International Criminal Court.

[26] Regulation 49 Regulation of the Trust Fund for Victims.

[27] See Trust Fund for Victims website, available at https://www.icc-cpi.int/tfv.

[28] See McCarthy 2012. See also Trumbull 2007–2008.

Africa Report (2021b) 'Nigeria risks another Embargo on sale of US Military Hardware over Human Rights Concerns' 02 August 2021. Available at https://www.theafricareport.com/114202/nigeria-risks-another-embargo-on-sale-of-us-military-hardware-over-human-rights-concerns/.

BBC (2021) 'Isa Pantami: The Nigerian Minister Haunted by his Extremist Views' 23 April 2021. Available at https://www.bbc.com/news/world-africa-56846948.

Cardenas J (1986) The Crime Victim in the Prosecutorial Process. (1986), 9, Harvard Journal of Law and Public Policy.

Council of Foreign Relations (2021) 'Boko Haram Capture of Military Equipment Fuels Lake Chad Insurgency', 09 September 2021. Available at https://www.cfr.org/blog/boko-haram-capture-military-equipment-fuels-lake-chad-insurgency.

Daily Trust (2021) 'How Boko Haram Survives on Weapons Stolen From Nigeria Military' 25 April 2021. Available at https://dailytrust.com/how-b-haram-survives-on-weapons-stolen-from-nigerian-military.

Deutsche Welle (2012) 'Nigerian President Warns of Terrorist Sympathizers in Government' 08 January 2012. Available at https://www.dw.com/en/nigerian-president-warns-of-terrorist-sympathizers-in-government/a-15653513

Garkawe S (2003) 'Victims and International Criminal Court: Three Major Issues'. (2003), 3(4), International Criminal Law Review.

ICIR Nigeria (2021a) 'How Pantami Inciting Sermon led to Sunday Achi's Death', 05 May 2021. Available at https://www.icirnigeria.org/how-pantami-inciting-sermon-led-to-Sunday-achis-death-former-atbu-students/.

ICIR Nigeria (2021b) 'Presidency Stands by Pantami Despite Pro-Terrorism Statements', 22 April 2021. Available at https://www.icirnigeria.org/presidency-says-stand-by-pantami-despite-pro-terrorism-statements/.

Los Angeles Times (2007) 'When is a Terrorism Figure no Longer One?', 28 November 2007. Available at https://www.latimes.com/archives/la-xpm-2007-nov-28-na-financier28-story.html.

McCarthy C (2012) 'Victim Redress and International Criminal Justice: Competing Paradigms or Compatible Forms of Justice' (2012), 10, Journal of International Criminal Justice.

MENA Rights (2021) Joint Statement Condemning the Inclusion of Four Emirati Activists and Members of the UAE 94 on the UAE Terrorism List. 17 September 2021. Available at https://menarights.org/en/articles/joint-statement-condemning-inclusion-four-emirati-activists-and-members-uae-94-uae.

National News (2021) 'UAE adds 38 People and 15 Entities to Terror List', 13 September 2021. Available at https://www.thenationalnews.com/uae/2021/09/13/uae-adds-38-individuals-and-15-entities-to-terror-list/.

NBC News (2005) 'Alleged Terror Financier Continues to Operate in Plain Sight', 01 July 2005. Available at https://www.nbcnews.com/id/wbna8421366.

The Guardian (2012) 'Nigerian Government Admits Islamists Have Secret Backers in Government', 09 January 2012. Available at https://www.theguardian.com/world/2012/jan/09/nigeria-islamists-government-backers-admits-president.

The Guardian (2021a) 'UAE Puts Six Nigerians with Ties to Boko Haram on Terrorist List', 14 September 2021. Available at https://guardian.ng/news/uae-puts-six-nigerians-with-ties-to-boko-haram-on-terrorist-list/.

The Guardian (2021b) 'Tension as U.S. Moves to Name Boko Haram Sponsors', 04 September 2021. Available at https://guardian.ng/news/tension-as-u-s-moves-to-name-boko-haram-sponsors/.

Thisday Live (2018) 'Danjuma Accuses Armed Forces of Complicity in Killings Across Nigeria' 25 March 2018. Available at https://www.thisdaylive.com/index.php/2018/03/25/danjuma-accuses-armed-forces-of-complicity-in-killings-across-nigeria/.

Trumbull IV C (2007–2008) The Victim of Victim Participation in international Criminal Proceedings. 29 Michigan Journal of International Law.

UAE Government (undated) 'The UAE Cabinet Approves the Inclusion of 38 Individuals and 15 Entities in the National Terrorism List'. Available at https://www.uaeiec.gov.ae/en-us/news/the-uae-cabinet-approves-the-inclusion-of-38-individuals-and-15-entities-in-the-national-terrorism-list.

Vanguard (2019) 'Alleged Collusion of Soldiers with Terrorists', 20 August 2019. Available at https://www.vanguardngr.com/2019/08/alleged-collusions-of-soldiers-with-terrorists/.

Vanguard (2020a) 'Borno Killings: Nigeria at Mercy of Terrorists, we're being Denied Weapons-Lai Mohammed', 30 November 2020. Available at https://www.vanguardngr.com/2020/11/borno-killings-nigeria-at-the-mercy-of-terrorists-were-being-denied-weapons-lai-mohammed/.

Vanguard (2020b) 'Give Us Weapons to Fight Terrorism: Lai Mohammed Begs World Powers', 13 August 2020. Available at https://www.vanguardngr.com/2020/08/give-us-weapon-to-fight-terrorism-lai-mohammed-begs-world-powers/.

Vanguard (2021) 'Presidency's Defence of Pantami', 16 May 2021. Available at https://www.vanguardngr.com/2021/05/presidencys-defence-of-isa-pantami/.

VOA (2020) 'Six Nigerians Sentenced for Funding Boko Haram Terrorist Group', 10 November 2020. Available at https://www.voanews.com/a/africa_6-nigerians-sentenced-funding-boko-haram-terrorist-group/6198178.html.

White House Archive (2001) https://georgewbush-whitehouse.archives.gov/news/releases/2001/11/20011107-6.html, 7 November 2001.

Worika I, Ozuru G (2018) 'The Nigerian Criminal Justice System: A Paradigm Shift to Victim Justice'. (2018), 21 (1), The Nigerian Law Journal.

Cases

Federal Republic of Nigeria v. Abiola (1994) FHCLR.

Godwin Josiah v. The State (1985) 1 NWLR.

Other Documents

ACJL Tracker—available at https://www.partnersnigeria.org/acjl-tracker/.

United Nations Security Council Resolution 1373 (2001) 28 September 2001 S/RES/1373 (2001) Available at https://undocs.org/S/RES/1373(2001).

United Nations Security Council Letter Dated 7 February 2007 from the Chairman of the Security Council Committee Established Pursuant to Resolution 1373 (2001) Concerning Counter-Terrorism Addressed to the President of the Security Council 08 February 2007. Available at https://www.refworld.org/pdfid/46de9f880.pdf.

Index

V. Ojo-Adewuyi, *Criminal Justice Responses to the Boko Haram Crisis in Nigeria*, International Criminal Justice Series 34, https://doi.org/10.1007/978-94-6265-615-4